Reader Response in Elementary Classrooms: Quest and Discovery

Edited by
Nicholas J. Karolides
University of Wisconsin–River Falls

LEA

LAWRENCE ERLBAUM ASSOCIATES, PUBLISHERS
1997   MAHWAH, NEW JERSEY

Lawrence Erlbaum Associates, Inc., Publishers
10 Industrial Avenue
Mahwah, NJ 07430

Cover design by Inga Karolides

Library of Congress Cataloging-in-Publication Data

Reader response in elementary classrooms : quest and discovery / Nicholas J. Karolides, editor.
     p. cm.
  Includes bibliographical references and index.
  ISBN 0-8058-2260-7 (pbk. : alk. paper)
  1. Reading (Elementary) 2. Reader-response criticism. 3. Literature—Study and teaching (Elementary)
4. Interdisciplinary approach in education. I. Karolides,
Nicholas J.
  LB1573.R2776 1996
  372.6'4044—dc20   96-20669
                                   CIP

Printed in the United States of America
10 9 8 7 6 5 4 3 2 1

DEDICATION

To my students,
who have been the crucible
of my learning
and
Louise M. Rosenblatt,
my teacher

Contents

Preface

Reading is a quest. Likened to an adventure, an experience—both metaphoric and real—the quest is a journey of discovery. The reader's search encompasses the sensations of the experience itself, accompanying emotions, sense, and meaning engendered by the experience, and understandings of the self, others, and the world around. Out of curiosity, readers also search for an extensive array of information. The journey can be envisioned and contemplated again and again after the reading act itself is completed. In a meaningful way, the reader's quest and its discoveries is life-enduring and life-fulfilling.

These ideas doubtless have a ring of familiarity. They are, however, qualified by a less recognized tenet that avows the central role of the reader in initiating the quest and experiencing the text. The transactional theory of literature—generally termed the *reader-response approach*—has recast the role of the reader from that of subordinated spectator to that of prominence as an equal partner to the text.

The recognition of the place of reader-response theory and practices in elementary classrooms blossoms in the midst of an explosion of attention to two other reconceptions of the elementary school curriculum: literature-based teaching and the integrated language approach. Indeed, the concepts and practices of these three are well integrated. Literature-based teaching, to be fully differentiated from basal-based teaching, involves not merely substituting literary texts for basal readers but also incorporating reader-response approaches. (The issues of basal readers versus literature-based instruction are effectively documented, particularly in chapters 2, 15, and 17.) An integrated curriculum likewise advocates authentic texts rather than basals, as well as strategies that integrate language and reading-process instruction across the curriculum. (These are illustrated directly and indirectly in the chapters of this book.)

The purpose of this volume is twofold: (a) to establish and explore the essential features of this theory and its rendering of the reading process, and (b) to acknowledge a philosophy of teaching and to illustrate teaching strategies to evoke and enhance readers' responses. Understanding the ways in which the reader affects the reading and how the reading happens will illuminate classroom pedagogy.

My discussions with students, undergraduate and graduate, and teachers reveal that there is generally a veneer of comprehension about reading as a process and the nature of readers' responses. They have a sense of several baseline principles but only partially recognize the theory's import. This level of understanding often leads them to misapply it in the classroom, limiting it to helping readers to relate to texts—to acknowledge their associations with characters and situations. These are expressive openings, useful motivational tools. However, as these discussions reveal, there is evident need to establish a deeper theoretical rationale and to develop methods to help teachers breach the surface of reader-response instruction, to mine the resources within the learning-to-read and response-to-literature processes.

The chapters in this volume portray a spectrum of teaching strategies. A case study format is used to illustrate them in action in real classrooms, rather than merely writing about the strategy in a general context. The author-teachers tend to focus on one teaching technique; however, others often are referred to and exemplified to present extending and enhancing activities. Among those displayed are whole- and small-group discussion; story drama; readers theatre; journal writing; scripts, letters, stories and other writings; and body punctuation. The classrooms that we are invited to visit span grades 1 through 6.

The chapters are arranged in four sections. Part I, "Transactional Theory and Literature-Based Teaching," essentially provides the theoretical bases for the text. In the introductory chapter, Nicholas J. Karolides illuminates the reading process and the role of the reader as an active participant in the reading act. Factors that condition or affect the reading—the reader, the text, the context—are explored. In chapter 2, Carole Cox differentiates between student/response-centered and teacher/text-centered classrooms as a basis for establishing the nature of literature-based teaching. She provides connections with whole language philosophy and several theories of learning as well as extensive examples of sound classroom practices.

The eight chapters in Part II, "Initiating and Developing Reader's Responses: Classroom Case Studies," present an array of strategies designed to evoke readers' responses and to effect and develop readers' interpretations. Shelley Allen, in chapter 3, exemplifies the operation of small group discussion in a fifth-grade classroom. Their dialogue expresses their interactions, how they build on each other's responses to make meaning. Interviews with their teacher, Peg Reed, reveal a consciousness of purpose and strategies. The application of drama—a class-inclusive role-play activity—to encourage responses of third graders is the focus of chapter 4. Patricia Enciso and Brian Edmiston provide situations in and around a story through which the children experience its text. In chapter 5, the wonder of a dramatic telling and a student-created choral reading introduce poetry to sixth graders. Arlene H. Mitchell elicits personal contact with and creates ownership of poems through response writing and performance. Spotlighted in chapter 6 is Readers' Theatre, an invigorating dramatic activity. Elizabeth J. Davis' second-grade class performs this response strategy after reading, rereading, and scripting—creating and writing dialogue—stories. Their attention engaged, their reading interpretation skills and their attitudes are affected. Chapter 7 focuses on the body language of response. Elizabeth B. Smith invites us into Cathy D. Nelson's fifth-grade classroom to observe body-language cultural markers used by the students to express their responses. Also acknowledged is the class atmosphere, the teaching philosophy, and style that encourage students' participation. Karen Hirsch displays, in chapter 8, the vitality and enthusiasm of third graders when given the opportunity to discuss their reactions in a small-group setting. She highlights the teacher's guide-on-the-side role and illustrates types of responses-generating questions. In chapter 9, Richard J. Meyer provides a panoramic display of life in the second grade: a classroom sketch, an outline of a daily program, a description of several writing activities, and vignettes of students in action. His camera zooms in on two students, documenting their responses—map-making and story writing. Paul Boyd-Batstone's third-grade bilingual class is comparably presented in chapter 10. His focus is on groups of students fulfilling the requirements of a literature plan, which encourages several types of responses, as well as questioning strategy and metaphor building.

Part III, "Exploring Issues: Content Area Applications" expresses, in the context of literature-based instruction, the premise of the integrated curriculum. Christine C. Pappas and Anne Barry in chapter 11 exemplify a read-aloud event with Ms. Barry's urban first-grade students. In a collaborative atmosphere, students initiate discussion through comments and questions in response to two information books on science topics. Ms. Barry redirects and expands the discussion with her initiations in concert with her teaching agenda—science and geography. In chapter 12 Alan Dean and Robert Small, Jr. express the teaching of nonfiction science—in conjunction with mathematics—through the responses of Alan Dean's first graders to a text about the life cycle of pumpkins. The students respond experientially, building their knowledge, clarifying their understandings. Elizabeth A. Poe and Nyanne J. Hicks' curricular focus in chapter 13 is social studies; their approach utilizes multiple literary texts and a variety of learning strategies—journals, letters, small-group dialogues, and others. The setting of this sixth-grade class' journey to the Eastern Hemisphere is family history and personal legacies. The interplay of informational and personal-experiential responses to texts is the focus of chapter 14. J. Kevin Spink observes the reactions of his first-, fourth-, and sixth-grade students, reporting the failure of traditional methodology and the exuberant learning that emerges from response-oriented approaches in the science, social studies and reading programs.

The orientation of Part IV is "Professional Development." In chapter 15, Lee Karnowski challenges teachers to consider the ramifications of their roles as process-oriented teachers and to examine and practice their skills to become effective. She illustrates the efferent approaches used by both traditional basals and literature-based basals in contrast to reader-response questions. Convinced of the necessity for teachers to become culturally alive, Kathleen G. Velsor and Jossie O'Neill in Chapter 16 propose reader-response journaling, discussion and retellings to develop meaningful sensitivity for the cultural "other." Their students reflect on their own responses as well as those of others, and they plan activities for their future students to achieve these ends. The concluding chapter focuses on a school district's decision to revise its reading/literature program. Connie Russell explains the procedures followed and the tasks accomplished: curriculum planning, book selection, reorientation of teaching philosophy and practices. She also provides insights about issues and problems encountered.

ACKNOWLEDGMENTS

The genesis of this book may be traced back to my undergraduate and graduate study at New York University. I am particularly indebted to Louise M. Rosenblatt, whose teaching, modeling the transactional theory of the literary work, inspired understanding and generated appropriate teaching practices. Over the years, her writings and her discussions with me have crystallized my thinking and encouraged the creation of this book. She has been a constant mentor and beacon for me.

To the chapter authors, I extend sincere thanks for their contributions of meaningful essays as well as their readiness to react to my editorial advice. I acknowledge with deep appreciation Laurie Pap and Eric P. Schmidt, students at the University of Wisconsin–River Falls, who read my theory chapter; their sensitive-to-language insights and thoughtful suggestions helped me to clarify my text for student audiences. Also, my appreciation is extended to R. Kay Moss, Illinois State University; Mary F. Heller, Kansas State University; Lee Galda, University of Georgia; Marjorie R. Hancock, Kansas State University; and Kathy G. Short, University of Arizona; who read the completed draft manuscript; their comments were meaningful, their encouragement reassuring. I also thank with much gratitude Sheri Fowler and LeRae Zahorski, who with great efficacy and efficiency accomplished numerous computer tasks, often under deadline situations. I acknowledge, too, with professional respect, my editor, Naomi Silverman, of Lawrence Erlbaum Associates, for her enthusiastic support of this book and for consistently sound advice.

My gratitude to Inga Karolides for her vibrant and inspired cover design.

—*Nicholas J. Karolides*

Part I

Transactional Theory
and Literature-Based Teaching

1

The Reading Process: Transactional Theory in Action

Nicholas J. Karolides
University of Wisconsin–River Falls

EDITOR'S OVERVIEW

The transactional theory of literature is *the formal name for what is commonly identified as the reader-response theory or reader-response approach. This theory of reading literature is significantly influencing the teaching of literature and reading. Reader response theory is in large measure responsible for the literature-based reading curriculum that is now a major presence in elementary schools.*

Recognizing the role of the reader in the reading act is the underpinning of the theory, along with the critical understanding that reading is a process. The role and functioning of the reader in this process in relation to the text is explored in detail in this chapter. How the process works and how readers achieve meaning are explained. Discussion of features of the meaning-making activity—selective attention, stance, validity, and the text itself—round out the discussion.

Two classroom scenarios demonstrate the theory in action. These, one set in the Virgin Islands, the other in the Midwest, illustrate the roles of students and teachers as they share responses to the text of a poem and an historical novel.

Consider the following:

1. *With a peer, try to evaluate the selective attention factors of your reading of a children's book. Try to imagine the variations in a class of students.*
2. *Search your memory to identify ways in which teachers in your past have either prescribed stance or allowed choice. How did these affect your reading? How will this awareness affect your teaching behavior?*
3. *The issue of validity of response is high on teachers' concern list. In what ways does the acceptance of a range of valid interpretations affect classroom principles and practices?*

The setting is a sixth-grade classroom in the Virgin Islands. The students, ringed by a group of teachers who have come to observe, are traditionally seated in rows. Robert Berlin, a master teacher then of New York University, is demonstrating the teaching of literature, specifically a poetry lesson.[1]

The text chosen for the occasion is Robert Frost's "Stopping By Woods on a Snowy Evening." At first mention, it seems an unlikely choice: What do these youngsters know about snow? But Bob's teaching purpose is to help these students make meaning beyond the visualization experience of the text, also to, in effect, advance their reading interpretation skills.

The children are stimulated by the occasion—the visitor from New York City, the surround of teachers. Excited, nervous, they shift in their chairs, whispering to one another, stealing glances at their teacher. But when Bob starts reading the text aloud, they settle down. He passes out copies and then reads aloud a second time.

Initially, the responses, not unexpectedly, are to the snow. The students have seen pictures, but they wonder about it—what it would be like to walk and play in it, to watch it fall. When the murmur of these comments breaks, Bob, piggybacking on their comments of watching the snow fall, scans their faces and asks, "What do you do that's like what the man in the poem is doing?" Smiling into the puzzled silence, he repeats the question, adding, "Think about all the things that you do."

At first, the children's responses are tentative, exploratory. They relate to the excursion: "Going for a drive in the country;" "taking a ride on a donkey cart." These responses are edged forward by a couple of developmental questions: "What else is the man doing?" "What do you do that's like that?" They know the answer to the first; the second is less immediate.

Hesitantly, Jenny asks, "Watch the rain?"

Bob nods encouragingly. "Does anyone else do that?" He pauses and acknowledges the signaling hands and voices. "Why do you watch the rain?"

"I watch to see if it's going to stop so I can go out to play," Phil says.

"Yeah, maybe there's nothing else to do," Martin interjects.

"Sometimes I'm waiting to go home. So, I watch 'til the rain slows down," Christina says, "so I won't get wet."

"Sometimes I just like to watch it," Matthew shrugs. "I don't know why."

"Anybody else who just likes to watch the rain?" Bob looks around. "Tomas?"

"Well," Tomas glances toward Matthew, " I like to watch storms when the wind is fierce and everything's blowing and the rain is splashing all over."

---

[1]Robert Berlin told the story of this teaching situation several times in my hearing. It is presented here as a recollection of his experience. Although the developmental sequence and key attributes of the discussion are true, the specific dialogue and students' names are invented. I also want to honor Bob for what I learned from his experience and from his teaching.

"Yeah! The trees bend over." "And the rain rattles on the roof." "And the wind makes things fly." Voices from around the room speak agreement.

"I watch storms like that, too," Bob says. "Storms in New York can have fierce winds off the ocean that toss the rain at the buildings. But I like soft rains, too."

A chorus of voices agrees. "Especially when the sun is shining at the same time," says Nora. "Then, everything glistens and smiles."

Bob smiles back at Nora. "Is there anything else that you do that's like what the man in the poem is doing?" He waits.

After a long pause, Carla says, "Well, sometimes I sit on the beach and watch the waves." She glances at Josie, who nods. "I don't know why. I just do."

"I do, too," adds Josie. "Sometimes with Carla, sometimes by myself."

"I like to watch the waves when the tide is coming in," exclaims Martin. "They roar and crash against the shore." He slaps one hand against the other, simulating the movement and sound of water against sand.

"In the morning the waves are quieter, like they're sleepy. They're nice to watch, too," Phil says.

"They sparkle in the sun," murmurs Carla.

Bob smiles at them. "I like the sound Martin makes—the roar and crash of the waves—and the look of sleepy waves. They remind me of some snow images in the poem." He looks at his copy, the students turning to theirs. "Do you see them?"

"There's *downy flake*," says Beth, "That's soft like *sleepy*."

"And," adds Joey, "*easy wind*."

"Oh, I like *sweep of easy wind and downy flake*," exclaims Jenny. "It reminds me of how the sand flies when I'm sweeping the sidewalk."

"Yes, those are soft snowy sounds." Bob nods and waits.

"How about *The woods are lovely, dark and deep?*" asks Joey. "That's kind of neat, the sound of it."

"Mmm, it makes me shiver," Carla says.

Bob nods again. He returns to the primary discussion. "Why do you watch them, the waves, I mean?"

"Like Carla says, they're sparkly and pretty," says Anne.

"Sometimes I count them," Marcos grins at the class. "It's crazy."

"That would make me dizzy, watching and counting. If I watch too long, I get sleepy." Tomas stares ahead. His head drooping, he pretends to drowse off.

The class laughs. "But it is relaxing," Josie agrees. "Sometimes I forget I'm supposed to watch my little sister. I watch the waves and can't seem to stop watching."

"How many of you are like Josie and Tomas, you can't stop watching and feel relaxed?" Hands go up, heads nod.

"Not when the tide is crashing and a storm is coming in." Martin again simulates the waves, adding sound effects. Marcos and Phil join in, laughing.

Bob leads them back to the poem, asking them to compare their reasons for watching with those of the narrator, and to measure the hypnotic pull of the waves in comparison to that of the snowfall. His final question, "Why do you stop watching?" draws forth another connection for them as they relate their sense of obligations: to get home for supper, to complete a chore, because it has gotten late. The students conjecture the narrator's tiredness, his need to complete his journey, and his *promises to keep*.

In traditional parlance, Berlin's demonstration lesson can be identified as *teaching a poem* to this class. In a manner of speaking, he has. However, by helping the students explore their connectedness with this text, he has helped them to connect with the heart of the text, perhaps to evoke and experience a *poem*. Concomitantly, he has potentially advanced a reading skill—going beyond words to the making and interpreting of meaning. Helping students to consider the relationship of their experiences to text and to suggest routes of connection and of understanding is consequential in processing reading. These students may have seen the scenic and narrative text broadened and deepened; they may have gained a strategy to open the mystery of that meaning hidden somehow "between the lines."

Further, Berlin has effectively led the students into the creation of a poem from the words. He has helped them envision beyond their initial responses to the scene and beyond their preliminary relatedness. Building bridges, he helped them fit their experiences into the words. The subsequent centering of attention gave impetus to both broader and individually specific responses. The student readers gained access to meaning.

RESPONSE-TO-LITERATURE BACKGROUND

Learning to read for most children starts with responses to stories, oral or read-aloud literature, or, in abbreviated form, responses to words. In the comforting ambience of parental attention and closeness, listening to words, often with the accompaniment of entrancing pictures, they develop language awareness and participate in language response. They experience the words, giggling, perhaps, at sound effects, repeating them for their own enjoyment; they experience wonder, their eyes wide, and experience joy at happy conclusions. They develop, too, subliminal awareness of story structure, being able, for example, to model and tell their own stories.

Such response-to-literature background is appropriately touted for its enhancement of reading readiness. Establishing positive, expectant attitudes about reading along with developing language and story awareness have significant learning effects. However, the responses themselves are equally significant; the giggles, the sighs, the exclamations reflect and enhance an increasing alertness to the effects of words, to the power that words in context have.

There are, of course, other language, nonliterary situations that promote experiences with words. Children are surrounded by symbols and texts—traffic signs, advertising symbols, billboards, food packages, and the like. Children, alive to situations, learn to "read" and understand these words situationally and experientially.

These early learning-to-read situations build word associations and broaden the children's language landscape. These experiences are the underpinnings of reading.

These preliminary statements have focused on the language-reading responses of children to call attention to the reader and the role of the reader in the reading transaction. The foundation idea: The reading act necessarily involves a reader *and* a text. Without a reader, text does not come into existence—does not have meaning or invoke feelings or sensations, but is just squiggles on a page, whether it is an unnoticed stop sign, an unopened letter, or a skipped chapter in a book. (The word *text* refers to the marks on the page, the words as symbols. *Text* is differentiated from *literary work* or *poem*; these are used in reader-response literary criticism to refer to what emerges and evolves from the transaction of a reader and a text.)

These ideas were first promulgated in 1938 (and in subsequent 1968, 1983, and 1995 editions) by Rosenblatt in *Literature as Exploration* (1995, fifth edition) and expounded in *The Reader, the Text, the Poem: The Transactional Theory of the Literary Work* (1976). In recent decades, theories of literature, termed *reader response criticism,* have emerged from the acceptance of the important role of the reader during the reading act. However, not all reader-response approaches are identical in their expression of the reader's role, some concentrating on the reader, others giving primary attention to the text. Rosenblatt's transactional theory insists on the reader and the text, each affecting the other (as will be explained). It forms the core of this book.

Traditionally, the reader's input in the reading act has been ignored; the text has been emphasized. Attention has been given to the decoding of words, the structure or characteristics of the text (What is the sentence structure, the plot sequence, the characterization? Does this poem use imagery, similes, or metaphors?), data from or comprehension of the text (Name some things Mimi can see using her fingers), and the author's meaning (What does the author mean when she says . . .?). This emphasis suggests that meaning comes from the text alone, that the reader is an outsider looking in. Also, it implies that the text is a constant, that is, unchanging. In part, these impressions have led to the notion that there is a single meaning to a given text.

THE ACT OF READING: TRANSACTION AND PROCESS

Reading is a process. The act of reading is much more complex than the decoding of graphic symbols and assigning meaning to words, or understanding the function of such words as *because* in a sentence, or even establishing the data within a text, leading to its comprehension. Factors of complexity include the reader and the text, as they are now understood, their relationship, the context of the reading, and the process—what happens during reading—itself.

Transaction

The central premise of the reading process is that the literary work exists in the transaction between a reader and a text. The active participatory role of readers encompasses—in conjunction with comprehension—discovering meaning, responding emotionally, developing interpretation. Readers are not passive spectators *of* the text but are active performers *with* the text.

The term *transaction* is meaningful in expressing the reader–text relationship. It signals a connection between them and the nature of the connection. One does not act on the other as a baseball bat hitting a ball. Rather, transaction denotes a situation of mutuality. During the reading activity, the reader and the text mutually act on each other, each affecting and conditioning the other. The reader's persona infuses the text; the text impresses the reader. While thus engaged in this mutual involvement and exchange, they cannot be separated and analyzed.

> . . . we need to see the reading act as an event involving a particular individual and a particular text, happening at a particular time, under particular circumstances, in a particular social and cultural setting, and as part of the ongoing life of the individual and the group. We still can distinguish the elements, but we have to think of them, not as separate entities, but as aspects or phases of a dynamic process, in which all elements take on their character as part of the organically-interrelated situation. Instead of thinking of reading as a linear process, we have to think rather of a complex network or circuit of inter-relationships, with reciprocal interplay. (Rosenblatt, 1985, pp. 100–101)

As can be imagined (and is described in the next few pages), all these particulars acting simultaneously, consciously and unconsciously, imply a complex and alive interaction.

A transaction between reader and text is not necessarily automatic. The reader must be able to decipher the marks on the page and must be willing to become engaged with the text. The latter may, in part, depend on the ability of the text to engage the reader's attention, to stimulate interest. A host of factors may short circuit this engagement: The situations, characters, or issues may be outside the maturational–experiential scope of the reader, the language may be beyond the recognition or experience of the reader, and the reader may use ineffective reading strategies. Also, the reader's distraction, inattention or indifference may block response. In such meager encounters, the readers may read words but will not acknowledge the text. They may in varying degrees comprehend it but will not evoke a literary work; they will not recreate and "live through" (Rosenblatt's expression, 1978) the experience of the text for themselves.

In this context, it is understood that no person can read/experience a literary text for another. A friend or teacher telling you about a book is not an act of reading—engagement—for you, nor is reading a summary an act of experiencing the text. Others can no more read or experience a text for you than they can relieve your hunger pangs by eating your dinner. (The reading–response situation of informational texts is different, as will be explained: For instance, a passenger remarking to a driver, "You just went through a stop sign," in large measure speaks for itself.) Only by hearing/reading the entire text of Steig's *Sylvester and the Magic Pebble* (1969) will readers feel the shock of surprise when Sylvester turns himself into a rock after he is frightened by a lion and, later, the chill of concern when text and illustration reflect the passage of time through the seasons. During winter, Sylvester's rock is covered with snow, a wolf is howling over him, and he is frozen fast. When, at the end, Sylvester becomes a donkey again and is reunited with his parents, the readers live through the surge of joy modestly expressed in the language and exuberantly depicted in the illustrations.

The Reading Process and the Reader

The relationship between reader and text is dynamic. And the reader responding is also dynamic, alive to stimulus and response. Further, what a reader makes of a text will reflect the reader's state of being at a particular time and place and in a particular situation, as well as the reader's relationship to the text.

Readers come to the texts imbued with their own personalities and character traits, their individual experiences and memories, their personal situations and concerns, their cultural background and perspective, and their backlog of language.

> What, then, happens in the reading of a literary work? Through the medium of words, the text brings into the reader's consciousness certain concepts, certain sensuous experiences, certain images of things, people, actions, scenes. The special meanings and, more particularly, the submerged associations that these words and images have for the individual reader will largely determine what the work communicates to *him*. The reader brings to the work personality traits, memories of past events, present needs and preoccupations, a particular mood of the moment, and a particular physical condition. These and many other elements in a never-to-be-duplicated combination determine his response to the peculiar contribution of the text. (Rosenblatt, 1976, pp. 30–31)

Thus, although the "medium of words" of the text appears the same, it will be read individually by each reader. Readers' responses may well vary in connotation, in focus or emphasis, in interpretation. Such variations may result from responses to individual words or images that may carry shades of meanings, experientially induced, differing from one reader to the next. A text's barking, leaping dog, for example, may be to one reader a yelping, nipping brute while another may envision a tail-wagging mutt, yapping an excited greeting. Past experiences—or lack of them—directly or indirectly connected to the text's situations, characters, or issues may lead readers toward distinct personal directions.

The reading situation is another dynamic factor. A particular stimulus, physical condition, a sense of purpose, a mood or preoccupation of the reader—each may affect the reading transaction. The context of the reading may be affective, as may be the actual setting in which the reading takes place, including whether the reader is alone or in a group. These factors suggest not only that a reading transaction is particular to each reader, but also that it is an "event in time" (Rosenblatt's term). Altering the stimulus, the purpose, the situation, or the reader's preoccupations will affect the response. As the passage of time changes the reader so, too, will the responses be affected. Thus, additional readings by the "same" reader of the "same" text will vary, the reader having been changed by events and insights, personal and cultural, that have occurred.

The reading response as an "event in time" thus happens with each reader each time—with the same book or different books. A class of 25 students reading the same book will emerge with 25 events because each reader brings a distinct personality and different experiences; each brings, as well, cultural variations that impact the reading response.

> Under the magnetism of the ordered symbols of the text, he marshals his resources and crystallizes out from the stuff of memory, thought, and feeling a new order, a new experience, which he sees as the poem. This becomes part of the ongoing stream of his life experience, to be reflected on from any angle important to him as a human being. (Rosenblatt, 1978, p. 12)

The range of possible readings of a given text is potentially infinite, considering the variety of personalities and the breadth of experiences among readers, these being augmented by the mobility and flexibility of the current culture. This potential for variation exists even among young readers of the same age, similar backgrounds, and circle of friends. The greater the complexity of the text, the greater the potential for variation.

Invitation 1.1

Select a text featuring an ethnic culture. Read it with your mind's eye focused on cultural features: situations, attitudes and language.

Try to determine through conversations with others inside and outside the represented culture what would / would not likely be responded to by individuals in either group. If this isn't feasible, try gender depiction and response.

THE PROCESS IN ACTION

The process of reading, comparable to the writing process, is evolutionary, a drama of quest and discovery. It, too, is a meaning-making, an experience-applying, experience-engendering activity. Just as writers do not at the outset know quite what they want to express, nor how, nor what insights will emerge, readers are not likely to predict the reading event, although they often anticipate. (They may predict about the text, even the probable happenings.) They are not likely to have an immediate flash of understanding like a cartoonist's light bulb over a character's head. Initial readings, especially if the text is short and relatively straightforward, may create strong immediate responses, of course, but as a reader proceeds to process the text, more refined insights may develop.

The reading process begins with the reader and words of the text. (Of course, in classroom settings as well as in some other situations—a friend summarizes and recommends a book—there may be a prereading introduction to the process.) The readers put the words together to elicit meaning; they react to the interplay of words, structures, and situations through their own persona. "The reader infuses intellectual and emotional meanings into the pattern of verbal symbols, and those symbols channel his thoughts and feelings. Out of this complex process emerges a more or less organized imaginative experience" (Rosenblatt, 1976, p. 25). Responses to additional words, characters, and situations create an unfolding effect. Expectations of the text are projected; later words, information, or events may solidify these impressions or may bring about a revision. Characters, too, are reconsidered in the light of additional behaviors.

In *The Pleasure of Children's Literature*, Nodelman (1992) conjectured about the minimum amount of information needed to evoke a reader's knowledgeable response. He identified in the first sentence of E. B. White's *Charlotte's Web* (1973) seven items of "a repertoire of knowledge of conventional behavior [needed] to fill in the many gaps."[2] The sentence under consideration: "'Where's Papa going with that ax?' said Fern to her mother as they were setting the table for breakfast." The readers acknowledge or fill in these seven items of information (ranging from Fern's gender and the relationship between Fern and her mother to the possible situation and date of the story) unconsciously in all probability, if indeed they are each acknowledged. The text proposes limits to the reading of this situation; the reader's imagination and experiences flesh out initial details, for example, of Fern's character and family situation through her cooperative activity and her act of questioning itself.

Nodelman's list does not reflect the emotional colorations that may also be part of the readers' responses except for the seventh: the ax as an element of surprise. "Its presence makes us think about its customary uses, and its oddity [i. e., during breakfast] evokes questions about what it might be used for here" (pp. 59–60).

Thus, readers begin their response. They construct a scaffold of feelings and understandings in response to the guidance of the text, attempting to account for its many features. Consciously or unconsciously, they conjecture about details, seeing how they fit an emerging pattern, and react to surprises. These may confirm or propel consideration of a new direction or dimension. The probable likelihood of some aspects being overlooked or understated on the one hand, or overstated on the other, is a reflection of the degree of involvement, reading maturity, and the limitations of the readers' experiences. The readers' personality, culture, and interests also come into play. The response will also resonate with the reading moment, that is, the reading context, the situational conditions in which the reading occurs.

The reading process is reflective and recursive—a forwards-and-backwards exploration of the text—rather than linear (again, comparable to the writing process). Recursiveness may be an actual turning back of pages or a thoughtful reflection to previous events or passages; these may be immediate glances back or returns many pages later. Readers may think back to a previous event, dialogue, passage, to savor the images or sensations. Perhaps provoked by another passage, they may turn back the pages to reread a segment to confirm or reconsider an impression, the implications of a situation or behavior. Such explorations, conscious or unconscious, immediate or prolonged, can reveal additional nuances and developmental understandings. These understandings confirm the complexity of the reading process.

SELECTIVE ATTENTION

During this processing, the readers make choices. Selective attention (attributed to William James, Rosenblatt, 1978) becomes operative: Readers may respond to some features of the text over others and may

---

[2] Iser in his expression of reader-response theory *The Act of Reading: A Theory of Aesthetic Response,* acknowledged the role of the reader in filling the gaps or blanks in the text. These unwritten aspects—background, unspoken dialogue, unstated relationships are filled in by the reader, who is reacting to the suggestions of the situations. It is a dynamic process in which the text imposes limits and the reader's imagination, activated by the text, works out the details. See also his essay, "The Reading Process: A Phenomenological Approach," in Tompkins' (1980) *Reader-Response Criticism: From Formalism to Post-Structuralism.*

heighten some responses over others. One word or phrase may generate attention; a particular connotation may be chosen, giving precedence to a particular feeling. Significant in this regard is the reader's interplay with connotative—private—language, which reflects personal nuances and associations, subtle individualized meanings related to life experiences. Close identification with a character, event or issue—socioculturally and otherwise—in contrast to perceived distance, may also intensify the response.

Social and cultural contextual differences are reflected in these choices. Interest and involvement are affected; markers are connected with and understood or given scant attention and, perhaps, misunderstood. What may be a rich reading experience for the cultural insider may be a poor one for the outsider. Certain historical texts can present comparable selective attention choices.

Invitation 1.2

In a small group, individually read and write a journal response to Roethke's "My Papa's Waltz," or another poem of your choice. Compare these. In particular, note the words that evoke individuals' responses and how these may direct the expression of meaning.

In this vein, the reader's stance, as explained next, may direct the very nature of the response or activate certain features, causing these to be highlighted. From the array of meanings and feelings that are conjured up, readers select those that seem to them appropriate, that fit the work that is being evoked, in relation to the reading situation. The created response is the realized experience of the reader.

STANCE

How—in what frame of mind, with what purpose or expectation—a reader approaches a text depends in part on the text, in part on the reader, and certainly, the two of them together. Consciously or unconsciously, the reader adopts a stance toward the reading of a text. The same text may be approached with different purposes or attitudes by different readers or by the same reader at different times.

The stance taken by a reader may be *predominantly aesthetic* (literary) or *predominantly efferent* (noniterary/informational) on a continuum of response possibilities between the two extremes. Rosenblatt (1988) explained the term *efferent* (from the Latin *efferre*, to carry away) as denoting the kind of reading that is concentrating on information or instruction. The reader attends to and draws from the text data that is important for whatever purpose or need. In contrast, the term *aesthetic* (its Greek source, *aisthetikos* refers to perception through the senses, feelings, and intuitions) denotes the kind of reading that focuses on the feeling states, "what is being lived through *during* the reading event" (Rosenblatt, 1988, pp. 12–13).

A reader's stance is adopted often in concert with the nature of the text. An efferent stance matches the text on the back of a baseball card or a bottle marked poison, a science textbook, and newspapers, the last somewhat dependent on certain pages. These are read to learn and retain information. Meaning is constructed by responding to the denotative, public aspects of language—the dictionary definition. In the aesthetic stance, relating, for example, to a novel or folktale, readers respond to dramatic moments and compelling characters through the connotative, personally associative language, bringing into play images, sensations, and emotions.

The cautionary word *often* used previously is deliberate. It is quite possible to read information-oriented texts with an aesthetic or partially aesthetic stance; the details of a battle or a baseball game in the newspaper or a textbook's account of the environmental crisis or the development of a litter of kittens may call forth emotions from the wellsprings of memory. In contrast, it is quite possible to read a literary text with an efferent or partially efferent stance as when an issues-oriented reading of Paterson's *Lyddie* (1991) seeks details of the lives of factory workers in 19th century New England.

A dualistic view of stance is inappropriate. Potentially, there are readings at either extreme end of the aesthetic-efferent continuum. However, as the words *predominantly* and *partially* suggest, along with the previous examples, readings are more apt to be a blend of the two stances. At the efferent end of the continuum, a reader whose primary purpose is information or instructional, say, about horses or hot-air balloons relies essentially on the denotative *public* sense of the words. Yet, images of a colt gamboling across a pasture or balloons floating on the horizon with the clouds may color the response with aesthetic nuances. Experiences with colts and balloons or wishful thoughts may intrude. Similarly, an aesthetic reading, responsive to connotative private aspects of language and image, can be modified with efferent understandings. Readers caught up in the experience of divorce or death, responding emotionally with the characters of Naylor's *The Solomon System* (1983) or Lowry's *A Summer to Die* (1978), may at least subliminally acknowledge, on an informational level, the grieving process and coping strategies of the protagonists. Indeed, these authors provide spokespersons for such strategies, inviting a partially efferent response. The degree of blending that occurs is variable from reader to reader, situation to situation, and is changeable over time. At the theoretical middle of the stance continuum, the reader would be applying an equal measure of the expectations, attitudes, and reading behaviors of the two stances.

As noted earlier, texts are party to the selection of stance. Authors have intentions and provide guidance to readers to promote or invite a stance appropriate to the material and purpose. For an efferent stance, the language choices to project a public, informational response will avoid emotionally laden connotative words; the structure and content will likewise signal an efferent response. The word *heart* will be presented differently in the context of a science or health fitness text in contrast to its expression in Conrad's *Heart of Darkness* (1965). Some authors seem to consciously seek a blended response as conveyed by their choices of language, style, and content. Other texts are more deliberately either informational or affective.

The nature of the text is influential but not entirely determinate. The idea that the text fixed the reading purpose, assumed in the past, denies the dynamics of the reading process and belies the role of the reader who is neither passive nor neutral.

The stance that the reader adopts affects the reader's activity. This choice results, perhaps, from the encouragement of the text itself, the reader's inner focus of attention or interests, the reader's cultural experiences and concerns, the situational context of the reading, or a directed purpose. Readers may blend their responses as affected by a combination of factors. How a response is generated and the nature of the evoked response is determined accordingly.

STANCE IN THE CLASSROOM

The dynamics of the reader's stance are particularly significant in a classroom situation. Directly or indirectly, the teacher or the textbook's questions and instructions can markedly affect the stance that operates in student transactions. Key ingredients are classroom atmosphere and teacher's expectations, selected texts and their integration, and questions and assignments. For example, the assignment of O'Dell's *Sarah Bishop* (1980) or the Collier brothers' *War Comes to Willy Freeman* (1983) in conjunction with the Revolutionary War chapter in the social studies textbook may readily lead to the integration of stances on the part of readers. Appropriate discussion and activities can assist readers in differentiating and applying stance in relation to the predominant purpose and language of the text, and in developing and enhancing their responses in keeping with that predominance. Expectations and assignments may promote the application of a blend of both stances or may direct emphasis to one or the other.

It is not unusual, unfortunately, for textbooks and teachers to focus their questions and examinations efferently—factually, despite the essentially aesthetic (literary) nature of the text. Such questions encourage readers to read efferently for details or formal aspects rather than for the experience of the text. The choice of this emphasis is especially significant because the classroom, in effect, projects a model for developing reading habits and attitudes. Several examples follow:

Consider the questions posed in this classroom reader in response to Mary O'Neill's poem "Mimi's Fingers":

I am blind. All that I can see
My enchanted fingers bring to me,
As if all sight were mingled with all touch
I do not mind not-seeing very much.
In Braille I read the words these fingers trace,
And with them come to know your smile, your face,
Your buckled shoes, the silk-thread of your hair,
The fabric of each suit and dress you wear;
All shapes, all sizes, how long, how far, how high,
How round a bowl, how gently curved the sky,
How pointed the far tip-top of a hill,
The narrow table of a window sill.
I know a snowflake as a melting star,
The sticky-thick of honey and tar.
Color alone my fingers cannot do.
Could you, could you, tell me about blue?

—*Mary O'Neill*

1. Name some things Mimi can see using her fingers.
3. How can Mimi tell the difference between the shapes and sizes of objects?
5. Could Mimi describe a sunset? Why or why not?
7. Why do you think Mimi would like to know about the color blue? (Ruddell, 1978, pp. 12–13)

"The Black Stallion and the Red Mare" is a short story about Donald who admires a wild stallion which roams the countryside with his red mare. Because the stallion "steals" farm horses, the local farmers form a tracking party to recapture their horses. Readers are asked to respond to the following:

Pre-reading questions:
A. 1. How would you describe Donald? What kind of person is he?
2. Why do you think the black stallion is so loyal to the red mare?
Concluding questions:
B. 1. How do you think Donald feels about the wild horses?
2. Why does Donald's father believe that the two horses have earned the right to be together?
3. In what part of the country does this story take place?
Thinking beyond:
C. 1. Do you think calling the horses outlaws is fair?
2. Do you think horses can communicate with each other? Why do you think so? What other animals can you think of that communicate and how do they do it? (Johnson, 1977, pp. 156–158)

Poems about seasons are used frequently in readers. "Winter is Tacked Down" by Sister Noemi Weygant exults in the first snowfall. Consider the stance of these questions:

1. In this poem, how many words rhyme with might?
2. What rhyming pair is in the last four lines?
3. How does the poet describe the way the snow looks on the ground?
4. What is this kind of figurative language called? (Johnson, 1977, p. 155)

An examination of these questions reveals that those affecting the poetry are efferent in their approach, focusing on lists of data and stylistic techniques. The questions about the narrative are comparable. Although the first one, describing Donald, offers the potential for aesthetic response, the suggested answers in the basal reader (implying right answers) focus on textual data. Indeed, the second prereading question about the horse's loyalty is predictive and suppressive of transactional response because it informs readers in advance of the loyal relationship of the horses. Again, the question about Donald's feelings offers the possibility of an aesthetic stance in proposing a discussion of those feelings; however, the instructions to the teacher seem to dissuade this posture. Finally, the thinking beyond questions relate to the readers' experiences or, potentially, research: The questions are beyond the text and, thus, do not help the readers to bring forth and expand their experiences *with* the text. Instead of helping students to construct and realize meaning, these questions are geared and limited to comprehension instruction.

Invitation 1.3

Select a story from a basal reader or a literature-based reader. Evaluate the questions to determine the directed stance. Prepare a set of questions that focus the reader's attention toward the opposite end of the efferent–aesthetic continuum.

THE TEXT

"The poem" comes into being in the live circuit set up between the reader and "the text." As with the elements of an electric circuit, each component of the reading process functions by virtue of the presence of the others. A specific reader and a specific text at a specific time and place: Change any of these, and there occurs a different circuit, a different event—a different poem. The reader focuses his attention on the symbols and on what they help to crystallize out into awareness. Not the words, as uttered sounds or inked marks on a page, constitute the poem, but the structured responses to them. For the reader, the poem is lived-through during his intercourse with text. (Rosenblatt, 1978, p. 14)

The text is a necessary counterpart of the reader, an equal component of the transaction through which the literary work—the poem—comes into being. It is the catalyst for the reading experience. In addition, the text acts as a mechanism of control or constraint, providing guidance for the reader. Its words, images, and structures propose stance, influence response, promote meaning.

Earlier in this chapter I noted that "traditionally . . . the text has been emphasized." With this focus, critics and teachers direct readers' attention to the text and/or to the author. Their assumptions are that the text is an entity, an object with a determinate meaning of its own: Thus, meaning can be achieved by close analysis of the structure and techniques of the text, and of the characters and events. The companion analysis that emphasizes text is that of the author's intention. This is accomplished sometimes by assessing clues in the text, sometimes by studying the life and times of the author. The reader's purpose is to attempt to discover/achieve the meaning that is somehow within the text or, perhaps, between the lines—a phrase that seems to convey mystery and encourage baffled resistance, particularly to the neophyte reader. (Readers' responses may be enhanced and deepened with selected strategies to evoke the impact of language—word play, structural and stylistic effects on the responses, as well as historical–cultural insights. These are usually most appropriate after the reader has responded, that is, has expressed the lived-through response during the process of developing the recreated literary work.)

As has been herein expressed, however, the text does not stand alone. A reader is required to activate the marks on the page. The emerging response, "'the poem' cannot be equated solely with *either* the text *or* the experience of the reader" (Rosenblatt, 1978, p. 105) but to a dynamic relationship between the two, each affecting and conditioning the other. The text plays a vital role, neither predominant nor submissive.

Authors create written texts out of their own experiences and imaginations. They process language, selecting words, searching for the right word to fit the emerging text; they select details, situations, and events, characters—attitudes and actions—to express their perceptions and feelings. Their expectation is to lead readers to share their insights. Authorial intention is operating. However, composition theory establishes—and writers themselves often attest—that composing is not altogether conscious; the subconscious also operates during the composing process. Composing research also indicates that the pattern of intention and understanding of the writer shifts as the text evolves, adapts as the writer discovers meanings. Indeed, the writer may not be altogether aware of revealed meanings. The text takes shape in an extraordinarily intricate fashion and is itself an intricately designed body of words, a multicolored tapestry, threaded with the author's intentions.

In a meaningful way the authors, too, live through the experience of the text—incubating it, processing, and reprocessing it. Authors are the first readers, engaging with the text from first draft through the revisions, and the final form. This final form, in a significant way, is removed from the writer once it is published. Readers process it without benefit of the immediate presence of the author. The text itself provides the stimulus for readers, encouraging them to create (or recreate) a literary work out of their linguistic and personal experiences and imagination.

The final form of the text at face value seems static, stable, unchanging; the words as they appear on the page do not change. Semantic study, however, informs us that language changes: Words are subject to shifts in denotative and connotative meanings, as well as to variations in image. These result from social, psychological, and environmental forces. Such shifts may occur across the age of a text, so that words chosen carefully by an author to particularly express an impression may no longer convey the meaning intended. Meanings are added to some words that maintain their usage; some original meanings may be dropped altogether. Some words fall out of the language mainstream. Such meaning variations may be regional as well.

Language flexibility is in part a personal semantic phenomenon in addition to being historical. As discussed earlier in this chapter, we cannot expect contemporary readers to experience language identically. Their responses to words will vary according to personal connotations imbedded in their private language; there may also be variant understandings in public language, personal colorations, or definitions at odds with the dictionary definition(s). It is notable, too, that changes occur in readers with age as word sense is affected over time.

Situations, incidents, actions, and characters in a text are subject to similar forces of changed response. For example, Sorensen's 1956 Newbery Award winning novel, *Miracles on Maple Hill,* in the past was frequently perceived as a gentle story chronicling a family's healing and integration after the father's return from war. Its characters come to terms with their strengths and values. Today's readers are apt to sense the sexism expressed in attitudes and behaviors, assessing these to reflect the dominance of the males, son and father, and the belittling of the females, daughter and mother.

Such understandings assert that the nature of texts is not fixed nor dominant in the reading act. Rather, they lend themselves to variations of response and interpretation in the eyes and minds of active readers.

VALIDITY

What each reader makes of the text is, indeed, *for him* the poem, in the sense that this is his only direct perception of it. No one else can read it for him. He may learn indirectly about others' experiences with the text; he may come to see that his own was confused or impoverished, and he may then be stimulated to attempt to call forth from the text a better poem. But this he must do himself, and only what he himself experiences in relation to the text is—again let us underline—*for him,* the work. (Rosenblatt, 1978, p. 105)

This often-quoted passage establishes the significant idea that readers make meaning—create the poem for themselves. It also suggests some of the revision stimuli outside and within the text that may bring about a reexperiencing of the text to recreate a fuller meaning. Additionally, it affirms, in the context of transactional theory, that a text can call forth different experiences, one reader from another, and in addition, not only different, but "better."

To some critics, theorists, and teachers, this may sound like license—an anything goes premise. In the paragraph immediately preceding the quoted one, Rosenblatt unequivocally rejects this notion: "Something encapsuled in the reader's mind without relevance to the text may be a wonderful fantasy, but the term 'poem' or 'literary work,' in transactional terminology, would not be applicable to such a mental experience any more than to an entity apart from a reader" (1978, p. 105). Thus, whereas a range of responses is recognized as probable and acceptable, some may be irrelevant to the text. Such a response may be valued by and valuable to the reader; it may reflect a heightened personal experience triggered by a feature of the text, but it has taken the reader far afield from the text. It may be "confused or impoverished," invalid or less valid than other responses in relation to the total text.

Resisting the idea of an anything goes response does not, however, enforce the position of a single, identifiable meaning of a text, one interpretation for the literary work. Such arguments are usually made in relation to the author's intention (discussed by Crosman, 1980, in "Do Readers Make Meaning"[3]) and suggested by such questions as "What is the author's purpose? What does the author mean by. . .?" Even if the idea of a fully visualized purpose were not contestable by what we have learned about the composing process and what authors themselves have to say (along with the near impossibility of absolutely establishing an author's purpose), it should be understood that most expert-identified purposes and meanings of texts are established by individual readers, that is, readers with "authority." It is not uncommon for one individual authority to promote an interpretation different from another's. This further belies the one-interpretation attitude.

---

[3] In "Do Readers Make Meaning?" Crosman (1980) argued that any word or text has meaning only when it is placed into a larger context, the context of the author's intentions being only one possible way of understanding a text. The difficulty is that for most texts, there is no author's stated intention and if there is it is "ambiguous or contradictory, and *it* must be subjected to the same process of reader interpretation. . . " (p. 161). Further, Crosman examines and refutes the assumption of one meaning implied by the author's intention concept.

The transactional nature of the reading act recognizes the mutuality of reader and text. Thus, validity and adequacy of interpretation are measured against the guidelines and constraints of the text: Are the situations and events, the behaviors and attitudes of the characters accounted for; are the language nuances and images appropriately reflected in the emerging response? Do the aspects of the response fit with the several features of the text without neglecting elements? Does the response include elements that are not discoverable in the text? To what extent have personal memories or images derailed the response?

Yet, under the guidance of the text, readers do read and experience differently, do discover more than one valid interpretation. These may have equal applicability as in the seemingly opposing poems created from Roethke's text, "My Papa's Waltz," (1973) one focusing on the father as a drunk and child abuser, the other imaging a playful, roughhousing parent-child relationship, animated, perhaps, by a drink. Arguably these are equally valid interpretations.

A pattern for measuring the degree of validity is suggested by Probst (1981): "The reader's experience falls somewhere on a continuum—at one extreme is a reading highly responsive to and closely controlled by the text, and at the other a reading triggered by the text but otherwise responsive to and controlled by the psyche of the reader" (p. 17).

Validity may also be construed as age or maturity-skill related. Naturally, the responses of younger children or less mature readers are influenced by their maturational–chronological age, reading experiences, and interpretive skills. Comparable to the continuum suggested by Probst, a growth–response continuum may be imagined: Third grade children responding to Frost's poem "Stopping by Woods on a Snowy Evening" (1946; it is actually labeled a third grade poem in a college children's literature text), are likely to envision the scene—the falling snow, the questioning horse in midjourney, the magic of the woods; middle schoolers (at least, many of those I have taught have so responded) will probably relate to the sense of responsibility, the need to accomplish things suggested in the closing lines, although they usually also maintain an orientation to the scene. College students (the poem is also anthologized in college textbooks) often go beyond this, arguing whether the repetition of sleep in the closing stanza refers to a much-needed rest after and before a day full of responsibilities, or to impending death. Each response is appropriate and valid for each group of readers.

SHARED RESPONSE

"Oh, but I didn't like the ending," Maggie complained, "that part where Caddie starts doing that sewing and stuff. I don't think it was fair to force Caddie to be like her sister."

Maggie's complaint broke into the class's discussion of *Caddie Wood-lawn* (1935). The students of Virginia Runquist's fifth grade class had already recounted tomboy Caddie's exploits and tricks with her brothers and exclaimed about her loyalty and heroism when she rode to warn the Indians of the impending attack.

A chorus of voices chimed in to agree with Maggie.

"Not fair?" echoed Ms. Runquist, glancing questioningly toward Maggie.

"Well, Caddie's too used to playing outside with her brothers. She probably won't like being inside with Clara and Annabelle."

"Besides," agreed Jessica, "she probably won't be able to stand all that sitting and quilting. And housework! I couldn't. No way!" She shook her head emphatically.

"And her brothers get to do the fun stuff," continued Maggie.

Ms. Runquist turned to the class. "Well, what do you think?"

"She doesn't mind, though," urged Amy. "I think she's having fun."

"How could it be fun if she's used to running and playing. I bet that housework was a lot of work." Liz leaned forward to emphasize her point. "They didn't have vacuum cleaners and microwaves and stuff.

"But her brothers are quilting, too. She's not by herself," answered Kristi. "They're still doing things together."

Voices around the room rose and fell.

After a pause, Paul, speaking cautiously, said, "Yeah, but the brothers are only—like, visiting. Caddie's going to stay." His voice gathered momentum. "They're going to fool around a little and then they'll move out."

"Yeah," Jason exclaimed. "They're going to be boys, do what boys do—uh, back then." Several male voices echoed Jason's "Yeah."

"What do you mean by that? What did boys do—and girls, too?" Ms. Runquist moved to the blackboard. "Let's make two lists." She wrote *Boys* on one side and *Girls* on the other and recorded as voices called out.

"The boys do lots of things like hunt and fish."

"And trap, maybe."

"Ride horses."

"Run around and play games."

"Chop wood."

"And carry wood. They're always filling the wood box for their mothers in stories."

"Probably farm chores."

"Scouting around."

"What about Caddie?" asks Ms. Runquist. "What will she be doing?"

"What her mother does."

"Well?"

"Well, she's sewing at the end—quilting."

"And housework. I suppose that means washing dishes."

"And cooking and cleaning."

"And baking. I like to bake; it's *fun*."

"She might help her mother with her chickens."

Ms. Runquist waited.

"I guess that's what girls did in those days," Jolene shrugged. "It doesn't sound like fun."

"Well, she's doing what her father wants," Amy's voice insisted, "what he says is right."

"And what her mother says she ought to do," added Jennifer.

"What is that? Let's find the page where her father talks with Caddie." Ms Runquist scanned her book. "It's page 215." She read the passage aloud.

> It's a strange thing, but somehow we expect more of girls than of boys. It is the sisters and wives and mothers, you know, Caddie, who keep the world sweet and beautiful. What a rough world it would be if there were only men and boys in it, doing things in their rough way! A woman's task is to teach them gentleness and courtesy and love and kindness. . . . A woman's work is something fine and noble to grow up to, and it is just as important as a man's. . . . I want you to be a woman with a wise and understanding heart, healthy in body and honest in mind. Do you think you would like to be growing up into that woman now? How about it, Caddie, have we run with the colts long enough? (Brink, 1935, p. 215)

The students read back through the passage. After a pause, his finger pointing in his book, Dan spoke. "He wants her to grow up to be a woman like her mother, wise and understanding and, uh, noble."

"Cause what women do is important." Liz smiled across the room at Dan.

"Men need them to make them better," said Kristi, "so they won't be rough."

"Yeah, the men are rough and the women are kind and gentle," Amy added. She straightened her shoulders as she spoke.

"Garrison Keillor says that women are strong and men are handsome." Kyle laughed at his own joke and glanced smugly around him.

"And all the children are above average," Ms. Runquist finished Keillor's line. She laughed with the class.

Maggie frowned. "I see what the father's saying, but I still think Caddie won't like it, and anyway I don't know why *she* has to *quilt* and *clean* to be those things. You can be wise and kind without washing dishes."

Ms. Runquist nodded toward Maggie and then scanned the class.

"Maybe she doesn't have a choice. Maybe she has to change to be like her sister and mother—back then?" Kyle's voice rose to his question.

"Well, my grandma says her mom helped with farm chores but mostly took care of the house," Jennifer remarked.

"And, during the war—I'm not sure which one, some war, when the men were soldiers, the women got jobs in factories. My grandpa told me," added Kristi.

"OK, but maybe Caddie won't end up exactly like her sister. She didn't grow up like her," said Paul. "She's been learning other kinds of things." "Yeah, she's a different person. Maybe she's still a tomboy inside," asserted Liz.

"Yeah, she'll be strong, like Garrison Keillor says." Kyle didn't laugh this time, but Virginia Runquist smiled.

CLASSROOM PROCESS

The students in this fifth-grade class are learning to read, that is, to advance their reading prowess. Through interactive discussion, they are exploring their evoked responses, attempting to understand and come to terms with the text. Individual speakers, reflecting an interior voice, relate their experience with the text. Others reveal impressions through reactions to previous speakers. Together they weave an interpretive tapestry, the weaving occurring within each individual as well as the group. Each reader, listening to the exterior comments, selects and makes connections with personal responses. Understanding is broadened, potentially deepened. Perhaps a preliminary response is validated and enhanced; perhaps, it is adjusted or even rejected.

Often, given the potential for shared emotions and for universal understandings, given also the dynamics of classroom personalities, there may emerge from response dialogues a core of common responses, a convergence of feelings and attitudes among readers. Such convergence may be encouraged by shared personal experiences as well as the stimuli of the text. A caveat: The seeming resolution of a group's discussion should not be construed as necessarily representing each individual's evolved experience, nor the group's correct answer. Such correct answers, such a convergence, need not be anticipated nor be directed. Often, too, responses may diverge, moderately or dramatically, again with the potential for individual variations.

It is probable that the learning-to-read factors attended to in this class experience are multiple. The teacher leads them to consider their comments, to reconsider and develop their reading through the interactive discussion that she promotes. She leads them back to the text to confirm their assertions and to amplify them. She encourages them to relate to the context of setting and character. The students are learning to be attentive to multiple voices, to reflect on subtleties expressed in the text. These skills, with practice, will become a part of the internal processing of texts. Equally important, although not communicated directly, these students are learning that responses may vary among readers.

The shared-response learning situation is a significant underpinning of reader response teaching strategies. With parallel significance for adult readers, it is especially meaningful for neophyte readers. The strategy exposes the building blocks of the responding structure, starting out with laying out of the materials at hand, the initial reader responses. With guidance from the teacher and active participation among themselves, the students begin to establish the design or designs of the structure, constructing it with the planks of their impressions and ideas. Discussion promotes expansion of the structure; reference to the text clarifies the details of the design and features of the structure.

Reading responsively is demanding. It requires an active, assertive intelligence. Readers must be willing to respond beyond the surface words and actions, willing to commit themselves to reflecting. They cannot depend on the teacher to read the story for them, summarizing the relationships and meanings in a lecture or drawing out prescribed ideas in a pseudodiscussion. Nor can they settle for comprehension.

Developing responsive reading is also more demanding for the teacher—and much more exhilarating and satisfying. Traditional procedures—the give-and-take discussion and comprehension-oriented workbooks that seek answers to data questions or textual details (often formatted by the text-basal reader along with suggested answers)—offer structure and management control. They do not provide the impetus for students to reflect on their experience with the text, nor to express their involvement and uncertainties. These teaching strategies, in effect, present the teacher as the dominant reader. They assume her expertise, experience, and greater skill in finding and making meaning; they provide the safety of a planned lesson and perceived interpretations, but not the excitement of quest and discovery. In contrast, the teacher's role in a reader-response situation is dynamic: ascertaining where the students' initial responses are, anticipating developmental responses, identifying passages in the text that may need clarification or that may be used to expand understandings, and preparing strategies for enhancing responses. And the top challenge is being in the mainstream of the discussion, initiating it, feeding it with queries and responses—not taking over ownership—thus, helping students grow as independent readers.

THE DEMOCRACY CONNECTION

There is no surprise in connecting literature to the humanities. It has long been acknowledged to be at the very heart of humanistic studies. Literature reveals the human condition, the foibles, struggles, and achievements of humankind. Focusing on individuals' reactions to challenges, literature expresses the triumphs and defeats of the human spirit. In tragedy, for example, humans are pitted against gods or social forces larger than themselves; brought to ruin, they struggle to emerge from under the yoke and express an indomitable will to prevail, to control their own lives.

An embedded promise of the humanities—thus, of literature—is the promotion of a democratic ideal. We need look no further, perhaps, than the current pedagogical emphasis on multicultural education that meaningfully centers on the use of literary texts. There is explicit recognition that the reading of such novels as *The Shadowman's Way* by Pitts (1992) and *Thank You, Dr. Martin Luther King, Jr.* (1990) by Tate will enlarge the perspectives of readers who may be limited by a restricted culture. Potentially, these readers will gain understanding and will become more accepting of differences, as well as recognize human similarities. Literary texts, of course, provide a vast array of people and concerns, situations and places across the human spectrum. Experiencing this array enriches readers, bringing them closer to the lives of others; indeed, when the transaction is strong, they may exchange lives with characters. Such possibilities are effected by the living-through experiences of literature, in contrast with the efferent-dominated responses to social studies texts.

The democratic impulse arises not only from the array of literary texts and from readers' growth to democratic attitudes through their responses to them; it emanates also from the reading process itself. The recognition of the role of the reader in making meaning, supported by classroom strategies that promote active reader behavior, encourages another democratic attitude. While transacting with the text, as has been explained, active readers relate to the evolving evidence in the text: They weigh the import of language nuances, of character behaviors and traits; they shift the direction of their responses in keeping with these evolutions. Later, when considering their total experience, such recursive weighing and balancing of details is a natural reaction in the process of sorting out their understandings and confusions, in reflecting on the resolution (or irresolution) of the stream of events, and their sense of reality. This pattern of weighing and questioning contains a democratic aspect, for it discourages automatic adherence to a presented idea.

The process of interacting with others is comparable. The reader-oriented discussion creates an atmosphere of empowerment for the students. They need not adhere to the authority of critic or teacher; she becomes instead a partner participant, providing an individual perspective! Students reacting to shared-response discussions comment on their feelings of being equal, that everyone's response is equally welcomed. In this regard, significant in a democratic sense as well as in reading interpretation, are the differences in social contexts—culture, race, ethnicity, gender—that the readers bring to the text and the discussion. The various perspectives within an open, equalizing forum promote acceptance of and insights about the reader-speaker, in addition to enriching and enhancing textual understanding.

The nature of these discussions, the implicit challenge of varied responses or direct disagreement with a stated view, ideally causes students to think through their responses and to find support or clarification for their assertions. This may provide the seeds for a habit of mind to be less willing to accept surface comments, to become assertive in expressing informed opinion, to be more critical and evaluative of language and ideas. Such processing of thought, reminiscent of the ideal of the town meeting, is at the heart of the democratic process: giving equal voice to all sides and testing these voices against our own.

THEORY TO PRACTICE

The theoretical assertions and the illustrations of this chapter reflect applications of the transactional theory of literature to teaching practice in the elementary classroom. Such applications project a shift in teaching style and purpose that correlates with the whole-language philosophy; they also correlate with the movement toward a literature-based reading curriculum in lieu of the traditional basal reading program. Chapter 2, "Literature-Based Teaching: A Student Response-Centered Classroom" discusses the principles of literature-based teaching and its connection to the theory of reader response. The implications for classroom processes and procedures are detailed against a backdrop of theories of learning. The subsequent chapters are case studies of classrooms in action. They represent an array of reader-response practices for a range of classroom levels and types of texts.

REFERENCES

Conrad, J. (1965). *Heart of Darkness*. New York: Dell.

Crosman, R. (1980). Do readers make meaning? In S. R. Sulleman & I. Crosman (Eds.). (149–164). *The reader in the text: Essays on audience and interpretation* (pp. 149–164). Princeton, NJ: Princeton University Press.

Frost, R. (1946). Stopping by woods on a snowy evening. *The poems of Robert Frost*. New York: Random House.

Johnson, M. S., et al. (1977). *Moments (Level M, Grade 5)*. New York: American Book Company.

Iser, W. (1978). *The act of reading: A theory of aesthetic response*. Baltimore, MD: The Johns Hopkins University Press.

Nodelman, Perry. (1992). *The pleasure of children's literature*. New York: Longman.

Probst, R. E. (1981). *Response and analysis: Teaching literature in junior and senior high school*. Portsmouth, NH: Heinemann.

Roethke, T. (1973). My papa's waltz. In J. Ciardi (Ed.), *How does a poem mean?* (p. 1003). Boston, MA: Houghton Mifflin.

Rosenblatt, L. M. (1976). *Literature as exploration* (3rd ed.). New York: Noble and Noble Publishers, Inc.

Rosenblatt, L. M. (1978). *The reader, the text, the poem: The transactional theory of the literary work*. Carbondale: Southern Illinois University Press.

Rosenblatt, L. M. (1985). Viewpoints: transaction vs. interaction—a terminological rescue operation, *Research in Teaching English, 19*, 96–107.

Rosenblatt, L. M. (1988). Writing and reading: The transactional theory. *Reader, 20*, 7–31.

Ruddell, R. B., & Crews, R. (1978). *Person to person (Level 15)*. Boston: Allyn and Bacon.

Tompkins, J. P. (Ed.). (1980). *Reader-response criticism: From formalism to post structuralism*. Baltimore, MD: The Johns Hopkins University Press.

CHILDREN'S TEXTS

Brink, C. R. (1935). *Caddie Woodlawn*. New York: Collier Books/Macmillan.

Collier, J. L., & Collier, C. (1983). *War comes to Willy Freeman*. New York: Delacorte Press.

Lowry, L. (1979). *A summer to die*. New York: Bantam Books.

Naylor, P. R. (1983). *The Soloman system*. New York: Aladdin Books.

O'Dell, S. (1980). *Sarah Bishop*. Boston, MA: Houghton Mifflin.

Paterson, K. (1991). *Lyddie*. New York: Lodestar.

Pitts, P. (1992). *The shadowman's way*. New York: Avon Books.

Sorensen, V. (1956). *Miracles on maple hill*. New York: Harcourt Brace.

Steig, W. (1969). *Sylvester and the magic pebble*. New York: Windmill Books, Inc./Simon & Schuster.

Tate, E. E. (1990). *Thank you, Dr. Martin Luther King, Jr.!* New York: Franklin Watts.

White, E. B. (1953). *Charlotte's web*. New York: Harper and Row.

2

Literature-Based Teaching: A Student Response-Centered Classroom

Carole Cox
California State University, Long Beach

EDITOR'S OVERVIEW

Student, response-centered. Teacher, text-centered. What do these mean? How do they relate to literature-based teaching or to the traditional basal-reader model? What does one choice over the other really mean in the day-by-day reading-instruction curriculum? This chapter focuses on defining these terms and answering these questions.

The title of the chapter identifies the direction the reading curriculum has taken. This movement is in concert with the whole language concept; it has been guided by transactional (reader-response) theory. Cox describes, through her own research, children's characteristic responses to literature, and considers the implications on learning of these responses, and, thus, on teaching style. She further grounds these implications by explaining the theoretical underpinnings of the two basic approaches so they may be compared.

Another comparison is offered: two classrooms, each representing one of the approaches. Drawn from Cox's several years of observing classes, students' responses to their teachers' pedagogical styles are expressed. They reveal the development of significant attitudes; they provide a contrast of learnings. Building on these, Cox provides an array of options for reading and responding.

Consider the following:

1. *Investigate the children's responses and behavior in each classroom. What do they reveal about attitudes and skills being practiced and learned?*
2. *A key word is discover. How does discovery apply to each of these teaching models?*
3. *Reflect on the theories represented in this chapter and consider the teaching/learning options each one offers and each denies.*

Literature-based teaching is a growing curricular movement in recent years, particularly in whole language instruction. There has been a shift from teacher and text-centered approaches that used basal readers and textbooks for other school subjects, such as social studies and science, to a student and response-centered approach that uses whole, meaningful texts such as children's literature and children's own writing for teaching language arts, developing literacy, and to integrate the curriculum (Cox & Zarrillo, 1993; Cullinan, 1987, 1992). This shift has meant that teachers change not only the type of texts they use, but the way they use them (Langer, 1992). Reader response theory has guided this shift (Beach, 1993).

RESPONSE AND READING

Reader response theorists explain that readers are actively engaged in the construction of meaning while reading. Because meaning is the creation of individual and unique readers, there is no single correct meaning of any text.

Transactions with Literature

Among reader response theorists, Rosenblatt's (1938/1983, 1978) transactional model of the reading process in particular has interested whole language elementary educators (Goodman, 1992). Rosenblatt (1994) called the reading process a transaction during which a live circuit is created between the reader and the text. According to Rosenblatt, although all reading occurs as experienced meaning, readers assume a stance, or focus their selective attention in different ways. *Stance* represents a reader's readiness to organize thinking about what is read according to a more efferent or a more aesthetic framework. Any text can be read efferently or aesthetically, and readers move back and forth on a continuum from efferent to aesthetic eventually settling on one predominant stance. During a more efferent reading, the reader's focus of attention is on the information the reader will take away from the text, or the more public aspects; for example, reading the label on a bottle of prescription medicine to find the correct dosage. During a more aesthetic reading, the reader's focus of attention is on the lived-through experience of the reading event, or the more private aspects; for example, reading a novel and picturing yourself as one of the characters. A more efferent reading focuses on what is in the text and a more aesthetic reading focuses on the associations, feelings, attitudes, and ideas that the text aroused in the reader. Most readings are a mix of both stances, and any text can be read more efferently or more aesthetically and readers may adopt a different stance toward the same text at different times and in different situations. Rosenblatt maintains that for most experiences with literature "our primary responsibility is to encourage the aesthetic stance" (1982, p. 275). Yet a study of teachers who made the shift from a basal reader to literature-based reading showed they are still using a more efferent, less aesthetic, teacher-and-text-centered approach (Zarrillo & Cox, 1992).

Children's Responses

A key to student response-centered teaching with literature is knowing how children respond as a basis for asking questions, giving prompts, and planning further experiences with literature. I have been reading and listening to the same group of children respond to literature from kindergarten through third grade, and analyzing their responses from a reader-response perspective (Cox, 1994a, 1994b). Some of the things I have observed are that children take a predominantly aesthetic rather than an efferent stance toward literature, resulting in a focus on personal meaning making; there is a dynamic interplay between both types of stances, and more efferent stances, usually associated with a traditional view of reading as understanding print and explaining a story, were always embedded in a broader aesthetic response; children frequently challenged the text by questioning something they wondered about, hypothesizing a possible explanation, and drawing on personal experience to provide or disprove it; children's characteristic response types in rank order are:

Questioning: Something that puzzled them, wondering, addressing an anomaly.

Focus on a part: Something that struck them, "I like the part when . . ."

Associations: Personal experience, intertextual, metaphorical.

Hypothesizing: Predicting, speculating, retrospecting—going back into the story, extending the story.

Explanations: Cause and effect, generalizing, concluding.

Print and language: Letters, words, sentences, rhyming patterns, reading independently.

Content: Retelling, listing, sequencing, summarizing.

Performance: Verbal and nonverbal acting out, role-playing, sound effects, pantomiming.

Analysis: Applying a critical framework to story facts, writing, illustrating, book design.

When unprompted, children's natural responses to literature indicate that they take a predominantly aesthetic stance (questioning, focus on

a part, associations, hypothesizing) rather than a predominantly efferent stance (explanations, print and language, content).

Obviously, paying attention to personal response in the classroom not
only gives young readers more choice, control, and an opportunity to use
their voices in response to literature, it gives them more responsibility
for their own learning and thus a deeper engagement and involvement
that may result in more learning. It means that the teacher may initiate
experiences with literature, but rather than set predetermined outcomes such as everyone coming to a single agreement on what the author
meant in the story, or doing a book report making sure to include setting,
plot, character, mood, and theme (remember those?), the teacher will
encourage children to respond openly, drawing on their own fund of prior
experience and impressions while reading to construct a meaningful
interpretation of the text.

The focus will be on student response, or personal evocation of the
text, rather than the teacher's ideas or those found in a teacher's guide.
In transactional teaching, teachers demonstrate this belief by asking
open questions—"So what did you think of it?"—and sharing their own
personal responses, and have expectations that the students will do the
same and will extend their responses to the book and develop interpretations through further language and literacy experiences. The students
make choices when responding, use their own voices, gain control over
their ideas and language, and share responsibility for their learning.

Reading as Experienced Meaning

In *Becoming a Nation of Readers: The Report of the Commission on
Reading* (Anderson, Hiebert, Scott, & Wilkinson, 1985), recommendations about the theory and practice of reading included a greater focus
on getting meaning from print from the very beginning of school, reading
aloud to children, providing a wide variety of experiences and talking
together about them, more time reading self-selected books and writing,
less time on worksheets, better libraries, more comprehensive assessment, and more use of good literature in reading instruction. These
recommendations came at a time when teachers were already making a
shift to literature-based reading guided by the classroom teacher rather
than dependent on basal-reading programs with an emphasis on teaching separate skills and student workbook exercises (Shannon, 1990).

This shift to literature-based reading grounded in reader-response
theory is supported by the whole language movement that advocates a
greater role for both literature and teachers in reading instruction, as
opposed to basal readers with teacher's guides (Altwerger, Edelsky, &
Flores, 1987; Goodman, 1986). Whole language is not a method but a set
of applied beliefs with regard to language development, curriculum,
learning, teaching, and the community. Edelsky, Altwerger, and Flores
(1991) described it as a professional theory in practice drawing from the
fields of psychology, child development, psycholinguistics and sociolin-
guistics, literary theory, composition theory, and the theory of literacy.

Goodman (1986) has described key ideas about whole language relevant to reading: (a) Literacy develops from whole (big chunks) to part (small increments) during functional, meaningful, relevant language use. (b) Readers construct meaning while reading, drawing on their prior learning and experience. (c) Readers predict, select, confirm, and self-correct as they make sense of print. (d) Three language systems interact in written language: the graphophonic (sound and letter patterns), the syntactic (sentence patterns), and the semantic (meanings). They work together and can not be isolated for instruction. (e) Comprehension of meaning is always the goal of readers. In a whole language classroom, literature and other authentic texts such as children's writing are the material for reading, and the teacher makes decisions about how reading is taught.

STUDENT RESPONSE-CENTERED VERSUS TEACHER TEXT-CENTERED CLASSROOMS

In a student and response-centered classrom, children are active and learn by doing. Students learn to talk by talking, read by reading, and write by writing. The teacher's role is to help children gain control over their own ideas and language through active engagement with learning experiences focused on the construction of meaning. Student and response-centered language and literacy experiences can be defined as those that originate with the ideas, interests, and language of children.

The theoretical underpinnings of this view of the classroom come from a social constructivist perspective that defines learning as an active constructive process during ongoing social and cultural contexts of the classroom, home, and community, and the transactional perspective that meaning is constructed during a transaction between the reader and the text. Reading is acquired through use. Children learn to read by reading, and children's literature becomes the main reading material along with other authentic texts like children's writing, language experience charts, magazines, newspapers, environmental print, and so forth.

The constructivist psychological theories of learning, or cognitive development, put forth by Piaget (1973, 1977) support the idea that learning is an active process of the construction of meaning by learners. Children discover or construct concepts through active participation with their environments. They develop a view of reality through the interaction of their internal maturation and their experiences. They learn through the exploration and discovery of new experiences, a process of adding new bits of information to what they already know. This means that the teacher's role is to be aware of how children learn and develop and to provide a classroom and environment where they initiate the kinds of experiences for children that helps them engage in the active construction of meaning and knowledge about themselves and the world.

The social interactionist theory of Vygotsky (1962) explains that children learn through meaningful interactions with the environment and other people, and these are both essential factors in the development of new knowledge. When compared to Piaget, who emphasized the importance of learning as an individual, internalized cognitive process not dependent on adult support, Vygotsky put much greater emphasis on the social contextual nature of learning and language. The children learn to read and write when others read to them, participate in shared story book readings and writing events, and eventually read and write on their own. A key idea in Vygotsky's theory (1978) is the *zone of proximal development*, which he defines as "the distance between the actual developmental level as determined by independent problem solving and the level of potential development as determined through problem solving under adult guidance or in collaboration with more capable peers" (p. 76).

This means that children learn when supported by others who know more than they do. Bruner (1983) described the support that adults give children as a scaffold for building new knowledge, moving children from one level of development to another. This support, or scaffolding, is temporary and withdrawn as the child develops and grows, but is then replaced by new scaffolding as new knowledge is constructed through meaningful social interaction. The adult or more capable peer takes into account what the child already knows and using that as a basis provides support or scaffolds in new problem-solving situations. It is a true interaction between the learner and the teacher.

A social constructivist framework also takes into account the unique cultural aspect of each classroom (Spindler, 1982) as well as the role of the family and the cultural and linguistic background of each child (Heath, 1983). Learning occurs in the situated context of a particular class, and this will vary from class to class, and year to year (Green & Meyer, 1990).

A different framework is a teacher and text-centered classroom that reflects a behaviorist tradition of learning. Most of us spent many hours in a classroom like this: in rows, raising hands to speak, listening to the teacher give directions, knowing that the correct response was the one the teacher wanted, doing the same worksheet as everyone else, and knowing that you were grouped according to ability in reading even though the groups might be called The Lions, The Tigers, and The Bears—you all knew which was the high, medium, and low group.

This type of classroom reflected a transmission model of teaching grounded in behaviorism. Educational applications of behaviorist learning theory were made popular by Skinner in the 1950s. Behaviorists believed that learning followed a formula of stimulus–response conditioning requiring reinforcement for acceptable responses. Teaching based on behaviorist laboratory research, often conducted with animals, looked something like the previous description of a classroom, based on the belief that children learned language through a process of environmental conditioning and by imitating adult models. Teachers conditioned students' learning by modeling behavior that students imitated. If they imitated it correctly, they received positive reinforcement. Language learning was not considered instinctive. It was learned in small increments, called skills. Mastering these individual skills meant that you built them up one by one until you could read and write. For example, children learned to read by first mastering the letters of the alphabet, then combining letters to master words, then combining words to master sentences. It was viewed as a step-by-step cumulative process, each step building on the previous one. Basal readers had scope and sequences of these skills, prepared for each grade by building on the grade before.

Invitation 2.1

Write down some memories of how reading was taught when you were in elementary school. How do they compare and fit with the reading models and learning theories expressed on these pages? What ideas do you now have about teaching with literature in your own class?

This is called a *bottom–up* or *part-to-whole* approach to learning to use language, which is quite different than the *top–down* or *whole-to-part* approach described in this book. This means that children learn to use language by using it when they are surrounded by print, have many rich and social interactive experiences with language, and a have focus on meaning, from the time they are babies through the school years.

This view is based on theories of learning like Piaget's and Vygotsky's, and literary theories like Rosenblatt's transactional model of the reading process. The landmark research of Loban (1976, 1979) also demonstrated that the language modes function together as children learn to use and control language. In a longitudinal study of the language development of 338 children K through 12, he found that there is a strong positive correlation among reading, writing, listening, and speaking abilities, but that the bottom line in learning to use language is to use it.

Let us look into two classrooms in the same school that reflect different perspectives on how children learn, develop language and literacy, and use literature. The school has a high percentage of language minority students, primarily native Spanish-speaking Mexican American children. Let's look at the experience of one student in the two classrooms. Anne is a native English-speaking child. Her first-grade classroom teacher uses literature to teach reading, but usually teaches whole class lessons with the Houghton Mifflin literary readers—a newer generation of the basal reader with excerpts of children's books. Each child has the same reader and pupil response booklets with prompts for the children to write after reading. The teacher uses a guide with ideas for teaching, with literature provided by the publisher.

A Text-Centered Lesson From a Literary Reader.   Before reading the excerpt from *Anna Banana and Me*, the teacher asks "Are any of you ever afraid when you try something new?" Children answer this question for a full 10 minutes. Anne does not participate. Then the teacher says "Today we're going to learn something about a person who follows someone else's action when they were unsure and afraid. I think it's exciting to read about somebody who has some of the same feelings we do." She passes out copies of the book that come with the series. First, she directed the children to look at the title and asks a series of questions: "What does it say? What is she? How do you know she's friendly?" She tells them to notice that the author and illustrator were related, what techniques the illustrator used (black ink and water color), to read the title page and dedication page. Anne still has said nothing.

After the teacher reads the book aloud, she says, "There were a lot of messages in this story." She tells them that the people who made the reader wrote some questions for children in the teacher's guide. She has written them on a piece of chart paper. She reads them and asks the children to answer:

1.   Where do you think they are?
2.   What does Anna Banana say about feathers?
3.   Why does the boy go home?
4.   Why does she visit him?
5.   What kind of building does he live in?
6.   What is he doing?
7.   Why does his voice echo?
8.   How do you think the boy is feeling about Anna Banana? (The teacher points out that this question doesn't have a right or wrong answer).
9.   What's something in the story that makes you think that?

Finally, she asks what she calls a thinking question, "How does she suddenly become brave?" There are many tentative answers to this question. Anne finally raises her hand and answers in a rather uncompromising way, "Because Anna Banana told him the feather was magic and made him brave." The teacher says, "Here is a big question. WAS IT MAGIC?" Anne answers, "Yes, because it really made him brave." The teacher says, "Anne says the feather was magic. What do the rest of you think?" Answers included: in the story, but not in real life; sort of, not really; sort of, but different; I think that it's not real, but he thought it was, and then it was, but not really; and so forth.

It is clear the teacher wants children to learn the difference between real and make-believe and come to the consensus that magic could happen in a story but not in real life. The children appear to sense that she is waiting for this answer. After no one disagrees that magic couldn't happen in real life, Anne speaks again, "I think he really believes that the feather is magic and it will make it happen. When I throw a coin into a wishing well, I believe my wish will come true." She says this in a rather uncompromising, even matter-of-fact way. She apparently has not been swayed by the teacher's implied answer, or the lack of support from other students. After this whole-class discussion, the teacher gives the students a writing prompt: "If the feather was really magic, I would . . ." She tells them to go to their seats and write.

This is an example of a text-and-teacher-centered approach to literature-based teaching.

Invitation 2.2

Reread this lesson. Characterize on a continuum from more efferent to more aesthetic, the teacher's questions, prompts, and the assigned after-reading activity.

OR

Write up a lesson plan for this lesson as it is described; then, write up a second lesson plan changing the emphasis from a more efferent, text-centered lesson to a more aesthetic, student and response-centered lesson.

A LITERATURE GROUP FORMS
IN A RESPONSE-CENTERED CLASSROOM

In third grade, Anne spends time in another teacher's room. It is a bilingual Spanish/English classroom. During a period called *Integration* throughout the school, native English-speaking children like Anne and children from bilingual classes go to each other's classrooms.

The teacher of the bilingual classroom Anne visits takes a student response-centered approach to literature-based teaching. He chooses not to use the Houghton Mifflin Literary Readers, although they are available for children to read in his room. Instead, he reads aloud and encourages students to do self-selected, wide independent reading. Frequently, the books students read and discuss become a focal point for integrated learning across the curriculum. This occurred in a literature group with Anne and several other students. One literature group had been reading and learning about Puerto Rico. Alfredo has asked the

librarian for books about the Caribbean, and she has given him Yolen's
Encounter—a story of Columbus' arrival and meeting the Taino people,
from the perspective of a Taino child. The group meets in a circle. Alfredo
tells them, "I went to the library and got this book. It's a sad story. About
how Columbus brought disease. The Taino people wanted to get along
with him, but he killed off the Taino Indians."

The teacher comes up with Anne and asks if she can join the group.
The students agree. He asks if she could read *Encounter* aloud to them,
because Alfredo is very interested in it and has been talking and writing
about it, and it's in English and Anne is an expert English user. (He also
wants Anne to feel a part of the group). Anne reads and Alfredo, Fabiola,
Eddie, and Laura listen. The teacher moves about the room, interacting
with other groups and students. When Anne finishes, the teacher
suggests they talk about it. They begin an animated discussion, pointing
and referring to the dramatic illustrations by Shannon. The teacher
notices this and joins the group.

Teacher:	Tell me about the book.
Alfredo:	He was little, a child. He was Taino, and Christopher Columbus was Italian, sent from Spain.
Anne:	He took the Taino and came back for more.
Teacher:	What happened to the rest of the Taino?
Alfredo:	Many died. Only one survived in the story.
Teacher:	Why?
Alfredo:	Because. . . (He reads part of the story and points to a picture with knives.)
Teacher:	Tell me more about the boy.
Anne:	He had a dream, and when he woke up. . .
Alfredo:	. . .the boy thought their skin was funny (points to picture of Columbus' crew), but he was afraid.
Teacher:	Why do you think?
Alfredo:	Cause he has his people and land taken away.
Teacher:	Have any of you ever had things taken away?
Anne:	We were robbed. TV, VCR, my Dad's tools and our bikes.
Eddie:	My Mom was washing clothes, and put outside to dry, and they were taken. They stole my overalls.
Laura:	(to Anne) How did they get in your house?
Anne:	Don't know.

Every student shares an experience of having been robbed, or having
something stolen.

Teacher:	So you've all been robbed, and the child in this book has been robbed.
Anne:	Yeah. Of his own people.

Alfredo:	They took him away from his land.
Teacher:	Did he ever come back?
Anne:	Let me read the last page (pointing to picture of child as an old man, telling the story).
Teacher:	What is he thinking?
Eddie:	Of his people.
Teacher:	Tell me more.
Laura:	He's wondering what they were doing (pointing to a picture of Columbus' ships as huge birds of prey).
Anne:	His dream about the ships.
Teacher:	Look at the picture. (A white bird like a ship). He is—he's dreaming of a ship.
Anne:	My favorite picture is his dream of flying ships.
Fabiola:	They look like parrots. My favorite picture is this one.
Teacher:	Do you ever have dreams?

The discussion continues, with students sharing their dreams and also talking about other books with dreams like *There's a Nightmare in My Closet* and *The Alligator Under My Bed* and *The Wreck of the Zephyr*. The teachers says: "We should write about our dreams." They also come back to the picture of the bird-boats in *Encounter*, talk about horror movies, and Alfredo tells about a story he heard in Mexico about being thrown in a hole with fire if you said a bad word.

Invitation 2.3

In pairs or small groups, compare the two classrooms with regard to:
 Role of the teacher and role of the student;
 Role of the text and role of personal response.
What implications might this have for your own teaching?

The teacher suggests they think about their discussion and something they could do, perhaps about Christopher Columbus or dreams. The literature group generates a list of ideas, and the teacher writes them on a piece of chart paper.

1. Make a story about what happened.
2. Do it on the computer like a book.
3. Make a musical play with songs.
4. Make poems about dreams of boats, or dreams, or boats.
5. Get some biographies of Christopher Columbus and read them.

This is what the students in this group, including Anne, actually did:

1. Read other books about Christopher Columbus.
2. Made a comparison chart of several books about Christopher Columbus and his meeting of the Taino people because they found these books had very different perspectives.
3. Invited a teacher who studied in Puerto Rico to talk to the class about the Taino and native people of Puerto Rico.
4. Did a play of *Encounter.* (Alfredo played Christopher Columbus, but wasn't very happy about it.)
5. Wrote poems about dreams, boats, and the ocean.

This is an example of a student response-centered approach to teaching with literature.

Keep these two classrooms in mind as you consider the conceptual differences between a traditional teacher and text-centered approach and a student and response-centered approach. Table 2.1 shows a comparison of what the teacher and student did in each one.

RESPONSE-CENTERED, INTEGRATED TEACHING WITH LITERATURE

Whole language, literature-based classrooms where learning is centered around students' responses don't all look the same, but many share a social constructivist view of learning and the transactional model of the reading process. Such classrooms are organized to provide time, opportunities, and an environment for children to read, respond, and ripple—develop further language learning experiences to ripple out across the curriculum, like waves after a pebble is thrown into a pond.

Language learning across the curriculum occurs within the context of the content areas such as social studies, science, mathematics, and music and the arts (Froese, 1994). It is based on three principles: All genuine learning involves discovery, language has a heuristic function (language as a means to learn), and using language to discover is the best way to learn it (Bullock, 1975).

In a student and response-centered classroom, language across the curriculum means an integrated approach to teaching. Students ask questions, identify and solve problems, use research and study skills, and discover the interconnectedness of subject matter. Teachers plan experiences to enable students to do this. Both teachers and students initiate themes of learning, or identify a topic of interest for individual inquiry. Students collaborate and teachers mentor them.

Thematic teaching goes back to the Socratic method of organizing instruction around meaningful questions. Today you will see terms like *theme study*, *theme cycles* (Altwerger & Flores, 1994), *thematic units*, and *integrated, cross-curricular, thematic teaching. Whole language*

TABLE 2.1
Teacher and Text-Centered Classrooms
Versus Student and Response-Centered Classroom

Teacher and Text-Centered Classroom

Teacher

makes all decisions for what is to be learned

basal readers, textbooks, and commercial materials used

uses teacher's guide for basals and textbook series

emphasizes part-to-whole learning

follows a sequence of skills to be mastered

evaluation based on questions with one right answer

Student

passive recipients of learning

imitate what teacher has modeled

follow directions of teacher or textbook

does the same assignment as other students

grouped by ability

evaluated on mastery of skills in hierarchical order

Student and Response-Centered Classroom

Teacher

provides opportunities for independent learning

children's literature and student writing used

observes and listens to students; student voice honored

emphasizes whole-to-part learning

ideas and interests of students generate thematic learning

evaluation based on individual growth and development

Student

learn by doing; active engagement; personal response

make choices: what to read, how to respond, what to learn

work in groups; discover things on own

interact, cooperate, collaborate, plan own experiences

---

generally means integrated teaching. I call these ripple effects of response-themed learning because I know that they are not totally planned ahead by the teacher but, like a pebble thrown into a pond, will send out ripples of their own that can extend across the curriculum depending on the ideas, interests, and experiences of students. Such ripples occurred, for example, when students formed a literature group around the book *Encounter*, and continued to read, think, write, research, and act out ideas about Columbus, the Taino people, and their own experiences with dreams.

Read

Literature-based teaching means creating a room environment and classroom library, and scheduling time and opportunities for reading.

Room Environment.   Classroom reading corners or libraries have designated spaces for shelves and book displays, tables, comfortable chairs—or floor pillows, bean bag chairs, or mats—or a rocker for the teacher. Children's work is displayed on bulletin boards, tables, or shelf tops. Art and writing materials are available.

Time for Reading.

1. Reading aloud. This can happen several times a day, to the whole class or a group, from picture books to chapter books, for sheer enjoyment or in connection with a theme like Christopher Columbus and the Taino people in *Encounter*.

2. Shared reading. Students participate in reading by following along in their own copy of a chapter book, or by reading the text of a Big Book guided by the teacher, or reading a teacher-made chart of poems or songs, which can also be written on sentence strips and used in a pocket chart.

3. Buddy reading. Students read in pairs. They may be reading for information to use for a project they are working on, like comparing different perspectives on Columbus, or simply because they like the same book and each other, or for one to share a favorite book with a friend.

4. Sustained silent reading. Everyone in the class, including the teacher, reads a self-selected book silently.

5. Wide independent reading. Students self-select books and read widely for interest and enjoyment, or they may read widely on a theme of interest. Much wide independent reading can take place when students work in literature groups during fairly large blocks of time.

Respond

Students respond to literature in many ways. One of the most natural is through discussions, talking together and with the teacher.

Talking Together.   Provide time and opportunities to talk before, during, and after reading for the whole class, small groups, or in one-to-one conferences, in what Peterson and Eeds (1990) described as grand conversations. This is some of the richest time for students to reflect on their own response while reading, and for you to know more about their response as a basis for planning further response-centered activities.

The type of questions teachers ask direct children to take a predominantly aesthetic or efferent stance towards any text. Ideally they should first direct them to take an aesthetic stance toward literature. Think about the children's natural responses described earlier as you develop questions and prompts for class or group discussions. Their preferred types were aesthetic. They questioned something they read about, focused on a favorite part, hypothesized and wondered, and made associations with their own experiences. Out of these broader, richer aesthetic responses leading to the development of personal meaning, more efferent concerns emerged such as developing explanations, attention to print and language, or content and analysis.

Table 2.2 shows questions and prompts based on children's responses. First, the more aesthetic that direct children to focus on the personal evocation of a text, and then the more efferent, focused on the text itself, which tend to emerge from the more aesthetic.

Invitation 2.4

Make a list of several children's books you like. Describe to a small group how you would introduce one of them in a classroom where you would use literature groups like the one described on the second lesson.

Writing in Response Journals.　Response journals are an important component of response-centered teaching with literature. Students can write in these before, during, and after reading. These journals can trigger discussions when talking together about books, during conferences with the teacher, or buddy reading.

1. What were you thinking about while reading? Tell about it.
2. What was your favorite part of the story? Tell about it.
3. Was there anything you wondered about? Tell about it.
4. What else do you think might happen?
5. Has anything like this ever happened to you? Tell about it.
6. Write anything you want about the story.

Students can just write, or you can suggest questions and prompts to get them started. Those listed here are primarily aesthetic, to encourage students to focus on the lived-through experience of the book.

Double-Entry Literature Response Journals.　Some teachers suggest double-entry journals, where a student writes down the part of the story that interested them and their thoughts about that part on the other side.

Left side: Interesting part of the book
Right side: Response to the part

Response journals are important in assessing students' engagement with and understanding of literature. They provide an authentic ongoing record of students' interests, responses, and personal explorations of literature.

Table 2.2
Aesthetic and Efferent Questions and Prompts

Aesthetic

What do you think about the story?

Tell anything you want about the story.

What did you wonder about?

What was your favorite part?

Has anything like this ever happened to you? Tell about it.

Does the story remind you of anything? Tell about it.

What would you change in the story?

What else do you think might happen in the story?

What would you say or do if you were a character in the story?

Efferent

What was the main idea of the story?

What did the author mean by—?

What was the problem in the story?

How did the author solve the problem?

Retell your favorite part.

Tell the order of the story events.

Describe the main characters.

Explain the characters' actions.

What other stories are like this one? Compare and contrast them.

How did the author make the story believable?

Is the story fact or fiction?

How do you think the characters felt?

Response Options.   Here are other options for children to respond
to literature. These should be flexible, with options for individuals and
groups. Ask students for ideas. Be cautious about directing children to
write or do a project after reading every book. Probably the best thing
to do after reading a book is—read another one.

1.   Read another book. If students enjoyed or were intrigued with a
      topic in a book, observe their response and talk with them and
      help them find more books: the same content, genre, author, or
      theme. Some students who read *Encounter* went on to read
      biographies of Columbus, looked for books about the Taino and
      Puerto Rico, and books with a dream theme.
2.   Read, talk, draw, write. Younger students especially like to talk
      and draw in response to a book read aloud or in a literature group,
      talk about the book or their picture, and either write or give
      dictation for a title or caption.
3.   Literature as a model for writing. Students draw on their own
      experience when writing, using a literary form.

4. Story dramatization. Students talk about the characters and how they act, analyze the story structure, and play the story. Students in the *Encounter* literature group wrote a script based on the book and produced it as a play.

5. Reader's theatre. Any printed text can be adapted for reader's theatre: picture books, excerpts from chapter books, traditional literature, or poetry (Silverstein's *A Light in the Attic* or *Where the Sidewalk Ends* are both excellent sources).

6. Storytelling. Students can retell the story in their own words, and also use a flannel board, props, music, and so forth. Traditional literature is excellent for storytelling.

7. Puppetry. Students can choose to make puppets to play a part of the story, the whole story, or to create their own story based on a story's characters and the puppets they make.

8. Artmaking. Options include drawing, painting, collage, constructions, murals, posters, mobiles, dolls, puppets, props for storytelling, costumes and backdrops for drama, masks, and so forth.

9. Mediamaking. Students can create a filmstrip, slides, or overhead transparencies of the story, or their own version of the story, by drawing directly on clear film stock with permanent pens. They can also respond to literature in a variety of ways by videotaping: role play characters, play a scene or dramatize the whole story, do their own version of the story, do mock interviews with story characters.

10. Computers. Students can write responses, stories, scripts, make books, or create hypertexts with print, visuals, and sound in response to literature.

11. Constructions. Students can build three-dimensional constructions of the story world on a cardboard or styrofoam base, or in a box with one side cut away. They can make dioramas, scenes, or landscapes; houses, buildings, or boats from a story; or papier-mache constructions.

12. Bookmaking. Students can write and make books based on their response to the story or a new version: stapling pieces of paper together with a construction paper cover, contact paper books, fold-a-books, pop-up books, and so forth.

Ripple

Listen to children's responses and questions during literature discussions. These will often indicate a theme, a focal topic of interest, a pebble that will set off a ripple effect of learning experiences. Ideas from students' response journals may also be a source of worthy topics. One easy way to develop these is to start a running list of ideas and questions about a book on a piece of chart paper. Another way is to do a cluster, or web of student ideas.

Literature Groups.   Literature groups are formed when children have a common interest in a book or theme and enjoy working together. Literature groups can be formed to read, write, and discuss the book with the teacher (Peterson, 1987; Watson, 1988). Or, they can be formed for a longer period of time, even several weeks or a month, for a ripple effect of response-themed learning. These groups require some self-direction on the part of students, who take responsiblity for control of their own learning.

Other names for literature groups are *book clubs, literature circles,* and *reading workshops.* Book clubs usually mean that a small group of children will read, write, and talk about a book without the teacher (Raphael, 1992). Literature circles are another way to describe literature groups (Short & Pierce, 1990). Reader's workshop is an entire approach to teaching reading and often writing in reader's/writer's workshop. There is no single way to do this, although these groups share certain characteristics:

1.   Groups are based on mutual interests: one book, several, or a theme.
2.   Groups are flexible and can change membership, amount of time they meet, or focus.
3.   Groups are social, cooperative, and collaborative.
4.   Groups can be led by teacher or students.
5.   Groups are student and response-centered and allow ample time and opportunity to read, talk, write, plan, and carry out further experiences with literature.

HONORING STUDENTS' VOICES

Teachers who use a text-centered approach to literature-based teaching often ignore the importance of student's voices when responding to literature. Children I have read to and observed over a 6-year period in a longitudinal study (Cox, 1994a) have demonstrated a natural freedom and eagerness to read and respond to literature. This seems significant when thinking about the future of teaching with literature in elementary schools. Children's ability and independence is not fully acknowledged in the development of the new basals like Houghton Mifflin's literary readers, where questions and prompts are provided for the teacher on the assumption that children need them to proceed further in their personal explorations of literature. I found children capable of asking and answering their own questions, a reflection of the dynamic interplay between efferent and aesthetic stances—first questioning the text, hypothesizing alternatives, verifying with personal associations, and explaining and interpreting on their own. I also see an inherent conflict between teacher and text-centered approaches to reading instruction and teaching with literature that ignore the authenticity and diversity of children's unique response process styles. They tend to reach immediately for a comfortable consensus rather than allowing for the tension and discomfort that seem to produce the rich, meaningful, and diverse responses students produce when they question or challenge a text. The children I have observed are most engaged with literature when something irritates them, like a grain of sand in the oyster that eventually produces a pearl. Encouraging children to respond authentically and aesthetically, to address the things they find anomalous, and accepting diversity of responses could provide a rich medium of growth for reading and language development as well as literary understanding, critical interpetation, and self-knowledge through transactions with literary works.

Anne and other students like her have been eager to respond to literature with me, or in classrooms where their voices are honored like the one in which she joined the *Encounter* literature group. They have been remarkably silent, however, in classrooms where the text and the teacher's questions drawn from the teacher's guide are more important. In fourth grade, Anne comments on her teacher's heavy reliance on Houghton Mifflin literary readers and the way much time was spent by students during reading instruction answering questions in pupil response booklets that were graded by comparing them to answers in the teacher's guide:

> I hate reading in school because you have to read what they make you. Unless it's a good book, but even if it's a good book you have to read certain parts when you have to. The only time I like reading in school is when the teacher's reading aloud and we can read along, or when we can read for fun—which is never. We never have time to read. And you have to write down the stupid thing. I hate that. You gotta write down everything you do. I don't get how that is reading. And one time I told the truth to one of the questions, and she put it wrong and counted it off. So I have to make up something which is real dumb. And they get mad at you when you get behind or something. Answering questions instead of reading is the dumbest thing in the whole entire world.

REFERENCES

Altwerger, B., Edelsky, C., & Flores, B. M. (1987). Whole language: What's new? *The Reading Teacher, 41*, 147–155.

Altwerger, B., & Flores, B. (1994). Theme cycles: Creating communities of learners. *Primary Voices, K-6, 2*, 2–6.

Anderson, R., Hiebert, E., Scott, J., & Wilkinson, I. (1985). *Becoming a nation of readers*. Washington, DC: National Institute of Education.

Beach, R. (1993). *A teacher's introduction to reader-response theories*. Urbana, IL: National Council of Teachers of English.

Bruner, J. (1983). *Child's talk: Learning to use language*. New York: Holt, Rinehart and Winston.

Bullock, A. B. (1975). *A language for life*. London: Her Majesty's Stationery Office.

Cox, C. (1994a, December). *Challenging the text: Case studies of young children responding to literature*. Paper presented at the National Reading Conference, San Diego, CA.

Cox, C. (1994b, April). *Young children's response to literature: A longitudinal study, K-3*. Paper presented at the American Educational Research Association, New Orleans, LA.

Cox, C., & Zarrillo, J. (1993). *Teaching reading with children's literature*. Columbus, OH: Merrill.

Cullinan, B. (Ed.). (1987). *Literature in the reading program*. Newark, DE: International Reading Association.

Cullinan, B. (Ed.). (1992). *Invitation to read: More children's literature in the reading program*. Newark, DE: International Reading Association.

Edelsky, C., Altwerger, B., & Flores, B. (1991). *Whole language: What's the difference?* Portsmouth, NH: Heinemann.

Froese, V. (1994). Language across the curricululm. In A. Puves (Ed.), *Encyclopedia of English studies and language arts* (pp. 693–694). New York: Scholastic.

Goodman, K. S. (1986). *What's whole in whole language?* Portsmouth, NH: Heinemann.

Goodman, K. S. (1992). I didn't found whole language. *The Reading Teacher, 46* (3), 188–199.

Green, J. L., & Meyer, L. A. (1990). The embeddedness of reading in classroom life: Reading as a situated process. In C. Baker & A. Luke (Eds.), *The sociology of reading* (pp. 141–160). Amsterdam: Benjamins.

Heath, S. B. (1983). *Ways with words: Language, life, and work in communities and classrooms*. New York: Cambridge University Press.

Langer, J. A. (1992). *Literature instruction: A focus on student response*. Urbana, IL: National Council of Teachers of English.

Loban, W. (1976). *Language development: Kindergarten through grade twelve*. Urbana, IL: National Council of Teachers of English.

Loban, W. (1979). Relationships between language and literacy. *Language Arts, 56*, 485–486.

Peterson, R. (1987). Literature groups: Intensive and extensive reading. In D. Watson (Ed.), *Ideas with insights: Language arts K-6* (pp. 32–45). Urbana, IL: National Council of Teachers of English.

Peterson, R., & Eeds, M. (1990). *Grand conversations: Literature groups in action*. New York: Scholastic.

Piaget, J. (1973). *To understand is to invent: The future of education*. New York: Grossman.

Piaget, J. (1977). *The development of thought: Equilibration of cognitive structures*. (A. Rosin, Trans.). New York: Viking.

Raphael, T. (1992). Research directions: Literature and discussion in the reading program. *Language Arts, 69*, 54–61.

Rosenblatt, L. M. (1983). *Literature as exploration* (4th ed.). New York: Modern Language Association. (Original work published 1938)

Rosenblatt, L. M. (1978). *The reader, the text, the poem: The transactional theory of the literary work*. Carbondale: Southern Illinois University Press.

Rosenblatt, L. M. (1982). The literary transaction: Evocation and response. *Theory into practice, 21*, 268–277.

Rosenblatt, L. M. (1994). *The transactional theory of reading and writing*. In R. Ruddell, M. Ruddell, & H. Singer (Eds.). *Theoretical models and processes of reading* (pp. 1057–1092). Newark, DE: International Reading Association.

Shannon, P. (1990). *The struggle to continue: Progressive reading instruction in the United States*. Portsmouth, NH: Heinemann.

Short, K. G., & Pierce, K. M. (Eds.). (1990). *Talking about books: Creating literate communities*. Portsmouth, NH: Heinemann.

Spindler, G. (1982). *Doing the ethnography of schooling.* New York: Holt, Rinehart & Winston.

Vygotsky, L. S. (1962). *Thought and language.* Cambridge, MA: MIT Press.

Vygotsky, L. S. (1978). *Mind in society* (M. Cole, Ed.). Cambridge, MA: Harvard University Press.

Watson, D. (1988). *Reading process and practice: From socio-psycholinguistics to whole language.* Portsmouth, NH: Heinemann.

Zarrillo, J., & Cox, C. (1992). Efferent and aesthetic teaching. In J. E. Many & C. Cox (Eds.), *Reader stance and literary understanding: Exploring the theories, research, and practice* (pp. 235–249). Norwood, NJ: Ablex.

PART II

Initiating and Developing
Readers' Responses:
Classroom Case Studies

3

Talking About Literature "In Depth": Teacher-Supported Group Discussions in a Fifth-Grade Classroom

Shelley H. Allen in Association with Peg Reed
Vanderbilt University
and Wickliffe Informal Alternative School

EDITOR'S OVERVIEW

A frequent concomitant of a literature-based reading program is the strategy of small group discussions. The use of the small groups in classrooms at all levels is not new. Their application, however, in developing the students' responses to literature, to enhancing those responses, merits particular attention.

Sitting in on a fifth-grade group's discussions of Incident at Hawk's Hill by Eckert, Shelley Allen spotlights the nature of the students' responses and their interactions.

The teacher of this fifth-grade class, Peg Reed, is experienced. Her classroom context reveals aspects of her teaching philosophy, particularly with regard to teaching reading and literature. Also evident are several organizational strategies, that is, ways of putting small groups together.

The discussions reveal the role and functioning of both the teacher and the students. Within Mrs. Reed's behavior and comments can be seen her teacherly concerns for developing the discussion strategies of the students, their reading strategies, as well as their understanding of this novel. The students reveal how they build on each other's initial responses to develop their understandings, how they make meaning in response to the text.

Consider the following:

1. *Review the samples of interactive student discussion. How do they work? What roles do the students play?*
2. *Study Peg Reed's language and discussion behavior. What dialoguing traits are evident?*
3. *What is the learning potential of both whole class and small group discussions? In what situations would each strategy be beneficial?*

A group of six fifth graders and their teacher, Mrs. Reed, had been reading and discussing the historical fiction novel, *Incident at Hawk's Hill* (Eckert, 1971), for several days in their classroom. I interviewed the students to find out what their perspectives on the literature group were.[1] Here are some of their responses:

Steve[2]: Well, it's [the group] different than just reading by yourself, and, if you don't know what parts mean, then when you talk in the group, you're gonna ask questions so you can know what that means.

Anne: Well, we would find out words we didn't understand and talk about what happened in the book. And we kinda had our own opinions, and there were a couple [of] arguments about different things, and we had to prove other people wrong or show 'um what was really true, 'cause sometimes they don't understand the book.

Diane: We talk about . . . how we felt and how the people in the book felt, and the characters. And how the things happened, and what your opinion was.

John: I think it was fun, because you got to tell about the book out loud instead of like in your mind, by yourself. (Allen, 1994a)

Students such as those in Mrs. Reed's classroom are enjoying the benefits of the growing number of literature-based reading programs that are burgeoning in elementary schools across the nation. Teachers are developing a range of techniques for use within these programs, techniques designed to help children learn by transacting with books. Literature has the power to challenge our thinking, expand our knowledge of human history, stretch the imagination, increase our social sensitivity, and provide a variety of vicarious experiences (Huck, 1990).

One literature-based instructional technique that is gaining widespread popularity is the use of literature groups–small groups of children and sometimes their teachers, who gather to talk about books they are reading (see Allen, 1994b; Peterson & Eeds, 1990; Pierce & Gilles, 1993; Short & Pierce, 1990). It is widely recognized that engaging in dialogues with others is a natural way for children to organize and

---

[1]Data presented in this chapter are drawn from an observational dissertation study I undertook in three elementary classrooms. The study's purpose was to explore how 3 teachers with experience in the use of literature groups viewed and conducted such groups. Teacher and student patterns of talk during group discussions, as well as teacher and student perspectives on those discussions were of key interest. Two combination 3/4 teachers and 1 Grade 5 teacher participated in the study. The grade 5 teacher, Mrs. Reed, and her focal group are spotlighted in this chapter. In each of the teacher's classes, I followed one small group of students as they read and discussed a children's novel from beginning to end with their teacher. The series of focal group discussions in each class lasted from 2 to 5 weeks. I observed and audiotaped these discussions, and I interviewed the teachers and participating students to solicit their perspectives on literature groups.

[2]Pseudonyms have been used for students' names to preserve anonymity.

reflect on their thinking (Barnes, 1976; Peterson & Eeds, 1990; Vygotsky, 1978). In *Literature as Exploration*, Rosenblatt (1983) wrote of the important role discussion plays in helping students reflect on their "lived-through" experiences with literature. She asserted, "awareness that others have had different experiences with it [the text] will lead the reader back to the text for a closer look. The young reader points to what in the text explains his response. He may discover, however, that he has overreacted to some elements and ignored others" (p. 286). Discussions in a small group, as opposed to talk in the larger, whole-class context, in particular provide opportunities for children to fully share, examine, and clarify their responses to literature.

In this chapter, I spotlight the literature discussion group views and practices of one fifth-grade teacher, Mrs. Reed, and a small group of her students. Mrs. Reed and her students attended Wickliffe Elementary, an informal alternative public school located in an upper middle class suburb of Columbus, Ohio. Wickliffe's population was predominantly Caucasian; for example, Mrs. Reed's classroom consisted of 22 Caucasian children and 2 children of Hispanic descent. Mrs. Reed is also Caucasian. Teaching and learning at Wickliffe were characterized by a child-centered approach based on the British integrated day model. Mrs. Reed's curriculum, like that of the school's, was literature-based. Mrs. Reed had been teaching for 27 years and had been conducting literature discussion groups, or "in depth" groups as she called them, for over 11 years.

THE CONTEXT FOR DISCUSSION

Mrs. Reed's Fifth-Grade Classroom

Mrs. Reed's fifth-grade classroom was a literature-rich environment. The 24 children in the room had access to hundreds of children's chapter books, arranged by genre, that filled bookshelves in a large carpeted area. Poetry books were arranged in a separate set of bookcases, and another bookshelf in a corner of the room housed a collection of one-title book sets. These sets were the books earmarked for in depth discussion groups.

Children in Mrs. Reed's room routinely read literature and wrote their own stories, poetry, and books. At the time of my research they were composing bird books as part of a large classwide study of birds. Students kept an ongoing record of the books they read in their Reading Notebooks. On a daily basis, Mrs. Reed read aloud chapter books, and students engaged in SSR (sustained silent reading).

Mrs. Reed said that "wide reading" was an integral part of her reading program. *Wide reading* meant that students were required to choose and independently read a chapter book a week (on average) from the classroom library. Mrs. Reed stocked the library with books with "meat," books she felt would make the children think and "stretch" them as readers. She was an avid reader of children's books herself. She strove to help students become aware of more sophisticated attributes of books, such as authors' writing styles; discussions during in depth group sessions, as well as during teacher-read-alouds, were opportunities to cultivate the students' awareness. Many of Mrs. Reed's comments to me during interviews suggested a focus on text in terms of her reading program purposes; however, she was open to, and mindful of, students' personal responses to literature as well, as was revealed in the in depth group discussions I observed.

Mrs. Reed's Approach to In Depth Literature Groups

In an interview Mrs. Reed explained why she decided to implement in depth literature groups in her reading program: "I just felt like the wide reading is not enough; they [students] need something where they look at the text more carefully than they do on their own" (Allen, 1994a, pp. 126–127). Mrs. Reed often assembled in depth groups to have students explore specific aspects of a book, such as setting, vocabulary, or author's use of language. She also put together in depth groups to encourage students to read a different genre or a more complex type of book than they were choosing to read on their own. Although participants in an in depth group usually read the same book, Mrs. Reed, at times, asked each student in a group to read a different book on a common theme or topic. (See Short, 1993, for a discussion of the strategy of using sets of conceptually related books, or Text Sets, for literature groups.) Literature groups also formed spontaneously at times in Mrs. Reed's room. For example, during the study Mrs. Reed pointed out that a group of boys was reading, informally discussing, and passing around a series of Brian Jacques books (e.g., *Redwall*).

In depth groups were flexibly formed and scheduled; all students in the class were not necessarily involved in an in depth group at the same time, and group membership was not static over the course of the year. When Mrs. Reed put together groups, she took into account such factors as students' reading abilities, self-concepts, and personalities. She strove for heterogeneous grouping in terms of ability. She stressed that she wanted to "lift" the students (challenge them as readers) but not to give them something so difficult to read that they felt degraded or embarrassed. Six (or occasionally seven) students was the maximum number for an in depth group. Beyond that number, children did not have adequate response time, nor were they sufficiently involved, according to Mrs. Reed. In depth group members typically met on a daily basis over a one to two week period to discuss the book they were reading.

Mrs. Reed expected students in an in depth group to be active discussion participants who moved beyond simply retelling a story. Specifically, she expected group members to voice interpretive disagreements with each other, to support their point of view by providing evidence from the book, and to discuss an author's (or authors') writing style, choices, and devices. Further, she wanted each student to "be an active participant in the story—it's not like television, that it kind of happens to you. Because there are shades of meaning, and people may interpret books a little differently . . . and some people get a lot more from a book than others" (Allen, 1994a, p. 128). Group members were also given the responsibility of deciding among themselves how much of the book to read before each group meeting. Finally, children typically created a project or presentation as a means of sharing their in depth book with the rest of the class.[3]

During in depth group sessions, Mrs. Reed's preferred role was that of a collaborator. "I like to be able to bring my questions in as one of the members of the group, rather than as the teacher," she said (Allen, 1994a, pp. 128–129). The reading abilities of group members, the difficulty level of the book, Mrs. Reed's goals for learning, and students' responses all shaped the kinds of questions Mrs. Reed asked during a group's sessions. Her level of involvement also depended on the individual group. She participated more actively in groups new to in depth reading and in groups that were not "gelling;" conversely, she participated sporadically, or not at all, in groups that were seasoned.

Mrs. Reed reported that she generally tried to follow the Rosenblatt model in her approach to in depth group discussions. Rosenblatt's (1978) transactional theory depicts the process of reading as reciprocal, a transaction between reader and text in which both contribute to the creation of a literary work. Rosenblatt (1983, 1991) asserted that the reading of literature should initially be an aesthetic, "lived-through" experience; she argued that later this experience should be reflected on and expanded.

Mrs. Reed interpreted Rosenblatt as encouraging teachers to let students do the talking about a story. She indicated that she did not want in depth group participants to feel that the discussions were teacher-question, student-answer sessions. Indeed, Rosenblatt (1983) wrote, "an atmosphere of informal, friendly exchange should be created. The student should feel free to reveal emotions and to make judgments" (p. 70). Mrs. Reed conceded, however, that there were times when she felt it was important to point out aspects of a book that students might miss. She cautioned against trying to point out everything though, "because . . . you just wear it to death and you have to be careful in in-depth that you don't do that to a book" (Allen, 1994a, p. 129).

Many of Mrs. Reed's expectations for in depth discussions were realized in the group I had the opportunity to observe and record. In the remainder of this chapter I discuss Mrs. Reed's strategies for interacting

---

[3]For reasons unrelated to my research study, students in the in-depth group described in this chapter did not do a project or a presentation.

with the focal group and the nature of the students' talk about the story
they read.

FIFTH GRADERS AND THEIR TEACHER DISCUSS
INCIDENT AT HAWK'S HILL

The Group and the Book

Mrs. Reed selected six students, four boys and two girls, for the focal
group. One child was Hispanic-American; the other five were Caucasian.
Group membership changed slightly over the course of the study. One
boy withdrew from the group midway through the series of seven
discussions, and a third girl took his place. Three of the children
attended a district program for gifted students. Mrs. Reed considered
all of the participating children to be readers who could comprehend a
story "beyond the surface level" (Allen, 1994a, p. 131).

The group met once daily over a 2-week period (seven total meetings)
to discuss the historical fiction novel, *Incident at Hawk's Hill* by Eckert
(1971). Meetings lasted from 30 to 45 minutes. Group members typically
sat in a circle in the carpeted area of the room, or at a table. Other
children in the class were usually reading independently (SSR), working
on student-made books, or participating in other in depth groups when
the *Incident at Hawk's Hill* group met.

Incident at Hawk's Hill is a 1972 Newbery Honor Book. Mrs. Reed
gave several reasons for choosing the book: It was challenging; it was a
story of survival, a topic not yet addressed in the class; and Eckert was
an outstanding writer. *Incident at Hawk's Hill* is set in Canada in the
1870s and is based on an actual event. It tells the story of a shy 6-year-old
farm boy, Ben, who becomes lost on the prairie and is adopted by a female
badger. Ben and the badger form an extraordinary bond and spend an
incredible summer together before Ben is reunited with his family. The
badger follows Ben home, a move that jeopardizes her life at the end of
the story.

Mrs. Reed's Discussion Strategies

When the book was introduced during the first group meeting, Mrs. Reed
made her expectations for in depth discussions clear. (The students were
participating in their first in depth group with Mrs. Reed, although most
reported that they had been involved in literature groups the previous
year.) Students were to take responsibility for leading the discussions.
Mrs. Reed told them to decide how many pages of the story to read before
each meeting. She asked them to suggest discussion rules, such as what
to do if someone did not complete the reading assignment for the day.
She also explained what in depth reading and discussion meant. She

mentioned that she wanted the group to address vocabulary in the book, too. The following excerpts from the first in depth meeting illustrate Mrs. Reed's strategy of explicitly discussing group processes:

Mrs. R: ... this is *in depth*, and that means that you talk about it [the book], and there are going to be arguments, you know why?

Steve: Because it's a hard book to read.

Anne: 'Cause some people may interpret the writing different ways than other people.

Mrs. R: In some ways we all probably are going to interpret it differently, and so one of the things you need to be able to do is to go back to the book to prove it when you get into it.—

. . .

Mrs. R: All right, any other things that you think would have to be done in order for you to discuss the book every day?

Diane: Well, if you think that like they're [other group members] wrong, and they just must have like read something wrong or something, then maybe you should, if you want, I was wondering if we were allowed to correct them?

Mrs. R: Well you can say "I don't agree," and then other people might not agree, or they might agree, and then how do you prove it?

Anne: You go back to the book.—

Tony: Go back and read it.—

. . .

Mrs. R: Does anybody have anything else that you think we need to do, or that you want to know about the in-depth reading? [brief pause] You may want to check back sometimes to see that you're getting all the detail, because detail gets brought out in this, and something else you need to think about is writer, what's the writer doing and why, why do you think he's doing it. Ah, the writing style, how that affects the story . . .

. . .

Mrs. R: When you're reading in depth, you're going to be looking at it [the story] a lot more deeply, so you want to do a lot more critical kind of reading, where you're thinking about it deeply. (Allen, 1994a, pp. 204–205)

At the beginning of the second meeting, Mrs. Reed further clarified her expectations; she told the children that she wanted to stay out of the discussion as much as possible. Throughout the group sessions, she reminded children to talk to each other, particularly when they focused their attention on her rather than on their peers. Consequently, it was not uncommon for students to talk for sizable stretches of a discussion meeting with minimal teacher input.

In addition to promoting student–student talk and explicitly discussing group processes and expectations, Mrs. Reed used several strategies to nurture children's responses to the story. She actively encouraged the sharing of personal responses, opinions, and background knowledge related to the text. For example, in the first in depth meeting, she distributed copies of *Incident at Hawk's Hill* and asked students to make inferences about the story by looking at the cover illustration. (The cover depicts a young boy and a badger on the prairie.) Children drew on their background knowledge to answer. Mrs. Reed listened to the students' comments and at times asked delving questions or made clarification remarks in response, as the following excerpts reveal:

Diane: Well, there's like a boy six years old, and I guess that he lives around a farm or something, and—

Mrs. R: Why do you think he's six years old?

Diane: Just be—, he doesn't look that old.

Mrs. R: Okay.

Diane: And um, that he's found this animal or something,—

Tony: [whispering] A badger. It's a badger.—

Diane: [continuing] and that it's not like around this time, it's around in the um, 1800s.

. . .

John: Um, well, usually you don't go that far from your house and he's far away from his house because you can't see the house.

Mrs. R: Oh [said with rising intonation]. Tony?

Tony: Um, he might be poor because he doesn't have any shoes.

. . .

Mrs. R: Steve?

Steve: Well, he's petting a badger, and it looks like he's made friends with the badger. The badger's not scared of him.

Mrs. R: Is that unusual?

Steve: Yeah, and he is about 6, 5, 7 [years old].—

Fred: Yeah.

. . .

Fred: Well I think it's um, a boy who went away from his house and he's been probably seeing this badger a few times, it's obviously not the first time because it's [sic] obviously made friends with him. And he's petting him, and ah, I bet it's around 1910s, 1910.

Mrs. R: Okay. Um, John?

John: Well um, I think he's lost because his clothes are pretty raggy [sic] and old.

Mrs. R: Okay, so you're predicting, that was my next question, what can you predict?—

John: Yeah, I'm predicting.—

Mrs. R: [continuing] So you're predicting that he's lost.—

John: I predict—, yeah, right, yeah.—

. . .

Mrs. R: Do you have any predictions? Can any of you predict anything? Tony?

Tony: I think he might live in America.

Mrs. R: All right.

Steve: Well, he might be close to his home, well because his hair's like, it's combed, and if he was running really fast, his hair would get all messed up.

. . .

Mrs. R: Anne?

Anne: Um, it kind of looks like the badger's gonna have something to do with the story, that he may come down to see this wild animal a lot, and maybe run away from home.

Mrs. R: Okay. Now some of you said you thought that he was far away from home because you could see no house, but he [Steve] thinks he's at least close enough that he hasn't been running, or gotten his hair all messed up.—

Steve: Yeah.—

Tony: Yeah.—

Fred: Because of his—

Mrs. R: [continuing] So why do you think we might not be able to see the house? (Discussion J1, pp. 5–9, Allen, 1994a)

Given the chance to draw on their general background knowledge and to explore and share their thoughts on the cover illustration, the students made several insightful inferences about the story.

Invitation 3.1

The student participants in Mrs. Reed's in depth group were by and large quite familiar with literature-based approaches to reading instruction. Discuss with peers how in depth group discussions involving students with little prior exposure to literature-based teaching might differ from the Incident at Hawk's Hill *discussions in Mrs. Reed's classroom. Establish potential guidelines or strategies for getting such students to understand and practice literature-response.*

Mrs. Reed revealed her awareness of the students' developing story responses during an interview with me. (In the interview I had asked her to talk about the participating students' reading abilities.) For example, she stated,

I think that another thing he [John] does in a group is he builds on other people's comments; it seems to open doors for him, doors of understanding, and he's able to reach into stories more deeply. It's like an oh! and then he'll pick up on something and take it a step further, and I think that's something that an in-depth group can provide for him.

Another of Mrs. Reed's statements during the interview showed her awareness of students' evolving responses to *Incident at Hawk's Hill*:

> She [Diane] seems to have a strong sense of character, and she identifies well with many of the characters in the book; however, she puts herself into—. While others [in the group] were trying to understand the father [Ben's father] she was saying, "I hate him, he's mean" in the beginning. There were some comments by others to that effect too; however, as they talked, they began to see, and began to say, the father . . . doesn't see how to do this [i.e., communicate with his son]. It may not be that he dislikes the boy [Ben] or that he's mean, but he just doesn't understand anything or anybody that's different or understand how to show feelings. So there was that movement on the other part of the kids; I didn't feel like she [Diane] made that leap.

Thus, Mrs. Reed indicated that some group members came to understand that the father in the story was not simply mean; rather, he had difficulty relating to his unusual son.

As well as inviting the students' responses and following up on their comments during in depth group sessions, Mrs. Reed sometimes initiated new topics for discussion. For instance, in the last in depth meeting she made the following remarks:

> Mrs. R: Let's talk about who some of the strong characters were.—
>
> . . .
>
> Mrs. R: Okay, now I want *you* to talk about what you think the main theme of the book was.—
>
> . . .
>
> Mrs. R: Okay, does anybody have anything they want to say about the guy [Allan Eckert] as a writer? (Allen, 1994a, p. 210)

Mrs. Reed's preceding remarks reflected her desire to encourage discussion that went beyond retelling, because they called on students to make inferences, generalizations, and evaluations about the story and author.

As another means of promoting in depth discussion, Mrs. Reed occasionally prompted children to refer back to the book to prove contested descriptions or interpretations of story events. She thus conveyed Rosenblatt's (1978) belief that "the transactional view, while insisting on the importance of the reader's contribution, does not discount the text and accepts a concern for validity of interpretation" (p. 151).

In conclusion, it is clear that Mrs. Reed took a facilitative stance during the in depth discussions. She fostered self-directed learning on the part of students by giving them decision-making responsibilities, inviting their personal responses, and advocating student–student exchanges. Furthermore, she encouraged thoughtful literary meaning-making by asking students to elaborate on their assertions, by summarizing or clarifying their remarks, and by prompting them to think about facets of the story not previously addressed. By supporting interaction among students, Mrs. Reed appeared to free herself to listen —and thus to attend to ways to extend the students' literary meaning making.

The Students' Interactions and Responses

Mrs. Reed's facilitative discussion strategies seemed to correlate with patterns in the children's interactions and responses during the *Incident at Hawk's Hill* group meetings. Student talk flourished in the group. The children delved into the details of the story with relish, describing, interpreting, and evaluating characters and events. They expressed their personal opinions and responses. They periodically talked about unfamiliar or unusual words in the book. They elaborated on each other's descriptions and showed concern for accurate retellings. For example, in the fourth discussion, Diane stated that the badger who adopted Ben left her den "for three days, or two"; to this remark Anne responded, "Four, it was four, she was gone for four days . . ." (Allen, 1994a, p. 213).

Students showed considerable engagement with each other during the discussions, often acknowledging, agreeing, or disagreeing with their peers' remarks. The following excerpts from the fourth discussion illustrate the nature of the students' interactions and reveal their responses to the story episode being discussed. In the episode, an obnoxious trapper, Mr. Burton, brings a dead badger to the home of Ben MacDonald and his family. Mr. Burton presses Ben's father to skin the animal and gives him a knife. When Mr. MacDonald reluctantly gets ready to do the task, Ben runs up to his dad and knocks the knife away. An already agitated Mr. MacDonald reflexively hits Ben in anger. When Anne asserted that Mr. MacDonald accidentally hit his son, the other children were quick to respond:

Tony: He [Ben's father] didn't accidentally—
Diane: No, he didn't accidentally—
Anne: Well he said he did when he went into the [inaudible]—
Diane: No he didn't, he said that—
John: He, he [inaudible]—
Anne: He acted like he accidentally—
. . .

Diane: . . . and he [Ben's father] said the only reason he hit him [Ben] [was] because he was mad at Mr. Burton, and he mixed feelings.
Nicole: Yeah.
Anne: Right.—
Tony: That's not an accident [inaudible]— (Allen, 1994a, p. 215)

In the previous excerpt, children indicated a willingness to voice disagreement as well as agreement with each other, using conversation maintenance signals such as "no," "well," and "yeah." As the discussion continued, Anne was apparently not yet convinced by her peers' arguments, and Mrs. Reed stepped in with a clarification question:

Anne: If he [Ben's father] said that he meant to hit Mr. Burton, [inaudible] he didn't.
Diane: He didn't mean to hit Mr. Burton, he was mad at Ben, but still I mean that was kinda rude to do, or like, oh yeah, smack somebody across the face, no that's okay.—
Mrs. R: You mean he hit Ben because he was mad at Mr. Burton and he had to take it out on somebody,
Diane: Yeah.
Mrs. R: [continuing] and he couldn't take it out on Mr. Burton?—
Tony: Yeah.—
Nicole: Yeah.—
Steve: Yeah.—
Tony: Well, he [Ben's father] said it clear out of the blue, so, this is the first person who came close [inaudible]—
Nicole: He [Ben's father] mixes feelings— (Allen, 1994a, pp. 215–216)

After a brief interlude in which one of the students began to retell the next part of the story, Mrs. Reed returned to the topic of Mr. MacDonald striking Ben. She asked a question that lifted the level of the discussion by prompting students to consider the incident within the larger realm of human experience:

Mrs. R: Do you think that people do violent things to people that they think can't um,
John: help you.—
Mrs. R: [continuing] retaliate, or can't help themselves?
Nicole: Yeah.—
Mrs. R: [continuing] Do you think people tend to hurt people who can't [paused]?
Fred: Well I think that happens.—
Steve: They take it out on other people instead of the person they really want to do it on, but they do it on someone else.
Mrs. R: Was it easier to do it to Ben because [inaudible]—?
Nicole: They have to take it out—
Fred: I take out [inaudible]—
John: Yeah, because—
Steve: He [Ben] couldn't do anything back.—
John: Yeah—
Mrs. R: What would have happened if he [Mr. MacDonald] had hit Mr. Burton?—
Diane: Ben was smaller and—
Steve: Then Mr. Burton probably would have hit him back.—
. . .

Anne: So it was kind of a [sic] accidental on purpose kind of.— (Allen, 1994a, p. 216).

Anne's last statement in the previous excerpt concluded the conversation about the encounter between Mr. Burton, Ben's father, and Ben. After the students explored this topic and Mrs. Reed extended it further with her remarks, Anne appeared to change her stance on Mr. MacDonald's motivation and action. She moved from believing that Ben's father hit him accidentally to conceding that perhaps his action was accidental on purpose. Rosenblatt (1978) stated that through interchanges with others, a reader "can discover how people bringing different temperaments, different literary and life experiences, to the text have engaged in very different transactions with it . . . . Sometimes the give-and-take may lead to a general increase in insight and even to a consensus" (p. 146).

Invitation 3.2

Consider how in depth group students from various cultural backgrounds might respond to works of historical fiction such as Incident at Hawk's Hill, Elizabeth George Spear's The Sign of the Beaver, *Jane Yolen's* The Devil's Arithmetic, *Mildred Taylor's* Roll of Thunder, Hear My Cry, *or Scott O'Dell's* Island of the Blue Dolphins. *What differing perspectives might students from parallel cultures bring to discussions of these books? What questions or strategies might you consider to help readers of nonparallel cultures respond more fully?*

Through their interchanges with each other and the teacher, the students mulled over and clarified their literary responses. Although they spent time simply retelling story events, they also shared interpretations and evaluated the author's choices. For example, in the last discussion Mrs. Reed invited the children to talk about the end of the story. The badger who adopted Ben returns with him to the family farm and is shot by Mr. Burton, the trapper. Whether or not the badger lives is inconclusive, however. Students expressed their responses to the ending and to the author's decision to be vague about the badger's fate:

Nicole: That [the end] was sad.—
Steve: The badger's gonna die.—
Anne: I kind of thought that the badger died at the end.
Nicole: It did.
Tony: Yeah, he probably was already dead,—
John: No he didn't, it never said.—

Tony: [continuing] 'cause he said he probably would have died 'cause
           he said it [the badger] probably won't make it through the
           night.—

. . .

Diane: I liked, what I like is that he [the author] gave you how you
           wanted to end it, but I'd like to know more pecific [sic, specific]
           like if he died.—

. . .

John: He [the author] could have put if the badger died or not and
           how, how old he lived or something.—
Anne: Yeah, an epilogue.— (Discussion J7, pp. 32–33, Allen, 1994a)

In the last discussion participants also discussed "strong characters"
in the story and the author's motivations for including one character in
particular:

Mrs. R: . . . Let's talk about who some of the strong characters were.—
Diane: Mr. Burton.
Nicole: Ben.
Anne: Mr. Burton.—

. . .

Mrs. R: Why did the author need George Burton?
Diane: To make—
Tony: To be the evil guy.—
Anne: You need a bad guy.
Tony: You have to have a bad guy.
Mrs. R: All right, it's a balance isn't it?—
Anne: Stories are good, stories are good if you have a bad guy, but if
           you don't have a bad guy, then—
Tony: But if you don't have a bad guy it's like an inner battle.—
           (Discussion J7, pp. 42–43, Allen, 1994a)

The previous excerpt also contains another example of Mrs. Reed
encouraging discussion that went beyond simple retelling to address
more sophisticated facets of a story.

In conclusion, students in the *Incident at Hawk's Hill* group actively
expressed, debated, and expanded their responses to the story. With the
gentle guidance of their teacher, they explored the book in depth. When
asked during an interview to explain what Mrs. Reed did and talked
about during the in depth discussions, Tony perhaps summed up best
the nature of the group's interactions: "we mostly do it by ourselves"
(Allen, 1994a, p. 268).

Invitation 3.3

*Select a small group of students (no more than six) in your class-
room to participate in an in depth group. Choose a children's*

chapter book that would suitably challenge and interest those students. Conduct a series of literature discussions with the group, selecting one or more of Mrs. Reed's discussion strategies—based on your goals and comfort level—to try as you interact with the group. What strategy or strategies did you find successful? What was the nature of the students' responses to the book? What is your assessment of your participation (as the teacher) in this group?

SUMMARY

This chapter illustrated one elementary teacher's approach to the use of literature groups, a popular instructional technique within literature-based reading programs. It provided an example of the rich context for response that can be created when a teacher and students gather in a small group to discuss a literary work. Mrs. Reed and her fifth grade students explored an historical fiction novel in depth during their literature group discussions. The teacher's facilitative stance actively promoted student-student talk, invited personal responses, and encouraged sophisticated literary meaning making. With her students, Mrs. Reed constructed a context in which the children made decisions about group procedures, talked amongst themselves about the story, and enriched their literary interpretations. As John stated about the group, "I think it was fun, because you got to tell about the book out loud instead of like in your mind, by yourself."

REFERENCES

Allen, S. H. (1994a). *Literature group discussions in elementary classrooms: Case studies of three teachers and their students.* Unpublished doctoral dissertation, Ohio State University, Columbus, OH.

Allen, S. H. (1994b). Talking about literary texts: Research findings on literature discussion groups in the elementary classroom. *Educational Reports, 24.* Columbus, OH: The Martha L. King Language and Literacy Center, Ohio State University.

Barnes, D. (1976). *From communication to curriculum.* New York: Penguin.

Huck, C. S. (1990). The power of children's literature in the classroom. In K. G. Short & K. M. Pierce (Eds.), *Talking about books: Creating literate communities* (pp. 3–15). Portsmouth, NH: Heinemann.

Peterson, R., & Eeds, M. (1990). *Grand conversations: Literature groups in action.* Ontario, Canada: Scholastic.

Pierce, K. M., & Gilles, C. J. (Eds.). (1993). *Cycles of meaning: Exploring the potential of talk in learning communities.* Portsmouth, NH: Heinemann.

Rosenblatt, L. M. (1978). *The reader, the text, the poem: The transactional theory of the literary work.* Carbondale: Southern Illinois University Press.

Rosenblatt, L. M. (1983). *Literature as exploration* (4th ed.). New York: The Modern Language Association of America.

Rosenblatt, L. M. (1991). Literature—S. O. S.! *Language Arts, 68*(6), 444–448.

Short, K. G. (1993). Making connections across literature and life. In K. E. Holland, R. A. Hungerford, & S. B. Ernst (Eds.), *Journeying: Children responding to literature* (pp. 284–301). Portsmouth, NH: Heinemann.

Short, K. G., & Pierce, K. M. (Eds.). (1990). *Talking about books: Creating literate communities.* Portsmouth, NH: Heinemann.

Vygotsky, L. S. (1978). *Mind in society: The development of higher psychological processes* (M. Cole, V. John-Steiner, S. Scribner, & E. Souberman, Eds. & Trans.). Cambridge, MA: Harvard University Press.

CHILDREN'S TEXTS

Eckert, A. W. (1971). *Incident at Hawk's Hill.* New York: Bantam/Little, Brown.

4

Drama and Response to Literature: Reading the Story, Re-Reading "the Truth"

Patricia Enciso
Brian Edmiston
The Ohio State University

EDITOR'S OVERVIEW

The children of Peter Spiegel's third grade class were challenged to deepen their literary experience with The True Story of the Three Little Pigs. Together with their teacher, Peter Spiegel, Brian Edmiston and Patricia Enciso involved the children in a "story drama" that took the children into the world of the story. The children become investigative defense attorneys intent on discovering "the Truth," as well as taking on roles as family, witnesses, police officers, and court personnel.

The story drama process requires role playing strategies. Everyone participates, the children and teachers taking on the roles of a variety of characters. Likely situations are created in which to play out encounters in and around the text, an "imaginary drama world." Through interviews, confrontations, considerations of evidence, and enacting a trial, the children create "stories within stories."

The processing of story drama takes these readers well beyond comprehension of the text, beyond, too, their immediate experiencing of it. Their investigations require scrutiny of the text, understanding and balancing of opposing points of view, and consideration of both the dynamics of decisions and the nature of truth.

Consider the following:

1. *Ultimately, what is the effect on readers of this response approach—role-play encounters with the story of the text and the stories within the text?*
2. *Establish the reading strategies and understandings that are potentially being developed through story drama with these students.*

3. *The authors indicate that, given more time, they would have incorporated writing strategies. What value, what additional learnings, might writing strategies have engendered? What types would you consider and at what junctures?*

Brian / teacher (to group of children):   Can I help you?
Chris: We're lawyers and we want to see the scene of the crime.
Brian: Oh. You're representing that wolf who's guilty.
Adam: He's not guilty.
Brian: Well we say guilty.
James: Well he might be guilty.
Anton: Who knows. We're not sure yet.
Chris: We just want to get more evidence.

The children and teacher quoted here had read and reread *The True Story of the Three Little Pigs* (1989), Scieszka and Smith's parody of the well-known folk story, *The Three Little Pigs*. In Scieszka and Smith's story, Alexander T. Wolf proclaims his innocence and testifies that, due to a bad cold, he merely sneezed when he arrived at the homes of the first two pigs. He found, each time, to his surprise, that the houses had collapsed and the pigs had died—so he ate them. As he explains, "Now you know food will spoil if you just leave it out in the open. So I did the only thing there was to do. I had dinner again. Think of it as a second helping" (n.p.). The story and illustrations are highly suggestive and full of innuendo, awaiting the careful reader's judgment. Indeed, the text and illustrations invite the reader to examine the wolf's confession for distortions and improbabilities.

We planned to use this story as the basis for a literature and drama workshop with Peter Spiegel's class of 8- and 9-year old children.[1] We assumed they would be appropriately suspicious of A. Wolf's testimony. However, we wanted them to become engaged with the story in a way that would not only give voice to their disbelief, but also require them to examine the effect of point of view on the creation and interpretation of stories. Of the 17 children in the class, 6 were involved in additional tutoring and special classes for reading, and/or oral and written language development. We chose to work through drama so that all of the children could find a way into the world of the story and find purposes and contexts for questioning the text. We began our work by using *story drama* (Booth, 1995)—drama that is generally focused on a single encounter or several brief encounters, drawn from a story, that are elaborated on and interpreted over time. Story drama and the more complex *process drama* are ways of "dramatizing at the edge of a text"

---

[1]We would like to express our gratitude to Peter and his students for their willingness to participate in this drama and to be the subject of this chapter.

where the students do not use a script but rather "improvise encounters which enable them to explore the ambiguities and possibilities of a text." (Wolf, Edmiston, & Enciso, in press). In our case, we used *The True Story* . . . as our starting text and developed encounters with A. Wolf and many other implied characters to extend our experiences of the roles of power and perspective in the construction of "the truth." Our work together extended over two, hour-long sessions with the whole class of third-grade students.

Drama, Literature, and Reader Response

Story drama's reliance on a text allows the teacher to explore with the students the problems and viewpoints inherent in the story. "Story drama occurs when the teacher uses the issues, themes, characters, mood, conflict, or spirit of a story as a beginning for dramatic exploration . . . of the meanings of the story" (Booth, 1985, p. 196). In doing so, the students and teacher adopt the perspectives or roles of specific or implied characters in a story. In addition, the setting of a story enables students and the teacher to more readily place the dramatic encounters in a shared, imaginary drama world. Although the original story is read and woven into the drama experience, students' interpretations through drama may alter the story (e.g., the ending) in significant ways. The pressing concerns of the drama world legitimate students' selective reading of a text. They may productively ignore textual details that they find confusing; equally, they may begin to delve into the implication of a few words that ordinarily they might skip over. Students are also encouraged to draw on their own life experiences and related reading experiences to help them interpret the àvents and actions arising through the drama. In short, story drama brings the story and the children's interpretations to life: Children meet and interact with characters in an imagined world that is built as much by the text as by their own perspectives, experiences, and ideas.

A teacher can adopt multiple roles within this form of drama. She organizes and facilitates the introduction of and interactions with characters, she considers what encounters might lend depth and breadth to children's interpretations, and she listens to children's interests and concerns so encounters can be created that will challenge assumptions and invite further inquiry (Edmiston, 1993). Often the teacher is in the world of the drama alongside the students. She may adopt the role of one of the characters who will enter into a dialogue with the students, or she may act as a colleague, working equally with the children, wondering what to do and say in response to a new situation. Clearly, this form of drama requires a flexible view of the teacher's relationships with children and stories. At its heart, the teacher is a player alongside the children, exploring perspectives and human dilemmas in the serious domain of make-believe. In our teaching, Brian was the lead teacher who facilitated the drama and also took on the roles of a defense lawyer,

A. Wolf, and a police officer. Pat video recorded the drama and occasionally interjected with a suggestion or question. Peter worked with the children primarily as a peer/defense lawyer; but he also took on the role of the wolf and a bus driver (who drove us to the scene of the crime).

Typically, with this book, children would be asked to discuss the credulity of the wolf's testimony. However, book discussions tend to be detached conversations where we stand back and look at events that happened to other people. In contrast, in drama "we can feel in the middle of events that concern us or are happening to us because in role we are in the same world as the story" (Edmiston, 1993). The drama offers students a primary viewpoint and purpose for reading while they encounter other viewpoints (Booth, 1994; Wolf et al., in press).

Transforming Texts and Readers: Preparing for Drama

The children in Peter's class had never worked through drama to interpret or develop stories but were part of a classroom community that valued cooperative learning and expression of ideas through art and extended personal writing. Based on our previous experiences with children, particularly those labelled learning disabled, we knew that the story drama would be an engaging, even empowering experience for many of the children in Peter Spiegel's class. Research conducted by Wolf (1993), Wilhelm (in press) and others (Kelley, 1992; Rogers & O'Neill, 1993) also supports the use of various forms of drama to create a more complex context for reading and responding to literature for students who may, otherwise, take very limited interest in or ownership of their own involvement in the world of a story.

The text of Scieszka and Smith's story had been typed and presented to the students as A. Wolf's signed statement to the police. The same statement was also read aloud by A. Wolf, as if he were on video. The video convention was set up by Brian, who appeared as A. Wolf, actually reading live to the children. However, because the event of reading aloud was seen by the viewers as video, they could rewind and fast forward the tape to review key statements and associated mannerisms. In her research, Wolf (1993) argued that it is as much the gesture and tone of voice that signals changes in meaning for children engaged in dramatic interpretations of literature as it is the words themselves. As children develop their own gestures, they interpret the text in complex ways; conversely, as they view and critique others' enactments of texts, they begin to explore the possible meanings a text implies; thus, children begin to regard text as more open to interpretation. *The True Story of the Three Little Pigs* could be read as a straightforward, uncomplicated truth. However, Brian's dramatized video reading carried with it a pleading tone and in some instances dismissive gestures and facial expressions when references were made to the pigs. Given these significations alongside the text, children were encouraged to interpret more than words alone.

In addition to the multiple signals of intent and perspective offered through Brian's reading, we gave the students a particular perspective and purpose from which to interpret and organize their readings. The students were asked to work together as though they were A. Wolf's lawyers. The task of the lawyers was to determine not if but how they would defend their client. In drama terms, they were "framed" (Heathcote, 1984) as defense lawyers, so that they would have a specific relationship to the text that carried with it certain responsibilities for the ways their interpretations might be viewed and construed. Developing this relationship with the text is a crucial first step in beginning a story drama because it enables students to establish social, emotional, and intellectual engagements with the imaginary world of the drama: In short, they begin to care about the characters, their own responsibilities to the characters and one another, and to the outcome of their situations. As Heathcote (1984), a leading drama educator stated: "I take it as a general rule that people . . . become involved at a caring and urgently involved level if they are placed in a quite specific relationship with the action [story], because this brings with it inevitably the responsibility, and, more particularly, the viewpoint which gets them into effective involvement" (p. 168). The students' relationship with the text was a professional one—they had to read the statement carefully because their client's very life depended on how a jury would interpret what he had said to the police. Their sense of responsibility was developed and sustained through a variety of situations that required them to investigate and interpret multiple versions of "the truth"—on behalf of A. Wolf.

Their first assignment was to listen to A. Wolf's testimony (Scieszka text) and then to mark their own copies of the text for indications of weaknesses and gaps in his story. They scrutinized the meaning of the truth as told and expressed by the wolf and as implied by the perspective of the wolf's jailors—the pigs. Even though the wolf claimed that he was telling the true story, they realized that he had reasons for not telling the whole truth—he had been charged with murder. As one student reasoned, "If he's lied before, maybe this might be one of his lies." However, that did not mean that the surviving pig could be relied on to tell the truth either, especially given the ongoing feud between the wolves and pigs, implied by images and headlines in *The Daily Pig* (a newspaper frontpage created by Smith for an illustration). Moreover, the police and news reporters were pigs and were unlikely to be sympathetic to the wolf's story; they might even be engaged in a conspiracy to charge him with murder.

Their underlined copies of the text showed further attention to the possible incriminating pieces in A. Wolf's story. In his statement, A. Wolf argues, "It seemed like a shame to leave a perfectly good ham dinner lying there in the straw. So I ate it up" (n.p.). One child underlined this statement and wrote in the margin: "He should have tried to help." In this case, the defense lawyer/child had to begin to reconcile two strong points of view of what constitutes appropriate action. She knew, despite her own convictions, that she would have to convince a jury that the wolf acted reasonably. Several children underlined his argument that he had a terrible cold and commented, as one child did, that "Even if he had a bad cold, it's just a cold. How could that make him blow the whole house down?" Although the wolf's arguments on his own behalf were questionable, the children/lawyers had to begin to develop a credible defense, using his story, reliable witnesses, and evidence. And throughout this work, they would come face to face with truths constructed from different viewpoints, experiences, and positions of power.

Invitation 4.1

Type out an extract from a version of the original story and introduce this as a piece of evidence from the third pig. Write a diary for the wolf in which he confesses to the crime. Have this sent anonymously to the lawyers and discuss if they should still defend the wolf.

Extending the Text: Encounters with the Truth

After this first close reading and exploratory dialogue about the wolf's statement, we worked with the students to designate potential witnesses—friends and relatives who might speak on behalf of the wolf and his testimony. This inquiry into other, related stories enabled the children to begin to expand the text in a way that allowed them to simultaneously create and investigate "stories within stories." Our list included the wolf's granny, the wolf's mother, his brother, neighbors, an uncle, and the grocer from whom the wolf bought cake ingredients. We then asked all of the students to work in pairs or threesomes and to select one of the characters on the list whom they would like to interview. Students were told to give themselves the letter A or B. After they had assigned themselves letters, we told them that A would be the interviewer/lawyer and B would be the interviewee. Students worked for 10 minutes describing and probing the details and events described by A. Wolf. The following are several children's accounts of their interviews. All of the children read and interpreted notes they had recorded during their interview:

I talked to his wife.

[Question asked by lawyer] Is her husband on a diet?

She said no.

I [lawyer] said if he was baking a cake for grandma. She said probably.

I asked had her husband ever got a cold. She said only sometimes around spring.

*   *   *

I talked to the wolf's other brother.

He told me that he sometimes has colds and he told me that when he sees a pig, he's going to eat it. And his brother . . . he [A.Wolf] wasn't just making a cake . . . his brother was making one, too. He did definitely go and ask for sugar.

*   *   *

[I talked to] The first little pig.

He had two bags of sugar and he got mad at him [the wolf] because he was watching his favorite show, Miss Piggy and the Muppets.

He said, I love kool-aid.

Evident in these three reports was a concern for corroboration of the facts that were part of A Wolf's testimony. In terms of response to literature, however, these reports also reflect the children's pleasure in elaborating on the characters and relationships implied by the text. Often, such elaborations are mentioned by children in discussions, but rarely are they allowed to develop into an adjacent text. The story-drama interviews gave the children an opportunity to revel in the possibilities additional characters' perspectives might pose. At the same time, the overall drama frame made the children accountable to the original text and to their peers' interpretations of the truths being constructed.

The wolf's granny was a favorite interviewee. To the delight of her peers, a student, who had been in role as the wolf's granny, agreed to be interviewed by the whole class. It was this whole group storytelling, modeled in many respects after A. Wolf's video, that heightened their scrutiny of the truth and their concern for placing details and perspectives in relation to one another.

During the session, several questions were asked that might confirm the relationship between the granny and the wolf and, at the same time, provide evidence for his "truthful" character. The children asked, "When is your birthday? Does he usually take care of you and bake you cakes?" [A. Wolf explained that he had needed a cup of sugar to bake a cake for his granny's birthday.]

"Has he had colds before?"

"Have you ever known him to lie?"

"Is he usually friendly?"

"Does he get along with pigs?"

The young girl who performed as the wolf's grandmother extended the story and the difficulties of discerning and judging the truth through several thoughtful, yet deliberately contradictory responses to her peers' questions. She was clearly fragile in her physical demeanor and indicated both through gesture and dialogue that she required her grandson's assistance. Her story, at this point, fit with the facts of the wolf's testimony. When asked to verify that A. Wolf had a cold at the time of her birthday, she could not recall that he was ill then or that he had ever been ill. The young actor had made a decision to play with the truth; to make fact-finding a more complex enterprise than it might have been. And her classmates, in turn, relished the opportunity to construct and deconstruct a tale full of conflicting details.

A. Wolf's grandmother had already implied that her grandson had lied about having a cold. But rather than appear to be aware of this lie, she proceeded to describe her grandson's loving ways and his difficulties since childhood with the other pig children. Her story of a young wolf who rarely played or had friendships created sympathies for him and insights into his psychology that had to be reconciled with the events and viewpoints, particularly the pigs' viewpoints, that landed him in jail.

The interview closed as the grandmother feigned tiredness and had to be taken home. All of the children gathered again, to relate the findings from their other interviews and to compare those findings with the interview they had just heard. We knew, at this point, 40 minutes from the time we had introduced A. Wolf's statement, that the children had more stories than they could manage to hold and compare by memory alone. We reminded them that, as A. Wolf's lawyers, they would have to defend him but that the jury and judge would have to decide if his story was believable. Rather than have the children retell all of the stories they had gathered through their interviews, we asked them to think of one statement or mannerism they had heard or seen so far that they thought would make anyone wonder about the truth of A. Wolf's statement.

The following excerpt from a 10-minute discussion exemplifies the kinds of questions raised by all of the children.

Tina: [holding the wolf's statement in her hand] Why is it the only time he sneezes is when he's by the little pigs' houses? He don't sneeze when he's by his house or nothing.

Christina: We should ask the grandma again if maybe he's allergic to pigs.

Tina: If he had a cold he would be sneezing all the way down. If you had a cold would you sneeze all the time? No. A couple of times a minute. It's very strange because it does not show him sneezing earlier in the story.

James: But we don't know how long it took him to eat the pig.

Aaron: She said her birthday was 25 days ago. The cake was for the other granny.

Lynn: Why did he eat up the two dead pigs if he only wanted sugar?

As can be seen, the wolf's story that his sneezes were the result of a cold was regarded with considerable suspicion. In reference to the sneeze, the children directly questioned the wolf's version of the truth while also creating hypotheses that might render his tale more believable."²ignificantly, the children also questioned the limits of their own perspectives and knowledge about the events of the story ("But we don't know how long it took him to eat the pig."). Other children drew on the stories within stories generated by their interviews to open up and interrogate A. Wolf's story even further ("She [the granny] said her birthday was 25 days ago. The cake was for the other granny.") Through their interviews and rereadings of the testimony, they were beginning to situate A. Wolf's story in relation to others' perspective, including their own.

It should be noted that the first two girls in this excerpt were involved in special reading and learning disabilities programs in the school. Neither Pat nor Brian was aware of the difficulties they had with print; in fact, we assumed that they were two of the more involved, insightful readers among their peers. They regularly contributed elaborate arguments, drawing on finer details of interviews and other evidence to support or challenge their client's testimony. Through the story drama, the girls' reading and interpretations had a purpose and relationship with the characters that gave them the authority to work as very astute readers, who could imagine and critique multiple, intersecting stories and points of view. In addition, the story drama, being a live, immediate context for reading and interpretation, gave all of the children a chance to develop perspectives and arguments from more sources than print. Thus, those children who are often lost in a discussion were included as active participants who were as able as everyone else to read the meanings of gesture and vocal intonation, alongside spoken and written words. In this sense, the drama context gave all of the children more meaning to create and interpret and therefore more possibility for offering their own ideas and suggestions.

Invitation 4.2

In small groups, create television news coverage of the trial for pig, wolf, and human television companies, complete with graphs depicting audience opinions, sound bites, and an anchor person / animal.

Concluding Day One: Taking a Stand on "the Truth"

Our purpose as defense lawyers was to work as a team to create a case for A. Wolf. They were not convinced, following our interviews, that we could build a coherent case. So, we decided to take a survey of the group to see who believed in the wolf's guilt or innocence. We asked the children to place themselves along a continuum, located along a line stretching from one end of the meeting area to the other, to indicate whether they were fully or partially convinced of his guilt or innocence. Once they had lined up, they presented their rationale for believing or not believing the wolf's testimony.

Our survey results were recorded under the three headings of *guilty*, *innocent* and *not sure* so we could refer to these arguments as we constructed our final case. Although half of the students did not offer extended explanations, it was important that they claimed an opinion, or took a stand, so they could begin to critique all of the information they had gathered and would continue to collect. Further, the standpoint could give them additional ownership of their work within the drama. Following are some of the reasons they gave for believing in his innocence or guilt or for feeling undecided one way or the other.

Innocent—
He was hungry.
His grandma said the same thing he said.
He does have a cold but he can't be allergic to straw.
I believe his story.
Not sure—
He ate the pigs. And how could a pig die just because of a sneeze from the wolf?
He couldn't resist the pigs—He's a wolf.
He didn't sneeze on the way to the pigs' house.
Maybe the pigs weren't dead and he said, "What a perfectly good ham."

Guilty—
I think he's guilty of two murders. . . . In the beginning, he wasn't sneezing at all, so I think the cold stuff is fake and the big bad wolf stuff is really true because he's not sneezing at all and if he had a cold he'd be coughing and sneezing.
A pig wouldn't just die from a sneeze.
His granny said he never gets sick.

As lawyers, they had to prepare for A. Wolf's defense at his upcoming trial. Some of the children immediately wanted to believe his story and thus his innocence. Some were ready to assume his guilt because of who he was; one student argued, "He couldn't resist [eating] the pigs—he's a wolf." However, most wanted to question his version of events. The drama supported delaying judgement and thus promoted detailed interpretations of the text. Preparations for the trial entailed reading and rereading his statement, gathering and interpreting multiple perspectives, and sorting through the corroborating and contradictory evidence.

From the point of view of lawyers, they needed to be skeptical of their client's interpretations. The prosecution would ask penetrating questions that the defense would have to anticipate. As the drama progressed, the students continued to explore their judgments as they dialogued with each other and with us about his possible guilt or innocence. Most important, at this point, the students did not assume that any one person possessed a complete truth.

Brian closed the first session with a reminder to the group that, regardless of their belief in the wolf's guilt or innocence, we would have to defend him.

Invitation 4.3

Brainstorm with your group or class about what influences our interpretations of the truth. Ideas can be written on index cards and then categorized as personal, social, or cultural.

Day Two: Collecting Evidence

Our second session with the children built on the story's ending and overall framework as much as it did on the wolf's testimony. The ending of the story leaves the reader with an illustration of a front page from *The Daily Pig*, featuring the headline "Big Bad Wolf!" and a silhouette of the wolf blowing or sneezing, with a cup falling from his hand; the "photograph" is subtitled "A.T. Wolf Big and Bad." Also on the front page is a close-up, technical picture of the mouth and teeth of a wolf subtitled "Canis lupus. Seen as Menace." A. Wolf's opinion of the news reporters is telling: "They figured a sick guy going to borrow a cup of sugar didn't sound very exciting. So they jazzed up the story with all of that 'Huff and puff and blow your house down.' And they made me the Big Bad Wolf." He concludes, "That's it. The real story. I was framed. But maybe you could loan me a cup of sugar." We decided, in the next session, to visit the scene of the crime, in hopes of finding evidence for building a strong case for A. Wolf. But we also wanted to make the pigs' viewpoint and statements strongly biased against A. Wolf (and wolves in general) to see how the children would grapple with the different parties' versions of the truth.

The closing illustration of the book shows a much older, graying A. Wolf behind bars, guarded by a pig/police officer. Implicit in the image is the fact of a guilty verdict at his trial. Despite this implied ending, we knew the children wanted to have a trial and to be responsible for A. Wolf's fate. Working as lawyers, judge, and jury, they could imagine and experience multiple interpretations of different, conflicting versions of the truth during the trial.

Thus, our second day involved a sequence of events that began with a pretend bus ride to the scene of the crime, followed by several encounters with police officers guarding the scene of the crime, collection of evidence, an interview with A. Wolf himself while heavily guarded in prison, a discussion of lab results and possible conclusions to be drawn from the evidence, and a final trial that required the services of several defense and prosecuting lawyers. Across these episodes we hoped to actively engage children in an imagined, "lived through" experience (Rosenblatt, 1978) of A. Wolf's story as well as the stories they had created together through interviews and their own conjectures and hypotheses. In addition, we hoped to create a purpose for critiquing the interpretations and evidence they gathered.

Our bus ride was a raucous 30 seconds of bumping and jostling and shouting directions. The children's teacher, Peter, was the driver and was reminded more than once to watch the road. This shift in relationship between the children and Peter was important because it allowed the children to begin to engage with him on terms other than child and teacher. Soon he would take the role of A. Wolf and be closely questioned, his every word scrutinized by the lawyers and police officers. On our arrival at the scene of the crime, the children were met by a police officer, Brian, who briefly stepped out of role to show them the final page of the book that features A. Wolf guarded by a pig police officer. Brian set the scene:

Brian: We have stopped at Pig Lane. I'm the police officer (Holding up the book); what can you tell from the picture in the book about the police officers?
Children (as a group respond):   They're pigs!
Brian: And who am I?
Children (as a group):   A pig officer.
Brian: I'm guarding where the crime took place. When you get off the bus, you'll have to talk to me.

It was at this point in the drama that the children's investment in being lawyers was actually put to the test. They had to confront an authority figure and maintain their own authority as lawyers if they were to continue their pursuit of evidence and a case. The children stood slightly back from Brian, appraising him.

Brian (to group of children):   Can I help you?
Boy 1:   We're lawyers and we want to see the scene of the crime.
Brian: Oh. You're representing that wolf who's guilty.
Boy 2:   He's not guilty.
Brian: Well *we* say guilty.
Boy 3:   Well he *might* be guilty.
Boy 4:   Who knows. We're not sure yet.

Boy 1:   We just want to get more evidence.

Boy 2 (hand raised, finger pointing to draw attention to his statement):   We need to gather blood samples.

Boy 3:   And we need to take pictures.

Their commitment to the frame of defense lawyer is indicated by the excerpt quoted in which the children challenged the authority of the police officer who assumed the wolf's guilt. The children paused following his statement but then, referring to their own authority as defense lawyers, reminded him that the wolf's guilt had not yet been determined. The statement, *"We're* not sure yet" is suggestive of one child's identification with his role; in addition, it reflects the tentative stance he had adopted toward the truth.

Brian agreed to show them the outside of the houses and led them to the crime sites. He stood next to the imagined site and declared: "This is where a poor innocent pig was eaten by a wolf." He added, "And you can see the blood on the ground. You can take samples if you wish. Don't touch anything. You can take pictures." In this exchange, the children not only heard a pig's point of view, they also heard their own ideas being incorporated into the world of the drama (they wanted to take blood samples and photographs). Unlike discussions of literature, the drama places children's responses to a story into an active encounter.

Back to the Scene of the Crime

They were eager to begin the pretend play of gathering evidence. Almost everyone started clicking a pretend camera as they huddled over the imaginary collapsed building. Several children exclaimed about all the blood on the ground. And again, Brian foregrounded their talk but placed it in relation to the pigs' perspective. He agreed that, yes, there was blood everywhere and that it was terribly gruesome.

After taking pictures and gathering evidence near the remains of the second pig's house, the children began taking blood and wood samples to the lab. Tina, described earlier, who had been engrossed in reading and interpreting the wolf's testimony, collected blood samples from the two pigs and found that, "The first brother's blood is 'A' but the second pig's is 'A and B'. They both have different blood." Pat engaged in a discussion with her about the significance of her finding:

Pat: Isn't that possible? I thought you could have two different blood types in one family.

Tina: They might not be related.

Pat: You'll have to ask forensics about that.

Tina: Where is he?

Pat: So you think the pigs might be lying?

Tina: Yes.

Pat: You'll have to take it back to the department and have the
            lab check that they are related.

At this point, Tina packed up her pretend samples and enacted
placing them in a bag that she lifted on her shoulder. As she walked
away she instructed Pat, "Tell them that I left early. I have to go to
forensics." And she strode across the room (but not out the door!). Tina's
experience, like that of other children within the drama, was a full-
bodied response to literature. Tina stepped into the world of the drama
to create a space that held the evidence she needed to work as a lawyer
and a serious reader. Drawing on her knowledge of blood types and
images of laboratory language and practices, she became, in Vygotsky's
(1966/1976) words, "a head taller", more able to control her knowledge
and language than she would in real life because play demands greater
attention to significations and meaning. As Wolf, et al. stated, "In . . .
action, students not only discover new possibilities, they also tranform
themselves in the process of transforming the words or situations of a
text" (in press). Thus, as a response to literature, Tina's dramatizing
allowed her to enter the implied world of the text with greater control
of and attention to meaning. And the meanings she made within the
drama were borrowed from her own life experiences while incorporating
the premises and characters of the original text.
    Our next stop (after another bus ride, of course) was the lab, where
we gathered to discuss our findings. Once again, new stories and
surprising evidence were uncovered. In addition to Tina's report on the
pigs' blood types and her conclusion that they were, in fact, brothers,
Christina reported that they reviewed photographs of A. Wolf's hands
and found an open wound. Peter asked, "Why would there be any blood
on Alex T. Wolf?"

Christina: I found a scratch. The pig bit him.
Peter: The pig bit him? So the pig must have been alive [implying
            the wolf was acting in self defense].
Christina: The [first] pig bit Alex.

This latter finding was added to the not guilty list of arguments and
evidence, to be used later during the trial. Our time was running out
quickly, as it always seems to do in extended work with children, so we
moved from the lab to the next encounter: This was an encounter the
children had been awaiting—the meeting with A. Wolf in his cell.

A Meeting with Power and Truth

Brian told the children that they needed to decide who would act as
police officers and who would continue to be lawyers. Those who would
be police officers were to stand by him (12 children, about three quarters

of the class). The others were to gather in the carpeted meeting area and consider what questions they wanted to pose to A. Wolf. The police officers then gathered with Brian in the back of the room to rearrange the chairs to create a cell. Brian decided to place their teacher, Peter, in the cell as A. Wolf. He knew that Peter would work with the orginal story's tone and viewpont but be responsive to the children's inquiries. The police officers were instructed to take their places near the prisoner and in the jail. On the count of three, the police officers froze in place; they were asked to tell what was on their minds:

The wolf is guilty.
He's a murderer.
We don't trust the lawyers.
I'm going to stop them.
I'm staying right here. No one will get past me.
IIe killed my friends.
All the wolves are killers.

As with the police officers, the lawyers stood and stated what was on their minds as they were about to enter the jail:

I'm nervous.
The pigs look dangerous.
I hope I can get in to talk to him.
I believe Alex T. Wolf.

This experience of freezing time and speaking thoughts out loud enabled all the participants to know what kind of situation they had created and what attitudes they might encounter. Clearly, in this case, the children were involved in their roles and in the world of the drama. Although their teacher was acting as A. Wolf, many of them were willing to accuse him of murder. They had moved into the world of the drama to explore their own perspectives and the possibilities implied by this tense encounter.

Brian unfroze the moment and directed the lawyers to request entry to the jail. (At this point, he was acting as a facilitator of the drama rather than as a member of the defense lawyer team). At once, a child acting as a police officer yelled out, "One at a time! One at a time!" while a child/police officer standing closest to the lawyers stepped in front of their path.

Greg: We're defense lawyers and we want to talk to Alex T. Wolf.
Child/Officer: One by one. One by one.
Chris: And we want to take pictures.
Child/Officer: Only one at a time. No pictures.

The children were creating the tension in this exchange entirely on their own. They recognized the rivalry between the two groups and worked to sustain it. Their command, "One by one!" was heard several times as the lawyers huddled together as a group to gain access to A. Wolf. In a sense, this was a game between the lawyers and the officers, one that the children understood immediately and enjoyed playing out. But it was not only a game, it was also a metaphor for the relationships implied by the text and final illustrations of the book. The police officer, foregrounded in Smith's illustration, holds considerable power over his prisoner; it was this same officer, representing all of the pigs, who had, for so long, been the purveyor of truth. The children created and met the power that could obstruct alternative versions of the truth.

Chris was escorted to A. Wolf by an officer who held an imagined bayonet or gun to his back. Both walked deliberately and seriously toward the prisoner.

A. Wolf/Peter exclaimed to the lawyer in a way that added to the authenticity of the moment:

A. Wolf/Peter: Where have you been? I've been waiting so long to talk to you.
Chris: What do you want?
A. Wolf/Peter: What do I want? I'm innocent. Let me free. Help me be free. Help me. This is terrible.
A. Wolf/Peter: They won't feed me.
Police Officer: He said he wasn't hungry. (To Chris)

Chris looked at the officers then asked to leave. He was escorted again to the lawyer's group, while Alex/Peter called, "Come back, come back." Brian urged Chris to report on his meeting:

Brian: Come tell us what you found out.
Chris: He said he was hungry and he hasn't been fed.
Tina: I'll go and see him.

The same boy who had shown such seriousness as he accompanied Chris also escorted Tina her meeting with A. Wolf. The police officers raised their chant as she came forward, "One by one. One by one."

A. Wolf/Peter was clearly distraught as Tina approached him. She was carrying a copy of his testimony in her hands.

A. Wolf/Peter: Are you going to help me?
Tina: Yes. We're trying hard. I have to ask you some questions.
A. Wolf/ Peter: Ok. Any questions at all.
Tina: Have you read your testimony?
A. Wolf/Peter: Yes. I told that to them. It's the truth.
Tina: Calm down. Calm down. Are you really on a diet? It says here, pigs are part of your diet.

A. Wolf/Peter: My diet? My diet is I love pigs.

Tina: Can I ask you another question? How did you know the pigs were dead?

A. Wolf/Peter: They were lying on the ground. They were roasts and they were so beautiful. They were dead. I'm sure they were dead.

Tina: No further questions.

After being ceremoniously escorted away, Tina reported to the group of lawyers that, "He can't eat." [Isn't allowed to eat]. Immediately a group of children decided that he needed a ham and that it would be delivered by his grandma. (The same girl who had enacted the role of his grandma stated, however, that she was not the grandma, but a friend who was delivering a ham that his grandma had prepared for him. Unfortunately, no one seemed to have heard her, so all the participants in the exchange assumed she was the wolf's grandma.)

She gave the pretend package to A. Wolf saying, " We have a ham. This is a package from your grandma."

A. Wolf/Peter replied, "I can't have anything. The guards take everything away."

However, their exchange continued, as the wolf pleaded again that he was innocent:

A. Wolf/Peter: I'm so glad to see you. I'm innocent. Those pigs wouldn't give me any sugar. They were dead.

Grandma/friend: It is so good to see you. What are you doing in here?

A. Wolf/Peter: I was making you a cake that's all and I needed sugar. I'm innocent.

A police officer interjected at this point and stated unequivocally: "He's a murderer."

A. Wolf retorted, "They were already dead."

In the interest of time, Brian interrupted this exchange and pronounced, "Your case is to be heard in the morning." As a transition to the trial and as a way of reflecting on this series of encounters, Pat asked the children to freeze where they were and to consider what they were thinking and feeling about the police officers or the lawyers. Several children from both groups offered their perceptions:

Lawyers: Too many people [police officers]. (Tina, a lawyer, said this and crossed her arms to punctuate her point.) I think that they're thinking about him running away. I think there's way too many of them. They don't trust us.

Police officers: I think there's way too many of you coming to the door. This wolf murdered our friends. Why should we feed him?

Invitation 4.4

Have each student write a few sentences on truth from their own perspective or from the point of view of a character. After circling a key phrase, all can share these as a group poem.

Throughout this episode, children formulated their own texts—extensions of the original story—and responded to them in role. Often children imagine scenes and dialogue as they read (Enciso, 1996) but rarely share these elaborations with others. Through the drama, these narrative possibilities, what Bruner (1986) refers to as the landscape of consciousness and the landscape of action, could be brought to life and enacted. Further, the drama invited the children to work with several kinds of texts and performances: a written testimony, a delivered testimony, their interpretations of the testimony, interviewees' testimonies, evidence they had collected, theories generated by the evidence, the police officers' commands and statements, the lawyers' questions, and A. Wolf's responses.

In our final episode, we brought these multiple texts and performances to bear on the fate of A. Wolf.

"Th Truth" at Last

"Order in the court!" called out one child in the midst of a flurry of chairs and congregating groups of children. The children had been instructed to set up the courtroom in preparation for the trial of A. Wolf. While some students moved chairs to accommodate the jury, witnesses, judge, and defendent, others began to clamber for the privilege of serving as judge, A. Wolf, a witness, or a member of the jury. The excitement was high as we entered the final episode of our work with the class.

Brian interrupted the calls for various roles, requesting that everyone sit down near the chairs they had placed in the courtroom. Then he calmly asked who would be judge. One child raised his hand. Six members of the jury had taken their seats (Tina and Christina were members of the jury). Four police/pig officers stood outside the courtroom holding A. Wolf, played again by Peter Spiegel. And three girls sat in the chairs designated for family members and witnesses (one of these was the wolf's granny who had been interviewed by the class). Last, two children raised their hands and stated that they wanted to be lawyers for the defense; one child agreed to serve as prosecuting lawyer. We were in our places, with testimonies and notes in hand and lists of arguments posted above the judge's head.

The judge took his seat in front of the jury and proclaimed, "Order in the court. Order in the court." As Peter/A. Wolf was escorted in, the judge commanded, "Everybody stand." Looking at his teacher/A. Wolf, the judge asked, "Do you swear to tell the truth and nothing but the truth?" Peter replied, "I do." and took his seat.

The children who wanted to be lawyers had reviewed the list of arguments in favor of A. Wolf's guilt and innocence and had decided to begin with testimony regarding A. Wolf's motive. Although we would have liked to engage all of the children in a review and discussion of the arguments and evidence, our time constraints urged us on to the courtroom encounter itself. Fortunately, the children's involvement in the story drama was high and they were willing to listen carefully to the unfolding arguments and refer to testimony, evidence, and questions that were already familiar to everyone.

Anton, the defense lawyer, striding back and forth in front of the defendant, began his inquiry. "When you were going to get a cake and get some sugar, did you need the sugar or did you ask . . . did you call on purpose or did you not call on purpose?"

Through this question, Anton expressed all of the children's skepticism regarding the wolf's motives. Had the trial been our first and only episode in response to the story, it would have been doubtful that the lawyer's question would have carried such weight and ownership. Through our story drama encounters, the children knew not only that the wolf's testimony was questionable, but that certain questions were more relevant than others. They had wondered about his sneezing, his cake baking enterprise, and his relationship with the pigs. Anton's question brought these encounters into a new context where competing versions of the truth mattered more than ever.

A. Wolf/Peter responded to the question with a pleading tone. "I needed sugar. I was making a cake. The rabbit was already in the pot and I just needed sugar. That was the ingredient I needed. And as I said before, I had a cold. I'm sorry for blowing down the house but I had a cold."

Anton listened closely to A. Wolf's response but led his client to another account of events, an account that the children had constructed in their earlier interviews with witnesses. He probed, "But your wife said you only have colds in the spring."

Peter replied, "Sometimes these colds just, usually it is the spring. But something in the air . . . I'd been having sniffles. I felt a cold coming on."

The jury and judge heard, once again, that the wolf's cold was not fabricated. Anton had realized that even though his questions could be potentially incriminating, they served the purpose of presenting the wolf's point of view. He pursued the wolf's motive when he turned to the part of the testimony that alludes to the relationship between the wolf and pigs. A. Wolf had previously testified (in the original story) that the third little pig had insulted his granny, an act that made him go crazy.

Anton inquired, "When that pig said something, that made you really mad didn't it?" And A. Wolf, using a high pitched, offended tone, offered his perspective again; at the same time, he directly sought the lawyer's and jury's sympathies, "Oh yes! The pig said he hopes my grandma sat on a pin. Can you believe that?"

Our courtroom scene continued with a pig as witness (who refused to say anything due to possible incriminations), family members who corroborated A. Wolf's story, and police officers who reported what they had observed on the arrest of A. Wolf. As the interrogation of witnesses concluded for both defense and prosecuting lawyers, it was evident that either pigs or wolves would be outraged by the verdict.

Rather than conclude the trial simply to have an answer, and an ending, Brian urged the children to consider, again, the ways a particular perspective contributes to the construction of truth . . . and justice. Brian asked, "Is anyone who is sitting on the jury a pig?" Several hands went up. He continued, "Would it make a difference if the jury were made up of pigs or wolves?"

One child suggested, "We should make it [a jury member] a regular person [neither pig nor wolf]."

Brian posed the question, "Is this a fair trial?" A number of children shook their heads no, and the defense lawyer, Anton, summarized the dilemma by stating, "All the pigs will vote for the pigs and all the wolves would vote for the wolves." Brian turned to the students and asked if they agreed. Everyone was nodding in agreement. It appeared, now, that despite the authority of a court of law, "the truth" would always be created and limited by those participants who have something at stake around the interpretation of events.

Brian suggested that instead of moving immediately to a final decision, that the children meet with reporters (Pat and Peter) who were waiting outside the courtroom to write the story of the trial for their respective newspapers, *The Daily Pig* and *The Daily Wolf*. Brian instructed those members of the courtroom who wanted to speak with the pig reporter to meet at one side of the room, and those who wanted to speak with the wolf reporter to meet at the other side of the room.

Again, due to time constraints, the adults, Peter and Pat, took notes and constructed stories based on the ideas offered by the children. It would have been much more valuable an experience for us all to have the children write and report back to one another. On the other hand, the adults listened carefully to the children and elevated their ideas by recording their thoughts and sometimes employing more sophisticated language. Peter's report included children's awareness of unfair practices within the courtroom and arguments that could be used to persuade readers of his innocence.

A. Wolf cannot be fairly tried in the current legal system:

1. All of the police are pigs.
2. Juries are almost always made up of pigs, even when the case concerns a wolf.
3. Wolves are carnivores. They should be able to eat meat when they need to eat it.
4. The whole wolf family has been treated roughly and unfairly.
5. The pig didn't even speak when he had a chance. That could mean that he is guilty.
6. We really haven't heard all sides.

The Daily Pig, held a strong opposing viewpoint:

A. Wolf is guilty of the brutal slaying of two brothers at their homes. A. Wolf claims that he had a cold and sneezed the pigs' houses down. That's impossible. No one could sneeze a house down, even if it is made of straw. Besides, we have seen A. Wolf in our neighborhood many times and he has stood around looking at the pigs. Everyone knows he eats pigs. The pigs were not dead: He murdered them. Why are we even having a trial??

Whereas the wolves questioned the legitimacy of the trial and implied that changes could be made to promote greater justice, the pigs assumed that the wolf was not even deserving of a trial. Their view of him as a predator made it impossible for them to even listen to his story, let alone provide for a hearing within the context of a trial.

After each report was completed, the children asked that each statement be read to the judge, who would have to make a final decision (the jury could not be trusted). Interestingly, no one asked whether the judge was a pig or a wolf! The judge listened solemnly to the reports offered by representatives of the wolves and pigs. He turned to A. Wolf/Peter and pronounced him not guilty. Even the wolves were surprised by the announcement, but accepted the judge's verdict. Given this surprise judgment, the children were able to see how capricious many of our decisions might be. When all perspectives and evidence are questioned, it is difficult to settle on the truth. In this regard, the "true story" will never be finished.

Returning to Reader-Response Theory

Reading literature is too often solely for efferent purposes—we want students to gain information from their reading; yet we often neglect the importance of students' aesthetic experiences—they need imaginatively to enter into a story world. Rosenblatt (1978) argued that readers must have aesthetic experiences out of which any efferent rereadings for information and reflections for interpretations can take place. Story drama is an aesthetic experience because it places the reader in the story—as if it is happening now. As Booth (1995) put it, the students "enter the story cave" in story drama (p. 31). Once they enter the cave, they can begin to interpret what they find there.

The students' relationship with and responsibility for A. Wolf created a kind of reading that, we would argue, was often simultaneously aesthetic and efferent. Peter's students did not act out the story in a chronological fashion but placed themselves in related encounters within an imaginary drama world that was implied by the original story. The "as if" world of the story became the pre-text or launching point (Booth, 1995; O'Neill, 1995) for the "as if" world of the drama so that the students were in the midst of the problems and possibilities posed by the characters and their predicaments.

The imagined, immediate context of the drama provided students with the range of experiences and perspectives through which they could raise questions, explore specific meanings and inferences, and place parts of the text in relation to the whole. In other words, their efferent reading was made more powerful and possible as they became increasingly more involved in the aesthetic world of the story drama.

The multiple texts and points of view that were brought together for these students through story drama created a dynamic, aesthetic, efferent, and critical space for reading and rereading of the text. In the excerpt that opens this chapter, Brian, working in role as a pig/police officer, embodied the implied meanings of the original story: Without a doubt, the pigs presumed the wolf's guilt. The children, on the other hand, working from the perspectives of defense lawyers and others, embodied the extended texts and perspectives that had evolved through their participation in the drama.

Through drama work, the students discovered that there are always multiple ways to read and comprehend a text—multiple meanings, texts, and truths are generated as we read and reread. "The truth" is subject to interpretation and reinterpretation as we revisit a text. Even factual truths, they discovered, are bound by the perspective or consciousness of the reader. As Bakhtin (1986) noted, "with comprehension there are [at least] two consciousnesses and two subjects" (p. 111). There is never a single way to comprehend or understand a text—understanding can always be contested and truth is always slippery. The drama enabled the students to comprehend the text by entering into more than one consciousness or point of view. This made them more critical in their reading and they began to critique the original text.

Bakhtin (1986) noted that "there never can be a first nor a last meaning; [the truth of one meaning] always exists among other meanings as a link in the chain of meaning, which in its totality is the only thing that can be real" (p. 146). We offer this chapter as a link in the chain of reader-response theory and hope that readers forge their own links as they use drama to explore literature with their students.

Invitation 4.5

Consider the impact of these extended responses to this picture-story book on the response experiences of these students. Discuss with your group or class and then write or use art to express your understanding of the development of the experience.

APPENDIX

Using Drama to Respond to Other Stories

Any piece of literature can be a springboard into story drama. The Invitation sidebars in this chapter contain suggestions for further drama activities with *The True Story of the Three Little Pigs*. We will now consider how you could use drama in ways similar to each of the invitations with the following four picture-story books:

Briggs, R. (1989). *Jim and the beanstalk* New York: Putnam Press.
Shart Hyman, T. (1983). *Little Red Riding Hood.* New York: Holiday House
Turner, A. (1987). *Nettie's Trip South.* Illustrated by Ronald Himler. New York: Macmillan.
Williams, V. (1981). *Three days on a river in a red canoe.* New York: Greenwillow Books.

Reading A Text In Drama

Some or all of the words in a book can provide you with a text to read in a story drama. You, or your students, need to think of who would need to read the text and where they would be. These are possible beginning roles, situations, and frames—a perspective, a purpose, and a need to read and interpret information. Students will read text from a book if it is presented as a coherent part of the drama world. Students will also read texts they have written or those prepared by the teacher.

Little Red Riding Hood. Frame the students as park rangers who have been asked to trap all wolves in the forest. Read the story as a record of what has happened in these woods in order to determine some of the difficulties for wolves and humans co-existing in the forest. Ask students to write other records of encounters between wolves and humans in the woods.

Three Days on a River in a Red Canoe. Frame the students as naturalists who are planning wilderness canoe trips. Read the book as a child's diary in order to determine potential dangers on such trips. Ask students to write and draw picture extracts from another child's diary.

Jim and the Beanstalk. Frame the students as social workers. Read about Jim and the giant as they plan their encounters with other giants who are old and infirm and who may need help. Ask the students to write something that the giant would need to read.

Nettie's Trip South. Frame the students as abolitionists in the pre-Civil War North. Read the book as Nettie's letter as they plan an incognito trip to the South in order to gather information about the difficulties faced by those who work on the Underground Railroad. Ask the students to write a reply by Nettie's friend Addie or some of the notes that her brother took on his trip to the South.

Other Ways to Extend the Text

In a drama, teachers and students can use any of the ways people in everyday life create and share the many stories that lie within and behind every other story. For example, they may talk to people, listen to gossip, read newspapers, watch television, analyze videotapes, or draw pictures. Each of these activities can involve preexisting written texts and images, or ones that the students create in class.

Little Red Riding Hood. In pairs, the park rangers could interview the little girl, her mother, neighbors, wolves, and other animals in the forest in order to discover their attitudes. They could write short reports of their findings to present to the Department of Natural Resources.

Three Days on a River in a Red Canoe. In small groups, one student is a naturalist talking to those who have important information; for example, parents who have taken their children camping in wilderness areas, children who have been canoeing, or animals who live in natural areas. The small groups could use their bodies to depict photographs of their experiences; the whole group interprets the photographs. They write accompanying guidelines for wilderness camping.

Jim and the Beanstalk. In pairs, one student as social worker interviews a giant neighbor for his/her views on older giants. Pairs share their findings by making documents, for example, a map of the giant's castle, giant food stamps, or a giant bill.

Nettie's Trip South. In pairs, one student as an abolitionist secretly contacts, for example, enslaved people and people in Underground Railroad safe houses to discover the dangers they face. Groups then create 10-second scenes of danger that at first are observed. Then observers as abolitionists plan precisely what they will say or do if they choose to interact with the people.

Classifying Information and Interpretations

You can help students classify whatever information and interpretations they share. Classification helps students to analyze and further interpret their understandings.

Little Red Riding Hood. As park rangers, they write key words on the chalkboard to summarize the attitudes of the people they interview; they look for similarities.

Three Days on a River in a Red Canoe. Small groups draw possibile ways of dealing with bears. The drawings are placed in three categories: Those that would/might/would not hurt the bear.

Jim and the Beanstalk. The social workers draw or write down what the giant may be doing when they arrive at the door; these are classified according to whether the giant will/might/will not want to be disturbed.

Nettie's Trip South. Abolitionists physically place the people who they found were taking risks along a continuum between what they thought were the most difficult and least difficult contexts.

Other Ways To Shape and Share New Understandings

Many students will orally share their ideas as they interact in drama. However, the arts provide us with many ways to shape and share our developing understandings.

Little Red Riding Hood. Make animal tracks out of Play-doh. Draw food webs that show how forest animals and plants are interconnected.

Three Days on a River in a Red Canoe. Make a tape recording of wilderness sounds. Write and draw warning signs to be placed at the entrance to parks.

Jim and the Beanstalk. Make giant-sized drawings of objects in the giant's house. Label these for potential danger spots for older giants.

Nettie's Trip South. Using their bodies, students can sculpt a contemporary statue entitled Slavery. They speak and then write the thoughts of several figures.

Exploring Questions

One of the questions that was implicitly explored in *The True Story...* was "How can we know the truth?" In order to avoid simplistic or merely factual interpretations of stories, it was critical that the drama explored a complex social question. The drama discussed in this chapter was sustained for so long because the question was not easily answered. This would not have been the case if we had simply asked, "Is he guilty?" Instead, we wondered about whether we could believe the wolf, and thus pondered on the nature of truth and how it is affected by perspective.

Little Red Riding Hood. Rather than ask, "What did the wolf do?" explore a question like "Can wolves co-exist with humans?"

Three Days on a River in a Red Canoe. Rather than ask, "Where could we go on a canoe trip?" explore a question like "How can naturalists lead safe canoe trips with children?"

Jim and the Beanstalk. Rather than ask, "What can old giants not do?" explore a question like "How can social workers help old giants live their lives in a dignified way?"

Nettie's Trip South. Rather than ask, "What was life like as an enslaved person?" explore a question like "What were people prepared to risk in their opposition to a society that promoted inhumane relationships?"

Resource Books

Readers who are interested in experimenting with the use of drama in their classrooms will find useful texts published by Heinemann in their series on drama education. In particular, the following are recommended:

O'Neill, C. & Lambert, A. (1983) *Drama structures*. Portsmouth, NH: Heineman.
O'Neill, C., Lambert, A., Linnell, R., & Warr-Wood, J. (1976). *Drama guidelines*. Portsmouth, NH: Heinemann.
Heinig R. (1992) *Improvisation with favorite fairy tales*. Portsmouth, NH: Heinemann.
Swartz, L. (1988) *Dramathemes*. Portsmouth, NH: Heinemann.
Ball C. & Ayers J. (1995). *Taking time to act: A guide to cross-curricular drama*. Portsmouth, NH: Heinemann.

REFERENCES

Bakhtin, M. M. (1986). *Speech genres and other late essays* (V. W. McGee, Trans.). Austin: University of Texas Press.
Booth, D. (1985). Imaginary gardens with real toads. In *Theory into Practice 24*(3), 193–198.
Booth, D. (1995) *Storydrama*. Markham, ON: Pembroke Publishers.
Bruner, J. (1986). *Actual minds, possible worlds*. Cambridge, MA: Harvard University Press.
Edmiston, B. (1993). Going up the beanstalk: discovering giant possibilities for responding to literature through drama. In R. Hungerford & K. Holland (Eds.), *Journeying: Children Responding to Literature* (pp. 250–266). Portsmouth, NH: Heinemann.
Enciso, P. (1996). Why engagement in reading matters to Molly. Reading and Writing Quarterly. *12*(2), 171–194.
Johnson, L., & O'Neill, C. (Eds.). (1984). *Dorothy Heathcote: Collected Writings on Education and Drama*. Portsmouth, NH: Heinemann.
Kelley, P. (1992) Two reader response classrooms: Using pre-reading activity and readers theatre approaches. In N. Karolides (Ed.), *Reader response in the classrom: Evoking and interpreting meaning in literature* (pp. 84–91). New York: Longman.
O'Neill, C. (1995). *Drama worlds: A framework for process drama*. Portsmouth, NH: Heinemann.
Rogers, T., & O'Neill, C. (1993). Creating multiple worlds: Drama, language, and literary response. In G. E. Newell & R. K. Durst (Eds.), *Exploring texts* (pp. 69–90). Norwood, MA: Christopher-Gordon.
Rosenblatt, L. (1978). *The reader, the text, the poem*. Carbondale: Southern Illinois University Press.
Vygotsky, L. (1976). Play and its role in the development of the young child. In J. Bruner, et al. (Eds.). *Play—Its role in development and evolution* (pp. 537–554). New York: Basic Books. (Original work published 1966)
Wilhelm, J. (in press). *Developing engaged readers*. New York: Teachers College Press.
Wolf, S. (1993). What's in a name? Labels and Literacy in Readers Theatre. *The Reading Teacher, 46*(7), 540–545.
Wolf, S., Edmiston, B., & Enciso, P. (in press). Drama worlds: Places of the heart, head, voice, and hand in dramatic interpretation. In J. Flood, D. Lapp, & S. B. Heath (Eds.), *The Handbook for Literacy Educators: Research on Teaching the Communicative and Visual Arts*. New York: Longman.

CHILDREN'S TEXTS

Scieszka, J., & Smith, L. (1989). *The true story of the three little pigs*. New York: Viking Kestrel.

5

If I Were A Poet, I'd Say Something Beautiful

Arlene Harris Mitchell
University of Cincinnati

EDITOR'S OVERVIEW

It is almost a given that a teacher who wants to introduce her students to poetry can anticipate their dismay and disinterest. Yet, young children, we know, adore poetry—rhythm and rhyme and the magic of sounds and words. They're natural metaphorists. Perhaps the disinterest results from our felt need to teach poetry. Arlene Mitchell, who can't abide such negative attitudes, takes us with her to a sixth-grade classroom so we can observe her revitalizing the students' perceptions.

She captivates them initially with drama and wonder, followed, then, by the surprise of activating their response-writing and performance. In the succeeding lessons, she hooks them more securely, first, by using popular, modern rhythms and lyrics—their selection—and, second, by introducing poems apt to engage their senses, emotions, and intellect. But it isn't just content that engages them.

The focus is on response, eliciting their personal contact and, subsequently, their self-ownership of a poem—establishing their self-knowledge of the poem. Mitchell waits for appropriate teachable moments to incorporate poetic elements that needed to be covered; these grow naturally out of students' responses and questions, promoting, thus, student commitment. In addition to writing responses to poems, students are encouraged to write poetry. By the end of the nine sessions, they're thinking—some of them, anyway—that they're "like poets."

Consider the following:

1. *What in the drama and surprise entices the students' positive reactions and engages their attention?*
2. *Recall your own history with poetry. What turned you on; what turned you off? What strategies will you consider for your classroom?*

Paul turned and shook his finger at one of the girls walking behind him, stating, "Well, Sarah, I tell you, life for me ain't been no championship game. It's had losses, and fouls called, but I'se still climbin'." As Sarah and her friends start laughing, my attentive ear picks up from another group, "The reason I like TV is because I can remote from MTV to PBS, and Mom thinks I'm smart; and I really like to be smart."

These sixth-grade students were creating parodies of two of the poems they had been studying through the year, "The Reason I Like Chocolate" by Giovanni, and Hughes', "Mother to Son." They were nearing the end of the school year and celebrating the end of our poetry unit. And it was apparent to all—the students, the classroom teacher, and to me—that we had had a successful, entertaining, and productive learning experience.

It had been in February when I had given a workshop on teaching poetry for the teachers and had offered the invitation to work with the students. Two weeks later, I received a call from Marta Jenkins, a third-year teacher, accepting my invitation and almost challenging me to get the students to learn about poetry and to enjoy the experience. The mention of the term poetry seemed to conjure resistance to learning, even at the tender ages of 10 and 11. I knew that this was problematic with older students, but for sixth graders to feel that learning poetry was one of the greatest chores in reading literature was beyond my acceptance.

Marta, on the other hand, admitted that she loved reading poetry but dreaded teaching it. The curriculum required attention to so many mechanical aspects that I could readily see that teaching poetry could be boring to the students and burdensome to the teacher. She reminded me several times that she had to *cover* the curriculum, and I assured her that students would *learn* the required curriculum and more. Our work was cut out for us.

The students were alike and different as most classrooms reflect. They were playful and serious. They were energetic when they liked the activity, and somewhat indifferent about routine lessons. They liked science for the most part, and felt that English (which was mostly done as part of reading lessons) was so-so. The district, situated on the fringes of a small urban area, was racially mixed with African-Americans the largest minority, but also with several Asian students. Economically, I later learned, the communities which the district served were basically middle class, but included both rural and upper-middle class families. The class I worked with had 11 boys, 12 girls, was predominately White with 6 African-American students.

I arrived one Friday afternoon, entering the room reciting, "Well, son, I'll tell you/ Life for me ain't been no crystal stair." I moved around the room, had not introduced myself, and was motioning to students to leave their desks and to line up along the side of the room. While I was having the time of my life, they were both amused and puzzled. (Remember, I knew where I was going with this little exercise, but they didn't.) After I completed reciting "Mother to Son," I gave out typed copies and invited the students to read silently. Two students then read the poem aloud. I briefly introduced myself (finally), explained that although most of them would be working at their desks, the small group assembled at the side would be preparing something different. I think this really took the side group by surprise and looks of apprehension came over some faces while full blown smiles came over others.

"I'm going to ask you two questions," I explained to the class. "You may respond to either one or both. You may respond in writing or by illustration, or in any other appropriate way. The students off to the side will respond in a different way."

"What does this poem remind you of?" was one of my key questions, and I put it into a prompt on the board: "This poem reminds me . . ." Many of the students began to write immediately. I continued with my second key question. "In what ways does this poem look like a poem?" which was translated into the prompt, "This poem looks like a poem ..." Some of the students who had started writing were now crossing out and writing down the second prompt.

Invitation 5.1

Clearly, leaping over the hurdles of negative attitudes of older students or getting younger ones started on the right track is a major teaching problem. Select a grade and an appropriate poem. Discuss your small groups' selections for the poems' engagement potential and, then, collaboratively consider the strategies each of you might use to introduce poetry to your classes.

The students on the side had begun to vocalize their apprehension among themselves as I ushered them to the hall. We sat in a semicircle on the floor. Two volunteers read the poem aloud for us, and I asked them if they could see a story in this poem. Several said yes. I asked them to tell me the story. Simple enough, they knew the story line. Basically, a mother was explaining to her child (son) that life is not always easy, but you have to continue working at it, not give up, but go on.

I then asked them to help me to divide the poem into three parts and to see how they could perform the poem for the class. "Do you think you can do that?" They were unanimous in their belief that it could be done with no problem. They easily saw three turns in the poem:

1)
Well, son, I'll tell you;
Life for me ain't been no crystal stair.
It's had tacks in it,
And splinters,
And boards torn up,
And places with no carpet on the floor-
Bare.

2)
But all the time
I'se been a-climbin', on,
And reachin' landin's
And turnin' corners,
And sometimes goin' in the dark
Where there ain't been no light.

3)
So, boy, don't you turn back.
Don't you set down on the steps
'Cause you finds it kinder hard.
Don't you fall now–
For I'se still goin' honey,
I'se still climbin',
And life for me ain't been no crystal stair. (Hughes, 1974, p. 30)

At the end of approximately 10 minutes, as the small groups worked on their skits, I went back to the larger group. "How many of you *wrote* a response?" Every hand went up. "Good. How many of you wrote a response *and* illustrated or thought about another way to respond?" One hand. "Good. Now let's count off one, two, three, four, and get into small groups, where we will share what we wrote or illustrated with each other."

There are some simple ground rules when we want children to respond willingly and to take risks. I reviewed these rules with the class and wrote key words on the board:

We must listen to each other; *Listen*

We must not criticize a response such as "that's dumb," or "that's not what she asked you to write about"; *Accept responses*

We must give time for everyone to respond who wants to respond, about two minutes; *Everyone gets a turn*

We want everyone to share, but will not force someone to share—that is a person has the privilege to "pass." *You can choose to pass*

Person number three in each group will be the reporter for the group. *Person 3 will report for the group*

Students were given about 12 minutes in their small groups while I checked on the skits.

When I returned, the reporters gave some of the comments from their group. Some of the comments around "This poem reminds me" included,

"When my mom tells me that I have to work hard so I can get good grades, even when I don't know the subject too well."

"My grandpa always tells us how he had to work hard when he was a boy, and he didn't finish school, so I have to."

Some responses to "This poem looks like a poem" included

"The sentences take more than one line."
"Some lines have only one or two words."
"The words aren't regular English."
"It doesn't rhyme like most poems. Does that still make it a poem?"
    (My response: That's a good question, we'll talk about that later.)

Validating all of these responses and not getting into the teachable moment was a strain sometimes, but Marta later showed me all her notes, including some of the dialect problems she perceived in the poem.

I asked the boy who had drawn something in addition to writing if he would share with us what he had done. His group was excited. They knew him; I didn't. They knew that he was very good at art. The picture he had started (he let us know that it was not completed) was a woman with one hand on her hip and one finger of the other hand pointing, as if in a scolding fashion. That was all. No boy. However, there was the caption: "I'm not scolding, just explainin."(sic)

The skits followed. The children were creative in what they had put together in 20 minutes. One group had made up lines to fill in; some groups used chairs, desks, books, and the blackboard for props; a narrator was used for one group; another group recited some lines individually and some lines in choral response.

Invitation 5.2

Choral reading or response (not just everybody reading the lines together) offers opportunity for expressive and subtle expression of meaning through oral interpretation. Select a poem that engages the members of your small group and, considering the resonant effect of your individual or grouped voices, devise an oral presentation. Discuss the various interpretations expressed by two or three groups presenting the same poem and the implications of this strategy for learning.

The students had been given the time to play with the poem, enjoy the richness of the words, come to some understanding of the meaning for themselves, and wrestle with interpreting the poem through a different genre. I took about five minutes to talk about the poet, Langston Hughes, and explained that he was African American, had written several hundred poems, short stories and plays. Did they know him? Yes. Many had read other poems and even this poem before. Did they think they could learn about poetry? Yes. Did they think that learning poetry would be fun. An apprehensive "yes." Did we have fun today? A more enthusiastic "yes." I then explained that I would be visiting each week for 5 or 6 weeks. Their teacher Marta and I would have assignments that they needed to bring in if we were really going to enjoy poetry. I encouraged them to participate by explaining that they were important to the process, their contributions would give variety and help all of us to experience songs and poems that perhaps others did not know. And I admitted that I was not up on the latest music, raps, and poems that they probably enjoyed today. This confession seemed to validate that they really did have something to offer.

The assignment for the next week was to find at least two poems or words to songs that they liked and would like to share with the rest of the class. They could write just a few lines using the prompts we had used or other ideas they wanted to share. They could illustrate, or they could use music, or whatever else they found appropriate to give a reaction to the poem. This introductory lesson took approximately 60 minutes.

The next session was more student-centered, as the students brought in their poems. In small groups of four or five, they read their poems to each other, shared their reactions (three had tried their hand at drawing) and four brought in tapes of songs that we all listened to. Each group selected one poem or song to share with the whole group and to talk about their reactions to that piece.

As a class we found that the songs had more rhyme than most of the poems they presented. So this became a teachable moment. We talked about rhyme and why that may be important in songs. We also discussed how rhyme sounds, and why that seems to belong to poetry, and especially in songs. Because some of their poems and songs had repetition of lines and others repetition of words, we talked about the element of repetition in poetry. One of the students commented that she found memorizing songs easier than memorizing poems. When asked why, several students talked about the repetition—simply hearing the song over and over. After some prompting, we also found that lines were often connected by the rhyme, and that the beat or music also helped them to remember the words. This led into a discussion about the rhythm of poetry. With these two important poetry elements, rhyme and rhythm, we beat out the iambic meter to a limerick someone had shared and found that the rhythm and the rhyme gave a sing-song feeling to the poem.

I had brought in "How to Eat a Poem," by Merriam, and we talked about mental pictures or imagery. We revisited "Mother to Son" to write about the images that we saw when we read it, as well as the images that we saw as the poem was performed and illustrated. For the next week, the students were encouraged to draw or find pictures that might illustrate, or ways to demonstrate, the images that a poem might present for them. They could use a poem we had already discussed or find a new piece.

Using the students' work almost exclusively, we naturally began to study and develop an understanding of four poetry elements that were required in the curriculum—rhyme, meter, repetition, and imagery. A few other elements had also been briefly introduced through their poems, which I saved for later mini lessons—simile, metaphor, personification, and hyperbole.

Although we also looked at, wrote about, and paraphrased what some the poems and songs were saying to us, we did not emphasize meaning or interpretation in these early sessions. The purpose was to get the students and the teacher to trust the process and to naturally find answers to the curriculum mandates. Because students can better understand what they know and what they don't know by writing it down, it was important for students to feel comfortable and to make personal notes for themselves as well as to take notes from lessons. With my prompting and Marta's encouragement, we decided at the second session that all of us, Marta, students, and I, would keep a poetry notebook that would include our poetry finds, our reactions, our drawings, our personal glossary, our attempts at our original poems, and any other related materials we wanted to keep. During the week, Marta gave the children folders that had clips for hole-punched papers and pockets on each cover. This type of notebook allowed us to add a variety of papers and other paraphernalia to help personalize and make the notebook our own. Many of the students drew pictures or created fancy writing on the covers.

Later in the term, we looked at three poems to expand our process for interpretation, another curriculum objective, and to give students structured practice to a concept introduced and worked through as a class previously. One of the poems, "The Reason I Like Chocolate," by Giovanni (1980) had been brought in by a student several sessions before. The students had found the poem especially enjoyable, and we had used it as a model for one of our creative writings. During this later session, I revisited this poem and added two new poems for them: "Those Winter Sundays," by Hayden (1973), and "My Brother Estes," by Carson (1989). Using three different poems allows for optimum interaction and discussion among students (see appendix). By revisiting poems we had previously shared in class, students who needed more security could participate, obtain more practice, and build their confidence by using a familiar poem. Also, because this was a poem brought in by a student, it showed students that we accepted their contributions. Although the students were given a choice, all poems were responded to by some students.

We began our study of these three poems by using the same technique of reading silently and several students reading each poem aloud that we had used during our first session and continued to use regularly. We then began our responses to the poems. The students were encouraged to choose one of the poems to concentrate on for this session. I requested that they "read, then read again," for self-ownership, and respond in writing for self-knowledge. These phrases are used to help students to understand that these are personal responses.

To get them started thinking about the poem, I had them make notes about anything that they found difficult, special, or unusual about the words or the style. They then joined other students who were working on the same poem to help each other and to get our help in clarifying, or just listening, to what they had found. Some questions about "Those Winter Sundays" included, "What does *banked fires* and *austere* mean?" I asked if anyone in the group could help and a student described keeping a fire going in a fireplace. I added to this by describing how we kept fires going in a coal furnace. (A new experience for most of these students.) Several students offered definitions for *austere* as "stern" or synonyms for *severe*, but it became necessary to look it up in a dictionary and a thesaurus in order to help us with the line. They found contradiction in using *love* and *austere* together, but offered good explanations of inverted word order, using one word that said many things, and one student offered, "I just like the sound of the word."

Following discussion of the apparent features of the poem, words, rhyme or lack of, and obvious elements of figurative language, the students responded to the first prompt: "When I read this poem, I think of . . ."

"The Reason I Like Chocolate" seemed to elicit literal responses such as, "I think of why I like to watch TV," and "I think of why I like to play the piano."

On the other hand, "My Brother Estes" (Carson, 1989) seemed to create images of relatives who did not live with the immediate family, or who were perceived to have strange or different habits. One girl, Sarah, wrote about her grandmother, who always brought peppermint balls when she visited and continuously gave them to the children and the adults, sort of like a prize, whether they liked peppermints or not.

Later, responding to the prompt, "Write a few lines about how the poem makes you feel," Sarah remembered collecting 22 little peppermint balls and wrote, "For weeks after my grandmother left, I remembered our times together. A time for each ball. Looking after my baby cousin, eating a snack together, and sometimes jus (sic) me talking to her. I still laugh."

"Those Winter Sundays" brought the widest range of responses on the next prompt, "Write a few lines about what you think the poem means. Remember these are your first impressions. You will be able to change or elaborate later."

"This poem is about a dad who gets up early and gets the house ready for the rest of the family. He works real hard all week, but he still gets up on Sunday to do this because he loves his family."

"This is a father doing something special for his son like polishing his shoes (or is this written by a lady so it would be his daughter). He gets the house warm for them, but they don't thank him."

[As stated earlier, I try not to give too much information about the poet so that students do not try to imitate what they think the poet meant, but rather will concentrate on what the words of the poem say and the form that is used. Once I revealed the name and background of the poet, we discussed whether or not a male poet could be speaking through the voice of a female, and decided that he could; however, it was unanimous among this group that the speaker was a male.]

Another response brought lots of discussion among the group later, and it wasn't until the next exercise that the student was validated for her ideas. She wrote, "This is a bad place to live; the father is mean (austere), and he is always angry. But he does work."

Working through interpretations is hard work for students and for teachers. Students from grade school through graduate school seem to want to find the right answer, to read the mind of the poet, and to tell the world his or her message. With this class, I continuously emphasized the need to hear their thinking, their interaction with the works, and encouraged them to use everything they could from their background knowledge to help them reach their individual responses.

Invitation 5.3

In your small group, read together "Those Winter Sundays" and "My Brother Estes." After each of you has written your personal response to these texts, share your reactions so as to expand and clarify your perceptions.

I ended this part of the lesson at this point because I wanted the students to have time to think through their responses, to make changes if they desired, to have an opportunity to revisit the poems and their responses, and to have release from the seriousness of the lesson. Each session, we had a "poetry find" session, and I strategically placed it at the beginning, during, or end of the planned lesson. This gave the students opportunity to share each week. That week, we purposely had planned to place it near the end. It was a better idea than I had anticipated. We needed the release.

Students were again reminded that they should look over their responses for the poem, make changes and additions, add to their list of special words and form, and to jot down additional questions, if any.

At our next meeting, we continued our process of guiding the students to interpreting or analyzing a poem by putting them into small groups where they could share their common poem. They were given time to again read the poem, and to discuss additions and changes they had made to their initial responses. Generally, they all had additional or revised statements. In fact, some of them had completely changed from the poem that they had started. After 20 minutes or so of small group exchanges, I offered the next prompt.

This prompt brings their initial interpretations to the center of meaning and usually creates the most discussion, disagreements, and validations. "Go back to the poem, and find the words or phrases or sounds, or form, which helped you to understand or to make meaning from the poem."

Irene had kept her response that "This is a bad place to live; the father is mean (austere), and he is always angry. But he does work," pretty much the same. But she highlighted and explained how words like *chronic angers, fearing, indifferently, austere,* and *lonely,* led her to her comments. That no one ever thanked him, she felt, was done because he was mean and that he was only doing what fathers should do. Although she listened to classmates and did make some adjustments, she stood firm. And we validated that stance for her as her findings at this time. (I made a note in my notebook, that I wish I could see her 7 years later to see if she kept that opinion or what changes she would make.)

The wording of the prompts is very important. Note that each prompt is personalized, requesting the student's reaction, not a definitive answer, and not the poet's answer. It's important for young readers to believe that they have something important to say about the poems they have read and that their reactions to and interactions with the work are valued. This exercise helps the students to validate for themselves whether their responses really reflect meaning, or if their responses were more of a guess or opinion. They must also understand that guessing and opinions are not inappropriate on the first tries of interpretation. What is desired, however, is that they develop strategies to test their answers for themselves. It also allows the student and the teacher to get into the thinking of students' responses and why they were made. Using these prompts as beginnings and our poetry notebooks as ongoing records, students turned several of their responses into longer papers or reports.

As part of our strategies to understand and appreciate poetry, we often wrote our own poems using one of the poems we studied as a model. During an early session, we talked about topics that could be used for writing our poems. We generated almost 40 ideas in about 10 minutes and decided that poetry could be about anything. Many of the poems we wrote were rhyming poems, but free verse was also popular. The students enjoyed forming concrete poems, keeping the simplicity of haiku, and playing with the rhyme and rhythm of limericks. We wrote poems about sports, animals, and people. I often used poems about people and animals for my mini lessons because the responses were broader, but we also wrote poems about school subjects such as math, and about school activities such as losing a wrestling match.

One of the more successful lessons was when we decided to generate our own lines and not use a model we had read (e.g., "The Reasons I Like Chocolate"). The students were accustomed to using brainstorming to generate ideas. When asked for topic ideas, they quickly began to respond as Marta wrote them on the board: hockey, soccer, basketball, dogs, kittens, grandmoms, babies. . . . Then Tommy shouted loudly,

"Poets." Some of the children laughed, and Marta wrote it down. Tommy went on as if his contribution needed explanation, "We're like poets."

We continued our brainstorming. Later, when we were ready to choose a topic to write about, I said, "All of these ideas, I don't know which one to choose."

Tommy knew immediately: "Write about poets."

Mostly to accommodate his eagerness, I said okay. Then I said, "I need help. How should I start?" I wanted students to see one way to develop writing a poem from ideas to final, edited copy. Similar to stories and other writings they see in published form, it's difficult to picture the process unless they see it for themselves.

Doris chimed in, "I am a poet." I wrote her suggestion on the board.

Then Tommy insisted, "We're not poets yet, but we can pretend."

"Okay," I agreed, and started, "I'm not a poet, I . . ."

Several of the students now began to brainstorm for me. "You'd be wonderful," "you'd like flowers." One student even suggested, "You'd be dead."

"Perhaps if you helped me, I could work this out," I suggested. "Let's get into small groups of four and try to come up with some ideas you can use for topics and lines for your individual poem. Help each other by brainstorming ideas and giving suggestions. Don't worry about spelling or form. This is an idea draft, just to get started. Remember, your first line may not be the first line of the final draft. It may just be a space holder today." I worked with three students, including Tommy, of course. After 5 or 6 minutes we shared our first attempts. The students helped me to brainstorm ideas to add: Smell the flowers, you love nature—the animals and stuff, and be a city poet. Taking into consideration the ideas of my group, I revised my first line to reflect that I was not a poet, but if I were a poet, what would I do? Just as the students helped me brainstorm ideas for my poem, we shared ideas with each other, suggested words when one of us would feel stuck, and listened to one another read a line that was special or that seemed problematic. We worked through our first drafts, collaborating and supporting each other, while allowing the poem to remain the product of the individual writer. Based on suggestions from my group, my feelings about the subject, and my desire to use the input of the group, my first draft looked like this:

If I was a poet,
I'd write about flowers in bloom
and about the birds' sweet song
about white winter snow and
autumn's colorful hues.
I'd write about something beautiful.

We began to develop a process for writing without ever giving it a name. We worked on our poems over several weeks, using 10 or 15 minutes each session and as much time at home as we wanted. We would often start new pieces or go back to old pieces. I used this poem as my model of collaboration and what it means in the writing process. At one session, I asked, "What form should this take, should it rhyme?" and received differing responses of "yes" and "no"; however, we did decide that I could change the form if this didn't work. We played with words and with rhymes. The English teacher in me at last took over, and I changed *was* to *were*, and we had a short lesson on using subjunctive expressions.

Reflections

Young adolescents bring so much background and imagination to the classroom. Their reactions to literature are often surprising, both in their insight and in their naivete. Slowly, students develop an appreciation and understanding about poetry through listening, reading, writing, and illustrating poetry. They begin to know why they like a work or not and to appreciate the effort that goes into writing poetry. Through the teacher-selected poems and through their own selected poems, they begin to see patterns that say, "This is poetry." They find that they can find meaning for themselves and can validate that meaning by going back to the work and using the poem and their own experiences to explain to others why the poem means what it does to them. They practice reading aloud because they know that there is a flow, a rhythm, to be achieved. In their own writing, they emphasize and de-emphasize words or lines to create a mood or to set a pattern. Almost without effort, they learn to recognize and use figurative language, and to value its effectiveness. They begin to understand the power of words—that so much can be communicated in such short space, if they choose their words carefully.

I spent nine focused sessions in Marta Jenkins' classroom. I was teacher, then facilitator, then observer, then student. I learned from Marta; I learned from the students. I realized later that I was fortunate during this setting in ways that I had not been during my school-based teaching days. Marta was at every session. She or I would take notes while the other interacted with the students. She and I separately wrote our reflections about the lesson, the children, the pace, and then shared our thoughts with each other; we shared a mentoring relationship. We planned together, keeping in mind our objectives, the goals of the students, and the curriculum requirements. We kept logs of these components and reviewed them as we planned together for the next meeting. We reaffirmed the need for time and practice. We talked through ways to revisit ideas that did not seem to work well the first time, rather than to abandon the technique. We were in constant contact with each other during the week as she kept me informed about what the children were bringing into the classroom. In addition, I visited the classroom when I was not teaching and when they were doing other activities and other subjects, just to observe and to allow the children to see a reversal in our roles—me in a passive role and Marta in an active role.

By the end of the 9 weeks, we felt confident that the students understood and could write poems using the elements defined in the curriculum. They could talk poetry, using language that expressed their meaning appropriately. We found that they already recognized and used metaphors and similes, probably from first grade, although some of them still confused which was which and consciously looked for the *like* or *as*. We pulled examples directly from some of their journal writings as a way of showing them that they do use figurative language on a daily basis. As they saw examples of poetry elements in newspapers, magazines, or heard examples on television or radio or among people talking, they added them to their poetry notebook. They found poems and songs that illustrated figurative language and wrote their own examples. And they also learned and deliberately created parodies, a term not required in the curriculum.

Now and then, I look at my poetry notebook with my comments in the margin and the doodling on the pages. I play with the words of my poem, "If I Were a Poet," and sometimes I work on revising the words or changing the form. The sentiment of working with the students, however, promotes a desire to keep it intact.

If I Were A Poet[1]

If I were a poet,
I'd say something beautiful—

Of birds
soaring to touch a cloud,
Or buildings
poised high and proud.

Flowers
in hues of red and gold,
Snow capped mountains
are sights to behold.

Alas, I do regret
My talent's pitiful
And yet—
If I were a poet,
In words bold and truthful,
I'd say something
beautiful.

—Arlene Harris Mitchell

---

[1]© Arlene Harris Mitchell. Permission granted to include with this article.

This is my story. Truly, "If I were a poet, I'd say something beautiful" about these wonderful sixth grade-students.

APPENDIX A

Mother to Son

Well, son, I'll tell you:
Life for me ain't been no crystal stair.
It's had tacks in it,
And splinters,
And boards torn up,
And places with no carpet on the floor—
Bare.
But all the time
I'se been a-climbin' on,
And reachin' landins
And turnin' corners,
And sometimes goin' in the dark
Where there ain't been no light.
So, boy, don't you turn back.
Don't you set down on the steps
'Cause you finds it's kinder hard.
Don't you fall now—
For I'se still goin', honey,
I'se still climbin',
And life for me ain't been no crystal stair.

—*Hughes* (1974, p. 30)

Those Winter Sundays

Sundays my father got up early
and put on his clothes in the blueblack cold,
then with cracked hand that ached
from labor in the weekday weather made
banked fires blaze. No one ever thanked him.

I'd wake and hear the cold splintering, breaking.
When the rooms were warm, he'd call,
and slowly I would rise and dress,
fearing the chronic angers of that house,

Speaking indifferently to him,
who had driven out the cold
and polished my good shoes as well.
What did I know, what did I know
of love's austere and lonely offices?

—*Hayden* (1957, pp. 120–121)

My Brother Estes

My brother Estes
and his cousin Ray
left here for California
the minute the two of them together
had enough money to buy a car.

They were leaving the god-forsaken mountains.

They were gonna make some money,
gonna find them California wives.
Well, they done right well,
both of them,
I gotta admit that.

But I got a phone call from Estes
just two days ago.
He's pushing into his fifties now,
and you know,
he wants to bring his California wife
and come back home.

All this time, he's called me
his hick sister,
I knew my chance was coming,
'cause the mountains speak the loudest
to a person in his middle years,
and no matter where he is
or what he's done,
he begins to think of them as home.

You know what I told Estes?
I told him to come on back and try it,
but not to get his hopes too high
'cause he don't talk right any more.

                                        —*Carson* (1989, pp. 17–18)

The Reason I Like Chocolate

The reason I like chocolate
is I can lick my fingers
and nobody tells me I'm not polite

I especially like scary movies
'cause I can snuggle with Mommy
or my big sister and they don't laugh

I like to cry sometimes 'cause
everybody says "what's the matter
don't cry"

and I like books
for all those reasons
but mostly 'cause they just make me
happy

and I really like
to be happy

—*Giovanni* (1980, p. 49)

CHILDREN'S TEXTS

Adoff, A. (Ed.). (1973). *The poetry of Black America: Anthology of the 20th century*. New York: Harper & Row

Agard, J. (1989). *Life doesn't frighten me at all*. New York: Henry Holt & Co.

Ambrose, A. (Ed.). (1973). *My name is Black: An anthology of Black poets*. New York: Scholastic.

Astrov, M. (1946). *American Indian prose and poetry*. New York: John Day Company.

Bauer, C. F., & Zimmer, D. (1988). *Windy day: Stories and poems*. Philadelphia: Lippincott.

Bennett, J.(1987). *Noisy poems*. Oxford: Oxford University Press.

Bodecker, N. M. (1985). *Snowman, sniffles, and other verse*. New York: Atheneum.

Breman, P. (1973). *You better believe it: Black verse in English from Africa, the West Indies and the United States*. New York: Penguin Books.

Brenner, B. (Ed.). (1994). *The earth is painted green*. (S.D. Schindler, Il.). New York: Scholastic.

Bryan, A. (1978). *I greet the dawn: Poems by Paul Laurence Dunbar*. New York: Atheneum.

Bryan, A. (1986). *Sea songs*. (L. E. Fisher, Il.). New York: Holiday House.

Carson, J. (1989) My brother Estes. In *Stories I ain't told nobody yet* (p. 17–18). New York: Orchard Books.

Cole, J. (Ed.). (1984). *A new treasury of children's poetry*. New York: Doubleday.

Cole, J. (1989). *Anna banana*. (A. Tiegreen, Il.). New York: Scholastic.

Cullen, C. (Ed.). 1993). *Caroling dusk—An anthology of verse by Black poets*. New York: Carol Publishing Group.

deRegniers, B. S., Moore, E., White, M. M., & Carr, J. (Eds.); Brown, M., Dillon, L., Dillon, D., Egielski, R., Hyman, T. S., Lobel, A., Sendak, M., Simont, M., & Zemach, M. (Ils.). (1988). *Sing a song of popcorn: Every child's book of poems*. New York: Scholastic.

Dunning, S., Lueders, E. & Smith, H. (1966). *Reflections on a gift of watermelon pickle ...and Other modern verse*. New York: Lothrop, Lee & Shepard. (2nd ed., Scott Foresman, 1995)

Espeland, P., & Wanik, M. (1984). *The cat walked through the casserole and other poems for children*. (T. Schart, H. Knight, N. Carlson, & P. E. Hanson, Ils.). Minneapolis, MN: Carolrhoda Books.

Farber, N., & Cohn Livingston, M. (Eds.). (1977). *These small stones*. New York: Harper & Row.

Feelings, T. (1978). *Something on my mind*. (N. Grimes, Il.). New York: Dial Books for Young Readers.

Frost, R. (1969). *Stopping by woods on a snowy evening*. (S. Jeffers, Il.). New York: Rinehart and Winston.

Fufuka, K. (1975). *My daddy is a cool dude and other poems*. New York: Dial Books for Young Readers.

Giovanni, N. (1980). *The reason I like chocolate in vacation time: Poems for children* (p. 49). New York: Morrow.

Greenfield, E. (1988). *"Nathaniel talking."* (J. Spivey, Il.). New York: Writers and Readers Publishing.

Greenfield, E. (1981). *Daydreamers*. New York: Dial Books for Young Readers.

Hayden, R. E. (1973). Those winter Sundays. In A. Adoff (Ed.). *The poetry of Black America: Anthology of the 20th century* (pp. 120–121). New York: HarperCollins Children's Books.

Hollowell, L. (Ed.). (1966). *A book of children's literature*. Chicago: Holt, Rinehart & Winston.

Hopkins, L. B. (1985). *Munching: Poems about food*. Canada: Little, Brown.

Hopkins, L. B. (1990). *Good books, good times!* (H. Stevenson, Il.). New York: HarperCollins.

Hudson, W., (Ed.). (1993). *Pass it on: African-American poetry for children*. (F. Cooper, Il.) New York: Scholastic.

Hughes, L. (1974). *Selected poems of Langston Hughes*. New York: Vintage.

Hughes, L. (1994). *Collected poems of Langston Hughes*. New York: Knopf.

Jones, C. (1985). *Poetry patterns*. (M. Baker, Il.). Indiana: Book Lures.

Joseph, L. (1990). *Coconut kind of day: Island Poems*. New York: Lothrop, Lee & Shepard Books.

Kennedy, X. J. (1982). *Brats*. (J. Watts, Il.). New York: Atheneum.

Kennedy, X. J., & Kennedy, D. M. (1982). *Knock at a star*. New York: Little, Brown.

Korman, G., & Korman, B. (1992). *The poems of Jeremy Bloom*. New York: Scholastic.

Lansky, B. (1991). *Kids pick the funniest poems*. (S. Carpenter, Il.). New York: Meadowbrook Press.

Larrick, N. (1990). *Mice and nice*. (E. Young, Il.). New York: Putnam.

Lawrence, J. (1968). *Harriet and the promised land*. New York: Simon & Schuster.

Lewis, R. (1966). *Miracles (Poems by Children of the English-speaking world)*. New York: Touchstone Center for Children.

Little, L. J. 1988). *Children of long ago*. New York: Philomel Books.

Livingston, M. C. (1985). *Celebrations*. (L. E. Fisher, Il.). New York: Scholastic.

Livingston, M. C. (1994). *Animal, vegetable, mineral: Poems about small things*. New York: HarperCollins.

Merriam, E. (1977). *It doesn't always have to rhyme*. New York: Atheneum.

Merriam, E. (1987). *Halloween ABC*. (L. Smith, Il.). New York: Macmillan Children's Book Group.

Merriam, E. (1967) How to eat a poem. In S. Dunning, E. Leuders, & H. Smith (Eds.), *Reflections on a gift of watermelon pickle and other modern verse* (p. 15). New York: Lothrop, Lee & Shepard.

Morninghouse, S. (1989). *Nightfeathers*. (J. Kim, Il.) Seattle: Open Hand Publishing.

Moss, J. (1989). *The butterfly jar*. (C. Demarest, Il.). New York: Bantam Books.

Nye, N. S. (Ed.).(1992). *This same sky: A collection of poems from around the world*. New York: Macmillan Children's Book Group.

Polhamus, J. B. (1974). *Dinosaur funny bones*. (M. Funai, Il.). Englewood Cliffs, NJ: Prentice-Hall.

Pomerantz, C. (1982). *If I had a paka: Poems in eleven languages*. (N. Tafuri, Il.). New York: Greenwillow Books.

Prelutsky, J. (1980). *The headless horseman rides tonight (More poems to trouble your sleep)*. (A. Lobel, Il.). New York: Greenwillow Books.

Prelutsky, J. (1985). *My parents think I'm sleeping*. (Y. Abolafia, Il.). New York: Greenwillow Books.

Prelutsky, J. (1993). *The dragons are singing tonight*. (P. Sis, Il.). New York: Greenwillow Books.

Rylant, C. (1894). *Waiting to waltz—A childhood*. (S. Gammell, Il.). New York: Macmillan Children Book Group.

Schecter, E. (1992). *I love to sneeze*. (G. Fiammenghi, Il.). New York: Bantam.

Sears, P. (Ed.). (1990). *Gonna bake me a rainbow poem: A student guide to writing poetry.* New York: Scholastic.

Sharp, S. (1991). *Soft song.* New York: Harlem River Press.

Sherman, J. R. (Ed.). (1974). *Invisible poets.* Michigan: Books on Demand.

Silverstein, S. (1974). *Where the sidewalk ends.* New York: Harper & Row.

Silverstein, S. (1981). *A light in the attic.* New York: HarperCollins.

Simcox, H. E. (1980). *Dear dark face: Portraits of a people.* Detroit, MI: Lotus Press.

Snyder, G. (1969). *Turtle island.* New York: New Directions Books.

Thomas, J. C. (1993). *Brown honey in broomwheat tea.* (F. Cooper, Il.). New York: Harper Collins.

Viorst, J. (1981). *If I were in charge of the world and other worries.* (L. Cherry, Il.). New York: Macmillan.

Withers, C. (Ed.). (1948). *A rocket in my pocket.* New York: Scholastic.

Wood, A. (1982). *Quick as a cricket.* (D. Wood, Il.). West Orange, NJ: Child's Play International.

6

Bringing Literature to Life Through Reader's Theatre

Elizabeth Jackowski Davis
Lakeway Elementary School

EDITOR'S OVERVIEW

Greeted by an unenthusiastic second-grade classroom atmosphere, the words, "I don't read. I don't know how and I don't want to," echoing in her head, Elizabeth Davis responded to the challenge with Reader's Theatre. This reader-response methodology engaged her students' attention and sparked their enthusiasm. More than attitude enhancement, the approach encouraged the development of their reading skills.

The strategies used with this second-grade class initiate with response discussion and are followed by reading, rereading, and then scripting the text or portions of it for performance. The scripting, accomplished by small groups, required still more rereading, and discussion-analysis of character and events. The last steps were creating and writing dialogue and performing their response script. The students graduate from picture storybooks to texts of greater length and complexity.

Also illustrated is the implementation of Reader's Theatre in a fifth-grade class. Applications are made in both language arts and social studies. The students' responses to Shakespeare's A Midsummer Night's Dream *through Reader's Theatre techniques led the class to staging a dramatic performance.*

Consider the following:

1. *How do the Reader's Theatre strategies exemplified here encourage readers' responses as well as reading skill development?*
2. *Explore the apparent impact of this approach, as well as that of story drama (see chapter 4, Drama and Response to Literature), on children with reading and learning disabilities?*
3. *Express the differences in expectations and, thus, processes and procedures evident for the two class levels represented in this chapter.*

"I don't read."

"Oh, sure you do. I love to read." I answered back calmly, dreading the very sound of such words.

"Nope, I don't know how and I don't want to."

"Don't worry Mrs. Davis, he's always saying that."

"Oh, Joshua, we are going to make reading an exciting adventure and you like adventures don't you?" The words were echoing in my head, I had to bide time.

"Nope."

It was October 5 and my first day. The class had been formed in September due to overcrowding of the second grade. I was hired and so began the best year of my life. In a desperate attempt to alter the unenthusiastic atmosphere and climate of the classroom, I searched madly for an exciting approach to literature. These kids were smart, street smart, and serious. Only second grade and many were already labeled with discipline problems and had obvious negative attitudes toward their academic achievement. Their neighborhood was tough. The urban school was surrounded by apartments and freeways, which allowed little space for recreation. A typical two-bedroom apartment might house two families or extended families. There was a large settlement of Nigerian families struggling to find work with a limited English-speaking background. Although I had many Nigerian parents who spoke only a little English, my Nigerian students were fluent in English. Single parents, double-income working families, parents working night shifts, all contributed to the children's raising themselves. Many second graders were already responsible for younger siblings or cousins. Drug related problems were affecting a large proportion of the community. The children were living in an environment where they were faced with hard realities and little fantasy. Their preconceived ideas (or experiences) had brought them here, at this special moment in my life, to expect boredom and idleness, whereas I was expecting great awakenings.

The challenge was to excite Joshua and the other students into reading literature. What I found was a reader-response methodology that transformed our ideas of reading into wonderment. Reader's Theatre worked in our classroom like magic. My research into the process of Reader's Theatre allowed me to adapt it to my specific needs. *Readers theatre* is defined by McCaslin (1990, cited in Wolf, 1993) as "the oral presentation of drama, prose, or poetry by two or more readers." The concept is to involve children in reading a particular selection, whether a story, poem, or textbook, and allow them to process it through their own schema. Then through group interpretation, discussion , rewriting, and performing, students can work their way through reading, rereading, understanding, and evaluating their understanding of literature. A great aspect of reader's theatre is that participants read from a script of their own words, not from memorized lines of a prewritten manuscript. In fact, there is no memorization involved, merely reading and oral expression (which developed nicely with practice). Even better, the words being read to the audience are words of which the students have ownership. These words have been processed through their background of knowledge and experience. These words mean something. They are their interpretation of the literature, their analysis and evaluation of the literature.

"So, how is this story of the *Three Little Pigs* different from the one you've heard before?" This was a typical way to start our class discussion, as we closed our copies of *The True Story Of The Three Little Pigs* (*by A. Wolf*) (Scieszka & Smith, 1989).

Calvin:	It's a lot cooler than the old story.
Devin:	I think the wolf isn't such a bad guy after all.
Erica:	I like the pictures.
Janika:	Really! They tell a lot about what the wolf thinks.
Teacher:	Any pictures in particular?
Erica:	On the page where the wolf is making Grannie's cake. See all the ingredients, the wolf could have told us what he was putting in.
Teacher:	What do you think the wolf should say on that page?
Devin:	Well look, there are rabbit ears coming out of the bowl. Yuck!
Teacher:	So how could we rewrite this part of the story ?
Ernest:	I think we should name a bunch of stuff that's in the cake. Also, on the next page the wolf is whistling and tossing the cup, maybe we should say something like "So I whistled and walked real cool like to my neighbor's for some sugar."
Calvin:	Yeah, let's make this guy too cool.

We were reading. And that was just the beginning. We were interpreting, analyzing, evaluating, rewriting scripts, and performing our scripts. We were implementing Reader's Theatre. Oral expression is a key part of this form of reader's response. Between their practices and performances, students read (perform) their scripts numerous times for various audiences. Developing these skills can often be difficult in front of one's peers; however, with Reader's Theatre, I find the students feel comfortable with their performances. Partly this is because they are reading familiar words, and because it became such a routine in our classroom. Even the most shy of my girls were excited about performing a script that they put together. The following is an example of how it effectively worked in my second grade class.

READING, SCRIPTING AND PERFORMING

The story of *Lon Po Po*, translated by Ed Young (1989), was first read to my class as a whole group. As a class, we designated certain times of our day to whole-group time, writers' workshop, and individual or group work. The children sat on the floor with books and we all took turns reading (even Joshua).

Latasha: This book is different.
Teacher: In what ways is it different?
Latasha: Well, sometimes the writer says things different from the way we talk.
Erica: Yeah, like, *close the door tight at sunset and latch it well,* instead of lock the door.
Ernest: And *eldest* instead of oldest.
Devin: That's because it's from China.
Joshua: What are *hemp strings* and *awl* anyway? And *gingko nuts*?
Teacher: Let's read that part of the story over. What do you think a hemp string might be?
Jordon: A wooden string.
Ernest: Straw, maybe.
Janika: Something like a broom or twigs.
Earl: I'll look it up. [Earl liked to look up everything.]

We all agreed that *Lon Po Po* was another version of *Little Red Riding Hood.* We talked of the parallels, and the differences.

Teacher: How are the two alike?
Joshua: They are both about a wolf wanting to eat kids.
Erica: They both have a grandmother.
Janika: The wolf pretends to be the grandmother in both stories.
Calvin: Yeah, but in *Little Red Riding Hood* the wolf eats the grandmother and in *Lon Po Po* the wolf visits the children's house, like in the *Three Little Pigs.*
Teacher: That's great! So what are some other important differences between the stories?
Joshua: Nobody wears a red hood in this story.
Erica: The mother takes food to the grandmother, not Little Red Riding Hood.
Latasha: And in this story the wolf doesn't eat anybody! I like this story better.
Teacher: That brings up a good point, what is an important difference in the ending of the two stories?
Joshua: Well, the wolf dies in both.
Erica: But in one a woodsman comes in and kills the wolf for Little Red Riding Hood and in this story Shang, Tao, and Paotze do it all by themselves.

Next we decided to summarize the book in our own words. I used chart paper and marker for this activity. I felt this was a good way to start Reader's Theatre with second graders, initiating a class script first, then modeling what they would later do in cooperative groups. We brainstormed for characters, events, and setting. We sequenced the main events and referred to the book for quotes. Some students were already thinking in terms beyond summarizing. They were adapting the story to their own world.

Jordon: I think we should take out the part where the wolf keeps blowing out the candles. Let's just say he sliced the wires outside the house before he came in.

Teacher: Well, later we are going to do this in smaller groups and you can write in more details, and you may choose to depict only a part of the whole story, maybe a chapter or a specific event.

An aspect that was to be developed further as we experienced Reader's Theatre was to get the students to think in terms of dialogue writing. This allowed great opportunity for students to see from someone else's perspective, a difficult task for children. After we rescripted the story, I asked for volunteers to read from the script, each with their own part or role. Without props, the children seemed to realize the importance of their voice and expressions. I had everyone volunteering and many disappointed faces when the characters were selected. I asked the students if they would like to do this again, and the response was unanimous.

We decided to split into groups of four, allowing for participation from each group member. I explained the steps to Reader's Theatre and we made a chart for reference. The first task on our chart of steps was for the group to reread the story, keeping in mind they would be rewritng it. I reiterated that reading the selection as often as 4 or 5 times might be necessary before they were really able to rescript it. (The rereading of the text makes the text more predictable. The predictability of the text helps support the reading strategies of the emergent or the ineffective readers.) The second step was for the group to decide which part of the story they would like to perform. This was a difficult task and called for compromising and some teacher-directed decisions. Later, with other literature selections, I often assigned chapters or events to particular groups, which allowed us to interpret longer books and have new material covered in each performance. Step three called for analyzing and summarizing the events, characters and setting of the part of the story they chose to perform. Also, it involved deciding which characters would have parts and who would play these parts.

Step four was the core of the writing aspect of Reader's Theatre, as it was rescripting and summarizing . Students seemed to be very enthusiastic about contributing to this part. Everyone wanted their words to be incorporated into the script. This is where I saw characters emerging from the book and coming alive in our classroom! We decided step five was practicing the actual script, which I reminded them would require reading and rereading until there existed a smooth and easy transition between the characters. I emphasized that memorization was not the goal, but reading the script with appropriate expression and gestures. With our chart made, our groups formed and our story (*Lon Po Po*) selected, read and discussed, we took off! We decided to allow the rest of the week, about an hour each day, for preparation.

Invitation 6.1

Choose a book and form groups—Lon Po Po or a comparable one with several characters. Read with students, then allow them to re-read in their groups. Have each group write a dialogue script for the text, then prepare a Reader's Theatre presentation. Perform it for your class.

We started the next day with a quick review of our chart, then went right into our groups.

Group 1:

Devin:	I want to be the wolf.
Calvin:	I want to be Shang.

I noticed that the designating of parts was foremost on their minds.

Teacher:	Well, let's reread the story, and think of what part of the story your group would like to perform.
Devin:	But Shang and the wolf have the best parts.
Teacher:	Remember you are rescripting part of the story, so Tao and Paotze could have more speaking parts.
Erica:	On the second page Tao and Paotze do a lot of action, we could make them say things, too.
Teacher:	Perfect. Can you give us an example.
Erica:	Well in the part when Tao and Paotze rush to their Po Po to get a hug, they could say something like, "Oh Po Po, we've missed you."
Calvin:	Hey, maybe they could say something when they let the old wolf in the door. Like "Come on Shang, let our Po Po in."
Teacher:	That's great! Remember your first step is to reread the story, then decide which part of the story your group wants to rescript.

I had to remind myself that this was a new approach for my second graders, and it would take time and practice before everything went smoothly. Part of their growing process is to learn social skills, decision making skills, and compromising skills. Reader's Theatre lends itself to these essential elements nicely.

I noticed different groups chose different methods for rereading the story. Some read in turns within the whole group. One group split into pairs to read quietly. I did notice some leadership skills forming within the groups. One girl decided to write down the characters as she read, and her partner would count the number of lines each character had. Whatever the method, I noticed intense reading going on, with great discussions among children who normally didn't choose to talk to each other.

Group 2:

Latasha: The boys are overdoing it. They want to make Shang into some super hero.

Teacher: Remember, you are just rescripting a story not creating a completely new one. Is there a way you can use some of the suggestions without changing the story too much?

Ernest: Well maybe Shang could be really extra strong.

Latasha: Okay, but how is that going to change the story?

Teacher: Let's reread the part of the story where the children pull the wolf up in the tree.

Ernest: Wow, I thought Shang was a boy.

Latahsa: He is.

Joshua: No, they are all sisters.

Teacher: Where in the story do we find out that Shang is a girl?

Ernest: Not at first because the mother just talks about her three children. And then they are all called by their names so we don't ever know.

Teacher: Does this change how you think of Shang now?

Ernest: Kinda.

I moved throughout the classroom, listening to various problems within the groups, most being solved without my intervention. The class was abuzz with talk, but it was talk of literature. I heard students analyzing predicaments and evaluating suggested changes. They were engaged and their energy was focused on learning.

Day three was spent settling parts and lines. I was beginning to see cooperative decision making.

Group 3:

Earl: Who wants to be the wolf?

Janika: I do.

Earl:	But the wolf should be played by a boy.
Sam:	Let's pick a number.
Earl:	Or we can just put the parts on pieces of paper and then draw them out of a hat.
Janika:	Okay, but no trading!

The method for recording the manuscript had not been discussed. Again, I was thrilled to see how each group handled this part of the process. One group chose to make one copy and pass it around during the performance. They highlighted each person's part in a different color. Another group wrote out individual parts on their own paper; however, they realized in their practice performance that they did not know their cues because they only had their own parts on their paper. They solved this by writting the previous character's line over their part. I think they still found this a bit confusing, and it showed during their performance. But I reminded them this was our first try, and we were learning as we went along.

The fourth day was divided. I allowed a few minutes of practice and then we drew group numbers out of a hat to see who performed first. The plan was for two performances that day and the other three the following day. Although each performance was a unique blend of student's ideas and interpretations, 3 of the 5 groups were very similar to the original story, with a mild language variance. In most cases, the formal tone of *Lon Po Po* became more relaxed. Group 5 changed the characters, giving each more dynamic personalities. Where Paotze originally says very little in the story, group 5 turned her into a rapper. Although they only gave her a few lines, she transformed into a character with whom they would easily associate. Group 3 was the risk-taker. They changed the house in *Lon Po Po* into an apartment complex and the setting from the country to the city.

Everyone was excited and surprised at the difference in each performance. I noticed that the more quiet students did better than I first expected. I believe it was due to their own input in the script and their comfort with the words they chose to perform. Again, the lack of memorization in this exercise allows for a less stressful environment. Joshua read his parts well, although he rebelled somewhat by not using any expression in his tonation. I'm sure this was his way of holding on to an image he couldn't quite give up. The group that passed the script around seemed more nervous. I thought perhaps this was due to their need of finding their place on the script and not having the words in their own handwriting.

CLASS EVALUATION AND FOLLOW-UP ACTIVITIES

After we finished our performances, we met for a class discussion. This was an incredible time of enthusiasm. Everyone had comments and suggestions. One girl tried to take notes, but there were too many ideas.

I was just as excited as they were, and we decided to write suggestions down on chart paper.

Teacher: What are some things you would change?
Sam: Let's make-up some more rules. I think it needs to be more team-like.

This particular child was typically quiet and had experienced his peers aggressiveness in their group work. He was considering a leadership role for future Reader's Theatre activities.

I led the discussion to the variety of interpretations that were performed. Everyone liked the way group 3 changed Lon Po Po's house into an apartment complex and the setting from the country to the city.

Teacher: What made your group change the setting of the story?
Earl: I don't know, it just seemed better.

This seemed logical, for many of the students had never been out of the urban environment and housing in the area was limited to apartment complexes. I was excited to see some risk taking.

Joshua: I'm glad somebody got rid of that gingko nut tree, too.
Erica: But apples don't grow in Houston.
Teacher: Well, what kind of trees would grow around here?
Earl: Pecan trees do.

Their interpretation was related to their world. The Chinese version of *Little Red Riding Hood* had become part of their world. Reader's Theatre had allowed these children to understand the story and interpret it into a real-life decision making predicament. Everyone agreed it was fun to see the different ways the groups performed. Requests were made for future Reader's Theatre. They asked if they could perform for other classes. They were begging me to let them read!

For a follow-up writing assignment, the students wrote about their favorite performance. They were instructed to choose a character in that performance and compare it to the same character in the original story. Characters were alive in our classroom. Students discussed *Lon Po Po* as if they had written it themselves, and essentially, in their minds, they had. Reader's Theatre was a hit! Our next adventure took on several of the *Amelia Bedelia* stories by Parish (1992). Each group read, interpreted, and performed a different selection of Parish's work. We did an author study on Roald Dahl and used Reader's Theatre for *The Magic Finger* (Dahl, 1966)

As we worked from week to week, incorporating Reader's Theatre into our classroom routine, I saw much more risk taking. Leadership skills were developing in everyone. Writing seemed less a task than before. I noticed an increase in the monthly book orders, although I knew money was an issue with many of my students. Cooperative group skills were practiced throughout the school day and seemed to carry through to outside classroom activities. Our class was becoming a family, through expression of ideas, through weekly performances, through literature. Mastery of oral skills was clearly evident. Expression was coming through in their oral reading and a new sense of understanding of words. Joshua no longer complained at reading time, but instead volunteered. In his grumpy way, he had found success and never declined an opportunity to read orally. Our classroom learning environment and climate were spirited and animated, as were the students. Their enthusiasm that was often before mistaken for bad behavior was directed toward learning. Reader's Theatre offered the challenge they needed. Literature was alive and well in our classroom.

FIFTH-GRADE APPLICATIONS

Since that wonderful year with my second graders, I have used Reader's Theatre with fiction, poetry, and nonfiction. Reader's Theatre is implemented by my current fifth-grade language arts and social studies classes daily. The children become pilgrims and colonists and rewrite the text in dialogue format. This allows nonfiction to become both exciting and informative. I have found increased conceptual understanding instead of fact memorization. Students are recalling events in chronological order after they have reenacted historical events. Class discussions are more enlivened and more students are active. One recent example is when two students explained the importance of the election of 1800. One student portrayed Thomas Jefferson, a Democratic-Republican, and the other student represented the previous government, the Federalists. The Democratic-Republican literally booted the Federalist out of center stage and then started to cut a piece of paper that represented Government spending. Not one student missed that question on the pop quiz.

Reader's Theatre emerged in my fifth-grade language arts class when I began reading William Shakespeare's *A Midsummer Night's Dream*. From the first few lines of the this wonderful classic, the students began to act out the characters as I read, for the purpose of understanding the rather confusing state of affairs with which Shakespeare engages his readers. I chose volunteers to act out the main characters as I read, so the students could follow the tangled relationship of this play. Through this quick and spontaneous reader-response technique, the students began to relate to the characters of the play. They recognized and responded to emotions they too felt and thus understood the basis of the plot. The natural course for these students was to rewrite Shakespeare in their own words. As a student remarked, "so other students in the school could understand it." What I anticipated as a week of Reader's

Theatre in our classroom turned into a dramatic retelling of *A Midsummer Night's Dream* to the entire school, costumes, stage sets, and all.

I was the facilitator. The students did all the work. They formed committees, the first being the writers. Who wanted to rewrite Shakespeare and in what form—contemporary, rap, or in Shakespearean? The two writing committees (one for each language class) spent 2 weeks on the computer, rereading, analyzing, and interpreting the summary I had given them of *A Midsummer Night's Dream*. They used a mixture of their own verse and some direct quotes from Shakespeare so that their audience would both understand the play and also get a good taste of Shakespeare's own words. I was amazed at their accomplishments, as I offered very little to their task. Every day I was astounded that they were reading sections of the story over and over, discussing them, and then putting their interpretations into dialogue form.

While they wrote, class after class, the other committees were working just as hard. The costume design committees from each class consulted with each other regularly, as we were going to have two different performances but share many costumes. They spent their time researching medieval costumes and on the floor making patterns for their designs. My students coordinated with the music teacher, who had a vast collection of costumes and props. The art teacher donated paint, brushes, books, and great ideas and encouragement for the set design. As the project grew, so did the support from the school. Our principal checked on our progress and watched as we practiced daily in the foyer. The students' reader-response to Shakespeare had ignited the appetite of the entire intermediate school for Shakespeare. I could see they were proud of themselves and their achievements.

As the weeks progressed, we spent much time analyzing the characters of the play, which contributed to the scriptwriting. Very often the scriptwriters would have the actors work through the scenes to edit dialogues. Students were problem solving the mechanics of their character's relationships through performing. They analyzed Shakespeare's word usage and intent. I saw actors and writers conferencing. From stages of comprehending, responding, analyzing, synthesizing, and evaluating, students were discussing 16th-century literature. Students dwelled on the thoughts of the characters and rejoiced at the contriving efforts of Puck, Shakespeare's mischievous elf.

We extended the literature experience by writing letters to Mr. Shakespeare, and asking him about his plays, life, and career. The response to literature from the two classes had spread to many parents, faculty members, students, and members of the community. Reader's Theatre had given the students a sense of ownership of Shakespeare's work. An improvement in their oral reading skills and tonation was evident. Reader's Theatre had taken a Shakespearean comedy and enabled the students to relate it to their world. They had dissected this play and put it back together beautifully.

The actual performances were wonderful and the students' experience well worth the weeks of preparation. They were the schools' experts on Shakespeare's *A Midsummer Night's Dream*. Although this experience had developed beyond the stages of Reader's Theatre, the successful outcome was evident to all. Reader's Theatre was the beginning. It allowed my students to find a path to lead them, a strategy to understand words, literature, expression, and knowledge. It started a pattern of success that felt comfortable, as it was processed through their world, their knowledge, their strengths, their excitement.

REFERENCES

Wolf, S. A. (April 1993). What's in a name? Labels and literacy in readers theatre. *The Reading Teacher*, *46*(7), 540–545.
Young, T. A., & Vardel, S. (Febuary 1993). Weaving readers theatre and nonfiction into the curriculum. *The Reading Teacher*, *46*(5), 399–405.

CHILDREN'S TEXTS

Dahl, R. (1966). *The magic finger*. New York: HarperCollins.
Parish, P. (1992). *Amelia Bedelia*. New York: HarperCollins.
Scieszka, J., & Smith, L. (1989). *The true story of the three little pigs (by A. Wolf)*. New York: V. King Kestrel.
Young, E. (Trans.). (1989). *Lon Po Po: A Red Riding Hood Story From China*. New York: Philomel Books.

7

Body Punctuation: Reader-Response in Motion

Elizabeth Bridges Smith
in Association with Cathy D. Nelson
Otterbein College
and Fifth Avenue Alternative School
for International Studies

EDITOR'S OVERVIEW

A keynote of reader-response theory is the individuality of the response, that is, the affective influence of personal experiences, attitudes, and backgrounds. Among these are culture and language. The focus of this chapter is a cultural marker, particular body language used by many African American students as part of their response process.

Body punctuation is displayed by African American students in Cathy Nelson's fifth-grade class in response to literature as well as in conversational situations. Elizabeth Smith defines the gestures, the exaggerated body movements, to clarify their intended meaning. She invites us into Ms. Nelson's classroom to observe her and her students, primarily African Americans, in action.

Teaching philosophy is identified; teaching techniques are explored. These are not limited to procedures but include processes. We are able to visualize Ms. Nelson's personal expression, how she creates an atmosphere that generates learning. It is this atmosphere and her expression that welcome response, that encourage these students to respond in their culturally situated manner. Smith suggests procedures and clues for processes that might be used by all teachers.

Consider the following:

1. *Reflect on what you know and can visualize about body language and its representation of meaning. What cultural and personal features are identifiable?*
2. *Put yourself in a literature-response situation, perhaps a small group discussion. Study the body language communication, the expression of meaning. How well do individuals understand and react to these?*
3. *Explore the procedures and process clues expressed in this chapter. Which of these can you adopt? What can you adapt in welcoming response to fit your style?*

"A people's story is the anchor dat keeps um from driftin'" (Yarbrough, 1989, p. 21). How that story is told and retold is the focus of this chapter. The discussion that follows is threefold; the first is to examine the relationship between culture and reader response; second is to define a specific type of cultural response pattern that I call *body punctuation*; and finally to describe the classroom and teaching method that supported this level of cultural response.

BACKGROUND—RESEARCH IN CULTURE AND READER RESPONSE

Research in the area of culture and reader-response tends to focus on outcomes. The emphasis has been on what a student says, writes, or draws during or after the reading of certain texts. In some instances, researchers have noted specific recall; in others, they mention the students' ability to relate what was read to their own lives. A few of these studies, quantitative and qualitative, are briefly discussed in the following paragraphs.

In working with Asian-Indian and American subjects, Steffensen, Joag-Dev, and Anderson (1979) determined that the schemata that persons have in their own background storehouse provides the framework for understanding the body of the text. Purves and Beach (1972) theorize from their research on culture and reader-response that readers are most interested in and involved with texts that are directly related to their own experiences. In 1990, Malik's study on reading comprehension and strategies showed that "the impact of cultural schemata may be evident not only in reading comprehension but also in reading strategies employed by the readers and in their reading speed while using culturally familiar and nonfamiliar texts" (pp. 207–208).

Sims Bishop (Sims, 1983) conducted a case study of Osula, a 10-year-old African American female. Bishop noted that Osula's preferences reflected literature choices in which there were experiences that were similar to her own. Osula sought out African American texts with strong, active, or clever female protagonists. These characters most closely reflected her own cultural schemata.

Spears-Bunton (1990) charted the changes in the responses of African American and European American eleventh graders in honors English classes. Her interest was to determine if exposure to a specific piece of African American literature had an impact on the historically documented animosity between these two groups within the context of this classroom. After reading Hamilton's *The House of Dies Drear* (1968), both Spears-Bunton and the classroom teacher noted a distinctly positive change in the attitudes of the students involved.

In 1993, Egan-Robertson examined the responses of Puerto Rican students to children's books with Puerto Rican characters and/or themes. The interaction these students had was replete with cultural markers including connection to family members and celebrations. This textual connection was evident in both discussion and story retelling.

These studies and others like them seem to support Applebee's (1985) assertion that "readers of a common age in a common culture will make sense of the text through a similar screen of linguistic and cultural conventions and presuppositions" (p. 89). It is the reader's cultural cohort that provides the lens through which text is viewed and understood.

As stated earlier, research in reader response has typically focused on the linguistic, or *what* the student says in writing or talk about text. Rarely has research emphasized the response process—*how* students talk about texts in a naturalistic setting. It was this that became one of the branches of a study I conducted in an urban elementary fourth- and fifth-grade classroom. Over the course of an academic year, I recorded the responses of African American students to literature, particularly literature with African American themes, characters and/or authors. It was during this process that I noted the cultural response pattern of body punctuation in the African American students' talk about text.

DEFINING BODY PUNCTUATION

"Frederick Douglass is Ms. Cathy's main man!" Tina giggled as she snapped the fingers of one hand high in the air.

Giving a twist of the neck and head, Olivia laughed and replied, "Ooh girl, you better shut up!"

More than conversation, this exchange between two African American fifth-grade girls represents one way they respond to literature. Most commonly seen in animated conversation, body punctuation is a culturally specific part of Black English. "Like exclamation points, periods and commas in print" (Smith, 1993, p. 68), these motions serve as punctuation for the oral responses and exchanges of many urban African American youngsters and adults. Abrams (1973) stated, "Black English is not just a linguistic system; it is the expressive system of Black Culture. This system includes not only linguistic features, but also paralinguistic traits which are recognizably characteristic of black speech" (p. 100).

The neck and head bob, the hand on the hip, and the snap of a finger are the most typical forms of body punctuation. The neck movement occurs when there is a repeated movement of the neck and head from side to side. It is often used to express attitude, the stance that accompanies self-assertion. This punctuation type occurs as the speaker is expressing himself or herself.

The hand-on-the-hip movement is an exaggerated circular swing of the hand to its final resting place on the hip. In many cases, the speaker swings the hip slightly to meet the oncoming hand. This punctuation type occurs when the speaker pauses or completes a thought.

Finally, the finger snap acts an exclamation point, adding emphasis to the speaker's message. It is a large movement combining the snap with swinging the arm across the body. The speaker uses this motion at the end of a thought or idea. Like the head and neck form of body punctuation, it often appears when extremes of emotion need to be expressed.

Invitation 7.1

Place yourself in a setting in which you can comfortably watch a conversation between African American children (a playground, McDonald's, etc.) Stay far enough away that you cannot hear the conversation. Instead, watch what is being said. What do the children do as they convey their message to one another?

CLASSROOM CONTEXT

What kind of a classroom structure, what teaching strategies not only permit but encourage these kinds of responses in African American students? The classroom was populated by 24 students: 17 African American, 2 biracial (African American and Caucasian), 4 Caucasian, and 1 international. Cathy Nelson, the classroom teacher, is also an African American.

The members of this classroom were encouraged to act as a community; building and class philosophy supported student involvement in curriculum planning and decision making. Global and multicultural education were strong foci. Cathy was strongly committed to the notion that students must be aware of their own history as well as the history and circumstances of others. Student readings were not limited to trade books; they were required to read newspapers, magazines, and developmentally appropriate selections from adult literature.

Cathy's commitment to community issues was reflected in her choice of instructional materials. It was not uncommon to walk into her classroom and see wall displays with student-produced posters tracing family roots, cooperative group research reports and maps detailing the American westward movement, or individual student biographical reports of African American historical figures.

The classroom was a strong example of a literate environment. Print was evident on every table and wall. Much of the print was student produced, some as a part of a class requirement, others as a result of a student interest or concern. Information that had been commercially produced or teacher-made had a direct relationship to the unit or thematic focus of the curriculum. Seldom did commercial materials stand alone; they were joined by writing or artwork that defined, supported, or enriched their intent.

Cathy used literature as an integral part of all classroom planning and work. The classroom library had well over 200 books, many of which had been purchased by Cathy. Additionally, she supported the class library with titles from area libraries, the school district's resource center, and the libraries of colleagues and friends. Her commitment to and interest in African American history is evident in the selections. Often as many as half of the books available were by African Americans or about African American issues and themes.

In many settings, fourth and fifth grade are the years in which some feel students are too old to be read to. Cathy took exception to this notion. She read aloud daily, often more than once, for multiple purposes. Her first commitment was to instill the notion of reading for pleasure. She would select a text because she enjoyed it and would bring that excitement to the class. Cathy is an expressive oral reader; students were captured by her tone and inflection. She had the ability to re-create the mood of the text and the emotions of the characters with her vocal interpretation of what was being read. Texts with dialect variations, character dialogue, and rich vocabulary were particularly pleasing to her. Cathy selected chapter books for reading aloud, a chapter a day, usually following the lunch hour. The day often started with a picture book or poem. At times, these would be related to the classroom theme; however, that wasn't always the case.

Read alouds were not limited to Cathy, nor were they always works of fiction. Fridays were Celebrity Reader days. Staff members, students (both in and out of this class), and community persons took part in selecting and sharing books with this classroom. Anyone who read was encouraged to bring a variety of genres to this group. Most frequently, students were exposed to contemporary realistic fiction or historical fiction. However, informational texts, picture books, and poetry were a regular staple in the literature supply.

Literature, in Cathy's classroom, was more than a vehicle for language arts. Fiction and nonfiction work emphasizing architecture became a part of the classroom library when the math focus was three-dimensional figures and area. Pioneer stories and biographies of Black cowboys were evident when the social studies theme was the westward movement. Books reinforced all aspects of the curriculum, even when there wasn't a specific thematic connection. For example, Cathy read *A Million Fish...More or Less* (McKissack, 1992) during her math review on place value. Literature was a source of information and an object of pleasure. Cognizant of the response potential, Cathy recognized the value of using literature for multiple purposes. She was aware of the factual knowledge students gained when using trade books as information sources. Additionally, she knew that using literature for pleasure was not a luxury. It evoked personal experiences and encouraged understanding. It increased comprehension, stimulated vocabulary growth, and encouraged students to become lifelong lovers of reading. Rather than being a dichotomy, using literature as a source of information and pleasure were complementary learning tasks in this classroom.

Body Punctuation In Cathy's Classroom

Because talk was a vital part of this classroom, discourse was always evident. Watching Janie and Olivia, African American students engaged in one such dialogue, I noticed that they added animated, often exaggerated, body movements to emphasize points in their conversation.

Later during independent book projects, I noticed many of the African American students, male and female, using these motions as they retold and talked about texts. As I began to note instances of these movements it became apparent that in relationship to textual responses, the African American students only used these motions when referring to books with African American characters and/or themes (Smith, 1993, p. 68).

The more I watched, the more I became aware of this body punctuation. In this classroom it was peer specific and gender neutral. Students rarely used these motions when conversing with an adult unless that student was using sarcasm or humor. They freely used body punctuation in the presence of adults; however, this usage was limited to oral presentations designed for their peers. Both male and female students used the finger snaps to punctuate thoughts and ideas, although the neck motions and the hand on the hip were typically used by the females.

Retelling Steptoe's (1987) *Mufaro's Beautiful Daughters* for an oral book report, Janie shared, "The sister, she was mean; she tried to get everything she could." As she spoke, she emphatically placed a hand on her hip and bobbed her neck from side to side. Later in her presentation, she added, "Now the prince, he was all right, but I didn't think he was really that cute," at which point she smiled and snapped her fingers with a broad gesture.

Kathy chose McKissack's (1988) *Mirandy and Brother Wind* for her oral report. As she described the dancing at the cake walk and the attitude of Mirandy and her dance partner, she exclaimed, "They danced like the wind!" She punctuated her statement with a hand swung round and placed on her hip.

The Frederick Douglass exchange described earlier between Olivia and Tina occurred after Carl, another student, reported on the book *Frederick Douglass: The Black Lion.* (McKissack & McKissack, 1987). Both girls were aware of the admiration their teacher had for the African American orator. Building on that, they made connections to the information Carl had provided in his report, accenting their conversation with the oral commas and moving exclamation points I call body punctuation.

Regardless of who used body punctuation in oral presentation or simple conversation, all of the African American students understood the meaning of the movements. Watching Janie retell *Mufaro's Beautiful Daughters* (Steptoe, 1987), students laughed and called back responses when she snapped her fingers. Kathy's hand on the hip was met with moans and exclamations of "Well!" characteristic of the call and response heard in many African American churches.

Although Caucasian students did not respond with call and response patterns to the body punctuation of their African American peers, they did converse with and react favorably to these motions. They registered mock surprise when Olivia and Tina conversed about their teacher, recognizing the playfulness with which the girls spoke. Body punctuation was racially or culturally specific in usage; however, it was not racially specific in who understood, was engaged by, and responded to this movement.

CATHY'S TECHNIQUES

What was it about this classroom that allowed students to use the cultural communication strategy of body punctuation in both formal and informal situations? How did Cathy's leadership, response, and facilitation support such response?

As an African American, Cathy shared a common cultural bond with many of her students. Although this was an asset, it was not the sole factor in the development of her supportive, collaborative classroom network. It was her conversation, her instructional material choices, and her curricular setup that made it possible for students to use body punctuation as a response form in the classroom.

Invitation 7.2

Keep a journal of your own physical responses to the reading of a children's book. Select Paulsen's Nightjohn *(1992) or Johnson's* Lift Ev'ry Voice and Sing *(1995). How do you respond? Do you notice yourself catching your breath or rocking in time to a rhythm? Compare journal notes with a collaboration group to extend/enhance body language resources.*

Talk That Talk—Conversation

Cathy talked in the classroom. Everyday, at every opportunity, she conversed with her students. It was not unusual to walk into her classroom and find her and a student engaged in a conversation about last night's dinner, the riots in Los Angeles, or an event she or the student had been involved in over the weekend. What made these conversations important was that they were intensely personal. Students talked with Cathy about anything.

It was in these conversations that I noticed Cathy's fluency moving from the Black English dialect to mainstream English. The more formal the topic of the conversation, the more formal her speech patterns were. When she was playful, teasing or chatting about issues related to home lives, there was evidence of dialect in her speech.

On one occasion Cathy told the students, "*Y'all got to know when it's okay to talk like this,* and when you need to speak like this." (Black English Variation [BEV] intonations and patterns are indicated in italics; mainstream, TV-talk, English is in roman.) In doing so, she was explicitly letting students know that there were appropriate times and places for both language variations. Following Cathy's lead, students moved in and out of dialect, with its vocal and physical characteristics, according to the formality of the setting. Cathy exemplified what Piestrup (1973) referred to as a *black artful teacher*. She allowed her cultural way of speaking and doing to become an integral part of her teaching.

During a read aloud of *A Williamsburg Household* (Anderson, 1988), students frequently interrupted to comment on or clarify story elements. As Cathy read a section focusing on the hardships of slavery, Michael responded with, "Mmmmm!" and a snap of the fingers. Cathy stopped reading and nodded toward Michael, encouraging him, although nonverbally, to continue or expand his thought. "I just couldn't do it. Couldn't live like that. It's just too hard." Several minutes of discussion followed before Cathy moved on with the text.

Cathy acknowledged Michael's finger snap as a response to the reading of the text. Recognizing it as representing something he was feeling, she invited him to expand his response as he felt comfortable. Instead of being seen as an interruption, Michael's snap was a contribution to the reading and discussion of the text.

Invitation 7.3

Spend time exploring classrooms. Make notes of ways that all teachers encourage African American students to respond to literature. Watch for specific signals that are given to encourage students to respond in ways that are culturally comfortable for them. Compare research notes with your collaboration group to extend / enhance your repertoire of teacher signals.

Putting Things To Use—Instructional Materials

As stated earlier, Cathy read frequently to her class. Her selections included a range of literature; however, she was always anxious to share African American literature with her students. It was this literature that provided another foundation to support students' use of body punctuation.

Over the course of an academic year, she read selections such as McKissack's *Flossie and the Fox* (1986), Greenfield's *Sister* (1974), and Hamilton's *Many Thousand Gone: African Americans from Slavery to Freedom* (1993). As she read, her fluency with Black English and her dramatic abilities made the listening an experience. Read alouds became more than silent times; they were times of engagement. She added physical embellishments and intonation emphasis to each text as she read. Although her physical movements were not identical to those of her students, they gave validity and support to student usage of body punctuation. Literature, in this classroom, was to be interpreted with sound and sight according to Cathy's model.

Literature was not the only instructional tool that supported the language patterns of the students in this classroom. Students were encouraged to watch the Civil War drama *Glory* with its historical dialect interpretations. Cathy used the local African American newspaper that, although printed in mainstream English, often had quotations from local persons which had elements of BEV. As a result, students were frequently exposed to dialect; they explicitly talked about its use, and they directly examined when it was appropriate or inappropriate according to the setting and audience.

Making Things Work—Curricular Set Up

Cathy was a firm believer in having an active, student-centered classroom. Projects that were student-designed and -driven were constantly being created in this classroom. Given a specific theme, students were permitted to explore their interests with certain basic parameters set forth at the onset. As an example, there were no reading groups in the traditional sense in Cathy's room. Students were permitted to self select literature that interested them. Her requirements were that students select a book from each major genre over the course of the academic year, and that students present each book orally, in writing and visually at an assigned time. This freedom to choose gave students the opportunity to be themselves. It was in this self-expression that instances of body punctuation were most evident.

Drama played an important part of the curricular design. Students were encouraged to become historical figures on one occasion; on another, the class became the figures involved in the Dred Scott court case. Cathy believed reenactment was a tool for helping students step into another person's perspective, increasing the understanding of a particular historical era or issue. Cathy rarely assigned things she would not do herself. It was not uncommon for her to appear in costume, speaking and acting like an African American female from the 1800s, always using primary source documents and pieces of literature as her information source. Students got to know African American history through Cathy's interpretation of Ida B. Wells and Susie Turner. The teaching and learning situation in this classroom was rarely stagnant; it involved putting talk and motion together.

CONCLUSION

Body punctuation, the art of physically punctuating speech, is a part of the African American urban dialect. Because this dialect was honored and deemed appropriate in certain settings, body punctuation became a part of the telling and retelling of tales and stories in this exciting classroom. Much of what happened in this classroom is not atypical of any other classroom. But it is not just the what that made the difference, it is the how.

Cathy serves as a model, not just for African American teachers, but for all teachers. Certainly Cathy's cultural connection and tendency toward Black artful teaching encouraged African American students to respond to texts in ways that included body punctuation. Although that connection is beneficial, it certainly is not the only way to promote this kind of response.

Cathy provided the students in her classroom with opportunities to use their voices in all their variations and movements. It is incumbent on all educators to follow this example if they desire this kind of classroom response. Teachers must recognize body punctuation as a valid response type, acknowledge the occurrences, and ask for expansion when appropriate. Teachers must make themselves aware of the body punctuation types and the meanings in order to facilitate non-African-American peer acceptance, understanding, and conversation. Cathy used and encouraged students to use literature for multiple purposes. They supported and expanded their knowledge base through reading and research, using fiction and nonfiction tradebooks. Finally, everyone in this classroom talked about books. They discussed, reported on, reacted, and moved to stories they read and heard. Any response, including that of body punctuation, was viewed as a valid contribution to the classroom discourse.

It has been said that language is culture expressing itself in sound. If that notion is expanded to include the concept of body language, there may be many forms of physical response, tied to a culture, that occur in the classroom. Stances, usages of hands, facial expressions could all be a part of a student's response to what they see and hear in texts. It is incumbent on the classroom teacher to observe and encourage this response from all members of the classroom community.

Invitation 7.4

Place yourself in a setting in which there is a significant population of a single culture other than African American. Begin to make note of their responses to texts. Do they respond differently when they hear or read texts from cultures similar to their own? Are there common physical responses among the students you encounter?

Overhearing some students complain about a Frederick Douglass literature extension, Michael felt the need to respond. Acting as a wise young African American fifth grader, he explained it best by placing his hand on his hip and stating, "It's our heritage. We got to know this to help each other!"

FINAL NOTE

Cathy Nelson's commitment to literacy and authentic response is evidenced not only in her relationship to the students she had at Fifth Avenue Alternative School for International Studies, but also in her willingness to participate in this project. She frequently gave feedback, expanded and explained situations, and opened her classroom to the inquisitive. She embraced anyone interested in actively becoming a part of her learning community.

REFERENCES

Abrams, R. D. (1973). The advantages of Black English. In J. S. DeStefano (Ed.). *Language, society and education: A profile of Black English* (pp. 97–107). Worthington, OH: Charles A. Jones.

Applebee, A. N. (1985). Studies in the spectator role: An approach to response to literature. In C. R. Cooper (Ed.), *Researching the response to literature and the teaching of literature: Points of departure* (pp. 87–102). Norwood, NJ: Ablex.

Egan-Robertson, A. (1993). Puerto Rican students respond to children's books with Puerto Rican themes. In K. Holland, R. Hugerford, & S. Ernst (Eds.), *Journeying: Children responding to literature* (pp. 204–218). Portsmouth, NH: Heinemann.

Malik, A. A. (1990). A psycholinguistic analysis of the reading behavior of EFL-proficient readers using culturally familiar and culturally nonfamiliar expository texts. *American Educational Research Journal, 27*(1), 205–223.

Piestrup, A. M. (1973). *Black dialect interference and accommodation of reading instruction in first grade*. Berkeley, CA: Monographs of the Language Behavior Research Laboratory.

Purves, A. C., & Beach, R. (1972). *Literature and the reader: Research in response to literature, reading, interests and the teaching of literature*. Urbana, IL: National Council of Teachers of English.

Sims, R. (1983). Strong Black girls: A ten year old responds to fiction about Afro-Americans. *Journal of Research and Development in Education, 16*(3), 21–28.

Smith, E. A. (1993). The anchor dat keeps um from driftin': The responses of African American fourth and fifth graders to African American literature. *Dissertation Abstracts International, 54*(08), 292A.

Spears-Bunton, L. (1990). Welcome to my house: African American students respond to Virginia Hamilton's *House of Dies Drear. Journal of Negro Education, 59*, 566–576.

Steffensen, J. S., Joag-Dev, C., & Anderson, R. C. (1979). A cross-cultural perspective on reading comprehension. *Reading Research Quarterly, 15*(1), 10–29.

CHILDREN'S TEXTS

Aardema, V. (1975). *Why mosquitoes buzz in people's ears.* New York: Dial.

Adler, D. (1992). *A picture book of Harriet Tubman.* New York: Holiday.

Anderson, J. (1988). *A Williamsburg household.* New York: Clarion.

Fitzhugh, L. (1974). *Nobody's family is going to change.* New York: HarperCollins Children's Books.

Greenfield, E. (1974). *Sister.* New York: Crowell.

Greenfield, E. (1978). *Honey, I love: And other poems.* New York: Thomas Y. Crowell.

Greenfield, E. (1988). *Nathaniel talking.* New York: Black Butterfly Books.

Hamilton, V. (1968). *The house of Dies Drear.* New York: Macmillan.

Hamilton, V. (1993). *Many thousand gone: African Americans from slavery to freedom.* New York: Knopf.

Johnson, J. W. (1995). *Lift ev'ry voice and sing.* New York: Scholastic.

Mathis, S. B. (1975). *The hundred penny box.* New York: Viking.

McKissack, P. (1986). *Flossie and the fox.* New York: Dial.

McKissack, P. (1988). *Mirandy and Brother Wind.* New York: Knopf.

McKissack, P. (1992). *A million fish . . . more or less.* New York: Knopf.

McKissack, P., & McKissack, F. (1987). *Frederick Douglass: The black lion.* New York: Scholastic.

Paulsen, G. (1993). *Nightjohn.* New York: Delacorte Press.

Ringgold, F. (1992). *Aunt Harriet's underground railroad in the sky.* New York: Crown.

Steptoe, J. (1987). *Mufaro's beautiful daughters.* New York: Lothrop.

Yarbrough, C. (1989). *The shimmershine queens.* New York: Putnam.

8

I Can't be Like Pippi 'Cause I'm Afraid to Live Alone: Third Graders' Response to Novels

Karen Hirsch
Eau Claire Area Schools

EDITOR'S OVERVIEW

Eagerness and energy describe these third graders participating in a literature response group using novels. They can't wait to get started; the class goes too fast for them. Recalling her first experiences with such groups, Karen Hirsch, a resource teacher providing for the needs of advanced learners, explains how she got started. She identifies key sources and provides provocative questions and helpful ideas offered by the authors of these texts.

The heart of this chapter, however, is the representation of the students' discussions. They portray what situations and characters third-grade readers react to, and what they think and feel about them. The discussions also exemplify a range of teacher questions, catalytic and probing questions, to promote student interaction without dominating it or being directive. Among the principles of response discussion that are illustrated are Socratic questioning, guide-on-the-side, metacognition, predicting, and relevance.

Consider the following:

1. Review the students' discussions to establish the nature and direction of their responses.

2. Reflect on the types of teacher's questions and comments to establish why they might have been used and to understand their effects.

3. At the chapter's close, suggestions are made for transferring these procedures and processes to a classroom situation. Explore with your peers these ideas and others to project reasonable plans of classroom operation.

GETTING STARTED

The children arrive early and peer through the window strip in the door of the small room where I meet my groups. They wave their *Ali Baba Bernstein* (Hurwitz, 1988) books and smile, waiting for me to beckon them in. As they burst into the room, they pause at the grumbling of the group already there.

"We couldn't wait," they say, apologetically, and they sit down the instant the others leave. They find their places in the book, flip open their journals, and begin a half hour of nonstop talking.

I started this group of six children a few weeks ago.

"We've got some incredible readers," Amy, a third grade teacher, said in December. "They love to read and could handle some more complex material than we're doing in the classroom."

I like those requests. As a resource teacher, it's my job to help provide for the needs of advanced learners.

"How about a literature response group using novels?" I asked. I'd recently been reading about reader-response and noticing its connection to two of my special interests: critical thinking and Socratic questioning. Since September, I had also been discussing literature response groups with the reading specialists. I was definitely eager to try.

"I'll be happy to do some literature discussion groups," I said. "But maybe later you'd like to put your whole class into small groups for awhile and let each group read a novel at their reading level."

"I know how to do that with the whole class reading a single novel," Amy said. "I had my kids read *The Flunking of Joshua T. Bates* in the fall." She opened the cupboard in her room and showed me the row of 24 copies. "But I think it'd be tricky with the kids in different books."

"I'll help you organize it," I said. "And I'll share some good ideas I found about how to keep a reading journal, too." I looked at her shelves of books. "Do you think that we could find enough duplicate novel sets in the Bridges Kits so I could work with four groups, one from each class?"

"Sure," Amy said. "Your four groups will be the strong readers from each of the third grades, so let's choose some books appropriate for them." We scoured the Bridges Kits, a collection of paperback novels in each of the four third grade rooms. The kit comes with our reading series and provides for a variety of difficulty levels.

We decided that I'd work with 4 groups once a week. We agreed on one group of six from each of the four third grades. We found enough copies of *Pippi Longstocking* by Lindgren (1988), *Ali Baba Bernstein* by Hurwitz (1988), *Homer Price* by McClosky (1943), and *Ellen Tebbits* by Cleary (1954), and I put together a Reading Journal for each of the 24 students. Now six of these children gather around the square formed by two tables pushed together.

I had recently read "Guiding Young Students' Response to Literature," by Kelly (1990), and was eager to try out what I had learned. Kelly discussed the child's need to respond to literature from a personal perspective, both orally and written. I was struck by the simple, yet potent, questions she suggested for encouraging students to respond to their reading:

What did you notice in the story?
How did the story make you feel?
What does the story remind you of in your own life? (p. 466)

I had also studied "Reading the Skeleton, the Heart, and the Brain of a Book: Students' Perspectives on Literature Study Circles," by Samway (1991). This article reinforced something I had noticed—that kids can get into meaningful discussions if their teacher will try an open-ended approach. I was impressed that the authors asked their students for advice. The children said that they wanted to have plenty of time to read the whole book, be able to talk about the book, and sometimes be given a choice about which book they'll read (p. 202).

I found some other good ideas from authors Keegan and Shrake (1991) in their article, "Literature Study Groups: An Alternative to Ability Grouping." I liked their thoughts of what helps make a discussion work:

- attending to the topic
- participating actively
- asking questions for clarification
- piggy-backing off others' comments
- learning to disagree constructively
- giving all members opportunities for input
- supporting opinions with evidence. (p. 544)

In fact, these seemed so sensible that I adapted them as discussion techniques for my students.

In one other article, "Teaching Children to Appreciate Literature," author Pugh (1988) compared two approaches to teaching literature: structural (traditional literary analysis) and reader-response. I found I agreed with her that it is more important for a reader to first respond on a personal level to a story rather than learn only about plot, setting, and point of view (p. 1).

I found *Invitations*, by Routman (1991) and *Journeying*, edited by Holland, Ernst, and Hungerford (1993) helpful in learning how to approach stories from the reader response perspective. *Readers' Workshop: Read Reading*, by Hagerty (1992), gave me some excellent "sentence starters" (pp. 24, 25), to which I added some of my own for use in my student reading journals. All of these readings appealed because they resonated in me as sensible and the most fun way to look at books!

THE READING JOURNAL

The Reading Journal that I put together for this project is simple. It's a stapled packet of 8 1/2 × 11 inch papers, some photocopied, others lined writing paper. It consists of:

Cover (my model simply reads "This Journal Belongs to_____.")
Discussion Technique
Discussion List
Prediction sheets (4 or 5 pages, depending on length of book)
Regular lined paper (4 or 5 sheets)

All of the Reading Journal pages presented in the appendix of this article are either adapted from things I've read or are self-invented. Because the idea of a reading journal is so open-ended, I alter what I include in it depending on the group with which I'm working. You can put together any kind of journal that you believe will work with your students. The important thing is that the children use the journal to write their reactions to what they're reading. If any of these pages seem appropriate for your situation, you are welcome to use them or tailor them in any way you wish.

They're dog-eared by now, these *Ali Baba Bernstein* journals, from life in the hands and desks of third graders. But not a single child shows up at novel-reading class without his or hers. I look at the group, reminding myself of the strategies and techniques I want to use with these students.

Remember Wait Time, I tell myself. Give the kids time to reflect, to process their thoughts, to respond to the story. Questions that probe, that promote deeper thinking. That's what helps kids think critically, I remind myself. It's also what makes me the guide-on-the-side, rather than the sage-on-the-stage. I know I won't be able to do *all* this stuff, but I plunge in, ready to try some of it.

WAIT TIME

"Who'd like to talk about your prediction for chapter seven?" I ask. I wait. Ever since I read about Wait Time, giving a class more than the one or two seconds teachers typically wait for an answer, I've been trying to incorporate it in my lessons. Rowe's (1987) research demonstrated that when teachers increase wait time to at least five seconds, some exciting things happen in the classroom:

- more, and longer, student responses
- whole sentence replies
- more student questions
- students making inferences

- students trying speculative thinking
- a greater variety of teacher questions
- greater teacher expectation of students (pp. 38–43)

It's hard at first to just wait. It's so tempting to rephrase the question, ask another question, or even give the answer myself! But waiting is a magic bullet. It stimulates active participation. If I wait, it works. Every hand is up.

SOCRATIC QUESTIONING

Ali Baba Bernstein is the story of a little boy who, in an effort to make his life more exciting, changed his name from David Bernstein to Ali Baba Bernstein. The name change seems to change his personality, as well, and his life becomes almost more exciting than he can handle. One of the girls in my novel group is eager to talk about Ali Baba.

"I predicted that Ali Baba would let his imagination run wild," says Anne. She has her journal open to the prediction record page. "And I think I was partly right." I try out my Socratic questioning.

I have to admit, I don't remember a thing about Socrates from my Philosophy 101 course. Lately though, I've gotten very interested in critical thinking through my participation on the Eau Claire Area School District's Critical Thinking Leadership Team.

In the fall of 1993, our committee presented our staff development plan for critical thinking to our school board, and it was approved. Since then, I have been involved in modeling concept attainment lessons based on Bruner's research of learning and thinking. I've also presented inservice on Socratic questioning, been trained in and taught Junior Great Books, and work with Creative Problem Solving and Talents Unlimited. I have discovered that all of these approaches include some common ingredients—the importance of validating and respecting students and their ideas, recognizing that all can become better thinkers, and questioning is one of the keys to involving students in their learning.

I have learned that probing questions can help students look within themselves for answers, instead of to us, their teachers, or other authorities, for the "right" answer. This kind of independent thinking provides the opportunity to examine assumptions, provide evidence, be aware of viewpoints and perspectives, and think with clarity—all especially appropriate skills in reader response activities. I keep a copy of Paul's (1990) "A Taxonomy of Socratic Questions" (pp. 276–277; Fig. 8.1) in my planbook at all times. I look at it now, under the Questions of Clarification section, as I think about Anne's comment about Ali Baba's imagination.

"Could you explain that further?" I ask. There are six categories on the Taxonomy, and I try to choose questions from several areas.

"Well, he invited all the David Bernsteins from the whole phone book to his birthday party," she answers. "I sure would never do that." I wait

*A Taxonomy of Socratic Questions

It is helpful to recognize, in light of the universal features in the logic of human thought, that there are identifiable categories of questions for the adept Socratic questioner to dip into: questions of clarification, questions that probe assumptions, questions that probe reasons and evidence, questions about viewpoints or perspectives, questions that probe implications and consequences, and questions about the question. Here are some examples of generic questions in each of these categories.

QUESTIONS OF CLARIFICATION

- What do you mean by _____?
- What is your main point?
- How does _____ relate to _____?
- Could you put that another way?
- Is your basic point ____ or ____?
- Could you give me an example?
- Would this be an example: _____?
- Could you explain that further?
- Would you say more about that?
- Why do you say that?
- What do you think is the main issue here?
- Let me see if I understand you; do you mean _____ or _____?
- How does this relate to our discussion (problem, issue)?
- What do you think John meant by his remark? What did you take John to mean?
- Jane, would you summarize in your own words what Richard has said?... Richard, is that what you meant?

QUESTIONS THAT PROBE ASSUMPTIONS

- What are you assuming?
- What is Karen assuming?
- What could we assume instead?
- You seem to be assuming _____. Do I understand you correctly?
- All of your reasoning depends on the idea that _____. Why have you based your reasoning on _____ rather than _____?
- You seem to be assuming _____. How would you justify taking this for granted?
- Is it always the case? Why do you think the assumption holds here?
- Why would someone make this assumption?

QUESTIONS THAT PROBE REASONS AND EVIDENCE

- What would be an example?
- How do you know?
- Why do you think that is true?
- Do you have any evidence for that?
- Are these reasons adequate?
- Why did you say that?
- What led you to that belief?
- How does that apply to this case?
- What difference does that make?
- What would change your mind?
- What are your reasons for saying that?
- What other information do we need?
- Could you explain your reasons to us?

- But is that good evidence to believe that?
- Is there a reason to doubt that evidence?
- Who is in a position to know if that is so?
- What would you say to someone who said _____?
- Can someone else give evidence to support that response?
- By what reasoning did you come to that conclusion?
- How could we find out whether that is true?

QUESTIONS ABOUT VIEWPOINTS OR PERSPECTIVES
- You seem to be approaching this issue from _____ perspective. Why have you chosen this rather than that perspective?
- How would other groups/types of people respond? Why? What would influence them?
- How could you answer the objection that _____ would make?
- What might someone who believed _____ think?
- Can/did anyone see this another way?
- What would someone who disagrees say?
- What is an alternative?
- How are Ken's and Roxanne's ideas alike? Different?

QUESTIONS THAT PROBE IMPLICATIONS AND CONSEQUENCES
- What are you implying by that?
- When you say _____, are you implying _____?
- But if that happened, what else would happen as a result? Why?
- What effect would that have?
- Would that necessarily happen or only probably happen?
- What is an alternative?
- If this and this are the case, then what else must also be true?
- If we say that *this* is unethical, how about *that*?

QUESTIONS ABOUT THE QUESTION
- How can we find out?
- What does this question assume?
- Would___ put the question differently?
- Is this the same issue as___?
- How would ___ put the issue?
- Why is this question important?
- How could someone settle this question?
- Can we break this question down at all?
- Is the question clear? Do we understand it?
- Is this easy or hard to answer? Why?
- Does this question ask us to evaluate something?
- Do we all agree that this is the question?
- To answer this question, what questions would we have to answer first?
- I'm not sure I understand how you are interpreting the main question at issue.

FIG. 8.1. Wait time. From Paul, R.: *Critical Thinking: What Every Person Needs to Survive in a Rapidly Changing World*. Santa Rosa, CA: Foundation for Critical Thinking, 1990.

again, Wait Time II. I remember when I heard about Wait Time II. I hadn't mastered Wait Time, when suddenly Wait Time II comes on the scene!

Invitation 8.1

Choose a simple book with a theme worth exploring, such as:

Best Friends, *by Miriam Cohen*
Ira Sleeps Over, *by Bernard Waber*
William's Doll, *by Charlotte Zolotow*
Ming Lo Loves The Mountain, *by Arnold Lobel*
The Art Lesson, *by Tomi DePaola*
Oh Were They Ever Happy, *by Peter Spier*
Frederick, *by Leo Lionni*

Read a book of this kind to your students and then ask them a question about the story to get the discussion started. Ask them a question to which you don't know the answer—something you're wondering about, something you and your students can chew on together. As your students begin to answer, go to your Taxonomy of Socratic Questions chart for your follow-up questions.

It's the quiet time after a student response that might trigger another student to jump in. Someone at a critical thinking workshop told me, "This strategy encourages the discussion to bounce between students, rather than always teacher to student and back to teacher."

So just when I want to say, "Good answer, Anne," or "That's right, David," I'm supposed to be quiet! I press my lips firmly together, conscious of how quiet I'm being.

GUIDE-ON-THE-SIDE

It's a most amazing thing when it works. You'll see when you try it. The ball flies from student to student, and you stand and watch, wondering for a moment if you should just leave and go to the lounge. But no! It is your careful planning, your guide-on-the-side status, your awareness of questions that promote reflective thinking, your ability to be an active listener that made it happen in the first place.

There are some interesting and sometimes confusing things that happen when we spend less time as the dispenser of knowledge, the sage-on-the-stage, and more time as the facilitator of our students' learning, the guide-on-the-side. It's more exciting for them, and sometimes they may be too loud in their enthusiasm. Sometimes you may wonder if you'll ever cover all the stories you wanted to. In one way, it's harder to be a guide-on-the-side than a sage-on-the-stage. It takes thorough preparation and all that self-discipline to WAIT. But seeing the children take some ownership of their own learning is satisfying and worth the effort. And if you don't cover as much as you thought you would, you can be comforted that the stories you did discuss, the children will remember for a long time. The thinking skills you see them demonstrate are instilled for a lifetime. Enjoy it and think, "This is what education is all about!"

I listen now as it works in this group.

"I think I'd be in big trouble," says Sarah. "Ali reminds me of the girl in the last book we read, Pippi Longstocking."

I speak up. "How do you come to that idea?" I ask her to clarify.

"Oh, you know, Ali does whatever he wants and so does Pippi, and they both get away with it," says Sarah. I wait.

"But Ali and Pippi are very different, I think," says Sam. "Ali's more a normal kid and has parents and everything. Pippi was like supergirl, and she lived alone."

"But they both did naughty things," says Anne. I wait, but nobody says anything.

"Does anyone see it another way?" I ask, choosing from the Questions About Viewpoints or Perspectives section of Paul's Taxonomy. Then I wait.

"I think both Sarah and Sam are right," said Kammy, the diplomat of the group. "Pippi didn't have anyone to take care of her, so she could get away with stuff. Ali's parents were there, but they were just too easy on him."

I hear the students responding to what they've read, telling how the story makes sense in their own lives, and I'm pleased. I can see them taking ownership of their learning. I listen to them discuss, and even argue a little, and I see independent thinking developing. I see them learning to read and to listen a little more carefully and critically. I hear them trying out comparing and contrasting, and changing their ideas when more evidence is given. I see kids relating to books and becoming better thinkers.

MAKING IT RELEVANT TO THEIR LIVES

"What would happen to you if you changed your name?" I ask. This is a Question That Probes Implications and Consequences. All hands wave.

"My dad would be mad," says Sam.

"They'd say, 'Forget it!'" says Kendall.

"My brother'd make fun of me," says Kammy. The discussion goes on awhile as we explore the various antics of Ali throughout the book, as well as antics of their own. I check the clock.

"Who'd like to read their sentence about the chapter?" I ask and the group turns to the back of their journals where I had stapled lined paper.

They choose a sentence-beginning from the discussion list I had provided in their journal. Each week, the children head their lined sheet with the chapter number and write one or two sentences responding personally with their thoughts about the chapter.

"I understand . . ." reads David, "how Ali feels. There are three Davids in my room, too."

"I think . . ." says Kammy, "that it would be cool if you could invite everybody that had the same name as yours for your party. It would be very fun if you ask me."

"I can't believe . . ." says Sarah, "that we are done with the book!!!"

"How do you feel about that?" I ask to a chorus of agreements with Sarah.

"I want to do a new book," Sarah says. I wait.

"Me too," says Sam. It's so much fun to have time to *talk* about the story."

"Why is that important to you?" I ask.

"Well, because," says Sam, "what happens in the story is what happens in our real lives. Like when Ali got that frog . . ." Sam tells about an adventure he'd had finding a garter snake.

"Is it always the case that a story is like real life?" I ask. This is a Question That Probes Assumptions. Anne's hand is up. I wait. Kammy's hand and Sarah's raise. I call on Anne.

"No—Pippi's not like real life." I look at my Paul sheet under Questions That Probe Reason and Evidence. I've covered five of the six categories and am satisfied.

"What happens in the story that makes you say that?" I ask.

"Remember where she lifts the police officer?" asks Anne. "And jumps from the roof to the tree? That's not real life." I try Wait Time II, and it is quiet awhile.

They need this time to think. If my questions or their comments and responses are worthwhile and valuable, we need time to think about them. In their book, *The Case for Constructivist Classrooms*, Brooks and Brooks (1993) talked about the importance of valuing the student's point of view, of seeing our students as thinkers, and of being interactive with our students rather than the giver of knowledge.

When we allow our students to be seekers rather than sponges soaking up what we give them, we are validating them, encouraging critical thinking, and in the words of Brooks and Brooks, "arranging classroom dynamics so that students are empowered to construct their own understanding" (p. 102).

METACOGNITION

"Yeah," says Sam, finally. "But Pippi does stuff we *want* to do, but can't."
I use a standard metacognition question, a ploy to get kids to talk about

how they're thinking. *Metacognition* means thinking about our thinking, and it's a good trick to have in our teacher bag.

"Can you tell us about your thinking when you say that?" I ask.

"Well, Pippi lives alone, right?" he asks. I nod.

"And so she gets to do whatever she wants because there's nobody to stop her." I wait, and Sam scrunches up his face.

"And even though I think it'd be fun to live alone, I know I really don't even like to stay alone when my parents go grocery shopping." He stops.

"Go on," I say.

"Sooo . . . I want to do what Pippi does and get away with it, like fooling the police or sassing adults." Sam grins. "But I can't because I don't want to live alone." He laughs at his own predicament and we join him.

"So, you're saying you want to do those things, but not if you have to go through the bother of living alone—is that right?" I ask. Sam beams.

"Yup," he says.

Invitation 8.2

Initiate a book discussion with a small group. As the discussion is in progress, be especially aware that you're going to concentrate on getting your students to think about and talk about their thinking processes.

Can you tell me about your thinking process in coming to that conclusion?

How did you happen to connect those two ideas?

Why do you think the event in the story triggered that thought in your mind?

Why do you think that you especially noticed that about the story?

What went through your mind when you had that feeling about the story?

I look around at the smiling faces as I bring out some new book sets: *Homer Price* by Robert McCloskey (1943), *Ellen Tebbits* by Beverly Cleary (1954), *Wizard of Oz* by Frank Baum and W. W. Denslow (1943), *Hello Mrs. Piggle Wiggle* by Betty MacDonald (1966). They are excited. They discuss which ones they've read, and which one they want to read as a group. Of course I don't always have enough books available to allow the children to make a choice, but I can clearly see that they like it when it happens. I've noticed that they seem to feel more subsequent ownership, too.

They are quite taken by the charming illustrations in *Homer Price* and decide that it's the one they'll read. *Homer Price* is the story of the people in the little town of Centerburg, where everybody seems to know everybody else's business. One enterprising young boy, Homer, always ends up in the middle of every Centerburg adventure and misadventure. I am delighted that the group chooses *Homer*, because I reacted to that book exactly the same way 43 years before.

The children hold the books in their hands now and we look at the first chapter title and its illustrations. I remember vividly reading about the broken doughnut machine, and I gaze at that drawing now, wishing I'd had a group to talk with about it when I'd first read it.

PREDICTING

"What kind of book do you think *Homer Price* might be?" I ask.

"Funny!" says Kammy.

"Maybe he makes a lot of mistakes," says Sam. "Like me." He laughs.

"And gets into trouble," says Anne. "There's a robber in the first chapter, I think, from this picture." She points to a drawing of four masked men.

"But it has something to do with a skunk," says Sarah. "The title is 'The Case of the Sensational Scent' and there's a picture of a skunk on page 20."

"It looks old-fashioned," says David. "The clothes."

"It is," I say. "I read this book when I was your age." They look at me, agog, and I feel like Methusala. I laugh. "Everybody write your prediction on the prediction-lines," I say. They start to write. "And write your 'why' too." They have their ideas down soon, have shared them, and are ready to read.

Predicting is another of those strategies, like Socratic questioning, that makes room for reflective thinking. It takes time, so it means you may not get as far as you hoped for in the lesson. But it's worth moving the content aside a little because something like predicting helps to do the really big work of education—encouraging, valuing, and respecting students' thinking, helping them grow in their ability to generate ideas, provide evidence, recognize assumptions, and relate in a perso.ial way to the literature they're reading.

READING ORALLY

We read aloud. At first when the students wanted to do this, and wanted me to take a turn, too, I felt nervous. Reading around the circle was a poor pedagogical technique, I'd always heard. But I met in a small room, in a back corner of the school, and nobody could see us. So, heck, I relented.

And I soon saw that reading aloud could be another exercise altogether than reading around the circle. It was a chance to react, an opportunity to respond, an occasion to interact. I found out, early on, that the students tend to interrupt their classmates in their eagerness to share an insight, change their prediction, make an observation, or ask a question. Their reaction is so immediate, almost urgent!

So what I do is let them know that we'll stop after every half-page, or page, to hear and discuss their contributions. It works—somewhat.

Kammy doesn't get halfway through the first page before Sam is waving his hand wildly. Oh well, I think. Nothing's perfect, and I let Kammy finish before I recognize him.

"I like it that Homer builds things," he says. "Look at the picture on page 11. That's what I wish my room looked like." He sighs.

"Why doesn't it?" I ask.

"I love to build, too, but whenever my room starts getting to look like Homer's, zap, my mom cleans it!" I laugh before I notice that Sam's face looks really sad.

"I'm sorry, Sam," I say. I realize that I hadn't taken Sam seriously. Taking a child's thoughts, ideas, and experiences seriously validates them and their thinking. Respecting their thinking is what reader response and developing critical thinking is all about. I had slipped. "Would you like to read next?" I say.

Page after page we read in spurts and stops.

"I wonder if the skunk is de-skunked," says Sarah.

"Why might you assume that it is?" I ask.

"I'm changing my prediction. I think Aroma has something to do with the robbery," says David.

"What led you to that thought?" I ask. The kids talk, pointing out the characters' actions, exclaiming over the turn of plot, and matching action to the drawings. Their ideas flow. They seem to think and speak with a delightful lack of self-consciousness, with such confident ownership of the story and its meaning to them. Homer Price is their pal.

And they like reading aloud about him, working hard at using expression that sounds good to them. They seem to pause and savor the story, to react more vigorously, and to discuss with more spontaneity if they can roll the author's words around in their mouths.

PUTTING IT TOGETHER

A couple of weeks later, we read and discussed what was destined to become the kids' favorite chapter, "The Doughnuts." Or maybe I'm projecting—it was my favorite, back in the Dark Ages. I decided to start that day with the three questions suggested in Kelly's (1990) article, "Guiding Young Students' Response to Literature" (see p. 139, this chapter). We had read part of the chapter the week before and they had finished it on their own. I looked around the group.

"So," I said. "What did you notice in this chapter?" Kendall's hand was waving.

"I saw that Homer gets in trouble," he said, his grin a mile wide. "Again!"

"But he gets himself out of trouble, too," said Kammy.

"I noticed that a lady lost her bracelet and offered a reward to whoever found it," said Sarah. I waited, but it was quiet.

"Anything else?" I asked.

"Well," said Sam, slowly, staring at the picture on pages 60 and 61, the one where hundreds of doughnuts are stacked up. "It seems like when anything happens in Centerville, it happens so *big*! " Everybody laughed. Several nodded. I didn't have to ask for clarification. We all got it.

"How does this chapter make you feel?" I asked.

"Fun. I like it," said David.

"Like I wish I lived in Centerburg," said Kendall.

"Oh, Kendall, you *would* like it," said Anne. "You're just like Henry." Kendall kept smiling.

"Why do you think Anne says that?" I asked Kendall. I had a feeling I wasn't going to have to ask the last Kelly question, "What does this chapter remind you of in your own life?" Kendall blushed.

"Oh . . ." he said. "I brought a couple of frogs to school last week and they got out in our room."

"*Five* frogs," said Anne. "And they got out all over the school!" We all laughed again.

"How is that like what happened to Homer?" I asked. Everybody sat thinking, and I waited for what seemed like forever.

"Well, our teacher said to bring in nature things," said Kammy.

"Is that like Homer in any way?" I asked. David's eyes lit up.

"Well, Uncle Ulysses did ask Homer to make doughnuts," he said. "It just got crazy with doughnuts." I waited.

"Like my frogs," said Kendall. "It wasn't Homer's fault the machine broke, and it wasn't my fault the frog box cracked open."

"Were you like Homer in solving the problem?" I asked Kendall.

"Wellll," Kendall began slowly, but Sarah interrupted.

"He sure didn't," she said. "Three are still loose."

"Mrs. Nicholson heard a croaking in the library," said David.

"So," I said. "Kendall is both the same as and different from Homer. Is that right?" They all nodded.

"Does this chapter remind anyone else of something in your own life?" I asked. I sat, waiting to hear about third-grade adventures. Rained-out camp sleepovers, maybe, or getting lost at the mall. Finally Sam spoke.

"Like I said before, I don't think stuff that happens to us is like in the book," he said.

"Can you explain your thinking on that?" I asked.

"Oh," he said, and paused. "Like when I caught a big fish at Half Moon Lake and won a prize. It was exciting, but it was only one fish. For Homer, everything is so . . .so . . ." He searched for the right word. "So much bigger than real."

"You'd say that this author exaggerates?" I asked.

"Yes!" said Sam. "Exaggerates!" I looked around the group.

"Does anyone disagree?" I asked.

"I do," said Anne.

"Me too," said Sarah. I waited.

"I think Kendall's frog story is like Homer," Sarah went on. "And when all my aunts and uncles and cousins and grandparents came for a family reunion to my house last summer, it was wild, like the doughnuts."

"What made you remember that when you read this chapter?" I asked. Sarah grinned.

"Oh, my Aunt Greta was allergic to our cat, and we had to keep her in the basement . . ."

"Who?" asked Kendall, laughing. "Your aunt?"

"No, silly. The cat," said Sarah. "Aunt Greta kept sneezing, and then my cousins—the *boys*— . . ." (She made a face at Kendall.) "decided to try to dig to China, in our backyard, and . . ." Sarah went on and on and ended by saying that Centerburg was a perfect place for *her* family.

We ran out of time before we ran out of things to say. So we agreed to disagree on how their adventures compared or didn't compare to Homer's. Then we went overtime a little to ruminate about what the next chapter, "Mystery Yarn," could possibly be about, and finally said our goodbyes.

IN YOUR CLASSROOM

Will what I've been describing work in Amy's classroom? Will it work in yours? I think so. You know your students' reading abilities. Maybe the hardest part will be finding sets of 5 or 6 novels at the appropriate levels.

Try your reading specialist or your central office bookroom. Maybe you have something like our Bridges Kit. Another way I've seen teachers gather extra books is through the free books teachers get from sending in class book orders. Or tell your principal what you want to try. Maybe there's money available.

Of course it's ideal to let the children choose from, say, two books, but if that isn't possible, okay—you plan which group will have which book. Put together a Reading Journal and tell the kids what they're going to be doing. Elicit from them what goes into a good discussion and then hand out the journals and let them see the Discussion Techniques you have. Maybe the children will have thought of one or two you missed.

Or, maybe you can wait to put the journal together until after you've gotten ideas from them on how to have a good discussion. Now that I think about it, I wish I had done that. It would've made the journal more theirs, would've generated more thinking, more ownership. It would take more time, of course.

You might use one or two reading classes a week for novel reading-and-responding. You might use a story in your basal with the whole class a few times to model predicting, reading, discussing, and using the open-ended sentences.

During a novel reading-and-responding class, you'd want to get around to every group for 15 minutes to help with the discussion, but maybe students could take turns being the leader when you're busy with another group. Or maybe, because you'll have the kids for a whole hour, they could use some of the time to respond in additional ways to what they've read—acting the chapter out or drawing a group mural for the whole book, adding action and characters at the end of each chapter. Or maybe they could expand on something from the chapter—like the doughnut machine in *Homer Price*. What other funny machine might there be, and what would happen if it went crazy the way the doughnut machine did? Or maybe they could draw an accompanying picture to go with their journal responses.

As far as oral reading goes, you'll probably have the children read the chapter by themselves. And that's fine. That's how I've done it in the past. The important thing is that the students get to respond to the story, get to relate it to their lives, get to identify with the characters, setting, action, and problems in the book. But do take the time to sit with a group and try the oral reading, even if it's only bits and pieces after they've read the chapter independently.

If it doesn't work to have all the groups reading novels on the same day, you might want to have the groups staggered. One day you meet with the *Ellen Tebbits* group, another day with the *Homer Price* kids, and so forth. And do train the children to help by being leaders. Certainly even a third grader could ask the group to look at the chapter, title, and pictures to predict what will happen. Use your own judgment. As you work with these ideas of reader-response and critical thinking, you'll find ways to mold them to your way of teaching and to your students' needs. Try it out. Have fun. Make mistakes.

TIME TO SAY GOODBYE

Today's discussion on *Homer Price* goes on and our time runs out. A tapping at the window disrupts the lively conversation in our little room. A group of fifth graders wait, students in a science group, and it's time to switch gears. The fifth graders hold orange owl pellet dissection kits and charts of mice bones in their hands. I wave them in and the third graders sigh.

"Our class goes too fast," Kammy says. I smile. What nice words to a teacher's ears.

"Finish chapter one," I say, "and then write what actually happened on your prediction page." They stand up. "And do a couple of sentences, too."

"Bye!" they call. "See you next Wednesday." They leave the room. One boy walks along with his book still open, reading as he stumbles along. I slip *Homer Price* onto the shelf, pull out the partly dissected owl pellets, and turn to the fifth graders.

APPENDIX A

Discussion Techniques

1. Stay on the topic.
2. Be active in the discussion.
3. If you don't understand what someone has said, ask them politely to explain further.
4. Listen carefully and piggyback off what others have said.
5. Don't be afraid to disagree, but do so politely.
6. Give everyone a chance to share their ideas.
7. Be ready to support your opinions with evidence from the story.

APPENDIX B

1. I began to think of ...
2. I can't believe ...
3. I noticed ...
4. If I were ...
5. My favorite character is ...
6. I felt _____ when ...
7. This made me think of ...
8. The problem here is ...
9. I disliked
10. Something I'm not sure about ...
11. It seemed like real life when ...
12. Now I understand ...
13. I'm confused ...
14. I wonder what would happen if ...
15. I think the author's reason for writing this book was ...
16. I love the way...
17. I wonder why...
18. I think ...
19. I'm not sure ...
20. I like the way the author ...
21. I wish that ...
22. Something I learned was ...
23. If I were in this story ...
24. The setting of this story...
25. The way I think a certain character looks is ...
26. If I were writing this story I ...
27. The funniest part is ...
28. I hope that ...
29. This reminds me of something in my own life ...
30. The character most like me is ...

You may also make up your own question or idea to write about!

APPENDIX C

PREDICTION CHART

Name of Story_____

	What I Predict Will Happen	*Why?*	*What Actually Happened*
Chapt. 1	_____	_____	_____

Chapt. 2 _____   _____   _____

Chapt. 3 _____   _____   _____

Chapt. 4 _____   _____   _____

This chart is designed with adequate space for each category for each chapter.

REFERENCES

Brooks, J. G., & Brooks, M. G. (1993). *The case for constructivist classrooms*. Alexandria, VA: Association for Supervision and Curriculum Development.

Hagerty, P. (1992). *Readers' workshop: Real reading*. Toronto, ON: Scholastic.

Holland, K. E., Ernst, S. B., & Hungerford, R. A. (1993). *Journeying: children responding to literature*. Portsmouth, NH: Heinemann.

Keegan, S., & Shrake, K. (1991). Literature study groups: An alternative to ability grouping. *The Reading Teacher*, *44*(8), 542–547.

Kelly, P. R. (1990). Guiding young students' response to literature. *The Reading Teacher*, 43(6), 464–470.

Paul, R. (1990). *Critical thinking: What every person needs to survive in a rapidly changing world*. Pohnert Park, CA: Sonoma State University, Center for Critical Thinking and Moral Critique.

Pugh, S. L. (1988). Teaching children to appreciate literature. *ERIC DIGEST*. Bloomington, IN: ERIC Clearinghouse.

Routman, R. (1991). *Invitations: Changing as teachers and learners, K–12*. Portsmouth, NH: Heinemann.

Rowe, M. B. (1987) Wait time: Slowing down may be a way of speeding up! *Journal of Teacher Education*, *11*(1), 38–43.

Samway, K. D. (1991). Reading the skeleton, the heart, and the brain of a book: Students' perspectives on literature study circles. *The Reading Teacher*, *45*(3), 196–205.

CHILDREN'S TEXTS

Baum, F., & Denslow, W.W. (1943). *The wonderful wizard of oz*. Indianapolis, IN: Bobbs-Merrill.

Cleary, B. (1954). *Ellen Tebbits*. New York: Morrow.

Hurwitz, J. (1988). *Ali Baba Bernstein*. New York: Scholastic.

Lundgren, A. (1988). *Pippi Longstocking*. New York: Scholastic.

MacDonald, B. B. (1966). *Hello, Mrs. Piggle Wiggle*. New York: Scholastic.

McCloskey, R. (1943). *Homer Price*. New York: The Viking Price.

9

Transactions in Action: Life in the Second Grade

Richard J. Meyer
University of Nebraska—Lincoln

EDITOR'S OVERVIEW

What is life in the second grade? Life in this second grade may not resemble what you have experienced. Its typical day is filled with options within a flexible structure. The children create options based on their interests; they make decisions. After the morning meeting—a reading followed by making meaning from it—Richard Meyer circulates among them to establish and consult about their work plans for the Drop Everything and Read and Write period.

Literacy activities fill the morning and often spill over into the afternoon. The children read, write, talk: whole language in action. They research; they experiment and think. Two examples—a pair of students and the whole class—portray the imagination and the dynamics of the class, the potential and power of literacy activity.

The extended focus on two students' transactions with books dominate the second half of this chapter. Lonna, enchanted with maps, decides to make a three-dimensional one of the setting of Just Grandpa and Me *by Mayer (1985). She shows us how she makes sense of this book. Keri authors books, transacting with her life through writing. The intriguing question is, "Where did these stories come from?" Two samples invite you to consider this question and evaluate her growth as a reader-writer with a reader-response classroom as a backdrop.*

Consider the following:

1. *Reflect on the diversity of reading transactions, aesthetic and efferent, encouraged in this class. Review the teacher's methodology.*
2. *Extrapolate the types of reading instruction infused into a typical day of this class. Evaluate the teaching methodology.*
3. *Review the reading–writing transactions of Lonna and Keri. What are they learning?*

In this chapter, I present transactional theory in practice in my second-grade classroom. I sometimes refer to the classroom as a *reading/writ-*

ing classroom (Butler & Turbill, 1984) and I also tend to use the phrases *reader-response theory* and *transactional theory* interchangeably because readers' responses are transactional in nature.

The chapter consists of two parts. The first part is a description of a typical day, showing our fairly predictable and dependable routine. The description of a typical day is provided to give an understanding of the context in which children relate with texts.

The second part of the chapter is a close look at two children's activities within our reading/writing time. The first child, Lonna, responds to a Mercer Mayer book in a way that extends beyond words into architecture, mapping, and sculpture. Keri, the second child, is an avid writer. I compare her first book with her thirteenth as a demonstration of a writer's growth in a reader-response theory-based classroom.

A TYPICAL DAY

The children arrive at the room between 8:30 and 9:00 in the morning and read the options of what to do until we formally begin our day. These options, clipped to an easel just inside the door and agreed on as part of our closing the previous school day, may include: *write in your journal, start the day's cooking activity* (cookbooks being one of our favorite reading genres, involving both reading and math), *finish something from the day before, check the progress of a science experiment, find a book to read, sing a song,* and more. The children always have the option of visiting with their friends in the class. They also may invite children from other classrooms into the room if the other children's teachers give permission.

The children are encouraged to add to the paper on the easel (and then engage in) other activities during the 8:30–9:00 time slot. For example, they might decide to play a game, something not listed as an option. They write the name of the game they will play and the names of the children involved on the easel. At the end of the day, we will plan for the next day and the children will refer to the present day's easel for information and ideas. Although it uses a full sheet of 12 × 18 inch construction paper each day, I like having the paper on the easel so that a child can take it home at the end of the day. It helps parents know what we do in school.

There is an agenda on a sheet of paper held to the chalkboard with a magnet. The agenda is also co-constructed with the children at the end of the previous school day. A typical agenda looks like Fig. 9.1.

A child, usually the person of the day, will take the agenda home so that parents can learn more about what we do each day.

Our daily formal activity begins at 9:00 when I read to the class at our morning meeting. Usually, I read a book, but there are days when I read parts of the local newspapers or magazines. The classroom subscribes to 11 different magazines. If we received a new *Sports Illustrated for Kids* or *World*, we choose an article to hear. We discuss the reading and the meaning

Agenda	
9:00	**Morning Meeting** Thomas' Snowsuit by Robert Munsch
9:15	**Drop Everything and Read & Write** Baking: Apple Crisp Who needs a conference?
10:00	**Lonna's project presentation**
10:15	**Lydia's book is ready to be read**
11:15	**Clean Up**
11:30	**Lunch and Recess**
12:30	**Afternoon Meeting**
12:45	**Chapter 3 of** Charlie. . .
1:00	**Math**
1:45	**Music (or other special class)**
2:15	**Science (or social studies) theme**
2:50	**Announcements** **Plan for tomorrow:** Easel, agenda

FIG. 9.1. Typical class agenda.

we make from it. Children might tell of ideas they got while listening, related stories, related things they saw on TV, or events from their own lives. I demonstrate the ways I respond to text.

One morning, I read *Thomas' Snowsuit* (Munsch, 1985) to the class. A conversation begins:

Teacher: This book is about a family, in my mind. It reminds me of funny things we can remember about our own families. I remember the time I squeezed under my sister's bed before she came upstairs to go to sleep. I hid there quietly until she turned off her nightlight. The whole bedroom was very quiet.

I waited, looking at the children.

Kesiah: What did you do?
Teacher (whispering):   I thought for a minute . . . I took a few deep breaths . . . and then I said . . . BOOOO!

All of the children jump, startled, and laugh. Notice that this morning we have forgone any discussion of the facts of the story and I have led the children to the aesthetic response that arose in me as a result of reading this book. This is a demonstration of one way to respond to books.

Eddy: Did you get into trouble?
Teacher: Well, she called to my mom and, well, my mom was sort of mad, but then we all laughed about it. I think my sister still checks under her bed before she goes to sleep even though we live 500 miles apart.

Our class shares stories that come from the stories we read. Good books remind us of our lived experiences.

Elizabeth: When I was two, I stepped on my birthday cake because my feet reached from the high chair to the table. We have that on video.
Tom: I once got my foot stuck in a chair and had to drag the chair to my mom for her to help me get out!

Invitation 9.1

Choose a book that provides potential for discussion within a family theme, a book that might stimulate children's connections between the lives of the character(s) and their own lives. Read this book to a class or small group (elementary level or college classmates) and conduct a discussion.

Other stories emerge from our memories, and we share them. Then I suggest that some of us might write these into stories to present at some other time. I will write mine in the evenings and share various drafts over the next few days. The children help me work through difficult spots, point out what doesn't make sense, and offer suggestions, just as I do with them when we conference. My writing becomes the focus of some minilessons and also serves as an ongoing demonstration of written language activity.

The reading of the book and the ensuing discussion rarely takes more than 10 minutes. When the discussion takes longer, we adjust our schedule accordingly. Because we have most of the morning to engage in literacy activity, we have become flexible with our use of time. Some days, I initiate discussion; other days, one of the children will begin. There are days when a discussion does not begin, but often the book will come up at some other personally or socially relevant time during the day or throughout the year.

Following the story, the children take care of all the business for the day. They fill out the lunch count sheet, take attendance, and run newstime (show and tell). There is one Person of the Day who decides how much of these responsibilities to delegate to colleagues and how much to do himself or herself. We are willing to allow newstime to extend into our Drop Everything and Read/Write time because newstime is a language activity.

We have a relatively uninterrupted morning through lunch at 11:30. The entire block of time is called Drop Everything and Read and Write (DEAR/W). We previously called it DEAR (Drop Everything and Read), but the children taught me that they needed time to read and write in a way that allowed the two to overflow into each other. Before we adjourn to start on the day's literacy activity, I use a sheet similar to Atwell's (1987) status-of-the-class sheet to get information about what each child will be doing. This is a class list with five rectangles next to each child's name. Each rectangle is sufficient for writing notes about the child's work plan for the morning time slot, with one rectangle for each day of the week.

During the status-of-the-class time, children tell what they will pursue for the morning. I know, by glancing at my clipboard, who is doing what they agreed to and who has strayed to other things. Some of those other things require me to edit what I wrote on the status sheet; other choices children make might lead me to remind them of what they agreed to be doing.

The afternoon is focused on math, special classes, science or social studies, and planning for the following day. It is not uncommon for social studies and science activities to be on the morning agenda because they involve reading and writing. The days become quite integrated as the year progresses.

Throughout the day, whether we are singing, doing math, involved in science experiments, or planning for the next day, the children are relating with texts in a variety of ways within the context of the classroom and the school. Quite often, during our science or social studies timeslots, the children read fiction as well as nonfiction, including historical fiction, science fiction, biographies, and autobiographies; and reference books such as encyclopedias, atlases, almanacs, medical dictionaries, and other textbooks. Sometimes the children ask for help in understanding technical texts; sometimes highly sophisticated texts are referred to solely for their photos, charts, and illustrations.

Invitation 9.2

Build a theme-related text set for children in any grade of your choice. You may want to follow up with family life theme, or select another life in school, for example.

I have included a rough map of our room (Fig. 9.2) to provide an understanding of the context in which we work. It is rough in that I cannot include the fluid movement of chairs, bean bag chairs, desks, books, activities, and (most important) children. We share in the care of our physical space and make decisions about bulletin board displays, placement of furniture, use of time (as our agenda evolves over the course of the year), and the nature of activity. Most of the map is self-explanatory; the cooking area has a large portable oven on the table near the refrigerator. The refrigerator is the type used by many college students in dormitories; it holds a dozen eggs, a few quarts of milk, some margarine, and a few other perishables used in cooking. The classroom library contains about 800 books and is constantly growing through book order bonus points used to purchase books. Although one corner houses writers' supplies, writing occurs wherever children wish to work.

By the second month of school, the children have learned much about themselves as learners. They plan and use their time carefully. We continually explore options for Drop Everything and Read/Write time. Cooking, for example, is usually a two-day activity. On the first day, the children in the cooking area are responsible for finding a recipe, copying

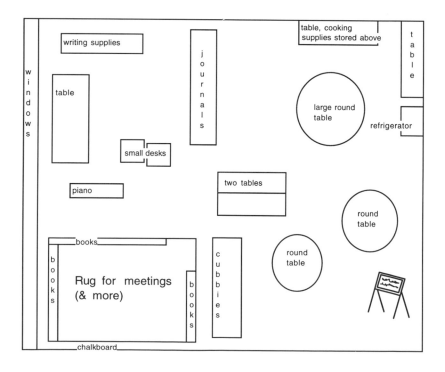

FIG. 9.2. Our classroom.

it onto a sheet of chart paper so the recipe will be more accessible, and providing me with a shopping list of food items not in our cupboards. I shop in the evening for what they will need the following day. On the second day, those same children cook, inventory supplies, and clean up. The inventory involves listing items that are used up or in short supply. This is reading and writing the way it might occur in a real kitchen; indeed, the children are in a real kitchen, very much involved with the reading and writing that occurs there. I view the measurement, use of fractions, occasional doubling of a recipe, and sharing of the cooked products as math lessons built into literacy learning.

Other children use this time to read, conduct research (which may overflow into science or social studies time), write in response journals, write in personal journals, or write in small pads (3 × 5 inch spiral bound) I provide for word study. Because conducting research, response journals, personal journals, and word study are integral parts of reading/writing classrooms, I describe each briefly.

Children and Research

I encourage and support children pursuing interests by helping them develop a clear question, finding resources that address their question, and developing a project based on that question. One day Chris and Cory said they wanted to do some research. They were unsure of the topic and wanted to peruse the encyclopedia to find what they might investigate. They took the volume with "F" in it and were about up to the "Fu-" words when I approached them.

Teacher: I see you are interested in F- words.
Chris: Yes, Cory and I . . . you tell . . .
Cory: Well, we were looking . . .

I knew they were looking for a word that they wouldn't find in this encyclopedia, but I was having too much fun to let them know I knew what they were looking for. Then Chris looked down at the book.

Chris: We are interested in studying the future.
Cory (also looking at the book):   Yes . . . ummm, the future. We want
           to know about . . .
Chris: houses!

The illustration on the page showed some futuristic-looking dwellings. I suggested they look under dwellings, too. A few minutes later, Chris approached me.

Chris: Mr. Meyer, is this word *geedeesic* or . . .
Teacher: It says "geo" in the beginning, like geography.

Chris:　　Oh, geodesic. I don't get it. What is a geodesic dome.

Luck had struck. I had just purchased a geodesic dome kit that could make a structure large enough for five children to sit in. Over the next few weeks, Chris, Cory, and other interested children built a dome, covered it with material, and wrote a report about Alexander G. Bell and Buckminster Fuller, the men who, respectively, had invented and later popularized the dome. The children were active researchers exploring their interests in small groups or as a whole class over the course of the year.

On another day during newstime, one of the children brought in the volcano that she found in a box of cereal. Kathy discussed how the picture on the box showed a dinosaur with a huge volcano erupting in the background. She had teased her mom until mom relented and purchased the cereal, a type the family preferred not to eat. The volcano was about 1-inch tall and had a depression in which the child was to place vinegar, baking soda, and a drop of red food coloring. Kathy and the rest of the children were quite disappointed.

I initiated a discussion of advertising and how it can be misleading. Later in the day, during social studies time, the children helped generate a list of commercials that they thought exaggerated their claims. We wound up discussing the "unsinkable Cheerio."

Was it unsinkable?
How could one tell because of all the milk?

Social studies was overflowing into science as we formulated questions about Cheerios. The next morning, I arrived with Cheerios, milk, plastic spoons, and cardboard bowls. Each child was given a bowl, a small amount of Cheerios and some milk. We waited.

Chad:　　　This is silly. No one takes this long to eat a bowl of Cheerios.
Teacher:　What do you mean?
Chad:　　　We've been sitting here for five minutes and in real life we'd be done with the bowl of cereal by now.
Teacher:　I hadn't thought of that.

We waited, thinking, staring at our bowls of soggy Cheerios.

Chris:　　　We need to time someone to see how long they take to eat. Then we can see if any sink by that amount of time.
Elizabeth:　I can't even tell if any HAVE sunk. They are in the way.

More issues emerge as we wonder about the submersing Cheerios. If we can't see the Cheerios, perhaps we should use clear plastic cups (which happen to be in the cooking center). Even then, we can't see so we decide to use water instead of milk. We watch and time five children eating bowls of cereal to find the average length of time that it takes to eat.

Chad: But when we eat cereal, our spoons tap the cereal that is left in the bowl. That means they're getting pounded and we should pound them, too.

We decide to put one Cheerio in a clear plastic cup of water for 2 minutes and 12 seconds (our average eating time). The Cheerio will be tapped with our plastic spoons 12 times. Although this is not what happens when we eat, it allows us to study carefully. The children have invented the scientific method. When the time has expired, the Cheerio had not. There is clapping as children lauded the honesty of the commercial. They are unsinkable. Even as we talk, in the time that follows the formal experimental time, the Cheerios stay afloat.

Teacher: This is an important finding and it has a lot to do with honesty in advertising. What shall we do about it?
Chris: What could we do?
Teacher: Share the information by letting others know about it . . .
Kathy: Like by making a poster that says they are honest?
Teacher: Yes, that's one way.
Cory: Are there other things to do?
Teacher: Do you want to write to the company and tell them what you found out?
Sean: That would be a good idea. They'd probably send us free Cheerios as a thank you.
Teacher: I don't know about that . . . but
Sean: I'm gonna try.
Others: Me too . . . yeah, let's tell them . . .
Teacher: I think the address is on the box.

The children write and send their letters informing General Mills of the success of their experiments on Cheerios. A few weeks later, when the excitement has died down, a package arrives at school from General Mills.

Teacher: Look at this . . .
Chris: From General Mills!
Sean: I knew it . . . free food.
Elizabeth: It's too small for that.

Inside the box is a note on bright yellow paper, the same color as a Cheerios box, from General Mills. They thank the children for the information and enclose a free (12 page) cookbook that offers ways to use Cheerios in cooking. The cookbooks provide excitement for the bakers in the class as they make a list of what we'll need to make a new dish with Cheerios.

The children read, wrote, experimented, and thought like scientists and consumer advocates. Their transactions with their world also affirmed their power and the power of literacy activity.

Response Journals

Response journals are stenographer's note pads that are about 4 × 6 inches with horizontal lines to write on, and a red line down the middle of the page. I don't know why the pages are laid out that way, but the kids love having a variety of types of pads and paper on which to write. Some children ignore the red line; others write in columns; others ignore all of the lines.

Their response journals were originally where the children responded to reading but extended beyond this during the year. I demonstrate possible ways of responding during brief whole-class minilessons that may be part of our DEAR/W time. On large chart paper, I have shown the children how to use sentence frames to respond to a reading. I do not provide a daily frame; rather, I encourage the children to invent their own frames if that helps them begin a written response to a book. Sentence frames that I have used include: *That book makes me feel . . .; Thomas' snowsuit reminds me of some things that happened in my own family when . . .; I'd never do what* a character in the story *did . . . . Children have invented frames such as: I wish . . . ; I hope. . . ; I wonder; This book makes me think. . . .* Some children prefer to respond by writing me a letter about something that happened in a book, writing a poem, writing a song, or free writing. Some of these ideas come from the children; others are suggested by me. I have encouraged writers who are stuck to sketch their understanding of a story (see *Creating Classrooms for Authors*, Harste & Short, with Burke, 1988).

One day, Mindy asked the class, "Don't you think we can respond to TV shows in our response journals? I saw Cosby last night and it made me think that they have a lot of money because he's a doctor and she's a lawyer." Mindy's suggestion was accepted by the group and opened up many connections as movies, videos, and other TV shows began to appear in response journals. Children made connections between various media (books, TV, movies) in their response journals. Short (1992) refers to this as *intertextuality*, a writer drawing connections between the various texts in his or her life.

Personal Journals

Personal journals are standard-sized, spiral-bound notebooks. I have regular- and college-ruled from which the children may choose. I share with the children some of the many types of journal entries that are possible. I show them how the journal may lead to a story or a poem. I demonstrate writing personal things in my own journal and reading it aloud to the class. Children may read journal entries to the entire class by signing up to do so during our DEAR/W time. They may opt to have one of their colleagues in the class respond to their journal, or ask me to respond. I demonstrate types of response, usually focusing on three possibilities: reflecting a little of the content in the journal, some of the affect that seems attached to it, and things that connect to what the writer wrote, such as books, stories, or my own personal experiences.

When Mindy wrote about her family's intention to move to Florida, I wrote, "I know we will all miss you if you move. I can see that the plan makes you sad, and I hope that you will find good friends once you get there. Will you write to me? I'll write to you."

Word Study

Word study may be part of a minilesson initiated by the children or me. It has focused on alphabetical order, prefixes, suffixes, big words, and more. These topics may sound dry, but they are rooted in the children's reading, writing, and curiosities about language. They study language with me; they study their growth and share their discoveries about language. I share my discoveries with them.

Second graders love composing lists. Word study takes advantage of this love and teaches children some of the conventions of our language. A small group of children found the pages in the encyclopedia that show the flags from countries around the world. They were excited and wanted to copy the names of the countries. My minilesson was virtually a microlesson, in that I saw them writing, suggested they use their word study pads, and pointed out that the countries' flags are shown in alphabetical order.

Kim: So what if they are in that order?
Teacher: Well, you can find a country's flag quickly if you can know its first letter. Find Iraq . . .

The children scanned the pages, some humming the alphabet to themselves, and quickly found Iraq. Other lists, over the course of the year, included hockey teams, dolls names, types of flowers, dinosaurs, songs we could sing, butterflies, last names of children in the class, foods, ice cream flavors, and more.

I also would invite children for minilessons using their word study pads. These lesson included: -*tion* as a suffix, *re-* as a prefix, homographs, homophones, and more. I invited children who I thought would gain from the lesson and also told the entire class what we were doing so that anyone could attend. These lessons remained brief, and the evidence of their usefulness was the children's written language. I feel obligated to offer lessons about the conventions of our language, but no longer feel insulted if kids don't learn what I teach. Studying their writing and their word pads helps me uncover what they are learning within our very scholarly second grade context.

A Close Look at Two Children

Transactions with books in the reading/writing classroom are personal expressions. I try to support children in expressing their understandings of books and being open to a variety of sign (meaning-making) systems. In this section, I describe Lonna who, after experiencing a book, makes sense of it through a physical construction. Then I present Keri's growth as a writer over time.

Lonna.   Lonna is from Iraq. She and her parents learned English together when they arrived in the United States when Lonna was a preschooler. She has attended our school since she was 3 because we have a half-day, 4-day-a-week program for 3-year-olds. The 4-year-old program is half-days, 5 days a week. Lonna attended our full-day kindergarten, was in a whole language first-grade classroom with Bryan Thompson, a wonderful teacher (and supportive colleague), and entered second grade considering herself a reader and a writer.

Lonna is a project person. When we studied maps early in the year, she suggested that we map the cupboards and took that task on as part of her reading and writing time one morning. She mapped our classroom and her bedroom at home, carefully drawing her bed, dresser, closet door, and other parts of her room. I felt that we had exhausted map skills for second grade, having mapped our classroom, playground, and invented imaginary lands.

One day in October, Lonna was reading *Just Grandpa and Me* (Mayer, 1985) for what seemed like the millionth time. Lonna had things to do with that text, still, and it was my obligation to honor that unfinished business. It is also my obligation to cultivate both Lonna's and my understanding of what that business is.

"You're reading that again," I say, smiling.

"Yes, I love these little critters."

We look through the book together. Lonna starts to read it aloud. "You know," she begins, "there's a spider and a grasshopper on every page."

"Yes."

"Well, in Mercer Mayer's other books there is usually one animal that goes through the whole book."

"Really?"

"Yes," she says. "In one book, there's a mouse on almost every page."

I like to allow silence for myself and children when we are together with a text. It gives us time to think, imagine, and rehearse our words. I let them know that I like to be next to them when we are thinking. Lonna is silent now. I am deciding whether to leave or sit a bit longer.

"Mr. Meyer, this book is like a map," she says after a few seconds.

"I don't get it," I say.

"Well, they start out at the house, then go to different places . . . like," she thumbs through the pages that she knows quite well as she continues, "to the ticket place, and then to the train, and then to the umm ... store, and then to the movies, and then out to eat, and then back to the train, and then home."

"What do you mean when you say, 'it's like a map'?"

"Uhhh, look." Lonna turns to the next page in the stenographer's pad that she uses for literature response. She lists the places the two critters travel, referring to the book for the sequence: home, ticket place, train, store, movies, eating, home.

"You see," she says.

"When you list these things, " I suggest, "you can get an idea of what their town is like. You know it has all the things you've listed here."

"Yeah . . . Can I make it?"

"Make the town?" I ask.

"No, umm, make the map."

"Sure . . ." I reply.

"I'll need a lot of things to do this, like clay and straws and maybe a box and . . ."

" . . . but I don't get it," I interrupt. "Isn't a map just a piece of paper with things drawn on it?"

"I want it to be three dimensional," Lonna says.

We had talked about maps being flat representations of a three-dimensional world. Lonna wanted to make a map that was a three-dimensional representation of the book. She had invented some type of relief map or model.

"Would you know how to go about this? Would you know what you need?"

"Yes," Lonna smiled. "I need a piece of cardboard to work on and some clay and paint and markers . . . and some other stuff, but I'm not sure what yet."

"See what we have," I suggest, "and make me a list of things I need to get."

Lonna's beginning of this project was important news to share. At the afternoon meeting, I asked her to explain what she was starting. She showed the book to us, then explained her idea. Lonna's idea would eventually lead us back to maps. We would build a city with an electric train running around it and deal with complex issues of city planning: trash, electricity, food, transportation, and more.

Lonna starts the next day as soon as she arrives, having placed her project on the easel as a morning possibility. She studies the book and the panel of cardboard from a large box that I brought to school for her. She decides that the brown cardboard color is acceptable and draws a road in pencil. She gets her stenographer's notebook and looks at that, too. She folds *Just Grandpa and Me* so that it remains open to the page that shows where the critter in the book lives. Other children watch, suggest ideas, and refer to the book to study Lonna's progress.

At this point in the year, Lonna is comfortable with the room and knows that the supplies in the writing area and in the various cupboards are available for use by the children. She gets some clay and then hears the morning song that calls us over for our morning meeting. Today we sing from a chart, a book is read, a person of the day is chosen by yesterday's person of the day, the lunch count is completed, we share at newstime, and children tell what they will be doing during our reading/writing morning.

By 9:25 Lonna is back to work on her three-dimensional map. She molds the clay to look like the tree in which the critters live. Satisfied with that, she uses markers to color a black road to the train station. The train station will be a milk carton saved from lunch. Lonna goes to the kitchen area and takes toothpicks from the cupboard. These are laid out and glued for a railroad track that parallels the pencil road that she has partially colored with marker. Lonna refers back to the text often. She flips to the front of the book, seems to reread large pieces of the book or even the whole thing, then returns to her map. This is a research project for Lonna; it involves constant reference to a text, cartography, construction, and more!

She makes the train out of a paper towel tube and the department store is a 1-gallon milk jug. Each new structure is placed on the cardboard, glued down, and has the road up to it colored black. It takes Lonna another two full days of work, including some time during our renewed study of maps, to finish her piece. The movie theater is a shoe box painted with a sign placed on the roof to resemble a marquee. The restaurant is also made of clay because, "I like to work with clay."

The map is circular and when we look at it, we know that the restaurant is quite close to the critter's home. But, as Lonna tells the story, she directs us to see it differently. The train might go around three or four times before it reaches (stops at) the store. There is a complex relationship between what appears before our eyes and the way the story unfolds. Everything, including the train, is glued down because Lonna wants to hang her map on the wall.

Lonna's experience with text is quite personal and reflective of what she is learning and what is important to her. She is intrigued with maps and, when given the time to do so, she will find mapness in many places. Her map is an intertextual (Harste & Short, with Burke, 1988) experience. She relates the oral, written, and drawn texts of our social studies unit to the text of the story she read. That transaction gives birth to a personal response—her map of the book. She gathers twigs and rocks at recess and also makes an aluminum foil lake.

Lonna also makes meaning through a variety of mediums. She uses architecture, mapping, and sculpture in her relationship with books. As the year progresses, she will explore various other mediums as she makes and shares meaning. Most important, to me as her teacher, is understanding that the projects that she invents to go along with her reading are not just art. They are Lonna making sense of books. She studies sequence, story, plot, theme, characters, setting, and metaphor in order to create her pieces.

I do a lot of kidwatching (Goodman, 1985) to make sense of what I am seeing. I watch her refer back to the book, ask friends, and study her own work as she internalizes each book and expresses that internalization through various mediums. I found my role to be one of guest in Lonna's work. I took the view of a visitor to an artist's gallery. With the artist present, I tentatively and politely ask questions of her work to see how she makes sense and meaning of texts in a very personal way. I am constantly surprised and invigorated by her learning and my own.

Keri. One very important part of working at my school is having parent–teacher–child conferences in August before school begins. This gives me an opportunity to learn about the children because I have virtually nothing to say about them. I discuss some plans for beginning the year and ask them about what they like to read and write. Then I invite the parents and child to talk about themselves: their likes, interests, dislikes, attitudes, feelings and concerns, or worries. Keri, a new-to-our-school second grader, Sue (Keri's mom) and I talk for a bit. Sue and my wife were friends about 10 years ago when they were both in college. I know Fred, Sue's husband, is in a local band and also teaches junior high school science. Keri has a younger sister, Jesse. Sue, Keri, and I chat for a while and then Sue asks Keri to wait outside of the classroom for a few minutes.

When Keri has left the room, Sue begins, "Fred has cancer. We're fighting this every way we can . . ."

I had heard that Fred was sick but didn't know the details. He was seeing many specialists in the beginning of the school year, but by early October all hope of survival was gone. I visited him at home a few times during the early autumn. He died during our winter vacation and my family attended the funeral and visited Sue, Keri, and Jesse a few times during the year.

The children in the class knew about Fred from the beginning of the school year. Keri mentioned him once at newstime and infrequently thereafter. She preferred not to discuss it; perhaps she was denying the situation. She had the love and support of Sue and Sue's and Fred's families. That support seemed to help her maintain what she wanted: her friends, knowing that she was loved, and a feeling of safety and security. Perhaps as you read Keri's writing in this section, you will sense some of the magic and dreaming that helped her heal throughout a personally tragic year.

While Lonna works on her map, Keri, a prolific reader and writer, is busily authoring a book. In this section, I compare her first book with the 13th book that she wrote. First, read the two pieces (Figs. 9.3 and 9.4). Then, I discuss some of the features of Keri's transactions as a writer.

This is the story about

I LOVE SINGING

by Keri Serfis
Illustrated by Keri Serfis

Dedication

To: Mr. Meyer

Once upon a time there lived a little girl name Ann.

She was five years old. She loved to sing.

But she wasn't very happy because she lived with a

witch, that was very very mean.

FIG. 9.3. Keri's first story: *This is the Story About I Love Singing.*

Ann ran up to her room.

At night the witch went out on a walk.

Ann was in her room crying. A fairy appeared in the room.

She said, "What's the matter, dear?"

"I live with a witch," said Ann. "She said I could never sing again."

She made Ann sleep in a cave. Ann had lots of friends. The witch a name was Matilda. She had been on a spell. Someone had cast a spell on the witch so she was mean. The witch said that Ann could never sing again.

"Make a wish, dear."

"Thank you, I wish my aunt was nice. And I wish I can sing."

Her wishes came true.

5

The End

Fig. 9.3 continued.

6   Readers Comments

About The Author

Keri Serfis is a student at the Campus Learning Center.

She is almost eight years old.

This is her first book.

What a super story! I especially liked the part when the fairy came to visit are. your illustrations are beautiful (the fairy is my favorite). I'm very proud of your first book. Sue Serfis

I like thes
book!!!!

Keri I like this Book Rachel

This Book is very
good I hope you
do alot more
Books Sarah

I Liked this book
very much Jessicah.

Fig. 9.3 continued.

172

FIG. 9.4. Keri's thirteenth story: *The Summer Vacation.*

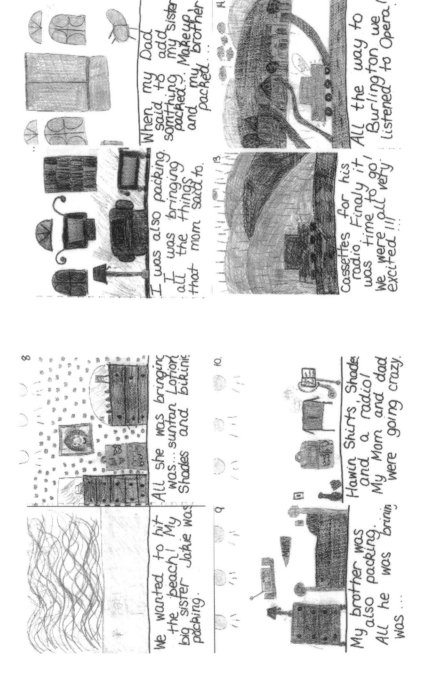

We wanted to hit the beach! My big sister Jake was packing.

8

All she was bringing was...suntan Lotion Shades and bikini.

10.

My brother was also packing. All he was bring was ...

9

Hawin Shirts Shades and a radio! My Mom and dad were going crazy.

I was also packing. I was bringing all the things that mom said to.

When my Dad said to something packed. my sister Makeup and my brother packed...

14

Cassettes for his radio. Finaly it was time to go! We were all very excited !!!

13

All the way to Burlington we listened to Opera!

Fig. 9.4 continued.

15.

16. I was the only kid that was hearing it because I was my brother & Sister going to be sick !!! had earphone.

17.

18. Our airplane ride was great! When we got to Mimi, I was thrilled. It was beautiful! I slept most of the way.

21.

When we got to the beach my sister was already hanging out with the 26 age boys!!!

Our hotel was gorgeous!!! We were unpacking to find our bathing suits when... mom screamed Ahh !!! There was a lisard in her suit case The brother said YIPPY! I'm going to scare girls with it

AHH! Help! A Lisard

23. The answer was NO! The next day we went to town and checked out the malls!

22. And my brother was also doing something he was nagging dad he wanted to surf.

Fig. 9.4 continued.

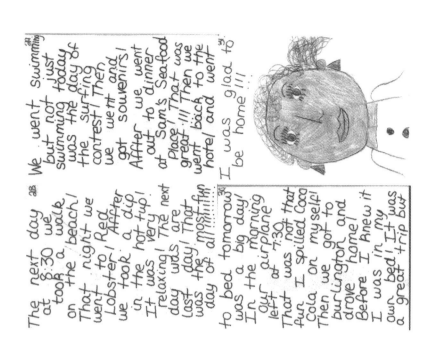

24 We went swimming but not just swimming today was the day of the surfing contest! Then we went and got souvenirs! After we went out to dinner at Sam's Seafood Place! That was great!!! Then we went back to the hotel and went

I was glad to be home!!!

23 The next day at 8:30 we took a walk on the beach! That night we went to Red Lobster! After we took a dip in the hot tub! It was very relaxing! The next day was last day! That was the most fun day of all!!!!!!!!

30 to bed tomorrow! was a big day! In the morning our airplane left at 7:30. That was not that fun. I spilled Coca Cola on myself! Then we got to burlington and drove home! Before I knew it I was in my own bed! It was a great trip but

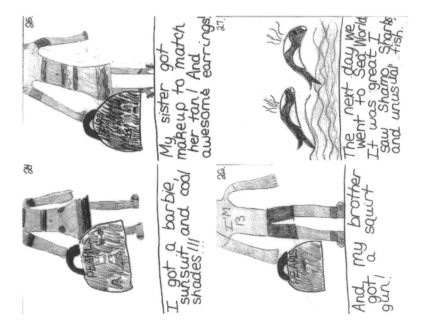

26 My sister got makeup to match her tan! And awesome earrings!

I got a barbie, sunsuit and cool shades!!!

And my brother got a squirt gun!

The next day we went to Sea World. It was great I saw Shamu. Sharks and unusual fish.

Fig. 9.4 continued.

About the Author

Heri Serfis is a
student at the
Campus Learning
Center this is
her 13th book.
She is eight...
She will be nine
September 20th 1989

THE

END!!!...

Reader's Coments

We completed with all the work I have had so big on her book been commplited abul implcment implment my problems

Keri I'm running away I will tell you Mom had been moved with me aer tree and I was all way with at was a wonderfull I was Grest will relay

This is your best book so far It's almost a noll I know you have you wanted it at aer the bepining plated of your dont have

**I Like the illustra-
tions. Nicole**

Keri,
This was your best
BOOK yet I like
THE illustrations

Fig. 9.4 continued.

Is the entire story of *The Summer Vacation* an allegory for Keri's family? I asked my graduate students, after they listened to me read Keri's book, what they could predict about her family life. "She's definitely the youngest," was the comment to which they all nodded agreement. They were quite surprised when they learned that Keri is the older of two children, the other a sister. "Where did that story come from?" is the next question. Keri says she, "just thought it up." And she did just think it up—out of the very difficult year she was living while a second grader.

Invitatation 9.3

Place yourself in Keri's classroom and pretend she has just finished reading her story. Take out your response journal and write an entry. (You may be yourself at age 7 or 8 or you may invent your own persona and family.)

Keri, Sue, and Jesse went to Florida during spring vacation in order to heal, rest, and escape the dreariness of the winter in our part of the country. Keri wrote the book on returning. It is a transaction with her life. It has to be. All of her writing is. Her writing is a vehicle for making sense of her life in a way that she can live with and share with others. It's very complex and relates to Rosenblatt's earlier work (1938/1976) in which she discusses literature (and I would add writing) as a way of exploring and understanding who we are.

Keri's books are powerful evidence of her growth as a reader and a writer. The elements of a story that she includes in each piece demonstrate her developing understanding of those elements. In *Grand Conversations,* Peterson and Eeds (1990) explained literary elements that teachers can look for and cultivate in children's reading and writing. These elements include layers of story meaning (possibility of multiple interpretations and symbolism), structure (including plot and tension), character, place (I call this setting), point of view, time, mood, and use of metaphor (pp. 2–46).

This writing is a barometer of the elements Keri understands in reading and its intersection with her lived experiences. As the year and her life progress, her reading, conversations, written response, and other ways of transacting with text help her internalize the complex and multiple elements in story writing. I used a chart, like represented in Fig. 9.5, to study her growth:.

The chart of story elements is useful for developing minilessons. For example, we did a minilesson on character development, and all members of the minilesson group invented a character because real authors do this.

Some authors create elaborate societies that the reader never sees. The creation of these allows the author to build a story that makes sense. But authors don't sprinkle literary elements into a story like spices in a stew. Child-authors don't have to reach a meta-textual level to use these elements. By meta-textual, I mean knowing and being able to identify specific elements as they are used. The chart of the elements is for me, as a teacher, to understand what the writers in my class are doing. It helps me decide what books to read and writing strategies to offer. In other words, we waste time and the children's time when we focus on literary elements as isolated areas of study.

I will only briefly compare the books using the chart. I encourage readers to use a chart like this to assess children's growth over time in their responses to texts that the children write as well as texts written by others. The chart is only a beginning, a point of origin, for further explorations in readers' and writer's responses and growth.

Layers of Story Meaning. In *This is the Story about I Love Singing*, I wonder if Keri is dealing with children as victims of the power adults have. It takes an adult to imprison Ann and it takes an adult to free her, each adult using magical powers that the child does not possess or necessarily understand. Perhaps, you are wondering, Keri did not

Book--> ELEMENT	THIS IS THE STORY ABOUT I LOVE SINGING	THE SUMMER VACATION
layers of story meaning		
structure: plot		
structure: tension		
character		
setting		
point of view		
time		
mood		
use of metaphor		
use of other sign systems (drawing, color etc.)		

FIG. 9.5. Chart used to chart Keri's growth as a writer.

intend to put this meaning into her story. As our class discusses stories, we talk about the personal nature of interpretation. We can find things in a story that an author did not intend to put there because once the story is published, the author loses a large degree of interpretive ownership. The author might say what she meant when she wrote a book, but our unique and personal interpretations are welcome.

In *The Summer Vacation*, do we once again see the theme of helplessness as the youngest child in a family must deal with the role of being the one least able to affect her world? Another possibility is that the youngest child offers wisdom and insights that only her unique perspective on the family can provide. As my students write, read, and share literature, I hope they understand this: Each of us may rely on our own experience, our understanding of the author's life, and other factors that we deem relevant as we write or interpret a story. Keri took that license quite seriously as she invented a sort of combined journal-and-story genre in *The Summer Vacation*.

Are there other layers of meaning in these two books? Absolutely. It's up to readers to discuss or write about them because they are very personal inventions. You might find issues of family tension, power and control, growing up and growing silly, and young children achieving noble goals.

Structure: Plot.   Keri shows her growth even in the way she uses titles. Her first book is kind of a summary title, beginning with, "This is the book about . . . " By the time she writes her 13th book, she knows more about what conventional titles look like. This is some evidence of her increased understanding, gained through our many elaborate discussions of texts, none of which focused specifically on how to choose a title. Her immersion in literacy in the reading/writing classroom provided ongoing demonstrations of titles from which she made decisions about her books' titles.

The plot unfolds quickly in *This is the Story about I Love Singing*. The action is over by the fourth page of the story. In *The Summer Vacation*, the plot unfolds gradually as we meet characters and learn them through descriptions of their actions. Notice that Keri uses dialogue in *This is the Story about I Love Singing*. She has intuited that dialogue carries a lot of information, and she uses it to be economical. When she writes, "I wish my aunt was nice and I wish I can sing," we can see, with delightful simplicity, the end of the story is in sight.

Keri shows growth in her sense of story (Applebee, 1978). Her first story begins with the very predictable, "Once upon a time." *The Summer Vacation* starts with the creation of a scene rich in mood, "The raining was falling down on the ground, Pit Plat. . . ." She shows what she is learning about stories in each one that she writes.

Structure: Tension.   Both of Keri's stories have tension, but the nature of the tension is different in each. In her first story, we are told of Ann, "She wasn't very happy. . . ." In the second story, the tension unfolds as Keri shows us a family involved in the various facets of vacationing. In the first case, we rely on the author to tell of a character's feelings; in the second case, we are shown the action and vicariously live the feelings. By her thirteenth story, Keri is comfortable with spending a few weeks on writing and illustrating. This is different from the eagerness she felt to complete her first book and to share it with friends and family. You might have noticed that her first book is typed. I type books for students on request when they have completed their editing. Perhaps Keri preferred having her first book typed because of the speed of my typing as opposed to the speed of her rewriting. It is the only book I typed for her during the year. She came to prefer the various pens and pencils available in the writing center.

Character. In *This is the Story about I Love Singing*, characters are described with words like *mean, wasn't very happy, had lots of friends*, and *nice*. These words are what Graves (1989) would call telling words because that is just what they do. They tell the reader about the character. In *The Summer Vacation*, Keri uses action to show us characters. We see a sister who packs bikinis and suntan lotion; we learn about Danielle's family members through their actions.

Notice that in *The Summer Vacation,* the narrator is a character in the story and, as such, she begins the story in the third person ("The rain was falling . . ."). Suddenly, on page 3, we meet the narrator when she introduces herself to us, and the voice of the piece shifts subtly. The absent narrator is present within the story. This is not something that I taught; it is evidence of Keri's accumulating understanding of the structures within a story and how they work together. She intuits from the reading, writing, and discussing that saturate our class.

The introduction of names for characters after the characters are introduced is also found in *This is the Story about I Love Singing* when Keri introduces the witch's name well after the witch appears in the story. In *This is the Story about I Love Singing*, the narrator retains her perspective throughout the piece. There are numerous other issues of character that I encourage readers find in these two stories.

Setting. Keri's use of a cave as a setting is remarkable in that the word *cave* evokes images in the minds of a reader. Keri relies on these images as economical ways of creating a setting with minimal words. The setting in *The Summer Vacation* is a mood that Keri establishes first, and then she slides her characters and the action of the piece into the setting. She also changes settings to affect mood.

Point of View. The narrator in *This is the Story about I Love Singing* remains outside in the telling of the story. As the narrator/character in *The Summer Vacation,* Danielle offers the reader the youngest child's point of view of the vacation. Asking, "Who's telling this story?" is sometimes confusing to children. After I read chapter 1 of *Charlotte's Web* (White, 1952) to the class, I asked who was telling the story. We had a discussion and the following day, one of the children brought in a Winnie the Pooh videotape in which the characters speak to the narrator. The children appreciate the humor, understanding that characters do not typically engage in discussions with the narrator. Intertextual discussions of this nature between books and videotapes help children understand the literary elements.

But it is not necessary for children to be able to discuss these metatextual issues. They listen to stories and intuit the literary elements long before they can explain what the elements are. Indeed, this is true for Keri. She put many facets of storytelling to work for her but could not explain those facets. My role is one of supporting her growing understanding by asking good questions:

Do you want to tell more about the character?
I wonder what the parents will say when the sister chooses to pack
    that way.
What does this witch look like?

There is no exactly correct time to ask such questions. I intuit when to ask and then carefully watch to see if my thoughts are helpful. This varies from child to child, making it quite difficult to know when and how to help. My questions for Keri are only my thoughts. She knows this and takes all of my suggestions as possibilities she may choose to follow or ignore.

Time.   Keri is comfortable with fictional time zones or modern time zones in her writing. I will not discuss time in great depth because it does not appear to be a salient issue in her writing at this point.

Mood.   Keri is clearly an expert on mood. She uses caves, dreary weather, bothersome siblings, and more to establish a mood. She changes moods from happiness at seeing a killer whale, to frustration at spilling a soft drink, to happy endings and resolution. I encourage readers to look at her stories to see how she develops moods. She uses powerful words and images in written text and illustration.

Use of Metaphor.   The use of metaphor and layers of meaning in a story often relate to each other. Metaphor may be something that occurs in one sentence or phrase like, "no brain brother." Metaphor may also be extended as we look for allegories between written text and Keri's life (as the one transacting first with the text). Is the cold, dark cave a metaphor for her childhood? Is it a metaphor for her understanding of the state of childhood? Or is it a metaphor for the way things generally begin on the road to happy endings? The possibility of *The Summer*

Vacation being metaphorical to the magic Keri might have wanted in her life was discussed earlier.

Other Sign Systems. By *other sign systems*, I mean other ways in which children demonstrate meaning-making. Keri is an outstanding illustrator of her books. She studies illustrators' styles as well as written text in a book. Her illustrations complement her stories. Lonna's use of other sign systems includes all the materials she used and the way she put them all together. Language, written and oral, is usually the thread that binds these systems and supports other readers and viewers in making meaning, too.

Keri's writing, like the writing of so many other children in the class, is a place where I learn. Each time I read the stories, I learn more!

Closing Remarks

While Keri works on her book and Lonna on her map, other children work on different projects that support the relationships they are building with each other and with written text. One group is cooking, one group is researching dwellings as we deepen our study of communities. Two girls who noticed a marker staining a paper towel have started a small book on chromatography (separating out the individual colors that make up the colors in a marker). There is reading and writing everywhere in the classroom. It is a living context in which relationships with texts are supported, growing, changing, and cultivated. It's hard to keep up with the children, but there is no other way I can see myself teaching second (or any other) grade.

APPENDIX A

Building Theme-Related Text Sets for Children

We can invite preservice teachers, inservice teachers, or children to read books that are centered around a theme. One of my favorite themes is life in our families. There is an incredible variety to such life, some lives being delightful, others hard, others sad. Our lived experiences can form a powerful text for our classroom. Getting children to write about their lives may begin with telling about our lives after listening to the lives of others portrayed in books.

Read any of the books that follow to a group of children. The lives of the readers and listeners are connected to the lives of the characters in the book as we recognize the similarities and differences across lives. Using the stories in the books as a starting point, we can tell stories of our own families as they resonate with the story in the book.

I often read one of the books in the list that follows to my undergraduates. We talk, laugh, cry, and reminisce; writing our stories is the next step. It's not always an easy one, but as we venture into such writing together, we can support each other in our endeavor. Enjoy the books that follow; then work with a group of children or adults and see where their writing (and your writing with them) takes you.

Suggested Books (For Use With Children or Adults)

Munsch, R. (1982). *The boy in the drawer.* Worthington, OH: Willowisp Press.
Munsch, R. (1983). *David's father.* Toronto, ON: Annick Press Ltd.
Munsch, R. (1985). *Thomas' snowsuit.* Toronto, ON: Annick Press Ltd.
Munsch, R. (1986). *50 below zero.* Toronto, ON: Annick Press Ltd.
Munsch, R. (1986). *Love you forever.* Ontario, ON: Firefly. (The only one that is not humorous, telling the story of a mother and child over time.)
Munsch, R. (1989). *Pigs.* Toronto, ON: Annick Press Ltd.
Munsch, R. (1990). *Good families don't.* Toronto, ON: Doubleday.
Munsch, R. (1990). *I have to go.* Toronto, ON: Annick Press Ltd.
Munsch, R. (1990). *Something good.* Toronto, ON: Annick Press Ltd.
Munsch, R. (1991). *Show and tell.* Toronto, ON: Annick Press Ltd.
Barbara Shook Hazen's *Tight times* (1979, New York: Puffin) is the tragic story of a family that loses an income source when dad loses his job. Many sad stories arise as children tell of their own tight times.
Mary Bahr's *The memory box* (1992, Morton Grove, IL: Albert Whitman) is the powerful story of a grandfather getting Alzheimer's and the impact it has on the family.
Faith Ringgold's *Tar beach* (1991, New York: Scholastic) is about a family's life as it is affected by their not being union members.

REFERENCES

Applebee, A. N. (1978). *The child's concept of story: Ages two to seventeen.* Chicago, IL: University of Chicago Press.
Atwell, N. (1987). *In the middle: Writing, reading, and learning with adolescents.* Portsmouth, NH: Heinemann.
Butler, A., & Turbill, J. (Eds.). (1984). *Towards a reading-writing classroom.* Rosebery, NSW, Australia: Primary English Teaching Association.
Goodman, Y. (1985). Kidwatching: Observing children in the classroom. In A. Jaggar, & M. T. Smith-Burke (Eds.), *Observing the language learner* (pp. 9–18). Newark, DE: National Council of Teachers of English/International Reading Association.
Graves, D. (1989). *The reading/writing teacher's companion: Investigate fiction.* Portsmouth, NH: Heinemann.
Harste, J., & Short, K., with Burke, C. (1988). *Creating classrooms for authors: the reading–writing connection.* Portsmouth, NH: Heinemann.
Peterson, R., & Eeds, M. (1990). *Grand conversations: Literature groups in action.* Portsmouth, NH: Heinemann.
Rosenblatt, L. (1976). *Literature as exploration* (3rd ed.). New York: Modern Languages Association. (Original work published 1938)
Short, K. (1992). Intertextuality: Searching for patterns that connect. In C. Kinzer &, D. Leu (Eds.), *Literacy, research, theory and practice: Views from many perspectives, forty-first yearbook of the national reading conference* (pp. 187–198). Chicago, IL: National Reading Conference.

CHILDREN'S TEXTS

Mayer, M. (1985). *Just grandpa and me*. Racine, WI: Western.
Munsch, R. (1985). *Thomas' snowsuit*. Toronto, ON: Annick Press.
White, E. B. (1952). *Charlotte's web*. New York: Harper & Row.

10

Learning to Walk Together in a Third-Grade Bilingual Classroom: From Transmission to Transactional Instruction in Literature

Paul Boyd-Batstone
Edison Elementary School and
California State University, Long Beach

EDITOR'S OVERVIEW

Developing students' English language prowess adds significant dimension to any teacher's objectives and tasks. Paul Boyd-Batstone's goal in his Span-ish–English bilingual class is biliteracy; that is, full competency in English and Spanish. Additionally, he discovers the need to shift from the transmission model to transactional instruction when his students encourage a change in his assump-tions about the nature of reading and, thus, the teaching of reading.

What changes does this entail? He reconsidered the needs of his students and their role in the instructional exchange. He broadened the range of materials. His own functioning in and relationship to his class shifted as he reorganized his teaching structure. Redirecting his teaching foci within the broad goals, he dramatically revised his classroom techniques.

Once his teaching world opens up, Boyd-Batstone's creativity comes to the fore. So does that of his students. They responded to literature aesthetically and efferently, writing poems and paragraphs; their curiosity piqued, they conduct research and write some more. The use of open questions leads them to compose songs and create metaphors. Examples of an array of activities express the nature of transactional instruction. Responsive teaching generates energy and enthusi-asm—and language skills: reading, writing and speaking.

Consider the following:

1. *What is revealed in this chapter about transactional instruction with literature (as opposed to the transmission model) that would be particu-larly effective with bilingual or English as a Second Language students?*

2. *Evaluate the various strategies illustrated in this chapter to determine their application in your classroom.*

"What you see, I can only half guess. From here we must walk together" was an Asian proverb next to a photographer's display at the local library. Captured in this simple saying is the essence of reading instruction. Assuming that the reading process is much more than a series of subskills and behaviors means realizing that we all engage in reading via our own paths to interpretation. The impact of this assumption has a profound effect on the way we teach. As teacher, I cannot enter into instruction without having my students first show me what they see and from there we can begin to walk together. Instruction then shifts from transmitting subskills to listening for student transactions and paths to reading.

One day without anticipating it, I made a radical shift from transmission to transactional instruction because of the resistance of my students. At Edison Elementary School in Long Beach, California, an urban school with 97% of the students identified as limited English proficient (LEP), I taught a Spanish–English bilingual class. Initially, I utilized a transmission approach as, what I saw as, an appropriate way to teach literature. I would have my students read through a selected story and identify the various conventions of story structure: setting, characters, events in order, problem, solution, and so forth. However, when my students began to challenge the text, the transmission approach was no longer the best tool for engaging them in the literature. Transactional instruction provided the students the creative space to respond to the literature and it gave me, as the teacher, a way of transforming resistance into an opportunity for creativity.

In my classroom, I met with my students in small groups during our Reading Writing Workshop time. We began the day's literature conference trying to define the problem of *The Rabbit and the Turnip,* a story about a hungry rabbit who finds a turnip in the snow at Christmas time; she encounters a hungry donkey and gives away the turnip; the donkey encounters another hungry animal and gives away the turnip . . . and so on, until the turnip winds up in the paws of the generous rabbit who shares the turnip with her friends. The problem was obvious to me that the animals were hungry and there was very little to eat in the dead of winter. But my students could not come up with my answer. In fact, they were restless, and discipline problems began cropping up. Javier's behavior was the worst; he was messing around and keeping other students from paying attention to the discussion.

Finally, the discussion came to a halt. Out of exasperation I asked: "Okay. What's wrong with this story?"

Javier, the discipline problem, spoke up immediately and said, "They don't know anything about turnips in this story."

"Oh really?" I said. "Why do you say that?"

"First of all," began Javier, "the color is all wrong. You're not going to find a turnip that looks like that anywhere."

"What else is wrong?" I prodded.

"Since when do you find a fresh turnip lying in the snow." He scoffed, "They don't grow in the snow." The rest of the students laughed.

"How did you learn so much about turnips?" I wondered.

Javier bounced his hand on his chest and said, "My grandfather grows turnips on our ranch in Mexico."

Suddenly, a whole new world opened up in our discussion. The group began talking about turnip farming in Mexico. I wrote their comments down on a chart that we read as a group. The following day, Javier brought a pile of photographs of his family's Mexican ranch that showed him and his brother riding a mule, working the land, and harvesting turnips. We made a display of the ranch pictures and wrote about life on their turnip ranch. What I began to realize was that transmitting notions of story structure was not the best approach for literature instruction. Transactional instruction, which looks for authentic responses to literature from the students, was a much more effective and enjoyable way to teach.

Invitation 10.1

When reading a compelling story, ask the students to tune into a personal experience that is evoked by the story. Try to figure out how the story and the lives of the students connect. Where are the live circuits between the readers and the text?

Transactional instruction invited Javier to bring to light the lived-through cultural experience that he brought to school. This is vitally important in light of the need for the bilingual educator to provide culturally responsive instruction. English-speaking students are readily perceived as having knowledge and experience to contribute to the discussion of a text. However, bilingual students and students of low socioeconomic status tend to be taught with the notion that they are at a deficit. Those who hold a deficit view of students call for transmission forms of instruction because the perceived deficient student is not seen to have enough knowledge to contribute to the learning process in an active way. Additionally, students who sense being perceived as deficient will resist instruction. The challenge for the bilingual educator is then to create the environment that invites students like Javier to share their lives and knowledge in the classroom. In the words of Bartolomé (1994):

The creation of learning environments for low SES [socio-economic status] and ethnic minority students, similar to those for more affluent and White populations, requires that teachers discard deficit notions and genuinely value and utilize student's existing knowledge bases in their teaching. In order to do so, teachers must confront and challenge their own social biases so as to honestly begin to perceive their students as capable learners. Furthermore, they must remain open to the fact that they will also learn from their students. Learning is not a one-way undertaking. (p. 182)

Freire (1985) complained that there exists a distorted view of literacy with regard to lower class students that "it is as if [they] were totally different from everyone else. This distortion fails to acknowledge their real-life experience and all the past and on-going knowledge acquired through experience" (p. 8). Students with greater cultural capital in predominantly White, affluent, English-speaking school settings are generally given permission to speak their minds. In fact, these students are readily encouraged to discuss, debate, and share their wide-ranging insights. Teachers tend to take time for their creative impulses to be exercised. But students like those in my classroom with less cultural capital, those of color, those of poverty, those who are also learning English as a second language, are rarely given the opportunity to discuss, to debate, and to explore the extent of their imaginations in the forum of a creative classroom context.

Learning becomes a two-way undertaking when transactional instruction happens in the classroom. Listening to students as they authentically respond to a text becomes the first act of instruction. Reader-response theory, as articulated by Rosenblatt (1978), emphasizes the "live circuit" that connects a reader to the text. When the teacher is tapped into a student's live circuit, following the student's path to interpretation, the student sheds light on what she or he is seeing and imagining. What Javier saw, I could only half guess. It was not until he turned on the lights via his live circuit and provided his insight into the text that we began to walk together. The discussion and language development that took place responding to his ideas and feelings was much richer than identifying preprogrammed conventions of literature. The benefits went both ways for students and teacher alike. Both student and teacher brought something to the text; both student and teacher entered the learning with anticipation of acquiring and sharing knowledge. And both began to walk together.

This chapter documents my emerging understanding of reader response in a bilingual classroom setting. As teacher, I found that I could not enter into instruction without having my students first show me what they saw, and from there, we could begin to walk together.

The chapter examines organizing a bilingual classroom for reader response; working with basal texts, literature books, stories; structuring for a reading/writing workshop. The bilingual classroom's organization is further illustrated with developing a literature plan with the book *Brother Eagle, Sister Sky* (Chief Seattle, 1991), using open-ended questions, and tugging at metaphors.

ORGANIZING A BILINGUAL CLASSROOM
FOR READER RESPONSE

My classroom was fashioned after a transitional bilingual program model. Transitional bilingual programs vary according to the ratio of Spanish-to-English instruction and to the duration of the processes of transistion from Spanish to English. Ramirez (1991) conducted a longitudinal study, involving several thousand language minority students, comparing three different program models: English immersion; bilingual early-exit, and late-exit transitional models. English immersion programs taught students exclusively in English; the other two taught the students in both languages with the early-exit moving to mainstream English instruction at third grade, whereas the late-exit program maintained two-language instruction through seventh grade. What Ramirez reported finding after eight years of study was that the late-exit program produced greater academic gains in Spanish and in English, in both language and content area development. Working from a strong research base and within the parameters of district policy, my classroom instruction began the school year with approximately an 80/20 ratio of Spanish-to-English instruction. As the year progressed and the students developed greater proficiency in English, the classroom instruction transitioned to more of a 50/50 ratio, Spanish to English. The goal of the program is biliteracy in both languages, full competency in Spanish and in English. This recognizes the value of the primary language in celebrating diversity, but it also has the added benefit of enriching the quality of English language development.

Just managing two-language instruction in a bilingual classroom, however, is only a piece of the pie. Responsive teaching calls on the teacher to see what the students bring to the classroom as the substance of instruction. However, it is impossible to respond to students' ideas and imaginations without creating a classroom where the teacher can listen to individuals and small groups of students. The students in my class were at the point in their language development in English and Spanish where they would freely select which language to respond in, either orally or in written form. I would maintain separation of English and Spanish in my language of instruction; however, the students' discussions and writing utilized both. This is not to say that the classroom maintained a kind of hybrid "Spanglish," although in natural language settings, that does occur; what happened more often than not was that Spanish would dominate a discussion one time and English the next. Students' writing would one day be in Spanish and the next day in English. Choosing to use either language at will, they provided evidence of their developing proficiency in two languages—not using one language as a crutch for the other. What was primary in my mind was that students were expressing their responses. Once the thoughts and ideas were out, it was a fairly easy undertaking to work with the conventions of how best to express their ideas.

My third-grade bilingual classroom evolved as my understanding of reader-response grew. This evolution in my classroom took place in four domains: working with basal texts, books, and stories; structuring for a reading/writing workshop; using open-ended questions; and tugging at metaphors. The process of change reinvigorated my classroom instruction and created an environment where learning was shared—a two-way undertaking.

Working With Basal Texts, Books and Stories

"If wishes were horses then beggers would ride." Since they are not, since really to satisfy an impulse or interest means to work it out, and working it out involves running up against obstacles, becoming acquainted with materials, exercising ingenuity, patience, persistence, alertness, it of necessity involves discipline—ordering of power—and supplies of knowledge. (Dewey, 1959, pp. 54–55)

Traditionally, language arts/reading instruction is organized around the scope and sequence of a basal text. The class objective is to plow through the stories in the basal text from beginning to end within the semester or school year. This approach forces the implementation of transmission strategies on students. The teacher plans for skills development according to the organization of the teacher's guide and the order of the selected stories. In turn, the students take on a passive role in their learning. What they read, what they are to discuss, and their conclusions have already been dictated by the basal reader. Not only do the students take a passive, nonthinking role in the process, but the teacher as well becomes a passive conduit of the learning. Dewey's encouragement calls on the teacher and the student to be much more active in the pursuit of learning, to use imagination and ingenuity following impulses and interests.

Ideally, classrooms should be filled with a rich array of books and stories. Multiple copies should be available for students to select for reading and study. Libraries should be inviting, well stocked and staffed, and easily accessible. The reality, especially for bilingual classrooms and schools in low SES environments, is that many classrooms are provided basal texts, a few trade books, and the library budget has just been cut. Resources can be scarce, particularily with primary language materials. The obstacles to quality instruction are always prevalent. Nevertheless, there are ways of working with basal texts, books, and stories.

In my classroom, basal texts in Spanish were provided by the school; I personally purchased many books out of my own pocket for the classroom, and the librarians from the school and public libraries worked to supply students with good books. Fortunately, the school librarian welcomed students into the library unannounced to select books or research a specific topic. I took the stance that sometimes the basal text would contain worthwhile reading material, but it was far from the exclusive resource for reading. If a group of students, on browsing through the basal, found a story that interested them, I would encourage them to form a group to study it. On occasion, students found literature selections in the social studies text that caught their fancy, so that became the focus of their reading. I would each day read from a book like *Baseball in April* by Soto (1990), which became a springboard for some students for further reading by the same author.

A single story was never enough to study in a group because students were constantly making connections between works of literature. What the students would begin reading and discussing would inevitably lead to other works from other sources. For example, one group of students began reading a story in Spanish out of the basal called *"Ma Lien y el pincel mágico"* by Kimishima (1989). The story was a Japanese fantasy tale about a boy with a magic paint brush; everything he painted came to life. They collaborated on painting a mural based on the story but became very interested in several art books of famous Mexican artists that I had on the shelf. After browsing the books, each selected a painting to reproduce with water color. They wrote poetry about their water color reproductions. Then one of the students found a children's storybook on Diego Rivera, the famous Mexican painter. The bilingual book *Diego* by Jeanette and Jonah Winter (1991) tells the story of the painter's life. The group enthusiastically read the book before I had a chance to read it myself. Our discussion became one of the students teaching me lots of interesting parts of his life that I did not know, such as Rivera being born a twin but his brother died young, and that he was raised by an Indian nursemaid who had a tremendous influence on the style and subject of his later paintings.

Part of the process of opening up the classroom to self-selection is trusting that students will follow a natural curiosity, an impulse. This impulse is at the discretion of the student, and not dictated by the basal or the teacher. Being attentive to that impulse and following the students' lead is fundamental to responsive teaching. Allowing for students to pursue their interests moves the student from being a passive recipient of knowledge to an active, self-directed learner. I would not have made the connection between a Japanese fantasy and the paintings of Diego Rivera, but the trail that the students blazed generated a rich learning experience for both the students and the teacher.

Structuring for a Reading/Writing Workshop

In the past, I took all the initiative in forming groups according to ability levels and the stories as sequenced in the basal reader. I planned the projects and the activities that the students were required to do. But I also spent an inordinate amount of time managing behaviors of students expressing resistance to my ideas and mandates. Students like Javier, cited earlier, forced me to rethink the underlying assumptions of my transmission mode of teaching. They showed me that their ideas and interests were advancing the goals of language and academic content development. As I began to look to the students' interests in their reading, I found myself questioning the arbitrariness of my criteria for grouping. And as the students demonstrated that I could trust their judgment, I progressively turned over much of the decision process to them.

The notion of structuring the classroom for a reading/writing workshop grew out of a change in my own thinking about the metaphor of classroom instruction. Rather than treating the classroom as an assembly line metaphor of dumping ideas into empty receptacles, I embraced the metaphor of an artist's or craftsman's workshop. Structuring the classroom for a reading/writing workshop meant reorganizing grouping for maximizing listening and responding. But more fundamentally, it recognized that language arts instruction is a creative time of working at reading and writing and imagination. The structuring of the classroom involved grouping strategies, collaborative planning, and a cycle of learning that would take approximately 6 weeks.

The following is how the students in the class collaborated to form their own groups around the books and stories that captured their imaginations. The process was designed to turn over more responsibility to the students with each new cycle. At the beginning of the school year, I had a heavy hand in the entire decision-making process, but as the year progressed, we moved toward self-directed learning with the teacher operating as consultant or principal researcher.

For the first cycle, I would provide the students with a list of six titles of stories that I considered appropriate for their reading. During the next 2 days, we would read through the six stories in small groups, in pairs and individually. Once the stories had been read, I would ask the students to select the story that interested them the most. We would form groups around the stories. The rules were that each group could be no larger than 8 students, and that there needed to be a representative number of boys and girls in each group. With stories of high interest, we sometimes formed several groups to study the same story.

With groups formed, the members of the groups had several tasks to perform. They were responsible to reread the story in pairs, as a group, or individually; they also were required to decorate their own story folder to hold their writing and project designs; finally, they selected a group liaison (to facilitate communication between the teacher and their group) and they selected students to be in charge of managing the workshop box (a storage bin to hold the folders and other projects the group was working on).

As each worked on reading, rereading, and decorating their folders, I would immediately begin to conference with a group of students to get them started on their Literature Plan (Lit Plan). The Lit Plan consisted of a cluster of individual and collaborative project areas that each student was required to accomplish. These Lit Plans were charted out on large sheets of paper and hung around the room by fishing line and alligator clips. The reason for this is to have the plans readily accessible for the conferencing and individual work, which I will discuss later.

The Lit Plan consisted of basically five sections: written expression, poetry/music, creative ideas, resources; and the group presentation (see Fig. 10.1). Each group was responsible for generating their own assignments as they bubbled up from the stories they read. The section on written expression required that each member of the group produce three pieces of written work. The poetry/music section required the group to either find poetry or music related to the story or compose their own work to teach the rest of the class. The creative ideas section is a wide-open section that asks the students to come up with their own way to represent or respond to the story. For example, students have produced murals, plays, research projects, community action, scheduled guest speakers—the list of possibilities is endless. In fact, the wilder the idea, the better. On one occasion, a group of students created a life size orca (killer whale) that we displayed in the school hallway—the orca was longer than the length of the classroom. As the group developed its projects, they kept track of the various resources they had drawn on under the resources section of the lit plan. The last component is the presentation section. Once all the projects have moved to completion, the group uses this section to begin to plan and think about how they are going to present their work to the rest of the class.

The goal of the first lit conference (small group meeting with the teacher) is threefold: to reread the story, to establish the group liaison, and to engage the story to provide direction for the first writing project. Once those tasks are taken care of, the group would be on its own for the next day to get to work on its writing.

The writing is developed in English and Spanish with prewriting clustering activities written on the back of the lit plan chart. Random

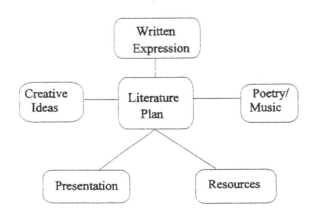

FIG. 10.1. The literature plan.

thoughts and impressions about a given story are written down on the chart paper. Once the students say what is on their minds, we look, as a group, at what was recorded on the chart, and color-code similar ideas. This way, ideas in the same vein are circled with the same colored pen. Once all the ideas have been color-coded, within each color group, we decide the sequence of the sentences. Each sentence within a color group is numbered in the order that the group agrees on according to their own logic. Finally, the group decides which color group should appear first, second, third, and so on. Thus, what is developed is an ordered essay of two to five paragraphs in length reflecting the students' thoughts about their reading. Normally, the entire process takes about 30 minutes. But occasionally the group is so engaged in discussing a story that time is taken to follow the students' lead. This kind of flexibility with time can happen because the other groups are generally engrossed in writing, reading, and creative projects.

The goal of the second lit conferences is not only to check up on the students' initial writing, but to delve into the more creative ideas that spring from a given piece of children's literature. It has been my experience as a classroom teacher that we often forget, when teaching children's literature, that we are dealing with a work of art rather than a chapter in a textbook. Echoing Rosenblatt, the students are responding aesthetically to this artwork. They are experiencing emotions of exhilaration, fear, and surprise as they empathize with the characters in the story, or identify with the poets' expressiveness. In the words of Rosenblatt (1986):

> The student should be helped to pay attention to the interfusion of sensuous, cognitive, and affective elements that can enter into the process of selective awareness and synthesis. No matter how limited or immature, this can provide the basis for growth. Aesthetic education should be rooted in the individual aesthetic transaction. The student thus can be helped to bring increasing sensitivity and sophistication to the evocation of "works of art," and can learn to bring to bear ever wider contexts for their interplay and study. (p. 127)

The teacher establishes whether the students will spend time exploring their aesthetic responses. Often, valuable instructional time is not taken for aesthetic responses. For an unexplained reason, we teachers feel like we are doing more teaching if we spend our time working on story structure or spelling lists. Teachers establish the learning environment with children's literature. Time spent helping students increase their "sensitivity and sophistication to the evocation of 'works of art' " can only serve to make the students better readers and interpreters of their own world. For this reason, considerable time is spent looking to students for their aesthetic responses and discovering how to represent those responses in poetry, music, and creative ideas.

Gallas (1994), in looking at her own students' languages of learning, asked her own second grade student to explain why she felt she needed to compose a poem to express her thinking. And this is what she said, "A poem is a little short, and it tells you some things in a funny way. But a science book, it tells you things like on the news . . . But in a poem, it's more . . . the poem teaches you, but not just with words" (p.136). There is something deeper in art, literature, music, poetry; deeper than the surface structure of language and its conventions.

Invitation 10.2

Select any children's book that captures your imagination. As you read the book, consider how you might represent the book using different visual and performing arts: drama, dance, music, visual arts, multimedia. How might you encourage your students to respond through these media?

Once the writing, music/poetry, creative ideas, and their various resources have been explored and developed, the group meets to develop a presentation not only for the rest of the class but also for the invited parents to celebrate the accomplishments of their children. I have used the following structure for the presentations. Students are paired within a group to share their writing and answer questions about the story that they studied. The paired students station themselves in designated areas of the classroom and the rest of the class and visiting parents are divided up into groups to sit at each station. A rotation sequence is explained and each group is given approximately 10 minutes to present their writing and answer questions. (The reason for the rotation is to give each student multiple chances in a small group setting to practice presenting their work.)

Having gone through an entire rotation, the whole class meets to see the creative ideas, hear poetry, and sing songs that were generated from the literature. This may take the form of a puppet show to a multimedia recreation of the story. There is a last time for questions and answers. And finally, students are asked to fill out one of two evaluation forms. The presenters fill out a form describing what they did and how they felt the presentation went. The students in the audience fill out a form describing what they learned, what they liked, and what they would do differently if it were their project.

This cycle will be repeated throughout the school year. The entire cycle takes about 6 weeks. One week to establish groupings, 4 weeks to work through a Lit Plan, and 1 week to plan and present the projects.

Each time the class worked through a cycle, they were given more autonomy over the process.

Developing a Literature Plan with *Brother Eagle, Sister Sky*

One example of the development of a Literature Plan is illustrated by the work of Adrianna, David, and Pedro. They discovered the book *Brother Eagle, Sister Sky* by Chief Seattle (1991), illustrated by Susan Jeffers. After reading the book several times in a group and individually, they met with me for a conference. They were all fascinated by the bald eagle and began a discussion in English by describing the bird. Each student contributed a sentence or phrase identifying the various attributes of the eagle. Their words were recorded on a chart in the random order that they occurred in their conversation. Once the conversation began to slow down, we looked at the sentences and phrases; we numbered them in order according to a more logical progression. They returned to their seats to write an essay on eagles, and Fig. 10.2 is what David wrote in English.

Two days later, the group came back to conference with me about the book. They had reflected more about the deeper meaning of the book and began discussing, in Spanish, about how an eagle's personality paralleled that of a human being. We took time to talk and I took notes on the chart paper. We ordered the thoughts for writing again and I sent them back to work. Figure 10.3 is what David produced in Spanish.

The group returned every other day or so to engage the book in a discussion. They wanted to study what eagles ate and their habitats. Their interests dictated a research project, so I sent them off to the library

DESCRIBING THE BALD EAGLES

The bald eagle is a powerful bird of prey. Bald eagles are built for soaring and speed, unlike the falcon that's only made for speed. The bald is equipped with a sharp hooked beak and sharp talons for killing its prey. The eyesight of an eagle is better than that of a human being. The eagle needs its eyesight because it helps to see small animals.

by David Pinedo

FIG. 10.2. David's essay in English.

El caracter de las Aguilas de cabeza blanca
Por DAVID PINEDO

Las aguilas de cabeza blanca tienen un caracter como el de una personas. Proteje su nido y sus crias como una persona. Ataca cuando siente que la van a atacar. El caracter del aguila es muy sensible porque de cualquier ofensa el aguila ataca. Las aguilas siempre parece que estan enojadas pero no es cierto.

FIG. 10.3. David's essay in Spanish.
TRANSLATION:
The Personality of Bald Eagles
by David Pinedo
Bald eagles have a personality like that of some people. They protect their nests and their young like people do. They attack when they feel that they are under attack. The personality of the eagle is very sensitive because any time they sense danger, they attack. The eagles always look like they are angry, but that may not be so.

to see what they could find out. Pedro and Adrianna returned with notes and ideas in an unedited form. We sat down to organize the material and to correct the spelling and grammar together. They wrote down their research, revised their writing, and Figs. 10.4 and 10.5 show what they produced.

At our next conference, I asked them what kind of poetry we could generate from the story. We discussed images of flying like eagles, the sense of connectedness to this magnificent bird, and dreaming. And Fig. 10.6 is a poem they wrote collaboratively in English and Spanish.

David was struck by the myriad of ways that the image of an eagle appeared in all aspects of life, so he wrote the reflective piece shown in Fig. 10.7.

As the literature plan developed, the group realized that they were amassing a wide variety of writings about eagles. Looking at their work, they decided to publish a book of eagle writings using the classroom computer. The striking feature of the plan was that it was generated by the group with a book that captivated their imaginations. The process of reader response was open to the students' ideas, and the plan flowed from their paths of interpretation. They knew that they had something significant to contribute to the learning. They needed a teacher to help organize their thinking on paper, to access materials and resources, and to give authority to the process. Figure 10.8 shows how the literature plan appeared as it developed.

As many as six different literature plans are developed simultaneously in my classroom. They are developed piece by piece. Approximately one to two segments of the plan are generated each week. While I am conferencing with one group, my aide is conferencing with another. The other groups of students are expected to work independently on their writing or creative projects. The students schedule time to conference with either me or my teacher's aide as needed. I take a few moments before and after conferences to supervise the entire class; but more often

The food of the Eagles
by Pedro Lopez

Eagles are predators that hunt for their food. They are carnivores because they eat other animals. Some of the eagles eat fish, salmon, baby deer, snakes, lizards, other birds and beavers. Some eagles eat different animals like sea lions that the sea has brought to the shore. The male eagle goes to scare a mountain cat so he can finish feeding his eaglets.

Eagles catch their food by soaring up in the air and looking down to the ground for small animals. They catch the animal with their talons and take it to the nest.

FIG. 10.4. Pedro's research.

Habitats for Eagles

by Adriana Navarro

Eagles are found on every continent except Antartica. Some of the eagles live in deserts, swamps, jungles, and high in the mountains. The mountains are a safe habitat for the eagles because high in the mountains no human can go to get to the eagle's eggs. Eagles live along the shores of large lakes, on the oceans, and in the forest. In the forests the eagles live in the canopy so no human or other animals can go up high in the tree to hurt them. When the eagles get cold where they live, they go south to live in a tree where it is hotter.

FIG. 10.5. Adrianna's research.

than not, I found that the students did not like me getting in the way of their work. Their work was self-generated, and thereby self-directed and intrinsically motivating. When they need my help, I hear about it, but I deal with whole-group concerns primarily during the conference time. The students came to realize that they got undivided attention from me during the conference. Listening to students, discussing ideas, and organizing thoughts was held as a sacred time in this classroom. The structuring of the classroom time and activities around the small group conferences was vital to make reader-response the focus of instruction.

Hermano águila

El águila planeando en el aire.
Planeando con gracia.
Me gusta imaginarme que él es mi hermano.
Me imagino a mi mismo volando en el aire,
Pero no es nada mas que un sueño.

FIG. 10.6. Pedro and Adrianna's poem in English and Spanish.
TRANSLATION:
Brother Eagle
The Eagle soaring in the sky,
So graceful.
I like to imagine that he is my brother;
I imagine myself flying in the sky;

It was during the conference where I was able to inquire about and
respond to the leads of my students.

Using Open-Ended Questions

Responsive teaching requires inquiry into what students are thinking
about their reading. The questions that are used by the teacher can
either function as an open invitation to dialogue, or they can act as a
kind of check for correct answers. On occasion, my questions have been
very closed and at times, embarrassingly silly. One of my students,

Daniela, taught me a vital lesson about my questions and their hidden assumptions. I had never considered Daniela to be one of my brightest students. One of the other teachers at the school told me that " . . . if Daniela just got through life as someone's housekeeper without getting pregnant as a teenager, she would be as successful as we could expect." And frankly, I believed it. But Daniela taught me how an appropriate open-ended question can make a world of difference in affirming the unique intelligence of each student.

One day in February, I tried to initiate a discussion for an English language development lesson about George Washington; I asked, "Who was Martha Washington's husband?" A poorly thought out question at best. Why that silly question occurred to me, I'll never know. What's more perplexing is, what did I expect to accomplish by asking such a question? Was I hoping to trick the students? Was I looking to display

The eagle as a symbol
by David Pinedo

Eagles have been used as symbols for a long time. The eagle is a symbol of wisdom, power, justice, and freedom. In the Middle Ages armys had shields with eagles on them. The bald eagle and the golden eagle were sacred to some tribes of Native Americans. People use the bald eagle on coins. The peso, a Mexican coin, has the golden eagle on it. The name of the rocket ship mission Apolo II was EAGLE. There is a medal for the U.S. army that has a bald eagle on it. Some time ago astrologers discovered a constellation that they called Aquila. For many years the eagle has been an important symbol for different cultures.

FIG. 10.7. David's reflective piece.

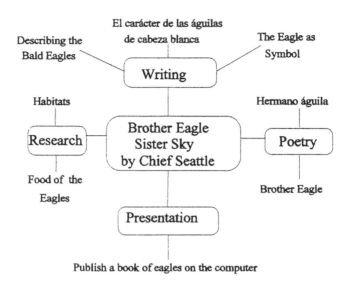

FIG. 10.8. The group's literature plan for *Brother Eagle, Sister Sky.*

my own knowledge? Hardly! Or was I looking to expose what I considered to be their lack of knowledge? Possibly.

"Who was Martha Washington's husband?" Admittedly a dumb question.

Daniela immediately raised her hand and blurted out, "Martin Luther King!"

Hearing her answer to my question helped confirm my belief that she was not going to catch on. Even so, Daniela's answer, apparently coming from left field, made me begin to observe her more closely to figure out what was going on in her mind. What I noticed was that during classroom discussions, she would often look up at the ceiling, her head would bob from side to side, and her mouth would move like she was whispering a song to herself. I thought to myself, there she goes again, daydreaming and not paying attention to the lesson. But then, I began to wonder if something else was going on inside her head.

Finally the day came when I began to ask a much more intelligent question. We were studying whales (*ballenas,* in Spanish). In their Spanish reading, the students found that whales communicated with each other through song and body movement. They slap their fins and their tails on the surface of the water to announce danger; they raise their heads out of the water and move them back and forth when in distress. In the middle of the discussion, I looked at Daniela and sure enough, she was looking at the ceiling, wagging her head, and mouthing some words to herself. I asked her a very simple and open-ended question, "Daniela, what are you thinking?"

This time, she spouted out, "*¡Baila la ballena!*" (Dance the whale!)

Another student suggested that it sounded like "*La Bamba*," the famous Mexican dance song. Before I knew it the group had reproduced the lesson about whales, *ballenas*, as a song to the tune of "La Bamba." The song is as follows:

La Ballena

Baila la ballena, baila la ballena, baila la ballena...
Para bailar la ballena, para bailar la ballena
se necesita una ballena grande,
una ballena grande y otra chiquita.
Ay arriba, ay arriba iré...
Yo no soy marinero, yo no soy marinero,
Soy capitán, soy capitán.
Por tí seré por tí seré

Para comunicar un mensaje
a las ballenitas
hay que mover la cabecita
y mover la colita.

Bamba, bamba . . .

[English Translation:

Dance the whale, dance the whale, dance the whale . . .
To dance the whale, to dance the whale
you first need a great big whale,
a great big whale and a small one too.
Kick it up, kick it up I'll go . . .
I'm not just a sailor, I'm not just a sailor,
I'm a captain, I'm a captain.
For you I'll be, for you I'll be.

In order to send a message
to the dear whales
you must move your head
and move your tails.

Bamba, bamba . . .]

What I realized that day was that Daniela had a gift. She was very talented at putting words together in creative, poetic ways. Thinking back to when I asked my closed question about Martha Washington, I realized that she was responding to the question on a more aesthetic level. She was playing with the words. As she looked up at the ceiling, and wagged her head, she mouthed the words back and forth: Martin/Martha. In a word, Daniela was a poet. She was an unrecognized poet. I did not recognize her gift; I could not see it until I began to listen openly for her aesthetic response.

Louise Rosenblatt's (1986) theory of reader response speaks to this very situation. Reader-response theory recognizes that all readers bring something to their reading, that each of us reads a text or situation according to the lens of our own experience. It is the teacher's responsibility to find that live wire in the students and connect instruction to it via the students' knowledge and experience.

In terms of Daniela, her live wire was tapped when I, as the teacher, became open to her way of thinking. When she took an active role in the lesson about whales, her learning increased and the entire class benefited from her creative contribution. In other words, a transaction took place as she participated in mutually defining the lesson on whales. It took the simple act of asking an open-ended question to listen for and respond to her wordplay and metaphor. But there is something more. I had certain perceptions about Daniela that kept me from seeing her as a poet.

Inviting Daniela's insights into the lesson was more than a question of how a student reads a text. The underlying assumption throughout my initial attempt at teaching was that Daniela had little to contribute to the lesson. Daniela, a young girl of color, an English learner, a child of poverty, who would think in unconventional ways, was not seen as having the knowledge and insight that called for a serious hearing. My closed questions only asked her to repeat back empty words. However, inquiring about her thinking with an open-ended question made learning a two-way undertaking.

Invitation 10.3

Create your own music based upon a favorite story. Take a familiar simple tune, such as "Are You Sleeping?" Line by line, write down the number of syllables in each phrase. With "Are You Sleeping?" there are either three, four, or six syllables per line. Divide a large sheet of butcher's paper into the corresponding sections. Elicit from the students words, phrases, sentences with three, four or six syllables based on a story. Fill in the phrases in the appropriate line of the music. Sing your songs about the story.

The way teachers use questions is a question of thinking, knowledge, and power. It is a question of thinking because it concerns the inquiry into the ideas of all students. It is a question of knowledge—of whose knowledge is invited into the classroom setting and whose knowledge is silenced at school. But it is also a question of power—of who has the power to impact the instruction in the classroom. The extent to which students like Daniela are heard from indicates how thinking, knowledge, and power are shared in the classroom. Designing questions to look for a preprogrammed response assumes that only the instructor has the insight and power to establish the parameters of knowledge. Asking and responding to open-ended questions, on the other hand, creates an ambience of openness to the collective wisdom of the students in a classroom of shared thinking, knowledge, and power.

Tugging at Metaphors

Ingmar Bergman (1960) described filmmaking in much the same way transactional learning takes place in the classroom:

> A film for me begins with something very vague—a chance remark or a bit of conversation, a hazy but agreeable event unrelated to any particular situation. . . . These are split-second impressions that disappear as quickly as they come, yet leave behind a mood—like pleasant dreams. It is a mental state, not an actual story, but one abounding in fertile associations and images. Most of all, it is a *brightly colored thread sticking out of the dark sack of the unconscious.* If I begin to wind up this thread, and do it carefully, a complete film will emerge. (p. 11)

Tugging at that "brightly colored thread"—my students' metaphorical thinking—made teaching an enlightening experience for me. These metaphors emerged in English or in Spanish and popped out unexpectedly at times. In a transitional bilingual classroom, even though students are quite fluent in English, the use of Spanish is not discouraged, especially when it helps provide the students and the teacher with multiple ways to tug at rich cultural metaphors. Rich metaphors like a brightly colored thread lead to the workings of the mind and heart. When those brightly colored threads pop up, they signaled for me an opportunity to tug at something deep in the minds and hearts of my students.

One day before school started, I was conducting my supervising duties on the playground. The night before, storm clouds had poured buckets of water on the city of Long Beach, but the morning was brilliant as the sun broke through the clouds.

A Salvadoran boy named Santos, standing near me, squinted as he looked up at the sky and said, *"El sol está enojado hoydía."* (The sun is angry today.)

Surprised at this statement, I asked, *"¿Por qué dices que está enojado el sol?"* (Why do you say that the sun is angry?)

"Porque," responded the boy, *"me está pegando como un gigante."* (Because it is pounding me like a giant.)

This brief conversation gave me pause. As I looked up at the bright sky, I, too, was pelted in the eyes by the sun's intense fury. Santos in a rather matter-of-fact way described the morning with a vivid sense of imagery. I could not help but think of unsuccessfully trying to teach lessons on personification, similes, and metaphors. And here, in a seemingly mundane conversation, a child was deftly applying personification to an angry sun, and the simile like a giant pounding his club down on earth. I wondered if my students talked like this very often. What I discovered was that I was not tuned into their use of metaphor, even though metaphorical thinking was present in their daily conversations.

Pugh, Hicks, Davis, & Venstra (1992) affirmed that metaphorical thinking is not only a higher-order thought process, but that it is pervasive, powerful, and generally ignored. They said, "Through metaphorical thinking, divergent meanings become unified into the underlying patterns that constitute our conceptual understanding of reality. Indeed, metaphor is so much a part of our thinking and learning processess that we usually do not think about the essential role it plays" (p. 3).

Metaphorical thinking provides an open window into the way one sees the world. Tuning into what students were saying metaphorically gave me insight into the students' understanding and background knowledge. Little education takes place with decontextualized instruction or learning situations that are foreign; however, building on students' prior knowledge is essential to effective instruction with English learners. Building instruction around the metaphorical thinking of English learners is a way of tugging at the cultural and personal understanding a bilingual student brings to schooling.

Not only does metaphorical thinking provide insight, but its affirmation and development in the classroom makes for more powerful speaking and writing. I once heard a radio commentator calling for a new business in Washington, DC, for marketing the creation of metaphors. The sound of their power resonates throughout our nation's capitol with phrases like iron curtain, a thousand points of light, desert storm, and contract with America. There is power in creating images that paint emotionally packed pictures in people's minds. Evocative and persuasive language skillfully applies metaphors to poetry and prose alike. Affirming and developing metaphorical thinking, speaking, and writing in the classroom adds power to the students' ability to express themselves. Therefore, I decided to begin tugging at my students' metaphors. And as metaphors appeared in our classroom discussions, I planned to structure the focus of instruction around their metaphors.

One example of this took place during a discussion of Cherry's (1990) fabulous book on the Brazilian rainforests, *The Great Kapok Tree*. I was conferencing with a small group of students in Spanish. In the book, a tree sloth tries to persuade a man not to cut the kapok tree down. In our previous conference, I asked the group to find out what they could about tree sloths. Now they were sharing what they had researched: how the sloth slept 18 hours a day, how a newborn would cling to its mother with its claws for the first 6 months of its life; then how it would go to live in the canopy of the rainforest by itself. Then out of the blue, Adrianna looked at the illustration of the tree sloth and said, *"Tiene la cabeza de coco* [It has the head of a coconut]."

Delighted with this entreé into her way of seeing, I asked, *"¿Qué más tiene?* [What else does it have?]"

She immediately responded with, *"Tiene la nariz de chocolate."* And she provided her own English translation saying that . . . "It has a nose like a chocolate bar."

I continued to encourage this line of thinking with, *"¿Y algo más?* [And anything else?]"

At this point the entire group jumped in with all kinds of similes about the tree sloth, comparing its eyes to coffee beans, its smile to a banana, its body to a melon. . . . This led the group to compose an original song about the newly created fruit sloth:

La Perezoza de Fruta

La perezosa de Fruta, La perezosa de Fruta
Tiene la cabeza de coco
Que nunca se puede abrir.

La perezosa de fruta, la perezosa de fruta
tiene el cuerpo de sandía
igual que un melón.

La perezosa de fruta, la perezosa de fruta
tiene la nariz de chocolate
que me gustaría comer.

Coro:
La perezosa de fruta
tiene el cuerpo de fruta
todo el cuerpo de fruta
de la selva tropical.
Cha, cha, cha.

[English Translation:
The fruit sloth, the fruit sloth
It has the head of a coconut
that can never, ever be opened.

The fruit sloth, the fruit sloth
has the body of a watermelon
just like a ripe melon.

The fruit sloth, the fruit sloth
has a chocolate nose
that I would love to eat.

Chorus:
The fruit sloth
has a body of fruit
the entire body of fruit
from the tropical rainforest.
Cha, cha, cha.]

The group did not stop there, however. They continued composing in English a song about the life and habitat of the tree sloth:

The Sloth

The sloth moves very slow
slowly moves the sloth.
The little baby sloth
holds its mother with its claws.

The sloth moves very slow,
slowly moves the sloth.
When it is six months old
it finds a way to live alone.

The sloth moves very slow,
slowly moves the sloth.
High in the canopy
it moves from tree to tree.

Chorus:
The sloth moves very slow,
slowly moves the sloth,
as slow as it can be,
as slow as it can go.

The students did not stop at writing songs about the sloth in Spanish and English. The following day, each one brought in a kind of fruit or edible item to create an actual fruit sloth. It had a coconut head, coffee bean eyes, a chocolate candy bar nose, a banana for a mouth, a large papaya body, cucumber arms, and green chili peppers for claws. That afternoon, the entire class sang their praises of the sloth, and then we all shared in eating a share of our metaphorical sloth and celebrating the students' ingenuity.

The centerpiece of the whole event was a work of art, a children's literature selection. The students experienced a delightful mix of reading, responding, researching, writing, sharing, creating, and making music. Their imaginations completed the circuit of Rosenblatt's live-wire between a reader and a text. The meeting of their minds around a juicy story made for a more human curriculum. One observer of the students told me, "I know that you could not have made that up. This really did come from the kids." It was an organic experience of teaching and learning, a two-way path to interpretation.

CONCLUSION

Conventional methods for teaching reading and language arts follow a plan written in a guide by someone who has never met my students. Javier resisted learning passively. He was knowledgable but needed an invitation to demonstrate what he knew about the agriculture of turnips. Reader-response formed a theoretical basis for hearing him speak his mind. The students who formed a connection between a fantasy tale from Japan and the paintings of Diego Rivera saw something that the teacher did not see until they showed me. Adrianna, Pedro, and David explored the manifold meanings behind the bald eagle, not because they were assigned to generate a book report outlining characters and plot. They were caught up by a story and responded as only they knew how. Daniela became a bona fide composer, not when she was asked closed questions, but when she was asked, "What are you thinking?" And each one of the students worked at sophisticated nuances of meaning as they generated and played with metaphors in English and in Spanish.

The wonder of their thinking, the beauty of their poetry, and the lyric of their song gave substance to their English-language development and enriched their proficiency in Spanish. As active participants in their own learning, they took time to learn to express themselves, acquiring language with deep meaning for themselves. Additionally, it was downright engaging and fun to be a part of the creative process. Both of us, students and teacher, found ourselves anxiously looking forward to where our imaginations would take us each time we met for a literature conference. Their learning and their insights opened up my eyes to what they saw as they read. Their leads showed me how responsive teaching can tap live wires.

Responsive teaching recognizes that, "What you see, I can only half guess. . . ." When a child sees a book or a story that captures his or her imagination, the teacher needs to follow. Following the student's lead is not a mindless, hands-off approach to learning; it is much more collaborative. The teacher works with negotiating student groupings together around a text. The teacher's job also includes creating a learning environment stocked with quality books and materials for projects and research. Conferencing with small groups and individuals is a major focus of instruction, where the teacher is listening, taking notes, offering suggestions, facilitating discussion, and arguing a point. It is in the conference where the imagination is stirred and ideas are generated. Guessing what the students think, want, feel, know is no way to teach. Asking open-ended questions, the teacher invites the students to express their thoughts, feelings, and critiques. Open questions, open eyes, open minds. Being attentive to their metaphorical thinking opens windows into their hearts and minds. But the entire process does not happen in isolation. Responsive teaching is a shared experience of walking together.

What each of these students initially saw as they read, I could only half guess. But as we began to think and imagine together, they opened up their way of seeing to me so that our learning could be a creative process of walking together. Bilingual students think and speak in vivid metaphors that provide rich ground for constructing meaningful learning. Even so, this requires that the classroom be structured to listen for their responses, that questions be open to their imaginations, and that their cultural metaphors be tugged at so that walking together can take place along their paths to interpretation.

REFERENCES

Bartolomé, L. I. (1994). Beyond the methods fetish: Toward a humanizing pedagogy. *Harvard Educational Review*, 24(2), 182.

Bergman, I. (1960). *Introduction to four screenplays of Ingmar Bergman*. (L. Malmstrom & D. Kushner, Trans.). New York: Simon & Schuster.

Dewey, J. (1959). Schooling and society. In M. S. Dworkin (Ed.), *Classics in education #3. Dewey on Education* (pp. 54–55). New York: Teachers College Press.

Freire, P. (1985). *The politics of education: Culture, power and liberation*. Boston, MA: Bergin & Garvey.

Gallas, K. (1994). *The languages of learning: How children talk, write, dance, draw, and sing their understanding of the world*. New York: Teachers College Press.

Pugh, S. L., Hicks, J. W., Davis, M., Venstra, T. (1992). *Bridges: A teacher's guide to methaphorical thinking*. Urbana, IL: National Council of Teachers of English.

Ramirez, J. D. (1991). *The Ramirez report: Executive summary: Longitudinal study of structured English immersion strategy, early-exit and late-exit transitional bilingual education programs for language-minority children*. Washington, DC: US Department of Education.

Rosenblatt, L. (1978). *The reader, the text, and the poem: the transactional theory of the literary work*. Carbondale: Southern Illinois University Press.

Rosenblatt, L. (1986). "The aesthetic transaction." *Journal of Aesthetic Education, 20*(4), 274–279.

CHILDREN'S TEXTS

Cherry, L. (1990). *The great kapok tree*. New York: Harcourt, Brace.

Chief Seattle. (1991). *Brother eagle, sister sky*. (S. Jeffers, Illus.). New York: Dial.

Kimishima, K. (1989). "Ma Lien y el pincel mágico." [Ma Lien and the magic paintbrush]. *Lima naranja, limón*. New York, Macmillan Publishing Company.

Soto, G. (1990). *Baseball in april*. Orlando, FL: Harcourt Brace.

Winter, J., & Winter, J. (1991). *Diego*. New York: Scholastic.

PART III

Exploring Issues:
Content Area Applications

11

Scaffolding Urban Students' Initiations: Transactions in Reading Information Books in the Read-Aloud Curriculum Genre[1]

Christine C. Pappas
University of Illinois-Chicago

Anne Barry
Jungman Elementary School

EDITOR'S OVERVIEW

There are many initiations going on in Anne Barry's urban first-grade classroom. There is the initiation into new material, two information books on science topics. There are the opportunities of the students to initiate discussion through their comments, questions, and humor; these represent the advancing of their reading skills, including responses to texts. Especially significant are the initiations that Anne introduces and orchestrates in her collaboration with her students to redirect or expand the discussion and to promote her own curriculum agenda; in this case, penguins and geography.

These children are not passive. They eagerly participate in response to the text and in learning. Their comments and questions activate the response process, feeding information and clarifying understandings for each other. These openly

[1]This chapter is fully coauthored and is based on collaborative university–school teacher research supported by grants to Christine C. Pappas from the Center for Urban Educational Research and Development at the University of Illinois at Chicago and Spencer Foundation. The major aim of the project is to document and study teachers' inquiry into their efforts to move away from traditional, transmission-oriented teaching and learning characteristic of recitation and rote-like instruction as they take on more collaborative, interactive student- and meaning-centered literacy instructional approaches.

stated responses also serve to inform the teacher of the connections they are making and the status of their learning.

The establishing of an atmosphere of collaboration among the class members, children and teacher, empowers these children to become students in their own right. It also empowers them to give to the text as well as to take from it, enhancing their experience with it. The evidence here is that the experience is indeed lived-through, a reward for the teacher's careful and conscious efforts.

Consider the following:

1. *Review the examples of the illustrative discussions. Establish the teacher's discussion strategies. What is she accomplishing? How?*
2. *What is the nature of these students' collaboration with the teacher? With the text?*
3. *How are these students' responses to nonfiction parallel to and different from responses to fiction?*

Anne Barry has important literacy hopes and goals for her Mexican-American first graders. Because she wants her students first and foremost to become lifetime readers, she has made the everyday routine or curriculum genre[2] of reading aloud a range of good children's literature the centerpiece of her literacy program.

A striking feature of these daily read-alouds is the extent to which her students have opportunities to initiate their own responses to these books that Anne reads. Instead of her dominating the discussion of these texts through her initiations, questions, and comments,[3] Anne encourages them to introduce the topics of talk. In doing so, she orchestrates a dance—a very collaborative dance (Oyler, 1993; 1996)—so that her moves or contributions can then be contingently responsive to her students' efforts in the joint coconstruction of meanings (Wells, 1986; 1994; Wells & Chang-Wells, 1992). That is, the reading-aloud curriculum genre enacted in this classroom supports—scaffolds—these young readers as active agents of the reading process. Indeed, their initiations represent a variety of transactions, ways by which they have "lived-

---

[2]We are using *curriculum genre*, a term suggested by Christie (1987; 1989; 1993), to name the repeated activities or routines that teachers and students construct and establish in each classroom. In doing so, we are emphasizing the sociocultural characteristics of classroom life and the teaching–learning relationship. See Pappas (in press) for a recent explication of curriculum genres from an integrated language perspective on reading instruction.

[3]Thus, Anne is challenging traditional classroom discourse formats whereby teachers control talk through an IRE pattern. This is the sequence by which the teacher initiates, usually by asking a question (typically a pseudo-question, one for which the teacher already knows the answer [Ramirez, 1988]), by calling on a child; then the nominated student responds to this initiation or question posed by the teacher; and finally the teacher evaluates the correctness or appropriateness of what the student has said, before calling on the next child, and on and on (Cazden, 1988; Edwards & Mercer, 1987; Young, 1992). (Two useful recent reviews and accounts of studies that illustrate this kind of interactions and others in book reading of stories in classrooms are Dickinson & Smith [1994] and Martinez & Teale [1993].)

through" experiences with texts (Karolides, 1992; Rosenblatt, 1978). Viewing reading as a transactional process argues that meaning is both a bringing to and taking from a text; that meaning is created out of the interaction of the text and the reader in a particular social situation so that different interpretations are possible (Bruner, 1986).

Our aim in this chapter is to illustrate the nature of these student transactions and Anne's role in relationship to them during the reading of information books. We have focused on the reading aloud of information books because we believe that too frequently teachers, especially at the primary grades, tend to limit their reading to stories. Believing perhaps that information books are too hard for their students to read, or that children would not find information books very interesting and therefore wouldn't be motivated to read them, these teachers, we think, rely on unacknowledged assumptions about children's abilities and preferences regarding this genre of books that just may not be warranted.[4] It certainly isn't the case in Anne's classroom, for she reads lots of information books and her students find them engaging and are eager to read them.

Although transactions are usually thought of as being related to the reading of literary or fictional texts, we believe that reading as a transactional process is easily extended to the reader-text relationship that is evoked in the reading of a range of genres (see Pappas, Kiefer, & Levstik, 1995, for such an approach). Thus, by providing actual class-room discourse examples of her students' initiations during her reading of information books, we hope to show the kinds of transactions that are possible in the sharing books of this genre.[5]

As we have already indicated, Anne attempts to share the control of the discussion with her students so that their initiations—their questions and comments—about books are valued and count as important knowledge about, and valid responses to, these texts. We have drawn our examples from a reading-aloud session in February where Anne read from two information books that were related to the class's current thematic unit study on winter. Actually, she read all of the first book, *Penguins* (Barrett, 1991), and only just the beginning of the second book, *Animals in Winter* (Fisher, 1982), so we'll be concentrating mostly on the responses on the first book. Nevertheless, because the children's initia-tions were so rich and varied on this book and the start of the second, we can still easily portray the potentiality of transactions with informa-tion books with such a limited text source. Moreover, because we will be limiting our examination to just one session, we can better convey more clearly what Anne's and her students' Reading-Aloud curriculum genre is like.

---

[4] More discussion on this narrative as primary ideology can be found in Pappas (1991a; 1993a; 1993b).

[5] Oyler (1993) and Oyler and Barry (1993) provide many other examples of initiations as transactions to informational books.

The Reading of *Penguins*

Today, Anne has brought to the read-aloud area a globe, which she has placed on the window sill. She stands and holds the *Penguins* book up high so all the children, who sit on small chairs around her, can see. Example 11.1 shows the beginning of the session. (The format conventions of the discourse examples can be found in the appendix at the end of the chapter.)

EXAMPLE 11.1   PENGUINS

1. Anne: Yesterday I was telling . . about where penguins live. Now
                  . .
2. C1:   They live in the South Pole.
3. Anne: They live in the South Pole. We talked about it.
4. C2:   (***) at the end of the earth and the (***) fall down.
5. C3:   [making a rumbling sound, addressing C2] Watch out you don't fall down!
6. C4:   (*** ***) book is on Artamerica?
7. Anne: Antarctica, Antarctica.
8. C1:   It's very dark and the moonlight's there.
9. Anne: What does that mean?
10. C1:   It's very cold and . . .
11. Anne: It is very cold.

. . . . [Conversation continues about the South Pole and then the North Pole.]

12. Anne: What animal lives up here? [pointing to the North Pole on the globe]
13. C: Penguins (***).
14. Cs: #Polar bears.#
15. Anne: #Polar bears.#
16. C: And uh . . . Rudolph the Red Nose Reindeer?
17. Anne: Yes! Can you find the reindeer? [referring to another book in the bookcase nearby, which they had read previously]
18. C: [singing] Rudolph the Red Nose Reindeer . . .
. . . .

19. Anne: Who lives down here? [pointing with hand to the lower part of the globe—Antarctica, Australia, New Zealand, South Africa, South America]
20. Cs: The penguins.
21. Anne: Penguins live . . .

22. Cs: (*** ***)
23. Anne: They live in here. [pointing to the globe] The warm waters of Australia. They live . . .
24. C5:   (***) Batman (***).
25. C6:   Batman.
26. Cs: (*** ***)
27. Anne: Oh, yes . . . Okay.

This example represents the Preamble,[6] an optional element of the Reading-Aloud curriculum genre, but one that is frequently found in Anne's class discussions. The Preamble is that part of the routine/discourse where teachers try to connect the book to be read that day to previous curricular topics or instructional experiences and activities, or provide some kind of rationale or purpose for reading the book. Here, in line 1, Anne begins by relating the book to yesterday's talk of penguins. Right off, however, in line 2, a child offers an initiation to state that penguins live in the South Pole. Anne confirms this contribution and then three different children offer ideas. Although parts of the talk is inaudible, C2 (in line 4) talks about the end of the earth and something "fall[ing] down." C3 makes a joke of C2's response by warning him that he needs to watch that he doesn't fall down. This cross-discussion—sometimes quite playful—between peers without teacher mediation (Cazden, 1988; Lemke, 1990) is another feature of Anne's read-aloud discussions. That is, not all the talk by students is directly addressed to her. Then, C4 has a question (line 4) as to whether the book is about "Artamerica," and Anne follows up on this child's approximation with the conventional pronunciation of it. Another initiation occurs in line 8 where C1 makes a claim of expertise regarding Antarctica, which Anne then attempts to extend.

At line 12, Anne has her own initiation in terms of a question. Answers are elicited—"penguins" and then "polar bears"—the latter being a contribution that is simultaneously made by Anne and students (this is based on common knowledge from reading a previous book on polar bears). Then, a child (line 16) tentatively offers "Rudolph the Red Nose Reindeer." Anne enthusiastically accepts the reindeer part by referring to another book on reindeers (which they can easily see on a nearby book rack) that they had read previously. In line 18, a child tries to reassert the Rudolph Reindeer topic by singing the beginning of the familiar song, but Anne does not acknowledge such extension. An effort is also made on the part of the children to link Batman (lines 24–25 and maybe

---

[6]Since the Reading-Aloud curriculum genre is seen as a human, cultural activity that is socially structured (having a particular sequence of actions, and so forth), the talk or text being used to perform that activity is also structured (Hasan, 1995; Lemke, 1990; Martin, 1992). We are using Pappas's (1991b; in preparation) description of the structural elements of the Reading-Aloud curriculum genre to characterize the organization of Anne's classroom discourse.

26, which is inaudible) to this reading of a book on penguins, and Anne says, "Okay," but her acceptance of this connection is done quite tentatively.

Several points might be made so far about the kinds of talk in Anne's read-aloud sessions. First, students offer a range of initiations. They claim their expertise on a topic; they also feel comfortable to offer ideas that they aren't quite sure of ("Artamerica" and Rudolph the Red Nose Reindeer). And, Anne, besides providing her own initiations, contingently responds to their efforts, thereby extending their present understandings on the topic at hand and motivating them to contribute their meanings in further discussions. Second, students also make intertextual links in the classroom discourse; that is, they juxtapose other texts—other books, songs, movies, personal stories from their home and community, and so forth—to the text being read. According to Bloome (Bloome & Bailey, 1992; Bloome & Egan-Robertson, 1993), for these connections to be considered as instances of intertextuality, they must be proposed, recognized, acknowledged, and have social significance for the participants involved. Thus, the Rudolph Reindeer and the Batman texts here might be seen as possible, partial cases because Anne follows up only on the reindeer aspect in the former and has an unsure acceptance to the latter. However, as we will see later, these Rudolph and Batman proposals of intertextuality are not finished in this read-aloud session. Moreover, many other initiations-as-transactions will achieve the status of intertextual links. As children know more and more books and are encouraged to offer texts from their home and community to book discussions, these connections grow and grow during the year in Anne's read-alouds.

Example 11.2 begins the Book Presentation, an element that always occurs in the Reading-Aloud curriculum genre. Here is where teachers officially present the book to be read. Sometimes the Book Presentation can be simply stating the title (and the author and/or illustrator) of the book. Or, Book Presentation can be more complex or elaborated, which is frequently the case in Anne's class.

EXAMPLE 11.2   PENGUINS

Anne has raised the book up again, ready to read.

1. Cs: PENGUINS.
2. Anne: PENGUINS.
3. C1:   How 'bout *Winter*?
4. Anne: Well, we're gonna get to it. We have to finish that book, don't we?
5. C1:   #You didn't read it.#
6. C2:   #It's a really book?#
7. Anne: It's a what?
8. C2:   It's a really book.

9. Anne: It's a *really* book. You're right.
10. C3:   It's a real book.
11. Anne: It means it's . . (***). Tell me again what C2 said. C3 got it, too.
12. C2:   It's a real book!
13. Anne: Uh huh.
14. C3:   It's 'cause, it's 'cause . . .
15. Anne: Because what?
16. Cs: (*** ***)
17. Anne: It's a not a fantasy, it's not a pretend story . . .
18. C3:   It's a real one.
19. Anne: And are these real pictures?
20. Cs: Yes. (*** ***)
21. Anne: Yes, (*** ***) with a camera.
22. C1:   Like in the *Winter* book.
23. Anne: Like the *Winter* book. You're right.

Anne signals the onset of the Book Presentation by raising the book, but it is the children who initiate the talk (in line 1) with their reading of the title of the book, which Anne then repeats as confirmation. So, instead of the teacher always reading the titles, students here are given more opportunities to take on this role, especially now that these first graders have become more and more adept in reading from print. Another child-initiation occurs on line 3 and serves as an intertextual link by bringing up another book, *Winter*, which apparently the class had previously begun to read but had not finished.

Then in line 6, C2 tells what the genre of the book to be read is—"It's a really book." After asking C2 to repeat the initiation to make sure she heard it right (C1 and C2 had been talking at the same time), Anne enthusiastically responds to this contribution. She repeats the child's wording—"really book"—and then follows it with, "You're right." Anne frequently says, "You're right," to her students' responses (see also line 23), but it is important to underline its role in the kind of collaborative talk that these read-alouds represent. That is, "you're right" evaluations can frequently occur in teacher-dominated initiate–response–evaluation (IRE) sequences, but these function by telling the child that he or she has got the "right" answer that the teacher is looking for. That is not the case here because "you're right" is Anne's response to the child's initiation; it is her acceptance of the child's claim of expertise. In other words, in teacher-dominated IRE talk, the ownership of knowledge is reserved to the teacher—the student is just to parrot or reproduce according to the teacher's agenda—whereas in collaborative talk, students' ownership of knowledge is acknowledged and appreciated by Anne and other classmates.

C2's initiation is then sustained and extended by two other students, who clarify that it is a "real" book (a more conventional name for the genre), and by Anne, who first contrasts it with other nonreal genres and then questions them to consider if the pictures are also real. And, at the end of the example, another intertexual link to the *Winter* book is made by a child, which once more, Anne acknowledges.

The Book Presentation continued by Anne reading the title page, listing the author, and so forth (not provided here). Today, it also included Anne's focus on certain particular features of this book that many information books have, namely a Contents page and an Introduction. Example 11.3 starts with Anne talking about these characteristics, and then she begins the actual reading (the reading element of the Reading-Aloud curriculum genre), in which is embedded the recurring Portional Discussion—another element of the Reading-Aloud curriculum genre where teachers or students interrupt a teacher's reading of a text to discuss some portion of it. You will see that more of Anne's agenda is reflected in this example as she talks about the book features and then relates ideas in the text to the globe she has brought to the reading-aloud. Nonetheless, her students' voices will still be heard.

EXAMPLE 11.3   PENGUINS

1. Anne: Now, this book also has a table of contents. That word up there says "Contents." So you can find different pages by—if you want to find out about a kind of penguins, you look up the page number and follow it across. If you want to know about the introduction, I'm going to the very first because we have not looked at this book yet. This is on page #six#.
2. C2:   #Six.#
3. Anne: So what am I going to do? I'm going to . . .
4. C2:   Go to page six.
5. Anne: Guess what? The first page I come to is page #six#.
6. Cs: #Six.#
7. Anne: And this says, "Introduction." That means the beginning of the book.
8. C: We have to go through that (*** ***). You have to go to the end.
9. Anne: I don't go to the end of the book. I go to the beginning of the book. PENGUINS ARE BIRDS THAT LIVE IN THE WATER AND ON LAND. THEY CANNOT FLY, BUT THEY ARE EXCELLENT SWIMMERS. THERE ARE SEVERAL KINDS OF PENGUINS. THEY LIVE IN BOTH WARM AND COLD CLIMATES . . .
10. C1:   In the summer . .
11. Anne: They live in some places that are very very cold . . .
12. C2:   Or very hot.

13. Anne: Or very warm. Warm and kinda in between.
14. C2: Hot and cold.
15. C1: [addressing C2] Between hot and cold.
16. Anne: BUT {THEY LIVE} ONLY IN WATERS AND LANDS SOUTH OF THE EQUATOR. Would you like to know where the equator is?
17. Cs: Yeah.
18. Anne: Okay, the equator is right here [pointing to the globe]. It is a pretend—an imaginary line and it is right in the middle of—What do we call this whole thing?
19. C: A globe.
20. Anne: What do we call this?
21. Cs: Earth.
22. Anne: Earth. Okay, there is an imaginary line that goes all the way around. The penguins live anywhere south of the equator.
23. Cs: (*** ***)
24. Anne: Remember, Mr. L [principal] lives . . . he comes from a country that is very near. It's named for the equator, Ecuador.
25. C1: Ecuador?
26. Anne: Ecuador.
27. C1: Huh. Where is it?
28. Anne: It's uh . . . right here [pointing on the globe]. Right here.
29. C: (*** ***)
30. Anne: Not—not any more. When he was growing up.
31. Cs: Oh.
32. C: Now he lives in Chicago.
33. Anne: Now he lives in Chicago.

. . . .

34. Anne: PENGUINS SPEND MOST OF THEIR LIVES IN THE OCEANS . . .

As already noted, lines 1 through 12 concern the "Contents" and "Introduction" features of the book, and Anne's beginning to read the book. On line 10, C1 interrupts her reading with a sparse initiation having to do with summer that evokes a debate about whether penguins live "in both warm and cold climates," which had just been read from the text. In line 11, Anne, in response to the summer contribution, reiterates that penguins live in "very very cold [places]," to be followed by C2's assertion of "or very hot." Anne then reacts (in line 13) by trying to lessen C2's extreme by moving to "very warm" and then suggesting "warm and kinda in between [very cold and very hot]." In line 14, C2 is still insisting "hot and cold," which is followed up by a cross-discussion response addressed to C2 by C1, who reiterates Anne's earlier compromise—"between hot and cold."

Line 16 has Anne returning to reading the text and then her explanation and demonstration of the equator on the globe. She also (in line 24) ties this information about the equator to the fact that the principal comes from Ecuador. This is then followed up by C1's questions about Ecuador in line 25 and 27, which enables Anne to return to the globe to locate it. Another inaudible initiation is offered in line 29, but from Anne's response to it, it must have had to do with whether the principal lived there now, which is clarified by Anne and then by another child-initiation in line 32—"Now he lives in Chicago."

Thus, although Anne has directed most of the focus of discussion in this example, it is also clear that her students are not passively on the ride—they challenge her and the text about where penguins live, and they show their interest in the geography lesson Anne has provided by elaborating on the connection she has made between the concept of the equator and where the principal had lived when he was young.

Example 11.4 comes from the reading of "Looking at Penguins," which follows "Introduction" as the next section of *Penguins*. This second section consists of a 2-page display depicting a large penguin on the left-hand page, and on the right, a circular, two-dimensional excerpt of a globe map showing Antarctica in the center, with parts of Africa, South America, Australia, and New Zealand, along with various small islands, around it. Other smaller picture inserts are also included on these two pages, as well as short little text explanations of various features of penguins. Anne did not usually read these little bits of text verbatim, but instead pointed to pictures and paraphrased (in a reading voice) what was written.

Example 11.4 is a long transcript on this section of the book that is full of child-initiated transactions, so we can't comment on all of them. We concentrate on certain portions of the discussion to examine three facets of their responses: the nature of their predictions; the importance of the questions that students offered here; and, at the end, how the earlier Batman initiation (see Example 11.1) became reasserted as a full-fledged intertextual link.

EXAMPLE 11.4   PENGUINS

1. Anne: [referring to a picture of a king penguin] So here's a picture about—this penguin that you see here is called the king penguin.
2. C1:   Where's his crown?
3. C2:   Where's his crown at?
4. Anne: Does it look like he might have a crown?
5. C1:   Yeah. He's still a bird (*** ***).
6. Anne: Do you think so?

7. Anne: [Anne is paraphrasing information in small little segments of text telling about the king penguin] "Then the king penguin keeps the egg at his feet."
8. Cs: [laughter]
9. Anne: "And the warmth of his body incubates the egg."
10. C1:   And then the egg hatches and babies are born.
11. Anne: That's right.
12. C2:   A little baby born in Bethlehem.
13. C1:   It's gonna be white. And then it will become black a little bit.
14. Anne: You think? Yeah, good prediction. I like that. "Underneath his skin and his feathers is a layer of fat. The fat helps keep him warm."
15. C3:   Is he real fat?
16. Anne: Because he's—because he's a bird what do you think—what do you call this outside of (***)?
17. C4:   I know, I know, I know.
18. Anne: What do birds have?
19. C4:   Skin, feathers.
20. Anne: Skin and . . .
21. Cs: Feathers.
22. Anne: Yes, the feathers are attached for warmth.
23. C2:   #Do they have fur?#
24. Anne: (referring to a circular picture of a section of the globe, with Antarctica in the middle and parts of South America, Africa, Australia, New Zealand and various islands) #Here's where they live#—I don't—Do they have fur? They—they're not a mammal. Birds do not have fur.
25. C: They live at the South Pole.
26. Anne: Here's where they live.
27. C: The South Pole.
28. Anne: The South Pole.
29. C1:   In the middle. In the middle. In the middle. All the way down.
30. Anne: Here and anywhere up to the imaginary line the equator.
31. C: Like Africa?
32. Anne: Could be.
           . . . . [Many children talk about the fact that a teacher is from Africa, then a classmate, then many where they come from—Mexico, California, America.]
33. C: (*** ***)
34. Cs: (*** ***)
35. Anne: I'm going to go to C1 now. Okay, I know what you're saying now. The penguins on the Batman series. The characters—like characters in the story.

36. C1:   They're dressed up. They're not real.
37. Anne: That's right. They're dressed up.
38. C1:   It's a movie. HBO.
39. C2:   Batman.

Lines 10 and 13, we believe, are good examples of child-initiated
predictions. It is quite common to talk about predictions in the reading
of stories, usually encouraging children to hypothesize or suggest what
the story might be about, the actions characters are likely to take next,
or how the story is going to end, and so forth. However, predictions occur
in the reading of information books, too, but they are different in kind.
For example, the transactions offered by C1 reflect a process of development: First (in line 10), that the egg that is being incubated will be
"hatche[d] and babies are born"; and then (in line 13), that the baby will
be "white . . . then . . . will become black a little bit." Anne accepts and
names the latter idea of changing color of babies to adult as a prediction
(in line 14), and this is one of the ways that she explicitly signals to her
students that predictive thinking can be applied to reading of this genre,
too. In doing so, she also promotes her students' future input regarding
them.

Asking questions about the information presented in the text is
another important type of transaction in such a genre. C3's question (in
line 15), "Is he real fat?" and C2's (in line 23), "Do they have fur?" show
how these children are critical of what's being read. In the first case, the
child is trying to make sense of the fat being said of penguins, because
she seems to realize that this word doesn't seem to be akin to her
lifeworld meaning of it. In the second case, the child is attempting to
puzzle out the connections between warmth and feathers versus fur,
relative to birds and penguins. In each case, these question-transactions
enable Anne to respond contingently to their queries, thereby providing
more clarification and better understanding regarding these fundamental concepts.

As already indicated, the topic of Batman had been offered by children
at the beginning of the read-aloud session. At that time, there was only
a provisional, tentative response from Anne regarding it. However,
beginning line 33, the efforts to make Batman a solid intertextual
connection is finally achieved. Lines 33 and 34 are inaudible apparently
because so many children are trying to bring this topic up again. Finally,
in line 35, Anne begins to sort out their meanings by noting the penguins
on the Batman series. And then, to further clarify and extend what they
and Anne had been saying, C1 (in lines 36 and 38) makes the point that
these penguins, although relevant to the topic at hand, are "dressed up,"
"not real," are part of a movie text, and therefore definitely not the
penguins in the book that they have been reading and talking about.

Our last example from the *Penguins* book comes from the next section
of the book called Kinds of Penguins. Some might think that the reading
about the various species or kinds of penguins might be boring. However,

this didn't happen in this class. Even in Example 11.4 (the very beginning lines), when Anne had pointed out that the penguin portrayed on the left-hand page was a king penguin, two children jokingly responded by asking, "Where's his crown?"

In Example 11.5, as you will see, children continued in this vein. Students' initiations-as-transactions have a playfulness about them, but at the same time, these responses indicate that children are also picking up information about the salient and distinctive features of the species of penguins. This example begins with Anne reading the first part of this next section of the book, and then shows various excerpts of these transactions.

EXAMPLE 11.5   PENGUINS

1. Anne: THERE ARE AT LEAST 16 DIFFERENT SPECIES {OR} KINDS OF PENGUINS. MANY PEOPLE THINK OF PENGUINS AS BEING ANTARCTIC ANIMALS, BUT ONLY TWO SPECIES {OR TWO KINDS LIVE IN} THIS ICY CONTINENT—THE EMPEROR AND THE ADELIE. We already saw the king penguin. Now we're going to look at OTHER SPECIES LIVE AROUND ANTARCTICA.
2. Cs: [laughter]
3. Anne: {THEY ARE} FOUND IN AUSTRALIA, NEW ZEALAND, SOUTH AMERICA.
4. C1:   And South Pole.
5. Anne: Okay, and the South Pole.
6. C2:   South Pole.
7. Anne: Here is the emperor right here [pointing to the picture on the left page of the book].
8. C3:   He's fat. He eats too much ice cream.
9. Anne: You think he eats a lot to be fat?
10. C4:   He eats a lot of fish.

. . . .

11. Anne: Now everybody's been real anxious. This is called rockhoppers.
12. Cs: [laughter] Rockhoppers.
13. Anne: Yes, rockhoppers. "He has a crest of yellow feathers."
14. Cs: [laughter]
15. Anne: "It is smaller than the other penguins and it has red eyes."
16. Cs: Ohhh.
17. Anne: "It breeds on the rocks of the coastlines."
18. C1:   He's a frog.
19. Anne: Oh. Here we go.

20. C1:   [laughter] He's a frog.

. . . .

21. Anne: Now this little penguin down here is very different. [referring to the chinstrap penguin in the picture] "He's keeping his little chicks warm." And I'm going to show you where he lives. "He lives in New Zealand and nearby islands." Find New Zealand.

22. Cs: [many children point to the globe, finding New Zealand] (*** ***) New Zealand.

23. C1:   How does he get across?

24. Anne: How do you think they get across?

25. C2:   (***) in the water.

26. Anne: In the water. How?

27. Cs: #They swim.#

28. C3   #In a big boat.#

29. Anne: A big boat?

30. Cs: [laughter]

31. Anne: Do they need a big boat?

32. Cs: No. (*** ***) [laughter]

33. Anne: Do you think they would take their babies before they were ready?

34. Cs: No. (*** ***)

35. C1:   Or they'd be crying, "Ohh, I want my mommy."

36. Cs: [laughter]

37. Anne: [referring to a picture in top, left side of book] Now these little—"this is called the little blue penguin."

38. Cs: [laughter]

39. Anne: "It's called the fairy penguin."

40. Cs: (*** ***) [laughter]

41. C1:   Fairy tail.

42. C2:   Oh if you put the nickel on his tail and then he get's it . . and and then he gives you nickels back?

43. Anne: I don't know.

44. Cs: [laughter]

. . . .

45. Anne: Right over here is another penguin called a macaroni penguin [referring to the top, right side picture]

46. Cs: [much laughter] Macaroni, macaroni.

47. C1:   Macaroni. Can we eat him if he's macaroni?

48. Anne: [much laughter]
& Cs:

It was clear in this example that the children thought these different penguins were hilarious because so many of their transactions were laughter. We have included their responses to five types of penguins. The first was the emperor penguin, which Anne mentioned and pointed out in the picture (in line 7). C2 remarks that, "he's fat," as well as offers the rationale of eating "too much ice cream" for such a state. Anne accepts this amusing idea by focusing on the "eating too much" aspect of C2's contribution. However, C4 make sure that they don't go too far on this ice cream hypothesis by stating the fact that "he eats a lot of fish." The second was the rockhoppers, which students appear to be quite inquisitive about because of the wonderful full-page picture of this penguin (which accounts for Anne's remark on line 11). Much laughter ensues around the name, and "ohhhs" are expressed as a response to the penguin's red eyes. Then, C1, presumably drawing on the "hopper" part of the penguin's name, suggests that "he's a frog." Anne accepts this as great fun with her remark, "here we go," which seems to give C1 license to reiterate this comic frog analogy.

Anne had gotten the children to predict, based on the picture (another full-page one), why the third type of penguin was called a "chinstrap" (note this discussion is not included in the example here), and then in line 21, Anne redirects the students back to the book by asking them once more to look at this picture. After the children's efforts to locate New Zealand on the globe are completed, C1 wants to know how the penguin gets across (line 23). Many mention swimming as a reasonable mode of transportation, but again a more humorous idea is put forth by C3—"a big boat." Then, when Anne asks them to consider their babies (presumably brought up in line 32, which was inaudible), C1 (in line 35) dramatizes the plight of these babies by crying, "Ohh, I want my mommy," which sends the children into much laughter.

The fourth penguin was the little blue penguin, also known as the fairy penguin (lines 37 and 39). This penguin is again met with great laughter, and then C2 suggests a quasi-riddle regarding it—"if you put the nickle on his tail . . . then he gives you nickles back." We are unsure about the source of this child's response, but it is important to note that the initiation centers around a particular physical characteristic (its tail), and is likely to be somehow connected to the fact that the fairy penguin is the smallest species of penguin. Then, the last penguin mentioned was the macaroni, which again led to much expressed delight. Children laughed and laughed as they repeated its name. And when a student asked, "Can we eat him if he's macaroni?" both Anne and the whole class once more began to laugh.

Thus, it is clear that the children found these various penguins extremely amusing and that their transactions reflected much playfulness. However, their responses also demonstrated that they seem to grasp the idea that different penguins are commonly named according to certain distinctive features of their physical appearance (chinstrap, emperor, fairy) or to a particular penguin's typical behavior (rockhopper).

Reading of *Animals in Winter*

The last example comes from the reading of the second book, *Animals in Winter*. We're going to skip the Book Presentation element, where the title, and so forth, were covered, to the beginning of the Reading part of the session. (There was no Preamble realized in sharing this book.) Anne had just read a little of the book when the children noted a picture of a deer. This spurred them to renew their efforts to initiate the Rudolph song text (see Example 11.1) into the present discussion. This time, however, their attempts were successful.

EXAMPLE 11.6   ANIMALS IN WINTER

1. Anne: BRRR! THE COLD TIME OF THE YEAR HAS COME.
             WINTER IS HERE!
2. C1:   Whoo. It's cold.
3. Anne: A HARE SITS VERY STILL IN THE SNOW. THE HARE
             MUST FIND FOOD AND STAY WARM IN WINTER.
             WINTER IS HARD FOR MANY ANIMALS.
4. C2:   Then they're going to die.
5. Cs: (*** ***)
6. Anne: C2 is right. [Anne has turned the page where there is a
             picture of a deer.]
7. C2   A reindeer.
8. C1:   A reindeer.
9. C3   A reindeer.
10. Cs: (*** ***) Rudolph deer . . #(*** ***)#
11 C3:   #That's a reindeer.# [addressing some Cs]
12. Anne: In the book, actually they say it's a deer. It reminds us of
             a reindeer. But there are many kinds . . .
13. C3:   How 'bout—how 'bout that's Rudolph Red Nose Reindeer
             with a nice (***) on his nose?
14. Anne: SNOW COVERS THE GROUND in this picture.
15. C1:   Maybe he . . Maybe he (*** ***).
16. Cs: Maybe (*** ***). [children begin to sing Rudolph the Red
             Nose Reindeer.]
17. Anne: Oh, you want to sing that song now? Real quick.
18. Cs: [Children sing the whole song. Anne sometimes chimes in
             on the parts in which some children seem to be unsure.]

When Anne turned the page in the book to show the picture of the deer, several children called out "reindeer." Then, in line 10, some say something about a "Rudolph deer," but C3 argues that Rudolph is a reindeer. Anne tries to negotiate this debate by explaining that the book had just said "deer," but also acknowledging that it would be reasonable if the picture reminded them of a reindeer. In line 13, C3 once again puts forth the idea of a particular reindeer—namely, Rudolph "with a nice . . . on his nose"—as a topic to talk about, although Anne tries to return to the text. Finally in line 16, quite a few of the children begin to sing the song, and when Anne finally gives explicit permission for them to sing it "now," they all chime in. Thus, the juxtaposing of the Rudolph song-text with the reading/discussing of the *Animals in Winter* text, which was initiated by the children, gets accomplished and has important social significance for all of the participants in the classroom.

SUMMARY

We want to summarize by making four interrelated points. First of all, there was a range of child initiations-as-transactions expressed in this session of the Reading-Aloud curriculum genre. This is not an accident, for Anne had not always read to her students this way. Anne has worked hard to encourage these initiations, which here served many functions for the students. Anne has argued that it has meant that she has had to take risks to give up control, to let it flow, to let the predictions, questions, intertextual links, and other kinds of initiations emerge in ongoing reading/discussion around books. But, because she has given children spaces to initiate and voice their responses to texts, these transactions serve a rich resource for assessing children's present understandings about the topics studied in the class and the ways in which various children are becoming members of the literacy club (Smith, 1988).

Second, how Anne responds to their initiations is important. Most of her contributions are contingently responsive to their efforts. They extend and sustain; they enable and empower. Even though the texts Anne has read are informational ones, and although one of Anne's purposes in reading these books is for children to learn about penguins and animals in winter, she does not believe that sheer accumulation of information by itself leads to knowledge. Her mediation—her scaffolding—encourages them to engage in texts in ways that promote critical and constructive thinking.

Third, although there were many student initiations, it is clear that Anne has her own educational goals that she brings to the reading-aloud sessions. She brought the globe so that she could have opportunities to integrate teaching geography and reading. She was also interested in her students' learning the content about the animals in the books, their being able to distinguish these books as texts of the information book genre, as well as their learning about certain features of the book language of this written genre, such as the contents and introduction. Thus, in collaborative curriculum genres, there is a negotiation of both teacher and student agendas. A collaborative style of teaching is the "search for the best fit" (Reyes, 1991).

Finally, underlying the collaborative talk that has been illustrated here is a perspective that views becoming literate as a cultural apprenticeship. For such a teaching-learning relationship to occur in the classroom, the discourse of curriculum genres has to privilege both teachers and students. This is hard work for teachers to accomplish after such a long educational tradition of behavioristic and transmission-oriented curriculum and teaching and learning. Because Anne is not from the children's language and cultural community, there is a constant challenge for her to try to understand her students' understandings—to learn from them about their ways with words (Heath, 1983). There is a common assumption that poor, urban Latino and other nonmainstream children like those in Anne's classroom, many of whom are also learning English as a second language, are somehow devoid of abilities and skills and suffer from a deficit of background experience. However, the examples provided here show that such a conception is completely erroneous. In Anne's classroom, children's participation in the Reading-Aloud curriculum genre demonstrate convincingly that they have ample language, cultural, and intellectual resources that can form the bases of their schooling. That is, if literacy instruction is organized so that teaching is more interactive and is more meaning-centered, these children can mobilize and share their funds of knowledge (Moll, 1992). They can predict, question, and connect a repertoire of texts or ways of constructing symbolic worlds learned both at their homes/communities and at school (Dyson, 1992; 1993), and teachers like Anne can then support, scaffold, and build on these present transactions to foster further empowerment in their literacy learning.

Invitation 11.1

To become more aware of the interactional patterns of reading-aloud sessions, collect some examples of the classroom discourse that is realized as teachers read children's literature—including information books—to their students. Transcribe as much as you can of your samples so that you can share them with others in your class. Now analyze and compare yours and your classmates' samples to determine the extent to which collaborative talk occurred. Did students have opportunities to initiate their own responses, questions, comments regarding the text? What kinds of responses did they offer? How did the teacher respond to those initiations? What ideas did the teacher provide to make the conversations about the book rich and meaningful for students? In other words, did the teacher scaffold students' understandings of text? Or, if the talk was not collaborative, why wasn't it realized? Can you point to specific teacher talk that prevented a co-construction of meanings between teacher and students?

Were there different patterns of interaction and response related to the genre or type of book—story, information book, poem, and so forth—being read?

Invitation 11.2

To better understand your own use of various discourse patterns in reading aloud, tape record your own discussions with students as you read books of different genres, including information books, to them. Again, as suggested in Invitation 11.1, transcribe as much as you can and analyze your strategies. To what extent were your interactions collaborative? Did you encourage and empower students to initiate their own ideas to these texts? How did you contingently respond to them? If your efforts in the sessions did not seem collaborative, can you determine why? What could you have done differently to promote collaboration? Finally, were there different patterns of interaction related to the genre of book read? Can you point to similarities and differences as they might affect students' learning language and learning through language?

APPENDIX: CONVENTIONS OF TRANSCRIPTION

Unit:	Usually corresponds to an independent clause with all dependent clauses related to it (complex clause or T-unit). Sometimes includes another independent clause if there is no drop of tone and was added without any pausing. Units here are punctuated as sentences.
Turn:	Includes all of a speaker's utterances/units.
Key for Speakers:	Anne is listed for teacher. *C, C1, C2,* and so forth are noted for individual children: *C* is used if a child's voice cannot be identified; *Cn*'s is used to identify particular children in a particular section of the transcript (so that *C1* or *C2*, etc., is not necessarily the same child throughout the whole transcript). Cs represents many children speaking simultaneously.
-	False starts or abandoned language replaced by new language structures.
..	Small/short pause within unit.
.. ..	Longer pause within unit.

< >	Uncertain words.
(***)	One word that is inaudible or impossible to transcribe.
(*** ***)	Longer stretches of language that are inaudible and impossible to transcribe.
Italics:	Emphasis.
# #	Overlapping language spoken by two or more speakers at a time.
CAPS	Actual reading of a book.
{ }	Teacher's miscue or modification of a text read.
" "	Paraphrasing of text spoken by a teacher in a reading voice.
[ ]	Identifies what is being referred to or gestured and other nonverbal contextual information.
....	Part of a transcript has been omitted.

REFERENCES

Bloome, D., & Bailey, F. (1992). Studying language and literacy through events, particularity, and intertextuality. In R. Beach, J. Green, M. Kamil, & T. Shanahan (Eds.), *Multiple disciplinary perspectives on language and literacy research* (pp. 181–210). Urbana, IL: National Conference on Research in English.

Bloome, D., & Egan-Robertson, A. (1993). The social construction of intertextuality in classroom reading and writing lessons. *Reading Research Quarterly, 28*, 305–333.

Bruner, J. S. (1986). *Actual minds, possible worlds*. Cambridge, MA: Harvard University Press.

Cazden, C. B. (1988). *Classroom discourse: The language of teaching and learning*. Portsmouth, NH: Heinemann.

Christie, F. (1987). The morning news genre: Using a functional grammar to illuminate educational issues. *Australian Review of Applied Linguistics, 10*, 182–198.

Christie, F. (1989). Language development in education. In R. Hasan & J. R. Martin (Eds.), *Language development: Learning language, learning culture* (pp. 152–198). Norwood, NJ: Ablex.

Christie, F. (1993). Curriculum genres: Planning of effective teaching. In B. Cope & M. Kalantzis (Eds.), *The powers of literacy: A genre approach to teaching writing* (pp. 154–178). Pittsburgh, PA: University of Pittsburgh Press.

Dickinson, D. K., & Smith, M. A. (1994). Long-term effects of preschool teachers' book readings on low-income children's vocabulary and story comprehension. *Reading Research Quarterly, 29*, 104–122.

Dyson, A. H. (1992). *Multiple worlds of child writers: Friends learning to write*. New York: Teachers College Press.

Dyson, A. H. (1993). *Social worlds of children learning to write in an urban primary school*. New York: Teachers College Press.

Edwards, D., & Mercer, N. (1987). *Common knowledge: The development of understanding in the classroom*. London: Routledge.

Hasan, R. (1995). The conception of context in text. In P. H. Fries & M. Gregory (Eds.), *Discourse in society: Systemic functional perspectives* (pp. 183–283). Norwood, NJ: Ablex.

Heath, S. B. (1983). *Ways with words: Language, life, and work in communities and classrooms*. Cambridge, England: Cambridge University Press.

Karolides, N. J. (1992). The transactional theory of literature. In N. J. Karolides (Ed.), *Reader response in the classroom: Evoking and interpreting meaning in literature* (pp. 21–32). White Plains, NY: Longman.

Lemke, J. L. (1990). *Talking science: Language, learning, and values*. Norwood, NJ: Ablex.

Martin, J. M. (1992). *English text: System and structure*. Philadelphia: John Benjamins.

Martinez, M., & Teale, W. (1993). Teacher storybook reading style: A comparison of six teachers. *Research in the Teaching of English, 27,* 175–199.

Moll, L. C. (1992). Literacy research in community and classrooms: A sociocultural approach. In R. Beach, J. L. Green, M. L. Kamil, & T. Shanahan (Eds.), *Multidisciplinary perspectives on literacy research* (pp. 211–244). Urbana, IL: National Conference on Research in English.

Oyler, C. J. (1993). *Sharing authority in an urban first grade: Becoming literate, becoming bold*. Unpublished doctoral dissertation, University of Illinois, Chicago.

Oyler, C. J. (1996). *Making room for students: Sharing teacher authority in room 104*. New York: Teachers College Press.

Oyler, C. J., & Barry, A. (1993, December). *Urban first graders' intertextual connections around informational books in the collaborative talk during teacher-led read-alouds*. Paper presented at National Reading Conference, Charleston, South Carolina.

Pappas, C. C. (1991a). Fostering full access to literacy by including information books. *Language Arts, 68,* 444–462.

Pappas, C. C. (1991b, April). *The reading-aloud curriculum genre: Book genre and teacher variation*. Paper presented at the annual meeting of the American Educational Research Association, Chicago, IL.

Pappas, C. C. (1993a). Is narrative primary? Some insights from kindergarteners' pretend readings of stories and information books. *JRB: A Journal of Literacy, 25,* 97–129.

Pappas, C. C. (1993b). Questioning our ideologies about narrative and learning: Response to Egan. *Linguistics and Education, 5,* 157–164.

Pappas, C. C. (in press). Reading instruction in an integrated language perspective: Collaborative interaction in classroom curriculum genres. In S. Stahl & D. A. Hayes (Eds.), *Instructional models in reading*. Mahwah, NJ: Lawrence Erlbaum Associates.

Pappas, C. C. (in preparation). *Learning written genres: A socio-semiotic perspective*. Cresskill, NJ: Hampton Press.

Pappas, C. C., Kiefer, B. Z., & Levstik, L. S. (1995). *An integrated language perspective in the elementary school: Theory into action*. White Plains, NY: Longman.

Ramirez, A. (1988). Analyzing speech acts. In J. L. Green & J. O. Harker (Eds.), *Multiple perspective analyses of classroom discourse* (pp. 135–163). Norwood, NJ: Ablex.

Reyes, M. de la Luz. (1991). A process approach to literacy instruction for Spanish-speaking students: In search of a best fit. In E. F. Heibert (Ed.), *Literacy for a diverse society: Perspectives, practices, and policies* (pp. 157–171). New York: Teachers College Press.

Rosenblatt, L. M. (1978). *The reader, the text, the poem: The transactional theory of the literary work*. Carbondale: Southern Illinois University Press.

Smith, F. (1988). *Joining the literacy club*. Portsmouth, NH: Heinemann.

Wells, G. (1986). *The meaning makers: Children learning language and using language to learn*. Portsmouth, NH: Heinemann.

Wells, G. (1994, April). *Discourse as tool in the activity of learning and teaching*. Paper presented at the American Educational Research Association, New Orleans, LA.

Wells, G., & Chang-Wells, G. L. (1992). *Constructing knowledge together: Classrooms as centers of inquiry and literacy*. Portsmouth, NH: Heinemann.

Young, R. (1992). *Critical theory and classroom talk*. Clevedon, England: Multilingual Matters.

CHILDREN'S TEXTS

Barrett, N. (1991). *Penguins*. New York: Franklin Watts.
Fisher, R. (1982). *Animals in winter*. New York: National Geographical Society.

12

Sharing the Responses of Readers: An Interdisciplinary Pumpkin Unit in the First Grade

Alan Dean
Macy McClaugherty Elementary School

Robert Small
Radford University

EDITOR'S OVERVIEW

In contrast to the primary status of fiction in school curricula to the near exclusion of nonfiction except in teaching content areas, Alan Dean and Robert Small contend that nonfiction may be more popular with young readers than is recognized by elementary school teachers, particularly those who teach primary grades. Because nonfiction is read with enjoyment and enthusiasm, using it can add excitement and intensity to school curricula.

Teaching nonfiction as literature, using a response approach, works. They prove this in Alan Dean's first-grade classroom in a pre-Halloween study of pumpkins—which did begin in part with carving jack-o'-lanterns, but did not end there. He combines lessons in science and arithmetic with responding to a nonfiction story of the life cycle of a pumpkin.

As he reads, Dean draws out his students' responses: questions to bring out their knowledge and expand their understanding, surprises and remarks to evoke their transactions. Creating individual booklets of the pumpkin's life cycle was the follow-up activity. Enthusiasm is evident from start to finish. The authors argue that the response apporach avoids the "boring and repetitious telling of the one right way" in favor of "a new discovery" for the students and the teacher. For the teacher, that discovery is based on the recognition that the students are different from each other and different from last year's students.

Consider the following:

1. Review the discussion in chapter 1 about stance; that is, the aesthetic–efferent continuum. In this context describe Alan Dean's teaching strategy.

2. *In the same vein, reflect on the responses of the students. What is their meaning mix?*

3. *In what ways can nonfiction find its place in your classroom in traditional (e.g., science and social studies) and nontraditional contexts?*

Far too many teachers of literature—and, therefore, readers of literature—believe that reading is a passive act. In that view, a reader opens a book as one might open a package, reaches down into it, and pulls out what the author put there. Therefore, some readers who are careful and perceptive get most or all of what is there to get and get it more or less accurately. Others do not. But all are mining for the gold that the author has deposited, all that and nothing but that. More than 50 years ago, Rosenblatt published *Literature as Exploration* (1938) in which she presented to teachers of literature a concept that is still not understood by many of us. In that book, Rosenblatt urged us not to think of the reading of literature in that way. Rather, she said, when a piece of literature is successful for a reader, that success comes from the fact that the reader brings to the selection all that he or she is and has experienced. When the reading is successful, a merger, a mingling of reader and work occurs. From that amalgam comes a new creation that never has been and never will be duplicated because it contains the unique qualities of the single reader. As she put it:

> The process of understanding a work implies a recreation of it, an attempt to grasp completely all the sensations and concepts through which the author seeks to convey the qualities of his sense of life. Each of us must make a new synthesis of these elements with his own nature, but it is essential that he assimilate those elements of experience which the author has actually presented. (1976, p. 133)

When we and our students read a recent work of nonfiction like Judith St. George's award-winning *The White House: Cornerstone of a Nation* (1990) or *Malcolm X: A Voice for Black America*, by Arthur Diamond (1994), our response is uniquely our own. We bring to our reading everything that we know and everything that we have experienced. As we respond to St. George's words about the White House, to Diamond's story of the life of Malcom X, we are continually creating our own stories. We may have been in a house like the one in which most of our Presidents lived; so we bring to the history of the White House that insight. We may have known someone we think is like Malcolm X; so we understand him in that light. On the other hand, another of our students may bring a different house, a different Malcolm. We all, students and teacher, bring to the reading of such so-called nonfiction our own experiences, beliefs, and prejudices. And so we create somewhat different works of our own as we read the story of the White House, the story of the civil rights activist. That individuality of response is the real glory of literature, including nonfiction, and probably the reason why so many people of all ages like to discuss literature, even if the only literature they have to discuss is soap operas, movies, and the nonfiction of the nightly news.

In *The Reader, the Text, and the Poem* (1978), Rosenblatt used the term *transaction* for the type of merging of text and reader that she saw as the essence of response. She defined transaction as "an on-going process in which the elements or factors are . . . aspects of a total situation, each conditioned by and conditioning the others" (p. 17). She went on to say, "What is perceived involves both the perceiver's contribution and the stimulus" (p. 19). When a transaction is taking place, the author and his or her intentions become unimportant: "The relation with the author becomes a transaction between the reader and the author's text. The transaction is between the reader and the direction he senses the text is leading" (p. 21). As we explain later, we believe that that transaction is every bit as much a relationship between reader and text in the literary genre usually termed nonfiction as it is in poems, stories, novels.

Rosenblatt is careful to tell us that there are responses that are true to the work of literature and responses that are just plain wrong. A good example of wrong reading appears in Squire's (1964) early study of response to literature. One of his students misread the word *musician* as *magician* and interpreted the story as about magic rather than music. Such a misreading, although seemingly superficial, is actually profound. The text might have presented a person for whom music was an all-consuming part of life. Although the young reader who read "magician" for "musician" could have concluded that magic was all-consuming, that it was worth a life of devotion, that it could inspire others with wonder, the text said nothing about magic. Other, more profound misreadings that, for example, assign value where no value is meant to be assigned, destroy the relationship between text and reader that Rosenblatt has shown us to be at the crux of response.

The creation that results from the merger of reader and work must be true to the work, just as it must be true to the reader. The work of literature is not reduced to a trivial part of the interaction. There is, therefore, potentially an infinity of valid creations; but there is also potentially an infinity of nonvalid creations. Let us try to represent that idea graphically, using an idea suggested by a friend who teaches philosophy. Suppose we put a set of dots on a blackboard, using a ruler to make them as much as possible in a straight line, placing one every inch or two apart. Then we asked someone to draw a line connecting them. Most people would probably draw a straight line through them. Consider, however, the fact that a curving line sweeping up through one and then down through the next and so forth also connects them, as does a jagged line going sharply up, then sharply down. There are, in fact, an infinite number of lines that connect those dots, all valid. Consider also a line that connects the first two and then wanders off down the board not meeting several, then darts back to touch the last dot. Valid? Not at all—although, if the line went on long enough, it might eventually wind its way back to those dots, which suggests that no interpretation can be said with final assurance to be, ultimately, a wrong one.

Still, truth to the literary work, like truth to the dots, is essential to response; but, after one's own discovery, the excitement of literature comes from the very diversity of valid responses. Although there may be a mild satisfaction in finding that a friend who has read a novel that you just finished agrees in every way with what you say about that novel, such a discussion is ultimately dull. What do you say to each other? "You're right." "I agree." Such a discussion is dull among friends; it is even duller in a class. Much more interesting is a discussion with someone who has seen the book differently, drawn different conclusions, found different insights. An argument may result, of course; but those readers will go away with new thoughts and new ideas.

READING LITERATURE

The reason that we teach literature, therefore, should not be that we give to students the one true interpretation. Such singularity does not really exist, although literature teachers have often acted as if it does. They have told us what Shakespeare meant to say about the lust for power in *Macbeth* and what Natalie Babbitt's message was in *Tuck Everlasting*. Instead of posing as authorities, teachers of literature should make possible a sharing of their students' personal responses, valid, semivalid, and erroneous. In that sharing, the readers can learn from each other; reconsider what they found in the book; keep, modify, or reject parts of their own responses; and go away to rethink their reactions.

It is not important or even desirable that student readers agree with the teacher's view of the work or with that of critics or textbook editors. What is important is that they share their responses, consider with respect the responses of the other readers, and think seriously about the entire array of reactions that they have encountered in the class. Although, as teachers, we might want to help our students to correct responses that are pretty clearly not true to the work by pointing out those errors, in fact, if a false interpretation or two slips through now and then, no great harm has been done. If the student who holds that probably false idea enjoyed the reading and discussing of the work of literature, he or she will probably go back to it later and, as a more mature reader, discover new, more relevant meanings. Or perhaps not. What, one wonders, happened to that reader who took the word *musician* to be *magician*? Was her life destroyed? Or did she value magic and magicians more than she might otherwise have? And was she worse for that? David Copperfield would surely argue otherwise.

Scholars themselves do not agree about what many works of literature mean. If it were not possible for even the best informed of us to disagree, there would not be a role for scholars. The Shakespeare section of any library makes diversity of view plain. He wrote in the 17th century. Yet, critics and scholars have been telling us what his plays mean ever since he wrote them; and, although each scholar may think he or she has it, just ask scholars who disagree.

From our own experience, we should know that there is not one, true meaning for a work of literature. Indeed, we sometimes disagree with ourselves. Rereading a piece of literature after several years have passed often provides that experience. For example, we have read Katherine Paterson's Newbery Award-winning novel, *Bridge to Terabithia*, several times since it was published in 1978. As we have grown older and changed, our responses to that novel have changed. Because we are not the same people we were 10 years ago, or even 2 years ago, we are not the same readers. Our reading of the novel is not necessarily better or wiser than it was when we first encountered the novel, but it is different.

And we know that readers bring to a work of literature, poem, essay, novel, history, or science, all that they are and have been. The children in the study that follows have begun their lives in a very rural, mountainous county deep in the southwestern part of Virginia. They have lived all their lives in a small town or in the country on farms. Many of them come to their school on school buses from rather isolated homes. They may see only the members of their own families from the time they step down from the school bus until the moment in the morning when they greet their school friends as they step back onto that school bus. What they bring to the works of nonfiction that they will read in their first-grade class will be very different from what a student in the urban center of Richmond or in an affluent Northern Virginia suburb of Washington, DC, might bring. The important point to remember, as Rosenblatt reminded us, is that their responses, although they know pumpkins in a very different way from their peers in that Northern Virginia suburb, are their own, wonderfully valid, although no more or less valid than those of a child who has only known pumpkins on the counter at a city market.

NONFICTION

In this chapter, we take a look at response to a type of literature, nonfiction, that is often overlooked in discussions of response, possibly because the name we use for the genre, that is, *nonfiction*, says that it is not fiction but does not state what its characteristics are. As Small (1992) wrote, "It is a 'non' something. It is as if poetry were called 'non-prose,' or drama, 'non-novel,' or you or I were termed 'non-turtles'" (p. 3). In *Using Nonfiction Trade Books in the Elementary Classroom: From Ants to Zeppelins*, Russell Freedman (1992) made the following comment:

> Someone else has said that fiction is a pack of lies in pursuit of the truth. As a corollary, I suppose you could say that nonfiction is a pack of facts in pursuit of truth. Unfortunately, facts can't always be trusted. Facts can be unreliable, misleading, ambiguous, or slippery. (p. 2)

This avoidance of nonfiction when selecting literature probably also stems from the fact that few of us have had an opportunity to study nonfiction as literature. Few English departments offer courses in nonfiction, certainly not in numbers approaching those devoted to the novel, the short story, drama, and major authors. When we do study works of nonfiction, we usually do so because some major writer of other genres happened to pen an essay, not because it represents a literary type with a history, with forms, with techniques used by successful writers.

Small (1992) pointed out that,

A few writers of non-fiction have sought a better term. Some have suggested 'informational prose,' but that name—besides suggesting writing of exhausting dreariness—really only applies to one small part of what is generally lumped under 'nonfiction': the presentation of mere information. Recently, at an IRA Conference, the term "faction" received a good deal of praise. That term, however, though intriguing, suggests that everything in every work is pure fact despite the fact (pun intended) that many types of nonfiction contain much that is speculative, judgmental, metaphoric, and narrative. (p. 3)

Indeed, in a study of what elementary school teachers actually do read aloud to their students, the researchers found not one work of nonfiction (Hoffman, Roser, & Battle, 1993). Yet, despite the fact that we as teachers tend to ignore it and it has such an uninteresting label, many young readers select nonfiction in place of the traditional stories that have been used to teach and promote reading. In their book, *Nonfiction for Young Adults: From Delight to Wisdom* (1990), Carter and Abrahamson documented the interest that young readers have in books. Indeed, they found in their research that many students who have the necessary skills to read say that they do not read. As Carter and Abrahamson explored this type of student, they discovered that many such students do read; they read nonfiction but do not report such an activity as reading. Why? Carter and Abrahamson suggest that, because such material is not a short story or a novel, these young readers see such reading as not really reading; and these students, it seems clear, have internalized that notion from the fact that their teachers emphasize fiction, poetry, and so forth and ignore nonfiction.

Nonfiction, then, despite the negative quality of its name, may well be the most popular form of literature for today's young readers. Offering great diversity of subject, approach, viewpoint, and style, the body of nonfiction available for young readers is rich and provides something for every student. Frances Dowd (1992), for example, in an article reprinted in *Using Nonfiction Trade Books in the Elementary Classroom*, pointed out,

Examining the trends and evaluative criteria of recent children's informational books indicates that writers are addressing a broad range of subjects—from the making of a crayon, to coral reefs, to bug collecting.

Considering this diversity, as well as the manner in which authors are treating nonfiction, it is not surprising that this literature is extremely popular with children and that it is experiencing a sort of renaissance. (p. 43)

By familiarizing ourselves with our students' interests and with the nonfiction that is available, we can introduce into the literature program an excitement and intensity that is often lacking for students who want to read about the real world of their interests, problems, and concerns.

FIRST GRADERS

Although there may be a slight movement in middle schools and high schools to recognize that "nonfiction could be written or read for pleasure" (Duthie, 1994, p. 588), that movement is seen less in elementary schools, certainly in the primary grades. Moss (1995) explained this lack of use in elementary schools as having three principal causes:

* First, in the past, a good deal of children's nonfiction was of mediocre quality. It was often characterized by inaccuracy, pedestrian writing, and minimal visual appeal.

* Second, in years past, children's reading interests did not typically include nonfiction; only recently have children expressed preferences for this genre.

* Finally, nonfiction has for many years been the "stepchild" of children's literature. Works of nonfiction were largely ignored: they received little recognition from the larger literary community. (p. 122)

Duthie (1994) began her article in a recent issue of *Language Arts* by stating, "In many elementary classrooms, nonfiction is used exclusively in content areas to generate learning of specific topics" (p. 588). In her study of nonfiction, Duthie approached the works of literature that her students read as well as the writing of nonfiction as a genre unit. The students brainstormed ideas about nonfiction, wrote about it, and wrote their own works. Duthie (1994), Pappas (1991), Smith (1992), Robb (1994), Mallett (1992), and others have each demonstrated that nonfiction can be read with enjoyment and enthusiasm by children in the primary grades and that a response approach works well with such material.

Moss (1995), in fact, argued that nonfiction is especially well suited to being read aloud to children. She supported this contention with five points about the nature of nonfiction:

* First, it expands children's knowledge, thereby contributing to schema development, a critical factor in comprehension.

* Second, nonfiction read-alouds sensitize children to the patterns of exposition.

* Third, nonfiction read-alouds provide excellent tie-ins to various curricular areas.

* Fourth, nonfiction read-alouds can promote personal growth and move children to social response.

* Finally, and most importantly, reading nonfiction aloud whets children's appetites for information, thus leading to silent, independent reading of this genre. (pp. 122–123)

THE FOCUS OF THIS STUDY

In the study that we carried out, the emphasis was on reading nonfiction as literature but not as a specialized genre. It seemed clear to us that first-graders do not make absolute distinctions between fiction and nonfiction. Information coming from stories is often as much fact to them as the facts they learn elsewhere in the curriculum, in mathematics and science, for example. In this belief, they seem intuitively to recognize what Eisner (1985) and others have recently been telling us, that is, that all writers, poets, and historians make meaning out of the chaos of reality through observing, finding explanations, and reporting, what Eisner terms "aesthetic modes of knowing" (p. 23).

But it seemed important to us to begin reading nonfiction with young children as a natural part of the entire reading experience so that they will incorporate such books into their selections as books read at home, as they asked for books as presents, as they began the use of the public library. As Duthie (1994) concluded after completing her nonfiction unit with first graders:

> The children's reading, writing, and final comments convinced me that nonfiction can be made more accessible to young children. I am also convinced that language arts teachers must give nonfiction attention as a genre long before students are required to use it to generate learning in content areas. With understanding and tools, young children can grow to be excited, competent, creative readers and writers of nonfiction across all discipline areas. If we, as educators, are to prepare students for life-long learning, then early introduction and analysis of nonfiction as a genre is a necessary piece of that preparation. (p. 594)

PRE-READING

It is a fall day in late October, a few days before Halloween. As in most elementary classrooms across the country, the students in Alan's first-grade class are excited about the upcoming holiday. The class is one of three in a small rural elementary school in the foothills of the Appalachian mountains in Southwest Virginia. There are 22 students, 8 boys and 14 girls, all of whom come from either small farms or a town of 4,000. They are a homogeneous group as far as race and culture are concerned,

White and from an Appalachian background; and about a fourth come from homes where college study, if not degrees, is characteristic of at least one parent. Also, about a fourth come from homes where parents are either merchants or professionals and where there is some degree of affluence. Each of the children has, since birth, been familiar with farms and farm animals, vegetable gardens and fall canning, and significant elements of country life.

In this unit, Alan chose to combine lessons in science and arithmetic with the reading of nonfiction about a key Halloween symbol, pumpkins. Bosma (1992) said of nonfiction science books, "Complex scientific concepts are clarified by capable authors. Trade books, therefore, can help students recognize causal relationships and analyze their own attitudes and ideas" (p. 51).

That passage describes Alan's goals for the unit, and he chose to follow a sequence suggested by Frank (1992) in "On the Road to Literacy: Pathways through Science Trade Books":

1. Explaining consists of interacting with a phenomenon and then articulating an explanation for this phenomenon prior to participating in learning experiences related to this phenomenon.

2. Experiencing consists of participating in learning experiences related to the phenomenon under study.

3. Evaluating, a third phase in the process of concept development, leads learners to reflect upon the path they have traveled. In this phase, learners review their initial explanations for the phenomenon under study and revise them in light of new understandings. (pp. 61–63)

He began by having his first-grade class weigh pumpkins, measure pumpkins, check to see if they would float in water, scoop seeds, carve pumpkins, count seeds, and graph seeds. On the day when we begin our analysis, he reviewed what they had learned about pumpkins from doing those things. The students seemed very interested and excited.

Invitation 12.1

Choose a nonfiction trade book to read with a group of students. Prior to beginning the reading, ask the students to list as many facts, beliefs, ideas, and attitudes as they can about the science topic of the book. Doing so will prepare them to think about the reading and related activities, and the list can also serve as a touchstone as the lesson progresses to determine what they are learning that is new or is different from their prior knowledge and beliefs.

Alan begins with a question: "Yesterday, what did we work with?"
Children together: "Pumpkins!"

They look a bit surprised that he should ask. Hilary gives Mary Anne a knowing look that says, "See, Mr. Dean can't remember as much as we do."

Alan: "Oh, that's right, we worked with pumpkins. Who can tell us the favorite of all the things we did with our pumpkins yesterday?"

He looks around the room expectantly.
Hilary raises her hand, waving it anxiously.

Alan: "Hilary, tell us something that you really liked doing with pumpkins."
Hilary, all smiles, pointing at the jack-o'-lanterns: "We carved them. We carved faces in them. I liked that!"
Alan: "All right! So did I! That's one of the things we did. We carved our pumpkins. What else did we do. Jennifer?"
Jennifer frowning intently: "We checked to see if they'd float."
Alan: "And did they float?" He raises his hands in a floating motion.
Children (together):   "Yeah! They floated."
Alan: "Okay. Now I don't remember. Did all four float?"
Children (together):   "Yeah! You remember."
Alan: "Sure. Now I remember. And what else happened?"
Benjamin raises his hand.
Alan: "Yes, Benjamin, what else did we do with the pumpkins?"
Benjamin: "We reached down inside and took out the seeds. I liked that. It was messy." He laughs. Several students wiggle and whisper, "Ugh!"
Alan: "All right! We scooped all the seeds out, and what would you like to do with those seeds today?"
A few children: "Eat 'em!"

They laugh. Others don't look as if they are sure they want to mess with the insides of pumpkins.

Alan: "Yup. We're going to eat some of them. But don't worry. I've toasted the seeds, each group's seeds."

He pauses, then asks,   "How many seeds were there?"
Several children: "Lots."

Alan: "Benjamin, do you think there were a hundred?"

Benjamin, looking worried: "I don't know. Maybe."

Alan laughs: "Well, Benjamin. I don't know either. So, I think we should count them. I think this afternoon we should have each group count their seeds. Remember those little pumpkins, those little paper pumpkins? Let's put those paper pumpkins on the chart to see how many seeds each group's pumpkin had. Wanta try that?"

RESPONDING TO THE STORY

Having gotten them interested in pumpkins as things to explore and wonder about, Alan explained:

I wanted them to enjoy reading about pumpkins and to respond to the story of pumpkins as told by the author and artist, Jeanne Titherington (1986), in *Pumpkin Pumpkin*. The book is basically nonfiction. It describes a boy planting pumpkin seeds and watching them grow to maturity, including one that becomes a really huge pumpkin. Then he carves the big pumpkin but saves some seeds for next year. It really tells the life cycle of a pumpkin, but it's a story the students can respond to with their own experiences with pumpkins, where they get theirs, how they carve them, that sort of thing.

Alan: "And right now, guess what I've found. I've found a book about—guess what?"

Children: "Pumpkins?"

They seem pretty sure where this is going.

Steven: "What else!"

Alan: "Right. And we're going to read it this morning."

Alan commented, "As we read, I asked the students questions designed to tap into their rural background. These students live in a very small town or in the country, and most of them have a vegetable garden or at least access to one."

Alan holds up the book so the children can see the first picture and
    reads: " 'Jamie planted a pumpkin seed.' And what do you see in the picture growing?"

Children: "Pumpkins!"

Alan turns the page and reads: " '. . . and the pumpkin seed grew a pumpkin plant.' Look at the pumpkin leaves in that picture. How many of you have ever grown pumpkin plants at home in your garden or have seen pumpkin plants growing in a garden?"

The children raise their hands and, jumping up and down, call out:
        "Me! Me! I have!"

Alan: "Me too. And what's this right here in the picture?"

Amanda: "A mole?" Several children laugh. Amanda looks distressed.

Allen: "Hey, Amanda, it does sorta look like a mole, and it lives in hole in the ground too. But it's bigger."

Joe calls out: "Groundhog."

Alan: "That's what it looks like to me. A groundhog." He pauses. "But how do they both look?"

Several children: "Surprised!"

Joe: "I'll bet that groundhog wasn't lookin' to see Jamie there."

Alan: "And how'd you think Jamie felt?"

Joe: "Well, I bet he didn't think there'd be that hog there either."

Alan: "I bet."

Alan explained:

We discussed how things grow and explored other plants that have flowers and fruit like a pumpkin. I was trying to relate the events in the story to their own knowledge and experiences with plants to help them see the story might be about more than just pumpkins, about how they felt about growing things, how they felt about pumpkins, especially at Halloween. The students were eager to share their experiences and shared what they knew about cucumbers and beans and other plants, but especially about pumpkins, as they listened to the story and looked at the pictures of the pumpkin beginning to form.

Alan: "Are pumpkins orange to begin with?"

Lewis: "No."

Alan, looking surprised: "No? What color are they?"

Children: "Green."

Len: "I saw one in the store yesterday that was part green. We didn't buy it. Who wants a green pumpkin on Halloween!" He looks scornful.

Alan tells Len: "Well, that's something to remember."

Then he turns the page and reads on: "'... and the pumpkin flower grew a pumpkin.' Look at that picture. It's a blue pumpkin. But what's that on the boy's head?"

Children, laughing: "A frog!"

Alan: "Now how do you suppose that got there. Would you like a frog on your head?"

Some children, laughing: "Ugh! No!"

Lewis: "I would." He looks proud of himself.

Alan laughs, turns the page, and reads: "'And the pumpkin grew ...'"
He asks, "What color is it now?"
Children: "Orange!"
Alan: "Yep, it's starting to turn orange. But do I see something in his shoe?"
Children, laughing: "A mouse."
Alan: "There sure are a lot of animals around these pumpkins. Do you think that's right? Are there lots of mice and frogs around?"
Lewis raises his hand: "Yeah. And turtles and lots of bugs."
Benjamin joins in: "My father has to put things, you know, traps and bug spray and stuff in his garden."
Alan: "That's something lots of people don't know."
He turns the page and reads: "'. . . and grew . . .' Look how big it is now," he says. "How big is the pumpkin compared to the boy?"
Amanda: "Very big?"
She holds up her hands as wide as she can.
Joe: "Lots bigger."
"Yeah!" Alan says. "And what's the boy doing with the pumpkin?"
Children, laughing: "He's sitting on it!"
Alan: "Did you ever sit on a pumpkin? I never have."
Several: "I have."
Alan: "I wonder what would happen if I sat on a pumpkin."
The children snicker.
Alan turns the page and reads: "'. . . and grew, until Jamie picked it.'" Then he asks, "Have any of you ever seen pumpkins this big?"
Some children: "Yeah, lots of times."
Other children: "No."
Alan: "Great! I never have. So how does this pumpkin compare to the pumpkins we carved yesterday?"
Children: "Bigger. It's bigger."
Alan turns the page and reads on in the book: "'Then Jamie scooped out the pumpkin pulp, carved a pumpkin face, and put it in the window. But . . . he saved six pumpkin seeds for planting in the spring.'" Then he asks, "What did we do yesterday?"
Children: "We did that."
Alan: "Yeah! We did all that yesterday. But look at the seeds in Jamie's hand."
Lewis: "One of 'em's falling down. Yeah, two, three of them."
Several others ask: "Can we save some to plant?"
Alan: "Well, I didn't roast them all."

RESPONDING THROUGH WRITING AND DRAWING

Alan explained:

> As a follow-up to reading and discussing *Pumpkin Pumpkin*, I guided
> students through making their own books that illustrated both the life
> cycle of a pumpkin plant and their own experiences with pumpkins. I gave
> each student a small blank book consisting of seven or eight pages. We
> then re-discussed the entire pumpkin process from planting pumpkin
> seeds through harvesting pumpkins.

Alan: "All right, now, you'll need to get your crayons out—and
           you'll need a pencil too for the title."

The students open their tables and rustle around looking for crayons
and pencils. Several begin to talk. "OK, let's get those crayons going."
The talking dies down.

After the students have their pencils and crayons ready, he continues:
           "You'll need a title for your book. Think about what you
           want the title to be, but be sure the title has the word
           pumpkin in it and write it on the front of your little book.
           You may have to write it fairly small to get it all in there."

After a pause while they struggle with writing their titles, he asks:
           "Has everyone gotten the title of the book?"
Children: "Yeah!"
Alan: "All right! Hold them up so we can all see."

They hold up their books, and Alan moves through the room, pointing
to each one and praising them. Then he sits back down.
    "Great job! Good titles! Now, open up your little books to the first page.
Yes, open the cover over to the first page on the inside." He pauses.
"Inside. Not the back of the cover. That's right."
    "Now, you remember Jamie. What was the first thing he did in
growing his pumpkin? Johnny?"

Johnny: "He got seeds."
Alan: "Right. So what goes on the first page?"
Lewis: "A seed."
Alan: "If you want to grow some pumpkins, would you only plant
           one seed?"
Johnny: "No, lots of seeds."
Alan: "Why?"
Johnny: "'Cause one might not grow."

Mary: "Should I draw Jamie and seeds?"

Alan: "Maybe you and seeds. Maybe how you felt when we read about Jamie and the seeds. Anything you want as long as the seeds are there. It's your book. Go!"

After they have drawn their seeds, he continues: "Now let's color our seeds. What color are pumpkin seeds?"

Susie: "Brown."

Alan: "Right, but you've got several brown crayons. What color do you plan to use?"

They hold up several different colors, but most choose a light brown.

He continues: "That very light brown one looks like seed color to me. I'd call it sort of tan."

They color for a minute, and then Alan says: "Let's turn the page. I know you're not all finished with your pumpkin seeds. That's fine. We'll come back, and you can finish your seeds. But let's turn the page."

When they all have turned to the next blank page, he continues: "After Jamie planted his seeds, what happened? Stephanie?"

Stephanie: "It grew into a plant."

Alan,   "All right! So on this page let's draw our pumpkin seeds underground. Anything else?"

Chris: "Jamie's had a little sprout."

Alan: "Great. Anything else?" When no one answers, he asks, "Is there anything else underground? When you dig in the dirt, do find anything else?"

Lewis: "Worms. You find worms."

Amanda: "I don't dig in the dirt. Why would anyone do that? Only boys would."

Several other girls agree.

Len: "I do. I find stones."

Alan: "There you go. Put in whatever you want. Just remember that sprout."

After they have finished drawing, he continues: "And now let's color those sprouts. Anyone have an idea for a color?"

Children: "Green."

Alan: "How about the dirt and the other things? Get those crayons going."

Invitation 12.2

*In small groups or with a class, consider how important the illus-
trations in reading were to understanding the topics being written
about. Take them to the library and have them gather a large
number of books on similar topics. Explore the use of illustrations
in nonfiction. Examine drawings and photographs, schematic
drawings, and impressionistic drawings. What does this picture
contribute to our understanding that isn't also in the words? For
example, Alan's students might have realized that the picture of the
seed sprouting underground was much clearer and immediate than
the lengthy description that the author would have had to include
of a sprouting seed.*

WHAT HAPPENED

And so the students retold the story of the growth of a pumpkin by
drawing a picture on each page of their books, illustrating their own
responses to and involvement with the story of Jamie and their own
stories of pumpkins. Alan explained:

> Since I was trying to combine a science lesson with enjoying and respond-
> ing to a story, as well as creating their own version of the story, as I said,
> I wanted to begin helping them see what you might call a cycle of nature.
> Later we talked again about other plants that have fruit and read a story,
> *Picking Apples & Pumpkins* by Amy and Richard Hutchings (1994), about
> a family visiting an orchard and pumpkin farm. Here again, we talked
> about picking apples and pumpkins. Most students had done both and so
> had lots of information and experiences to share. I thought this book would
> extend the story since the family returns home and makes an apple pie,
> so we talked about using things like pumpkins as jack-o'-lanterns and
> apples and pumpkins as pies.

Alan's intention in this lesson was, as he said, to combine a science
lesson about the life cycle of plants, a bit about gardens and garden
animals, some mathematics about weighing, floating, and counting,
with student response to a piece of nonfiction that draws on a genuine
interest of the students, Halloween. He also wanted to start the students
off in their education believing that they could talk about books, write
books, create books. Here is his assessment of what happened:

> Students' responses to both of these nonfiction books were amazing. So
> many of the books we read to primary students and they read to them-
> selves are fiction. I rarely get as many questions and as much relating of
> experiences from students after they read fiction as I heard from these

students after we read these two works of nonfiction. My students had so much previous knowledge and so many previous experiences with small animals and with the raising of vegetables that they couldn't contain their excitement and enthusiasm. They all wanted to tell about their experiences that were similar to those described in *Pumpkin Pumpkin* and *Picking Pumpkins & Apples*. I think the key to the excitement was their being able to add new knowledge to a knowledge base they already had.

When students made their own pumpkin books, they were able to express their previous knowledge along with their newly acquired knowledge. They were proud of their accomplishments.

I consider the lessons based on these two nonfiction books to be great successes since the students were able to develop a very strong, positive appreciation for nonfiction, not just as a source of information but also as a source of entertainment fairly closely related to their own lives and experiences.

OUR CONCLUSIONS

After the reading about pumpkins was finished, we agreed that the glory for teachers of literature from what is sometimes called *The Response Approach* is that, as teachers, we are not locked into a boring and repetitious telling of the one right way, an interpretation that they have told their students year after year. Rather, each reading we do together of a piece of literature, fiction or nonfiction, is a new discovery because we have changed and, more important, because our students who read the work with us are different people, different from the students in last year's class and different from each other. Nowhere else except in our classes are our students likely to be able to share their responses to what they have read and had read to them. We can, in the primary grades perhaps more than anywhere else, say to our students, "Reading is a personal thing; you are what reading is all about; look at pumpkins, what do they mean to you? Read about them in science. Read about them in mathematics. Read about them in a story. What is important is that you read about them. What is important is what you do with what you've read. Plant a seed. Carve a jack-o'-lantern. Write about what your family does on Halloween. Your response is what it is all about."

When we accept Rosenblatt's view of reading literature, we can bring our students together for sharing, for rethinking, for a trusting sharing of what works of literature mean, but also what those works mean to each of them. Providing that opportunity is, for us, the reason for teaching literature.

Alan took his class of 6-year-olds through a look at pumpkins, a topic in which, before Halloween, they had a high level of interest. He guided their response to a book about pumpkins, but he regularly helped them bring their own experiences and reactions to the book. Some students thought a frog on the head was disgusting. Others thought it might be funny. He asked them questions that tapped into their own lives as country and small-town residents. If he had been teaching the book in an urban setting, he would have looked to different sources—pots on window sills, perhaps, or grocery stores, or plastic pumpkins.

And he asked them to write—draw for these first graders for whom writing a title was still a major challenge—a book of their own about pumpkins, but also about their own reactions to the growing and carving of a pumpkin. Alan explained his rather directive approach to the writing assignment this way:

> In selecting this activity of making a booklet of the life cycle of a pumpkin plant, I wanted the students to come away with a specific understanding of what happens from seed germination until the pumpkin is picked. Most of my students had general knowledge of a pumpkin growing on some kind of plant, so I wanted to concentrate on their more newly acquired knowledge of a seed sprouting and growing into a huge vine. I thought the best way to do this, short of spending lots of time trying to grow a pumpkin plant, was to direct them through their look at growing things. My goal was that everyone would gain similar, specific knowledge of the growing process, rather than allowing students to be completely creative and coming away from the lesson with only vague ideas of pumpkin plants and plants in general. One of my goals in this lesson was to teach information about pumpkin plants specifically, and also how seeds sprout and grow into full-sized plants generally. Therefore, I wanted students to think about specific ideas through this guided lesson. The science part of the lesson was, therefore, pretty directive.

> However, when they laughed at the frog or found it disgusting, when they talked about their family's gardens or seeing pumpkins in supermarkets, they were responding as individuals. They were really uninhibited in that response. Remember, they laughed at me when I asked what would happen if I sat on a pumpkin.

> Their little books were really very different. Girls drew girls, of course, and boys drew boys. But the farm kids showed pumpkins growing in cornfields, mostly. The town kids drew what were clearly little vegetable gardens. Len even included what was clearly a picture of a market on one page in his book. It wasn't connected with the rest, but I understood. You remember, he was the town kid who talked about buying a pumpkin in a supermarket. So, I'd say they were responding as individuals who'd read a book about pumpkins, sticking to the facts—which, if I understand Rosenblatt, is important—but bringing themselves to the whole idea of growing, growing pumpkins and jack o'lanterns.

As Alan explains, their response to the science and mathematics part of the study, to the reading of the book *Pumpkin Pumpkin*, and to writing their own book was positive. As the class moved on to other topics, other books, other seasons, this look at pumpkins shaped their attitudes toward studying something, measuring something, reading about something, writing and drawing about something.

ACTIVITIES FOR USING
NONFICTION SCIENCE BOOKS

Teaching ideas for incorporating nonfiction science books into the elementary curriculum abound. Alan combined the reading of a book about growing pumpkins and turning them into jack-o'-lanterns with writing and drawing activities; science activities such as discussions of how plants grow, weighing the pumpkins, and considering their displacement of water as they floated in a tub; and mathematics activities such as counting seeds and measuring pumpkins. What follows is a small sample of other activities that might be used with science books in elementary classrooms. Other ideas can be found in the books and journals listed in the section at the end of this article titled "Other Sources of Nonfiction for Teachers."

Try This

Prior to the reading and related activities, ask each student to look for a topic that he or she would like to learn more about as the activities are carried out. Help each student to find such a topic. Take the students to the library and work with the librarian to find a book or books that provide additional information and show the students how to use the library to find out information and answers to questions. For example, Alan might have had a student who wanted to know more about what the new leaves of different plants look like.

Try This

After the reading of the nonfiction science books, ask the students to make a list of how the authors might have found out about the topics they wrote about. Consider the list together, using such questions as, "How hard would it be to gather all that information?" "Could I write a nonfiction book? Could I do that research?" "How much experience does the author have to have with the topic before starting the research?" "If I were going to write and illustrate a nonfiction book, what would it be about?" For example, Alan's students might have chosen such topics as horses and flowers, and might have decided that experiences with them would be very helpful but that some information, such as that about how a pumpkin seed grows underground, would have to come from some special research.

Try This

Divide the class into groups of five to eight and ask them to plan what they would put on a large picture on the wall to show what they now know about the science topic that is the subject of the reading and related activities. Tape large sheets of paper on the walls and boards of the classroom and assign each group a sheet. Before each student begins drawing and coloring his or her part of the picture, the group should have a plan that shows how the parts fit together and what understandings each part illustrates. Conclude with an art show to which parents and others are invited and during which each group explains what its picture illustrates. For example, Alan might have had a picture that showed the different roles that pumpkins can play in Halloween.

Try This

Divide the students into groups and ask each group to develop a short play in which some aspect of the science topic under study is illustrated. Be clear that mere statements of what has been learned do not make a play, that the play should show people involved with a topic. For example, Alan might have had a group that carried out plays illustrating planted plant growth (the plant played by a student), and so forth.

Try This

Ask each student to keep a list of important words that he or she has used as the reading and related activities have progressed. With students who are just learning to write, some help with spelling and letter formation may be helpful, although this may also be a place for invented spellings. If students are having problems deciding on what words to put on their lists, identify a few such words as they come up as ones that might be important. Then ask the students to pick a few words to illustrate by pictures or a story or other writing. Have them put these into small books. For example, Alan's students might have identified such words as *sprout*, *seed*, *size*.

Try This

Ask each student to identify one topic they know a lot about such as their favorite sport, animal, car, and so forth. Then ask each one to make a list of all of the words that he or she knows that relate to that topic. Then using a dictionary appropriate to the level of the class, explore what a dictionary would tell about those words and help each student to turn his or her word list into a simple specialized dictionary of words on that topic. For example, Alan's students might have picked topics such as horses and flowers and might have been able to use their increasing knowledge of the alphabet to arrange the words in alphabetical order, give their spelling, and provide a definition in everyday terms.

Try This

Ask the students to look at how authors of nonfiction arrange what they are presenting. Again, explore a number of works of nonfiction and list ways such as chronology, by size, by type, by function, by age, and so forth. Ask the students to consider a topic they might like to write about and illustrate, such as horses or flowers, and decide what way of organizing the presentation would best suit that topic. For example, Alan's students might have discovered that both of the books they read presented the information as a story, that is, used time to organize the nonfiction content. They might also have decided that the same information might have been presented by how pumpkins and apples are used or by a history of pumpkins.

REFERENCES

Bosma, B. (1992). The voice of learning: Teacher, child, and text. In E. B. Freeman & D. G. Person (Eds.), *Using nonfiction trade books in the elementary classroom: From ants to zeppelins* (pp. 46–54). Urbana, IL: National Council of Teachers of English.

Carter, B., & Abrahamson, R. F. (1990). *Nonfiction for young adults: From delight to wisdom*, Phoenix, AZ: The Oryx Press.

Diamond, A. (1994). *Malcolm X: A voice for Black America*. Springfield, NJ: Enslow Publishers, Inc.

Dowd, F. S. (1992). Trends and evaluative criteria of informational books for children. In E. B. Freeman & D. G. Person (Eds.), *Using nonfiction trade books in the elementary classroom: From ants to zeppelins* (pp. 34–43). Urbana, IL: National Council of Teachers of English.

Duthie, C. (1994). Nonfiction: A genre study for the primary classroom. *Language Arts, 71*, 588–595.

Eisner, E. (1985). Aesthetic modes of knowing. In E. Eisner (Ed.), *Learning and teaching the ways of knowing*, 84th Yearbook (pp. 23–36). Chicago, IL: National Society for the Study of Education.

Frank, M. S. (1992). On the road to literacy: Pathways through science trade books. In E. B. Freeman & D. G. Person (Eds.), *Using nonfiction trade books in the elementary classroom: From ants to zeppelins* (pp. 55–64). Urbana, IL: National Council of Teachers of English.

Freedman, R. (1992). Fact or fiction? In E. B. Freeman & D. G. Person (Eds.), *Using nonfiction trade books in the elementary classroom: From ants to zeppelins* (pp. 2–10). Urbana, IL: National Council of Teachers of English.

Freeman, E. B., & Person, D. G. (Eds.). (1992). *Using nonfiction trade books in the elementary classroom: From ants to zeppelins*. Urbana, IL: National Council of Teachers of English.

Hutchings, A., & Hutchings. R. (R. Hutchings, Photographer). (1994). *Picking apples & pumpkins*. New York: Scholastic.

Mallett, M. (1992). How long does a pig live? Making facts matter. *English-in-Education*, *26*, 26–31.

Moss, B. (1995). Using children's nonfiction tradebooks as read-alouds. *Language Arts*, *72*, 122–126.

Pappas, C. (1991). Fostering full access to literacy by including information books. *Language Arts*, *68*, 449–462.

Paterson, K. (1977). *Bridge to Terabithia*. New York: Avon.

Robb, L. (1994). Second graders read nonfiction: Investigating natural phenomena and disasters. *The New Advocate, 7*, 239–252.

Rosenblatt, L. (1976). *Literature as exploration* (3rd ed.). New York: Noble and Noble.

Rosenblatt, L. (1978). *The reader, the text, the poem: The transactional theory of the literary work*. Carbondale: Southern Illinois Press.

Squire, J. R. (1964). *The responses of adolescents while reading four short stories*. Urbana, IL: National Council of Teachers of English.

St. George, J. (1990). *The white house: Cornerstone of a nation*. New York: Putnam.

Small, R. (1992). Nonfiction and young readers. *Virginia English Bulletin, 42*, 3–15.

Smith, F. (1992). Reading the bear facts: Information books and learning in the primary classroom. *English-in-Education, 26* , 17–25.

Titherington, J. (1986). *Pumpkin pumpkin*. New York: Scholastic.

OTHER SOURCES
OF NONFICTION FOR TEACHERS

Anderson, P. M. (Ed.). (1994). *Reading and writing nonfiction*. *(New York State English Council Monographs)*. Schenectady, NY: The New York State English Council.

Children's Science Book Review Committee. *Appraisals: Children's science books for young people*. Boston, MA: Children's Science Book Review Committee. (published quarterly).

Hoffman, J., Roser, N. L., & Battle, J. (1993). Reading aloud in classrooms: From the modal to a model. *Reading Teacher, 46*, 496–505.

Kelly, P., & Self, W. (Eds.). (1992). *Teaching nonfiction. Virginia English Bulletin* [Special Issue] *42*.

National Science Teachers Association. Outstanding science trade books for children. *Science and Children*. (Included in the March issue each year)

Poe, E. (Ed.). (1995). *Focus on nonfiction/informational literature. SIGNAL Journal* [Special Issue] *19*.

Shugert, D. (Ed.). (1984). Nonfiction. *Connecticut English Journal* [Special Issue]. *61*.

Zvirin, S. (Ed.). (1992). *The best years of their lives: A resource guide for teenagers in crisis*. Chicago, IL: American Library Association.

CHILDREN'S TEXTS

Titles Selected from National Science Teachers Association. "Outstanding Science Trade Books for Children," *Science and Children*, March Issue of the Year on the pages noted for that year.

1990 (pp. 34–36)

Arnosky, J. *Come out, muskrats*. New York: Lothrop, Lee, and Shepard Books.

Coldrey, J. *Strawberry* (G. Bernard, Illus.). Morristown, NJ: Silver Burdett.
Dunrea, O. *Deep down underground*. New York: Macmillan.
George, W. T. *Box turtle at long pond* (L. B. George, Illus.). New York: Greenwillow Books.
Lyons, G. E. *A C cedar: An alphabet of trees* (T. Parker, Illus.). New York: Orchard Books.
Parnell, P. *Quiet*. New York: Morrow.
Rockwell, A. *Apples and pumpkins* (L. Rockwell, Illus.). New York: Macmillan.
Ryder, J. *Where butterflies grow* (L. Cherry, Illus.). New York: Lodestar.
Turner, D. *Potatoes* (J. Yates, Illus.). Minneapolis: Carolrhoda Books.
Turner, D. *Bread, eggs, and milk*. Minneapolis: Carolrhoda Books.

1991 (pp. 34–36)

Hirschi, R. *Winter* (T. D. Mangelsen, Illus.). New York: Cobblehill.
Parnell, P. *Woodpile*. New York: Macmillan.
Robbins, K. *A flower grows*. New York: Dial.
Ryder, J. *Under your feet*. New York: Four Winds.
Watts, B. *Tomato*. Morristown, NJ: Silver Burdett.
Wienwandt, T. *The hidden life of the desert*. New York: Crown.

1992 (pp. 24–26)

Allen, M. N., & Rotner, S. *Changes*. New York: Macmillan.
Ehlert, L. *Red leaf, yellow leaf*. San Diego: Harcourt Brace Jovanovich.
Fife, D. H. *The empty lot* (J. Arnosky, Illus.). Boston: Sierra Club/Little Brown.
Florian, D. *Vegetable garden*. San Diego: Harcourt Brace Jovanovich.
Hirschi, R. *Fall* (T. D. Mangelsen, Illus.). New York: Cobblehill.
Hiscock, B. *The big tree*. New York: Atheneum.
Jasperson, W. *Cranberries*. Boston: Houghton Mifflin.
Leslie, C. W. *Nature all year long*. New York: Greenwillow Books.
Parnell, P. *The rock*. New York: Macmillan.

1993 (pp. 32–34)

Holmes, A. *Flowers for you: Blooms for every month* (V. Wright-Frierson, Illus.). New York: Bradbury Press.
King, E. *Backyard sunflower*. New York: Dutton.
Rudolph, M. *How a shirt grew in the field* (E. Weihs, Illus.). New York: Clarion.
Tresselt, A. *The gift of the tree*. New York: Lothrop, Lee, and Shepard Books.
Wilkes, A. *My first garden Book: A life-size guide to growing things at home* (D. King, Illus.). New York: Knopf.

13

Journeying Through the Eastern Hemisphere: Listening and Responding to Many Voices

Elizabeth A. Poe
Radford University

Nyanne J. Hicks
Blacksburg Middle School

EDITOR'S OVERVIEW

The many voices in the title of this chapter have multiple dimensions. There are the many voices of a multicultural sixth-grade classroom, the students representing a variety of regional and international cultures and ethnic groups, as well as diverse economic and social backgrounds. The many voices of adults are inclusive of educators and educators-in-training; they encompass the voices of parents and grandparents and the language that emerges from family and personal legacies. The multiple texts selected from regions of the eastern hemisphere provide an array of vital, international voices. These, in effect, bring the world voices into the classroom.

The dynamics of the use of multiple texts form the core of this chapter, including the introduction of the books, their processing, and a variety of response activities. Readers' responses are illustrated. A larger context, however, is provided. Elizabeth Poe and Nyanne Hicks take us into Hicks' classroom to participate in the development of a unit focusing on ancestry and cultural heritage. From discussions of personal origins, the unit offers learnings of cultural geography based on the student-selected regions of the eastern hemisphere.

The unit's teaching is steeped in practice of reader-response strategies and the whole language concept. Indeed, active language is a constant. The activities are natural outgrowths of the investigative-response format, so natural that the sense of assignment is minimized.

Consider the following:

1. Identify the various reader-response activities and how they are used. What is the developmental impact on student learning of these activities?

2. *What learning values emerge from the use of class-common literary works
    and the use of multiple literary texts? When might either strategy be used?*
3. *Consider the developmental design of this unit. How is it at once diversified
    for individualization and unified for the community of learners?*
4. *Study the connections evident in the unit discussed in this chapter between
    fiction and nonfiction. What learnings are generated from each; in what
    ways does the reading and response to fiction color learning in the social
    sciences?*

It's September and a new group of 11-year-olds find their way into their
sixth-grade language arts/social studies classroom. Most of them live in or
around a small town in rural southwestern Virginia that is also the home
of a major university. Some of them have lived in this part of Appalachia
all their lives, and others have migrated from all over the United States
and other parts of the world such as Egypt, Korea, Chile, Puerto Rico,
Germany, India, and Iraq. Of those who were born in the United States, a
few are African-American and most are of European descent.

Many come from families with parents who are professors or university students, and others come from families where one or more parent
did not finish high school. Some may be world travelers, and others are
experts on local culture. Some live in single-family neighborhoods, some
live in government-subsidized housing, some live in apartment complexes, some live on multiacre farms, some live in low-income trailer
parks, and some live in homes in the nearby mountains of Appalachia.
When they talk, they reflect a mixture of the regional dialect, as well as
first generation English and conventional speech. But whatever their
backgrounds, they are all apprehensive about starting their middle-
school years.

When they enter their classroom, along with other anxious sixth graders, they find several adults who will also be part of their learning
community. These adults are Nyanne Hicks, the lead teacher, and Chris
Vestal, the special education teacher assigned to the team, and may also
include parents, students from local universities, parents, retired teachers,
and other interested community members who will join them on a regular
or intermittent basis. The adults in the room have planned a community
for learning where all voices are heard, developed, and valued. This type
of community is possible when all members of the group question as they
share, read/write, and respond to learning.

SHARING INFORMATION WITHIN THE
CLASSROOM COMMUNITY

The year begins with the first of many invitations. The adult leader
invites all learners to begin a search throughout their homes with the
hope of creating a *Legacy Box.*

Invitation 13.1

Think about what you would select as your legacy to share with the learning community in which you are presently involved. Share these things among small group members.

This Legacy Box (container, sack, bag, etc.) will include items that help tell what each class member values from gifts given to them by people in their lives. The adult learners share their legacies by explaining why they value the items they selected. Often the value comes from the giver, thus helping each class member know about the adult's past and present relationships.

The student learners then share their legacies. Over the years, students have brought items such as china that great-grandmothers have handed down, pictures of loved ones, Bible cards earned at a church camp, a meat cleaver that was used by a grandfather and great-grandfather who were both butchers, violins, cellos, books, and toys. During this activity, students often question the word *legacy*. What makes a legacy? Can any gift be a legacy? Does it even have to be a gift? Who decides if it is a legacy, the giver or the receiver? Does the item have to be old? What makes each selection a valued item? As the community discusses questions like these, a sense of familiarity and trust begins to build.

Instead of beginning the sharing of their legacies with the whole group as the adult learners did, the students begin by talking with a partner. Each pair finds a private place where they can examine each other's legacy and discuss its importance. After they have shared, the owners may want to tell the whole class of their treasures or quietly close their containers. Some class members leave their legacies in the room whereas others carry theirs home to a safe haven among other keepsakes. In any case the conversations, both informal and formal, create an atmosphere that nourishes risk-taking. Those legacies that are left in the classroom, in addition to the family pictures each member brings, help identify the individual members of the community while establishing a homelike environment. Because students have discussed the selection of their legacies with their families, the community at school has expanded to include the home as well.

This connection with home helps students enter into conversations about their cultural heritage. Based on knowledge of family backgrounds, students locate a spot, sometimes from several possibilities, on the map where they identify their roots and about which they want to become a class expert.

Invitation 13.2

Realizing that we all have diverse cultural backgrounds, even if our families have lived in the United States for generations, investigate some aspect of your personal heritage. Share this information with your community to determine the cultural diversity and variety of expertise within your group.

As the map fills with student names attached to yarn leading to places of origin all around the world, students and adults recognize they are part of a diverse classroom community. This information serves as a bridge to the eastern hemisphere, the required social studies course for sixth graders in the district. Although many children find they are geographically connected to the eastern hemisphere through their ancestors, few have extensive cultural knowledge about the continents of Europe, Asia, Africa, and Australia.

Building on what they do know about this part of the world, community members pool their knowledge about the eastern hemisphere. In an effort to deepen their knowledge, students are invited to select a place in the eastern hemisphere where they have an interest in becoming an expert. This place may or may not be part of their individual legacy, but very often is. For example, some students may be particularly interested in Northern Europe, South Africa, various parts of Asia, or Middle Eastern countries.

As groups form around areas of the world that interest them, the students list what they already know (or think they know) about this region. This knowledge has many sources, from talks with relatives to movies and books to past explorations. From here, each group generates a list of questions that will guide future research. Typical questions at this point are usually concrete geographical inquiries such as, What are some of the land formations in this area? or, What are the surrounding countries? What are the surrounding bodies of water? What is its climate like? Through discussion, the students are also encouraged to ask more abstract questions about the gifts of this culture. For example, how do these people celebrate births, deaths, rites of passage? Are any of these rituals part of life in this country? What is it like to be a child in this culture? How has life changed for them over time?

With these questions in mind, as well as others they develop as they read, the students set out to find information about a part of the eastern hemisphere that connects with their roots or holds some other particular interest for them. Students begin with the class text, *Eastern Hemisphere* by Beyer, Craven, McFarland, and Parker (1991), but soon realize it cannot answer the questions sufficiently. After many trips to the school and town libraries, materials about the eastern hemisphere fill the room. These materials include poetry, short stories, informational picture books, magazines, newspapers, and young adult nonfiction and fiction. Learning community members with access to electronic information also add to this collection.

Students immerse themselves in the materials and read and respond orally by talking with a partner or in writing by recording what interests them. After much reading and notetaking, they list questions from their inquiries so they will know what they have discovered in order to help them formulate where they want to go next in their reading. For example, Rebecca, who is investigating Italy, responds to the materials she read by asking the question, Is there any racism in Italy? Joe, who is studying Wales, wants to know: Were any of the castles haunted? and, Do the people in Wales believe in dragons? Because this classroom is a learning community, all students are obligated to bring the knowledge they discover to the whole group. This sharing is done in the form of authoring circles where students gather in small groups to share their knowledge gained and plans for future exploration. The written version of this information takes the form of a friendly letter. This is Laura's friendly letter to the class:

November 1, 1994

Dear Fellow Students,

The following letter tells about the country of Ireland. I first got interested in studying my heritage of Ireland last year in fifth grade, when we had our Heritage Fair. I enjoyed studying Ireland before, so I am glad I am going to become a more knowledgeable person on Ireland this year.

One topic that interested me while I was doing my research was the Irish holidays. Three holidays that children look forward to in particular are First Footing Day, Little Christmas, and Puck's Fair. First Footing Day is on January 1. Little Christmas is on January 6, and Puck's Fair takes place on Lammus Day. Unfortunately, I couldn't find what day of the year Lammus Day falls on. The people say there are so many holidays there is one almost every day.

The capital of Ireland is Dublin. Dublin is also Ireland's largest city. Cork is the second largest city. I could not find the populations of these cities.

I found little information about Irish schools. I wish I had found more because I think it would be neat to find out what children do in their schools. Anyway, I just found out that children must go to school when they are ages 6-15. I would like to know what kinds of things they do in school. Also, how big is their average school?

There are four main political parties in Ireland. Fianna Fa'il is the Republican party. Fine Gael is the party for Gaelic people. The Gaelic people have their own language. The two main languages in Ireland are English and Gaelic. Anyway, the third party is the Labour Party, and the last is the Progressive Democratic Party.

Other things about Ireland are that it's in northwest Europe. It's often called the Emerald Isle because of how green the land is. Because of that, the Irish have large deposits of peat. Peat is dead plants that are mixed with mud. They use it for fuel, and 10 percent of Ireland is made of it.

Ireland seems like a very kind and wonderful country to me. Someday I hope to visit there.

Sincerely,
Laura

Letters like Laura's are based on the facts students gathered about their cultural roots. The next phase takes students back to their personal experiences with their heritage. In subsequent class discussions, the teacher and students engage in conversations based on survey questions students have shared with their families. Once again, students write friendly letters to the community to express their personal connections with their learnings. In response to a question about how food reflects a family's cultural traditions, Enmar describes his family's feasting at the end of Ramadan by writing:

November 14, 1994

Dear Black Hawks,

It has been just about two weeks since I have written you. The last letter you received was about Iraq if my memory serves me correctly.

As you may recall, in my last letter I noted that my family has something called Aeid. Well, let me tell you about that tradition. It is a celebration of the end of the fasting month called Ramadan which occurs once a year. That is when we start grocery shopping for some special foods. During that time we make a big feast where we eat sitting on a mat on the floor, using our first three fingers, not spoons or forks, to eat with. We have to put Mish Mish, our dog, in a room with the door closed or she would join us for dinner.

The foods we eat are Arabic and are delicious. We all help out with the cooking; my sister and I make different dishes—like I might help make the hummus betina and she would help make the dolma (grape leaves stuffed with onions and tomatoes), and my dad would make the baklava (a pastry dessert), and so on. We drink something special—laban—made of yogurt, water and ice blended together, and it's delicious!

Hummus betina is the first dish we eat after we are done with all the cooking and the dishes are in the oven or on the stove. This is my favorite!! I talked a lot about it in my recent letter, so you remember what it is. Then we go on to the main course and end with honey and nuts put together with many layers of flakey pastry for dessert. That dinner lasts us at least a week. While we eat my dad tells us stories about his family, his culture and values and traditions important to all of us.

Well, I better be wrapping things up now. I hope you will write back and tell me some of your rituals!

Sincerely,
Enmar

All friendly letters are filed in the *Experts Box* from which students can add and borrow materials from each other's folders. The Experts Box is important because it provides an opportunity for the give and take of information throughout the year. As new countries are studied, folders are added to the box. From these folders, each student selects a piece of inquiry of particular interest and offers it as a contribution for the class *bulletin board*. This bulletin board, which is displayed in the hall outside the classroom, is a collage that invites as well as informs the larger school community of the class's collective expertise and emphasizes their belief that they learn individually and share collectively.

LEARNING TO RESPOND TO LITERATURE
IN A CLASSROOM COMMUNITY

At the same time students are learning about themselves and each other as they begin to study the Eastern Hemisphere, they are also learning to respond to literature and share their responses with other members of their learning community. The first pieces of literature they encounter are *daily read-alouds*. Lowery's *The Giver* (1993/1994) was this year's first selection, followed by short stories and poems with culturally diverse themes. In order to help students connect, or form transactions, with these literary selections and with literature in general, the teacher makes a variety of suggestions to enhance their aesthetic responses with literature. For example, she guides the development of visualization skills by encouraging them to ask themselves questions about what they specifically see and feel as they listen. She invites them to express their thoughts, feelings, impressions, and questions, and relate these ideas to their prior experiences. She leads them to explore the actual words the author used to create the images, thoughts, and feelings, and helps them to discover personal connections with the story. In addition, she helps them establish practices that develop avenues of expression that will continue through the year. One of these avenues is the *personal journal* in which students record their private thoughts about what they see and feel, both about literature and the world around them. These written responses, which are shared only with the writer's permission, serve as a place to preserve initial thoughts, a rehearsal for class discussions, and may also provide raw material for future written pieces.

Sharing responses about common literary works is an important concept within the learning community. Because all responses are valued, an atmosphere that fosters risk taking occurs and convinces students that their responses are pieces of their own learning. As they share their insights, the community affirms the similarities of its members as well as honors its differences. The recognition of this knowledge is not only vital for the learning community, but it also sets the context for studying cultures of the Eastern Hemisphere through literature.

Once the reader-response approach is internalized, students expand their opportunities to transact with literature in a *reading/writing workshop* setting. Now they add to their response strategies by writing in a three-part *reader's notebook*. The first section of this notebook is designated as a *dialogue journal* in which students develop and share their initial responses to their own individually selected books by writing back and forth with other learners in the community. The following excerpt is taken from the journals of Megan and Ivy:

October 4, 1994

Ivy,

I have started reading a book called *The Night White Deer Died* by Gary Paulsen. When I read the first part of the book, I felt excited to find out what Janet had as a dream. In her dream she would wake up in the night and start to walk down to a lake, but a white deer would walk out to the lake just then. I felt worried for the deer, because an Indian brave would appear in the trees, aim an arrow at the deer, and then Janet would wake up. She has that dream very often. I'm excited to find out what happens next! Good-bye!

Megan

October 4, 1994

Dear Megan,

Your book sounds very interesting, and maybe I would like to read it sometime. Thank you for telling me.

Sincerely,
Ivy

Dear Megan,

The book I'm reading is called *Starring the Babysitters Club* by Ann M. Martin. Almost everything in this book is believable, because it has girls that live in a town. The girls have girl problems like almost all girls. The story has real things going on in town, so the story is very life-like. Well, I have to go. See you later!

Sincerely,
Ivy

October 4, 1994

Ivy,

I have seen many of the movies of *The Babysitters Club*. I started reading one of the books, but never finished it. I hope to read one of those books sometime.

Megan

The second section is devoted to recording *information*, or students' efferent responses, either from fiction or nonfiction, which relates to the study of the Eastern Hemisphere. When recording information about Egypt, Nufyal says that "without writing, we wouldn't know how to communicate, or even learn about ancient Egyptians. That's why writing was a great achievement in ancient history." Later, when students are asked to formulate and answer their own questions about what they read, Jill asks: "Do you think the ancient Egyptian government system was fair to the lower-class citizens?" Her response is based on information from the text, as well as a comment an African-American student made during class discussion. Jill answers: "Yes . . . I think the labor was part of being religious. I guarantee if M. were in Egypt, then she would do labor because it was her way to show respect. It was their life. Although she said she wouldn't've done labor, she would've." Information recorded in the second reader's response journal is often shared and narrowed by consensus in small groups before it is offered to the group at large.

The third part of this notebook is dedicated to collecting *words and passages* readers love and want to share with others. The room comes alive with words such as *abate*, from Paulsen's *Woodsong* (1990/1991) which Kate chose and defined as *to stop or end*. Ryan selected *saga* from *The Brothers Lionheart* by Lindgren (1973/1975), which he says means *continuing stories of past adventures*. Trevor liked the word *solitude* which he found in *Maniac Magee* by Spinelli (1989/1990) and defines it as *peace and quiet*. This reader's notebook becomes a vehicle for response in the next stage when the study of the Eastern Hemisphere is intertwined with literature as students are invited to regroup and join one of seven literature circles.

CONNECTING LITERATURE AND THE STUDY OF THE EASTERN HEMISPHERE

The members of each of the seven literature circles, or small groups, all read the same book. These books have been selected by the teacher because of their cultural–geographic connections to the Eastern Hemisphere. The books vary each year according to student interest in specific geographic areas. This year's books represent Pakistan, China, Cambodia, South Africa, Turkey, and North and South Korea, as well as the concept of cultural bias toward immigrants in America. The forming of the eastern hemisphere literature circles is a negotiated process between students and classroom adults. Students are introduced to one book each day through *book-shares* given by adults who have previously read the books. In these book-shares, the reader briefly describes his or her personal response to the book. This response informs the class about the book's content by telling enough to intrigue them to read it, but not enough so they feel they don't have to. Book-shares take on many different forms, limited only by the reader's imagination. To introduce *Against the Storm* by Hicyilmaz (1990/1993), a coming-of-age story set in Turkey, a student teacher creates an oversized book jacket using scenes depicting the terrain on the cover and information about the story and the author on the book flaps. The teacher shares her love of Staples' *Shabanu: Daughter of the Wind* (1989/1991), the story of a contemporary adolescent in Pakistan, by reading aloud a letter to a friend about the book. A parent volunteer presents a set of thought-provoking questions about Yep's *Dragonwings* (1975), which tells of early 20th-century Chinese immigrants' struggle for acceptance in America. The student teacher and the teacher collaborate in a simulated TV interview with Sheila Gordon, the author of the South African tale of interracial friendship, *Waiting for the Rain* (1987/1989). A university undergraduate education student explains the meaning of the title of Ho's *The Clay Marble* (1991/1993) and provides background information about the political climate in Cambodia at the time the story takes place. For *The Year of Impossible Good-byes* (1991/1993), Choi's story which takes place during the Korean Conflict, the special education support teacher reads a journal entry that could have been written by the main character when she was separated from her father. In the final book-share, the teacher becomes a journalist who recounts the recent human rights demonstrations in China that form the backdrop of *Forbidden City* by Bell (1991/1991).

As with all book-shares, these presentations entice others to read the books. They also demonstrate both efferent and aesthetic literary responses; they model possible formats for ongoing book-shares throughout the year; they stress the books' geographical connections with the Eastern Hemisphere; they situate the adults in the classroom as members not only of the general learning community, but also of specific literature circles; and they provide information that will assist students in their choice of literature circles. Because honoring choices, matching students and books, and creating a genuine interest in the book are crucial, forming literature circles is a multistep process. Therefore, as each book-share is given, copies of that novel are placed in *Book Baskets* throughout the room. During these seven days, community members are invited to examine the books at their leisure and add other material, such as maps, picture books, newspaper articles, informational books, or other novels related to that book's cultural–geographical setting. On the eighth day, students enter the room to find a map covered with the familiar titles of the books they have been exploring.

The next step is a *book-pass activity* in which individuals examine each of the seven books and, using a form the teacher has constructed, write comments about each title and rate it according to their first and second choices. For example, Brandon, who lives on a farm on the outskirts of town, rates *Waiting for the Rain* as his first choice because "the cover looks like it is going to take place on a farm, and I like that." Jill notes that not only has *Shabanu* been recommended by her mother, but it also has a glossary of Pakistani words and the cover art reminds her of Ringold's picture book *Tar Beach* (1991).

Invitation 13.3

Using the literature circle concept, select a topic of importance to you (or your students) and five to seven books from which they could form literature circles. Identify and discuss the common thread that ties these titles together. Don't forget to include poetry, nonfiction, short stories, or picture books to enhance your exploration. Prepare a book talk for one of the texts.

Students discuss their opinions in small groups prior to a whole-group discussion so all possible impressions can be considered before individual students make their wishes known. By listing their first and second choices as well as noting books that are objectionable for any reason, students make their voices heard. The adults then form the *literature circles* based on student preference, students' different strengths, and the type of support available from group members. The next day, students excitedly enter the room to discover which book they get to read as they locate the Book Basket with their name in it. The teacher assures those who did not get their first choice that they will have opportunities to read any and all of the other titles if they like.

When they first meet as literature circles, members' eagerness to read determines the reading pace for each group. Although the group decides on the minimum number of pages to be read for each discussion, students who wish may read ahead, but they can only discuss what the whole group has read. The first day, students read in class and conclude the period with a general discussion of their responses and a negotiated commitment to the next day's minimum reading assignment. The following day, the circle opens with a minilesson on responding to the book in dialogue journal form in the first section in their reader's notebooks. These responses might discuss what readers notice and care enough about to want to share. Although students don't use the terms, they understand that both aesthetic and efferent responses are welcome. After writing, the students share their responses with their circle members, determine the next night's minimum reading assignment, and share a few comments with the class as a whole about their book to keep the learning community informed. These comments typically involve general information about the story and character development and whether or not readers like the book so far. This process continues for a week to a week and a half until each group finishes reading the book.

When they finish reading and discussing their initial reactions to the book, it is time to delve deeper into the cultural and geographic characteristics of each novel. The next week is spent generating and answering three types of questions which will be discussed in the literature circles and recorded in the second section, the information portion, of their reader's notebooks. Adult members of the groups may assure the quality of these questions by adding their own as group members. The first set of questions is specific to each novel. For instance, in *Shabanu*, the readers might compare their thoughts and feelings about arranged marriages or parent–child relationships as they are presented in this novel about Pakistan. The second group of questions is more general in nature and could be applied to each of the novels. These questions might involve cultural issues such as values, traditions, relationships, religion, customs, clothing, social structures, and gender roles. These questions are posed to each literature circle, which responds as a small group, then reports its collective understanding to the whole group. The third set of questions is those that cannot be answered completely within the novel itself, but requires readers to examine their own views as well as search other sources. An example of this third type of question is: "What is the origin of the term *Forbidden City* in the Chinese culture?" To answer this type of question, student learners may begin with the Book Basket for their novel, the Experts Box for that region, individual experts in the room, or informational books in the classroom library. Beyond the classroom, they might seek interviews with experts in the broader community, electronic assistance through e-mail, the Internet or computer programs, or current information provided by the news media. In the case of the question about the term *Forbidden City*, Meg interviewed a teacher who had been to Beijing and invited her to come talk to the whole class.

After posing and exploring these questions, literature circle members return to their novels and each reader selects his or her favorite passage. Readers record these passages and why they liked them in the third section, collecting words and favorite passages, of their reader's notebook as well as on 3 × 5 cards to share with the rest of the community. Jill, for example, likes this passage from *The Clay Marble*:

> "Don't tell me I don't understand war," I said fiercely. My hands seemed to have a life of their own, kneading and rolling, shaping that cool ball of clay. "I understand that [Jantu] will never wake up in that hammock again. I understand that Father will never come home to us again. I understand war kills people who aren't even fighting in it." My eyes stung

and when I blinked, I could feel the threads of cool tears streaking my cheeks. But my hands were still shaping the marble, smoothing it, and I did not bother to wipe my tears away. (p. 151)

Jill writes, "I like this part because it shows how much she changed in the past year or so because of war and Jantu. Jantu and war combined for a purpose to make Dara understand and change. It really showed how war changed her."

Megan selects this passage from *Shabanu*:

His hands are gnarled and his beard wispy. He folds back the last piece of paper and pulls out an exquisite gray-colored piece of cloth as light as a spider's web.

"My father gave this shatoosh to my mother," he says. "Would you like it?"

Pale pink and green embroidery so fine I can't see the stitches curls along the edges of the gossamer shawl. It is the most beautiful thing I have ever seen or touched. (pp. 72–73)

Megan explains,

I like this part because it is so descriptive. I could see everything that was written. If I had been offered something like that, I would be so joyous, happy, and amazed. I would *really* love to own this. I am glad for Shabanu that she was offered that shatoosh. She is very lucky. If I owned this shatoosh, I would treasure it always.

Sharing these passages and comments on why they were selected adds another layer not only to readers' personal responses to the books, but to the whole learning community's appreciation for both the book and its individual readers.

In addition to the students' entries made in their reader's notebooks that represent effort and involvement in the project over time, each literature circle develops a working folder for the purpose of assessment that contains evidence of individual and group growth. In the working folder, each circle member places at least one piece of work that demonstrates knowledge he or she acquired through the literature circle experience. This offering of an individual's learning could be a painting, a piece of poetry, an essay, a photo essay, an interview, or anything the circle member negotiates with the group. This contribution needs to be accompanied by a personal letter that describes to the class the knowledge the student acquired and reflects on the process involved in his or her journey. For her contribution to the group folder, Alicia included the excerpt from *The Clay Marble* she memorized and interpreted to the class. She also included this letter about what she gained from this book:

12/19/94

Dear Mrs. Hicks and Mrs. Vestal,

I read the book *The Clay Marble* by Minfong Ho. For my individual offering I'm doing a monologue. When I chose the dialogue for it, I looked for things that showed emotion and things that show how war can change personalities without telling whose personality changes.

I chose to do a monologue because I can show how I think the characters feel when they say what they say, without knowing how they really feel, just by the setting and the words.

What I learned from this book is war changes personalities, some for the worse, some for the better. I also learned to like what you have, because some people don't have what you have.

This book made me realize some things too. Number one was how much those people valued families, friends, and food. And number two was how nice people are to people who are not exactly like them.

Your student,
Alicia

P.S. I really enjoyed the book.

Evidence of group growth includes a communal list of what the group now knows about the geographical region to which its novel is tied, group record-keeping about assignments completed and daily individual commitment, daily collaborative notes on what will be shared with the whole group, and a plan for its group book-share. The *group book-share,* another form of assessment, represents the belief that individual learning is shared with the total community. Each book-share needs to meet specific criteria. Because collaborative book-shares are expanded versions of individual book-shares, they will not only inspire others to read the book, but they will incorporate a brief overview of the book, information about the author, cultural understandings gleaned from the book, and learnings about the book's geographical location, as well as shared transformations that could be informational or aesthetic and are often a combination of both. Group book-shares should involve everyone, use the strengths of the group members, and turn the book into something new. For example, a literature circle might transform the book into a play, a readers' theater, a trial scene, a poetry reading, a game show, a newscast, a fashion show, a guided tour of an art gallery, a travel brochure, a video or slide show, a collection of board games, a traditional meal, a model of a geographic location, several character monologues, a musical demonstration, or a combination of these or any other possibilities. Group members need to demonstrate effective public speaking techniques. Prior to the book-share, the groups should identify the areas of their presentation in which they have collective pride.

With these group book-shares, the learning community has come full circle. From adult book-shares to group book shares that emphasize students' voices, the classroom has become a dynamic environment that provides many forums for sharing thoughts, feelings, impressions, questions, and knowledge. Through these forums, reasons to share emerge; students acquire ownership and direction of their learning; they increase respect for their own ideas, as well those of others; they gain confidence in their ability to respond to literature in a variety of ways; and they form connections between themselves, literature, and other cultures as they journey through the Eastern Hemisphere and the world.

General Invitations

Think about the question: Where do we go from here? Devise strategies to take your students beyond this unit. How do you encourage ongoing reading on a certain topic? What else did these authors write? Are there sequels available? Could nonfiction continue to play a role in future investigations? Are school or family field trips an option? How do you provide opportunities for continual sharing of learnings throughout the year? Share your ideas with your classroom community.

Using the suggested novels, form seven literature circles in which all readers keep a reader's-response journal and discuss their transactions with other circle members. Culminate these literature circle experiences by preparing individual or group literary transformations for the class.

Select a historical novel and investigate its setting(s) by researching its cultural and geographical characteristics. Using this newly found information, create a short story, film script, or picture book that shows your understanding of this time and place.

REFERENCES

Books Used This Year

Bell, W. (1991). *The forbidden city.* Garden City, NY: Doubleday. (Paperback edition published 1991, New York: Bantam)

Beyer, B. K., Craven, J., McFarland, M. A., & Parker, W. C. (1991). *The eastern hemisphere: The world around us.* New York: Macmillan/McGraw.

Choi, S. N. (1991). *The year of impossible good-byes.* Boston, MA: Houghton Mifflin. (Paperback edition published 1993, New York: Bantam)

Gordon, S. (1987). *Waiting for the rain*. New York: Orchard. (Paperback edition published 1989, New York: Bantam)

Hicyilmaz, G. (1990). *Against the storm*. Boston, MA: Little, Brown. (Paperback edition published 1993, New York: Dell)

Ho, M. (1991). *The clay marble*. Toronto: HarperCollinsCanada. (Paperback edition published 1993, New York: Starburst [FSG])

Lowery, L. (1993). *The giver*. New York: Houghton Mifflin. (Paperback edition published 1994, New York: Dell)

Staples, S. F. (1989). *Shabanu: Daughter of the wind*. New York: Knopf. (Paperback edition published 1991, Borzoi Sprinter)

Yep, L. (1975). *Dragonwings*. New York: Harper & Row.

Books Used in Other Years

Choi, S. N. (1993). *Echoes of the white giraffe*. Boston, MA: Houghton Mifflin. (Paperback edition published 1995, New York: Dell) (Korea—sequel to *The year of impossible goodbyes*)

Chrisman, A. B. (1925). *Shen of the Sea*. New York: Dutton. (China)

Crew, L. (1989). *Children of the river*. New York: Delacorte. (Paperback edition published 1991, New York: Dell) (United States/Cambodia)

Filipovic, Z. (1994). *Zlata's diary: A child's life in Sarajevo*. New York: Penguin. (Paperback edition published 1995, New York: Penguin) (Sarajevo)

Fritz, J. (1982). *Homesick for my own story*. New York: Putnam. (Paperback edition published 1984, New York: Dell) (China)

Heide, F. P., & Gilliland, J.H. (1990). *The day of Ahmed's secret*. New York: Lothrop, Lee & Shepard. (Paperback edition published 1995, New York: Mulberry) (Middle East)

Hesse, K. (1992). *Letters from Rifka*. New York: Henry Holt. (Paperback edition published 1993, New York: Puffin) (Russia)

Kronberg, R., & McKissack, P.C. (1990). *A piece of the wind: And other stories to tell*. New York: Harper & Row. (Short story collection—Europe, Africa, America, etc.)

Laird, E. (1991). *Kiss the dust*. New York: Penguin. (Paperback edition published 1994, New York: Puffin) (Iraq/Iran)

Mahy, M. (1991). *The seven Chinese brothers*. New York: Scholastic. (Paperback edition published 1992, New York: Scholastic) (China)

McGraw, E. (1991). *The striped ships*. New York: Macmillan. (England)

Nhuong, H. Q. (1982). *The land I lost: Adventures of a boy in Vietnam*. New York: Lippencott. (Paperback edition published 1984, New York: HarperTrophy) (Vietnam)

Nye, N. S. (1992). *This same sky: A collection of poems from around the world*. New York: Macmillan. (Poems representative of 68 countries)

Rochman, H. (1988). *Somehow tenderness survives: Stories of southern Africa*. New York: HarperCollins/Harper Keypoint. (Paperback edition published 1990, New York: Harper Keypoint) (Short stories—South Africa)

Service, P. F. (1988). *The reluctant god*. New York: Atheneum. (Paperback edition published 1989, New York: Fawcett Juniper) (Egypt)

Speare, E. G. (1961). *The bronze bow*. Boston, MA: Houghton Mifflin. (Paperback edition published 1973, Boston, MA: Houghton Mifflin) (Rome)

Staples, S. F. (1993). *Haveli*. New York: Knopf. (Paperback edition published 1995, New York: Random House) (Sequel to *Shabanu: Daughter of the wind*—Pakistan)

Tan, A. (1992). *The moon lady*. New York: Macmillan. (China—Picture book)

Yardley, Y. U. (1976). *The bracelet* (J. Yardley, Illus.). New York: Philomel. (Paperback edition published 1993, New York: Philomel) (Picture book—United States/Japan)

Yolen, J. (1986). *Favorite folktales from around the world.* New York: Random House. (Paperback edition published 1988, New York: Pantheon) (World)

Sample Books Used in Preparation for the Unit

Lindgren, A. (1973). *Brothers Lionhart.* Stockholm: Raben & Sjogren. (Paperback edition published 1975, New York: Viking Press)

Paulsen, G. (1990). *Woodsong.* New York: Delacorte. (Paperback edition published 1991, New York: Dell)

Ringold, F. (1991). *Tar beach.* New York: Crown.

Spinelli, J. (1989). *Maniac Magee.* New York: Scholastic. (Paperback edition published 1990, New York: Scholastic).

14

The Aesthetics
of Informational Reading

J. Kevin Spink
Mountain View Elementary School

EDITOR'S OVERVIEW

The underlying premise of this chapter is that reading nonfiction affords pleasure to its readers. As such, it can involve both aesthetic and efferent aspects of a reader's stance. Young readers exhibit excitement and delight. They make personal associations and provide experiential references. These responses are critical to their remembering information and developing understandings of the expository texts.

Kevin Spink's first graders initially taught him these principles. He reflected on their spontaneous, expressive responses to storytime, which often included nonfiction; he contrasted these to the minimal attention and retention during reading instruction, sometimes with the same materials. These observations were his catalysts for change. The changes then spilled over to the teaching of science and social studies when, again, the didactic forced-march approach was leading to disinterest and limited learning.

The point is doubly made. Having switched to the intermediate level, Spink found his fourth-graders to have seemingly lost their curiosity and hunger for learning. Reinstituting the pedagogical principles of reader-response, he again turned this situation around. An integrated social studies unit about family history was particularly engaging. Involving response reading and response writing in the contexts of personal history, historical fiction, biography, history, and geography, it sparked the deep understandings and intelligence of the students.

The interplay of aesthetic and efferent responses to texts, rather than their dualistic distinction and separation, speaks to a meaningful pedagogical understanding. It recognizes the flexibility of a reader's stance and the variation of stances among readers. Cognizant of the nature of reader engagement, teachers are led to apply this interplay advantageously.

Consider the following:

1. Explore your responses to nonfiction. When and how does the interplay of the aesthetic and efferent stance have effect?

2. Consider the pedagogy of developing students' responses to and understanding of nonfiction materials. How can personal responses be introduced and applied to support and enhance an information-oriented (predominantly efferent) text?

3. *What learning advantages emerged from complementary use of fiction and*
   nonfiction as detailed in the unit described in this chapter?

Some enjoy without judgment;
others judge without enjoyment;
and some . . . enjoy while they judge

       —Goethe (cited by Slezak, 1993, p. 74)

The Aesthetics of Informational Reading refers to an important lesson
about reading that I first learned as a young reader, forgot as a student,
and was retaught by my first-grade students. Watching my first-grade
students eagerly turn to informational books and magazines with a
fervor and frequency equal to their interest in fictional stories reminded
me of my own early preference for informational books at home and
continual frustration with the lack of exciting, real books in my primary
grade classrooms. It wasn't until I had entered the fourth grade and was
allowed to cross over to those shelves in our elementary school library
that held books with numbers on their spines that I sampled in school
from my favorite genre of literature, nonfiction.

My main interests then were tanks and battleships, reptiles, and
anything else remotely horrifying and potentially gory. As soon as I
discovered that books could be more than the sanitized, homogenized
pretend stories from our basal reader about unnaturally wholesome
families or overly protective fairy godmothers, I became hooked. This
marked the beginning of a lifelong passion for nonfiction books and
journals on an ever-widening range of topics. So it shouldn't have come
as so much of a surprise to me that my first grade students were
requesting articles from *Ranger Rick* and other fact-filled texts just as
frequently as they asked for fictional stories during our daily read-aloud
sessions.

Perhaps the reason why I miscalculated the kinds of reading selections that would appeal to my 6-year-old teachers was that I had fallen
into that very common logic trap of viewing reading as being either
informative or pleasurable. This cultural tendency toward dualistic
thinking, or, put another way, our propensity for seeing things in terms
of either–or propositions is a problem that plagues much of educational
theory (Dewey, 1938, p. 21) and it certainly has created troublesome
distortions in our understanding and application of reading theory.
Almost any intellectual process involving thinking and learning is far
too complex to fit neatly into tidy, uncomplicated theoretical boxes.
When I looked at and listened closely to these beginning readers, I began
to understand that my first graders were reading almost everything,
fiction and nonfiction, exposition and narration, as both potentially
informative and enjoyable.

Any problems related to my students' attitude toward what they were
reading were usually caused by my overly simplistic conception of what
their purposes should be. I assumed that we would be reading stories

for fun and reading information books to learn. In so making this assumption and basing my teaching decisions on this misconception, I shortchanged the full range of potential benefits offered by both genres. I now believe that stories can be highly informative without losing their appeal to our imaginative and aesthetic sensibilities, and that informational texts can fuel our imaginations and fill us with delight while at the same time provide us with empirical knowledge and concrete answers to specific questions.

For the four years that I taught first graders, I learned over and over again that successful learning was largely a process of connecting new knowledge and experiences with what was already known. The 6- and 7-year-olds whom I taught seemed predisposed to associate stories and new information with their prior direct experiences and the vicarious experiences that their reading and being read to had provided. These past four years, I've been teaching intermediate age students (in many cases, the same students who were in our first-grade classes). When shifting to fourth, and more recently to sixth grade, I was initially convinced that older students read and learned in a less personal way than their first-grade versions. This impersonal learning approach appeared to be particularly dominant in the so-called content subject areas of science and social studies. What follows is the story of how I've come to no longer believe that learning, generally, and reading, specifically, in a personally dissociated way is natural for learners of any age or for any subject matter or literary genre.

Reflecting on my own reading tendencies, and observing my students and my own child, when they were deeply engaged in a wide variety of reading experiences, has convinced me that genuine understanding of stories or informational texts depends on the links that we are able to make between our experiences and what we are reading.

My recognition of the readers' need to personally construct their understanding of a text was first acquired in the context of using fictional stories with first-grade students, and I was then later able to extend and adapt this knowledge when reading nonfiction with students. With intermediate age students, I've continued to search for ways to help us find connections between our interests, our experiences, and fictional, scientific, and historical texts that we read.

Reflecting back over changes that I made in my beliefs and practices as a teacher, two factors stand out. First, what I discovered about teaching my students matched what was already true for me as a reader-learner outside of school and second what started as a new realization about learning in one curricular area eventually spilled over and changed my understanding of student learning across all curricular areas. I began by changing the way that fiction was experienced by students in our class, and the success of this change led me to change the way that I presented scientific and historical texts. In both cases, the catalyst for the change was largely the discrepancy between my personal satisfaction with and enjoyment of reading both fiction and nonfiction, and the students' lack of enthusiasm for and success with either genre. As an avid reader, I knew what reading could be. And after experiencing success with a personal approach to teaching fiction, I became convinced that nonfiction reading experiences could be similarly enhanced.

STORYTIME VERSUS READING INSTRUCTION

Early in my teaching career I began to notice and become uncomfortable with the distinctly different way that stories were received during reading instruction time in contrast to storytime. Each afternoon, following lunch and recess, we would meet together on the floor to listen to and talk about stories, poems, and informational selections. Generally I would begin by reading from books and magazines requested by the students, either in excerpt form or in their entirety depending on the length of the text and the students' interest level. At that time, I did not view these sessions as a part of reading instruction, but I mostly used storytime for what I hoped would be its sedative effect following afternoon recess. At most, it seemed like a logical closure to our morning choice reading time and a way to expose students to books that might appeal as possible choices for our home reading program. It wasn't long, however, before I began to notice that the discussions about books that took place during our story sharing time were generally of a much higher quality and more enthusiastic in tone than the formal discussions that I was staging during our reading group times. After lunch and recess, we would gather in a circle on the floor for read aloud and choice book discussion time. With each student bringing at least one favorite book from the free choice book tub to discuss, we spontaneously discovered similarities between books, eagerly pointed out diffrences or variations on the same topic across books, and insistently sought out and discussed connections between the stories or information pieces that we were reading and our own past experiences and future plans.

At about this time I was introduced to the theories of Rosenblatt, through her writings and through an opportunity to study with her colleague and personal friend, Bob Probst. Bob's theoretical explanations of the first grader's behavior during storytime created a floodlight of understanding. This thing called reader-response theory was exactly what the 6- and 7-year-old kids had been demonstrating as we sat around comparing stories with each other and simultaneously weaving our own experiences into and around these discussions.

Reading and discussing the ideas of Rosenblatt allowed me to build a framework of understanding that has in turn affected literally every instructional decision I make as a teacher, whether it be with reading instruction or in other curricular areas such as science and history. A central tenet of Rosenblatt's theory is expressed by Steinbeck (1961) in the following passage from his novel, *The Winter of Our Discontent*:

> . . . a story has as many versions as it has readers. Everyone takes what he wants or can from it and thus changes it to his measure. Some pick out parts and reject the rest, some strain the story through their mesh of prejudice, some paint it with their own delight. A story must have some points of contact with the reader to make him feel at home in it. Only then can he accept wonders. (p. 89)

When I allowed for this process and encouraged each reader to find a way to feel at home with each story, it was nearly impossible to get through an entire story, or frequently even a single page, without someone in our class announcing their point of contact with the story. If there was a pet, it reminded someone of their pet or their cousin's pet. The monster might have been similar to a nighttime visitor to someone's dreamworld, and the story's hero was almost as heroic as a parent or grandparent in the eyes of some of the listeners. After directly or imaginatively finding points of contact between our lives and the stories, we each strained out what was most important to us, colored it according to our liking, and constructed our unique but interrelated versions of the same story. Storytime seldom seemed to drag, discipline was rarely a problem, and the stories themselves were almost never quickly forgotten and left behind.

Of course, storytime wasn't succeeding as a sedating activity, but this objective was frequently being achieved during our official reading instruction time. At this time of the day, when readings were assigned, gone over closely so that we could first comprehend the literal meaning of the words individually, then collectively, and later used to teach phonics, sight words, and vocabulary, the student response was very different. Attention spans were short, decorum often broke down, and factual retention was minimal. I can even recall occasionally reading a story in our reading book that we had previously encountered and enthusiastically received during storytime and being amazed at how differently the students responded to, or more accurately, didn't respond, when the same story was used as the basis for reading lessons.

My teaching experiences are, I realize, closely matched by countless other teachers of literature from preschool to graduate school settings. Like many of these teachers, I have gradually learned to trust the power of good stories working together with the imaginations of my students to guide me in structuring reading experiences in our classroom. We spend most of our time reading books we've chosen. We begin consideration of our books by looking for points of contact between our lives and the books, and we collaboratively construct our version of the stories through formal and informal, planned and spontaneous discussion of what we're reading. Skill instruction does take place, but I try to never allow the direct teaching to overshadow the process of figuring out what the story means to my students and to not allow anything to interrupt the aesthetic, lived-through experience (Rosenblatt, 1976) that stories can provide for us when we fall under their spell. Essentially, storytime has become the cornerstone of our reading program and teacher-directed instruction is brief and designed to enhance the process of reader response, not interfere with it. This is just as true for me today as a sixth grade teacher of big kids as it was a few years back when I was teaching those little kids who convinced me of the validity of reader-response theory.

Invitation 14.1

Read and / or view provocative fictional works (poems, plays, movies, novels, and short stories) centered around teaching, as a means of gaining multiple perspectives on our profession and as a way of raising to a conscious level and articulating our theories and ethical beliefs about teaching. Keep a free-response journal that focuses on personal memories evoked by the literature, in addition to any other intellectual or emotional reactions. Analyze your journals by comparing your experiences with the experiences of a main character in the story (in some cases a student and in others, a teacher). Finally, through lists, charts, and discussion, try to infer what a story character and, perhaps indirectly, the author, believes about the process of education and the effects of a particular relationship between a teacher and student(s). As a last step, compare the lessons to be learned from the story with the lessons that your own life experiences as students and teachers have imparted to you.

IT'S ALL "STORY," FICTION OR NONFICTION

Having been convinced of the importance of permitting students to have opportunities to experience stories on a personal level, I became intrigued with how similar my students' spontaneous response was to both fiction and nonfiction during storytime. I also noticed that these first graders referred to most of what we read together and discussed as story. They distinguished between true stories (nonfiction) and made-up or fake stories (fiction) but almost everything, even texts that were clearly expository, were referred to as story. Furthermore, our discussions about factual texts on a variety of topics were in many important ways indistinguishable from our discussions about fictional stories. The students sought connections between their experiences along the ocean shore and a factual description of tidepool creatures. They told personal stories about slipping on the kelp-covered rocks or touching the tentacles of an anemone as we read such scientific texts. They also appeared equally inclined to go under the spell of these true stories and frequently had intense, highly personal associations with these scientific accounts.

One particulary vivid example of this personal involvement that my students frequently had with nonfiction occurred the day that Dawn requested a Golden Press *Rocks and Minerals: A Guide to Familiar Gems, Ores and Minerals* (Zim & Shaffer, 1957). It was Dawn's turn to choose the book for story circle and I remember wincing at her selection. I probably thought, "Okay, hotshot, you'll have to be really creative with this text to hold the class's attention!" but I needn't have worried. As I began leafing through the pages and showing some of what I considered to be the more eye-catching photographs, Dawn started weaving in the story of her family's camping adventures as weekend gold miners. Her father liked to pan for gold and the rest of the family enjoyed exploring for unusual rocks and minerals. This natural process of blending memorable experiences together with the information from the expository text created a dynamic and fluid hybrid of narrative and exposition. Rather than have the class lose interest in the book about rocks, other students began interrupting with personal accounts of rock collecting expeditions and spontaneously speculating on and wondering about gold mining or geology in general.

From this and countless similar experiences of this sort with expository texts, I began to recognize the central role that narrative and personal association played in the learning of my students. That students referred to almost everything we read as story wasn't simply due to a lack of refinement of their understanding of what a story is. Nor was it a result of a lexical gap or a lack of the proper term for expository writings. Instead their deliberate lumping together of both fiction and nonfiction as story reflected the fact that they were building their understandings of both types of texts through a narrative thought structure. When information books were written in a narrative form, they got caught up in the story and retained much of the information and conceptual structures as a by-product of enjoying a good story, albeit a true story, and when the form was expository, the students frequently translated or filled in around the information with their own real or imaginative narrative adventures. Almost everything was seen as either being a story or as informational fuel for their imaginative abilities to construct stories.

By this time, I had abandoned my teacher-dominated dissections of stories during reading time. Following the student's lead and Rosenblatt's (1976) suggestion, I was allowing for and encouraging the students to discover personal meaning in the stories we were reading together. As a means of doing this, my students were engaging in far more of the so-called higher-order thinking processes than they had ever done during my highly teacher-directed discussions. They were continually returning to the text in search of support for their interpretations. They were frequently pausing in midthought to jump ahead and predict which way the story would turn or who the villain might be. They were expressing disapproval with some of the character's actions and occasional suspicion regarding the hidden motives of some of the more unsavory characters. They were also seriously weighing the merits of the author's choices regarding the plot twists, the story endings, and the accompanying illustrations. Some of this sophisticated thinking was happening as a result of planned, structured activities, but much of this deeper critical thinking was simply the spontaneous natural outcome of authentic reading experiences and literate discussion carried on amongst personally engaged readers. In short, the students were doing everything in the way of thinking that we could possibly hope for at a graduate literature seminar level, much less in a first-grade classroom.

Of course, at no single moment did I ever see every child deeply engaged in critical thinking, and even when most of the students were thus engaged, the learning often looked disorderly and uneven. But more and more, I've come to see that this seeming messy quality to learning and thinking is an indication of how real and lasting the learning actually is. Conversely, I've come to see that insisting that we proceed through identical learning activities in lock-step fashion often leads to little more than the illusion of learning. I've had to accept that the most genuine, lasting learning experiences look messy, proceed at different rates for different learners, and seldom hit home with equal impact for all, or even almost all of my students. Of course, these observations also hold true for me and my adult friends when we are engaged in learning experiences. This recognition has allowed me to relax about my students' nonuniform and unpredictable responses.

APPLYING READER RESPONSE THEORY
TO NONFICTION

Knowing this, I became increasingly troubled and dissatisfied with my science and social studies lessons. Here the students were reading the same assignments, following the same procedures, and having similar reactions: boredom and frustration. They also weren't learning very much by any measure that I could conceive of. No matter how often we went over definitions, dates, and data findings from our experiments, little of it was sticking. And there clearly was even less going on for the students at a conceptual level. They were generally unable to see connections between our staged experiments and what we were reading or discussing, nor were they very willing to try. These frustrating attempts to read or learn about science stood in sharp contrast to the informal science discussions that we were having when a science article or chapter was read and responded to during storytime. A parallel contrast between science instruction and storytime similar to the contrast between reading instruction and storytime was developing.

At about this point one of the students brought Carson's *A Sense of Wonder* (1956), to our story circle time. In her autobiographical account Carson observed that,

When Roger visited me in Maine and we have walked in these woods I have made no conscious effort to name plants or animals nor to explain to him, but have just expressed my own pleasure in what we see , calling his attention to this or that but only as I would share discoveries with an older person. Later I have been amazed at the way names stick in his mind, for when I show color slides of my woods plants, it is Roger who can identify them. "Oh that's what Rachel likes—that's bunchberry!" Or, "That's juniper but you can't eat those green berries—they are for squirrels." I am sure no amount of drill would have implanted the names so firmly as just going through the woods in the spirit of two friends on an exciting discovery. (p. 18)

This quality of friends going along "on an exciting discovery" was precisely what I believed to be missing from our science and social studies lessons. Once again, I returned to the theories of Rosenblatt and the implicit suggestions of my students during storytime to guide my decisions about changing our classroom practices. Reader-response theory draws a distinction between reading as a vicarious experience and reading as a means of extracting out specific information. Rosenblatt (1978) used the now-familiar terms, *aesthetic* and *efferent*, respectively, to denote these two fundamentally different purposes for reading, which she refers to as the reader's stance. This much referenced distinction is, I believe, also much misunderstood or at least frequently oversimplified and, consequently, often misapplied. Although Rosenblatt pointed out that reading a novel or a poem as a means of getting inside of or living through the text (aesthetic) is different from going to a reference book purely to gather predetermined factual information (efferent), she also pointed out that most reading experiences contain elements of both aesthetic, or living through, and efferent, or carrying away, mental processes. She described the reader's stance as falling somewhere along a continuum between the most extreme poles of aesthetic versus efferent reading and was careful to point out that reading is not usually purely one nor the other. Moreover, she also cautioned us that it is both the text and the reader's predetermined sense of purpose that determines the appropriate stance or where along this continuum that a particular reading experience will fall.

This theory is generally interpreted and applied in the context of fictional literature and is rightfully used to explain the importance of allowing and encouraging readers to personally experience, rather than academically dissect, stories and poems. Instead of reading a work of literature with an eye toward remembering names and places so that one can pass the teacher's quiz or fill in the workbook blanks, students should be experiencing literature as a work of art and they should be bringing their experiences and dreams for the future to their reading encounters, as they have a form of transaction with the literary text. As Steinbeck suggested, readers should be straining the stories through their unique mesh of prior experiences and personality traits to build their own version of the story. In so doing, the story or poem is both shaped by and helps shape the reader. This transactual potential of literature is what gives it its timeless, universal power. So far, so good. But many of us tend to misconstrue Rosenblatt's theory as applying only to stories and poems and not to nonfiction literature of the sort we ideally are able to use when we teach science and social studies.

This misinterpretation is perhaps inevitable because of previously mentioned tendency to form either–or dichotomies rather than to see theoretical distinctions along continuums. It is also likely the result of Rosenblatt's natural emphasis on stories and poems. This is, after all, her major concern. But, it is my belief that we as teachers have tended to define literature too narrowly, and we have also mistakenly predetermined scientific and historical texts as purely efferent reading experiences with the same deadening, low-retention results that workbook style teaching wrought in our literature classes.

An example of this assumption is Loban's (1987) statement:

> Teaching literature is fundamentally different from teaching the other academic subjects. It is different because, as has been insisted by Louise Rosenblatt . . . literature makes a direct claim on the emotions and imagination of the pupils. In social studies or science class, a body of information can be accurately conveyed in a didactic manner—by lecture or by demonstration. (p. 45)

My own experiences as a learner with a fascination with science and history, coupled with the responses of my students when I attempted to teach them in a didactic manner, would seem to refute Loban's claim. Once we begin to see that literature does encompass high quality writing in the fields of science and history (and it is encouraging to note that nonfiction is the fastest growing genre in juvenile literature), and we begin to reexamine this supposed fundamental difference between the language arts and science or history, we will, I believe, see new possibilities for extending Rosenblatt's reader response theory into curricular areas other than English class.

Invitation 14.2

Using journal articles or short works of nonfiction, select a text that is either personally relevant to your experiences or your interests (actually the ideal is to find a piece that meets both criteria) and that is written in a narrative format. Then read the text as more of an adventure story to be vicariously experienced and enjoyed rather than as a collection of facts to be memorized or ideas grasped and

mentally filed away. After, or periodically throughout the reading,
make diary type entries that have the tone of you actually being in
the story and that capture both your thoughts and feelings through-
out this imagined experience. (Many young readers seem to naturaly
respond to nonfiction in this manner and other readers [even adults]
are capable of experiencing and enjoying nonfiction after a certain
amount of deprogramming has taken place.) Compare your degree
of remembering the general concepts and even the particular details
to those times when they've read informational texts, written notes,
taken the test, and then deleted that particular mental file.

SCIENCE AS AN ADVENTURE
RATHER THAN A FORCED MARCH

After reading Carson's description of her walks through the woods with her nephew, I began to observe similar kinds of learning experiences taking place inside and outside of our classroom when I encouraged the students to both aesthetically and efferently read and/or write about our experiences with science. Perhaps it was the increased emphasis on experiencing science that triggered important changes, but as I shifted my teaching emphasis in science away from teaching about science toward having my students do science, I noticed a pronounced switch in their attitudes toward science time. We began going on weekly nature walks through our neighborhood wood lot, growing plants in our classroom, and populating our terrarium with insects and other bugs, along with lizards and other reptiles.

The next step was to stop assigning whole-class reading selections to be consumed and later regurgitated for a test, but instead to simply make available as much high quality nonfiction literature as I could find to help all of us satisfy our curiosity about all of the animate and inanimate creatures and objects in our woods and in our classroom. At the same time, students started keeping scientific journals in which they based their decisions about what to research and write about on their curiosities, observations, and questions. Their experiences as scientists on a journey of discovery, rather than as students didactically being taught about science, had dramatically positive effects on their attitudes toward science and on how much they understood and remembered about scientific topics.

Their journal writing also revealed another interesting change in the way that they viewed science as a school subject. They began to react to our science activities just like they reacted to information books shared during storytime. In their journals, they frequently used narrative structures to record their observations and conclusions. They told personal stories in response to science experiments or our nature walks.

And they made imaginative connections across other academic disciplines as they commented on the scientific accuracy of storybook illustrations, interwove our class collection of wildlife into math story problems and wrote fictional accounts starring their meal worm or petite marigold.

Karen Gallas (Tchudi, 1993), a first grade teacher in Massachusetts, made similar observations about her students' use of science journals,

> Through the medium of science talks and science journals, I have seen children develop ways to make their thinking visible in narrative . . . Students also gained a stronger identity as scientific thinkers. . . I noticed that the children I taught did not naturally confine their conceptualizations of science to include only natural or physical science, and they did not communicate in ways that I associate with scientific language . . . they used oral—written language devices that were sometimes more literary and poetic than expository . . . Metaphor, analogy, literary allusions to stories and folklore—six and seven year-old children were thinking and talking about their world in ways that forced me to revise my conceptualizations of the purposes and potential of the scientific journals and science talks. (p. 12)

Hanging around with first graders and watching how they go about figuring out the world and expressing their thoughts will change lots of ideas for us. We will either revise our concepts about how they learn, or we will be forever going against the tide. They will remind us that it is with a sense of wonder that science is best approached and that carrying away information and understanding results from having lived through experiences as scientists and not from didactic presentations.

THE EMOTIONAL CONNECTION
WITH FACTUAL TEXTS

When my oldest son, Conor, who was then a first grader, was given a hamster, he immediately wanted to go to the library and check out everything available that might help him in his new role as parent of a small rodent. He studied the illustrations, read what he could on his own, and begged us to read all that applied to his new baby hamster. As I would have predicted from my experiences with the first-grade students, Conor absorbed an amazing amount of information, grasped the basic concepts of hamster care, and generated more and more questions as we read together. His response was strongly efferent in nature. That is, he carried a lot away from his reading. But, at the same time, he had a strongly aesthetic experience with the books about hamsters. He imagined the story of his own hamster's growth. He wanted to know when and how his hamster would be able to reproduce, and he became upset at the prospect of his hamster contracting illnesses such as those described in the library books. He also, with difficulty, confronted his hamsters mortal nature when he read that hamster's typically live to be only 2 or 3 years of age.

Just as the first-grade students showed a capacity and a preference for reading information from a personal as opposed to an academic point of view, Conor further demonstrated the potential for fusing efferent and aesthetic stances into the same reading experience. Related to this point is the observation by Eisner (1994) that affective and cognitive processes are interdependent strands that, when not fragmented by faulty instructional design, lead to unified understandings on the part of the learner. My experiences as a learner, a teacher, and as a parent confirms Eisner's basic premise. That is, we all seem to have deeper and more lasting learning experiences when the concepts and information have personal relevance and when we are not kept at an antiseptically safe emotional distance from the subject of our study.

In her collected writings on education and drama, Heathcote (1984) referred to most of the so-called learning that takes place in schools as "over there" learning. She compares this to "in here" learning that she says takes place when the learner is either allowed or led to discover the personal significance of what is being learned. She claims that, ultimately, all real learning, or those experiences that have a lasting effect on what and how we think, are a matter of "seeing with significance" (p. 33).

I learned or was changed by reading Rosenblatt's ideas because they had tremendous significance for me as a frequently floundering beginning teacher. My first-grade students learned more readily when they were given the freedom to match the topics of study to what they had fixed their senses of wonder on. And my son, Conor, took in more information and retained it longer when the information focused on an actual exigency in his personal life—caring for his baby hamster.

At this point, it is important to be reminded of a caution that Rosenblatt (1978) issues regarding the danger of confusing our reading stances when the logical purpose is primarily either aesthetic or efferent. That is, when students read a novel, they should be helped to realize that focusing too much on the superficial details of the story interferes with the desired lived-through experience with the text. Just so, when the point of the reading is to rapidly and precisely assimilate information or instructions, too much emotional involvement can distort the information and mislead the reader. They should be helped to adopt the predominant stance in some measure.

Having witnessed examples of both types of failed reading experiences, I would still emphasize that we should encourage for the vast majority of reading experiences that we will provide for our students, a blend of aesthetic and efferent reading stances. With fiction and poetry, the natural inclination of the student to go under the spell of the story or poem should be balanced by a critical, judging disposition so that both the beauty of the language and the value system of the artist are brought to light. For rarely, if ever, does art exist as a purely aesthetic expression, devoid of an underlying persuasive intent. Likewise, science and history, no matter how prosaically expressed, have an inherent potential to capture our imaginations because of our human capacity to wonder about our physical universe and our human history. And it is because of, not in spite of, our personal interest and emotional involvement with the topic of study and their concomitant texts that the learning experience becomes coherent and memorable.

RECAPTURING OUR LOST SENSE OF WONDER

I refer to this universal human sense of wonder knowing full well that for many of us who spend our time with children in classrooms, there are days when wonder and curiosity seem to be rather endangered, if not altogether extinct. After a year's leave from teaching first grade to attend graduate school, I returned to my school as a fourth-grade teacher. In a very short amount of time, I recognized that although my students were in many ways more skilled than the earlier grade students had been, there was also some intangible desire for learning that seemed to have been lost. The spark of curiosity, the constant wondering, and the hunger to know more were much less evident. I speculated that this apparent loss might be a developmental change, but I also suspected that the students' school experiences had played a large role in bringing about this change. Many of my experiences with, and observations of, the fourth-grade students throughout that year added credence to this latter hypothesis.

For over a month, we met daily in school with no obvious changes in the students' disposition toward learning. They were well-behaved but passive. They became easily frustrated with open-ended assignments. Some even complained at the imposition of choice on their academic menu. One very academically talented girl stated directly that, by asking her to participate in choosing topics of study, I was shirking my job and pushing my teacher responsibilities off onto them. I was stumped as a teacher and more than a little cynical about the practical value of my year spent in graduate school.

Finally, a small breakthrough occurred on a Friday nature walk. Remembering how fruitful these walks had been with the first graders, I announced the resurrection of that tradition on one of our last warm Fridays in early October. As we were strolling along, Thomasina, a former first-grade student, wondered out loud about the absence of mosquitoes on such a warm afternoon. Clutching at the first sign of genuine curiosity, I decided on the spot that our first science topic would be insects and their response to seasonal changes in Alaska. It might not have been much to start with, but gradually we began to restore the spirit of inquiry that had driven our first-grade curriculum, and over the next two years with the same students, my faith in their capacity to question, to think deeply, and to care about learning was restored.

I slowly began to realize that my students hadn't lost their fascination with learning as much as they had lost their belief that what happens in school is at all relevant to their lives and the bigger world outside of school. This example of miseducation might be particularly likely to occur at a school such as ours, where most of the students have different ethnic, language, and economic backgrounds than their teachers. The less we know about our students' whole lives, the more difficut it is to help them to see the significance of their learning. But it is also a very great danger in any school or in any classroom where the learning experiences are structured without regard for the learner's needs, interests, or past experiences and there is no attempt to assist the students in connecting the threads of their experiences with the school curriculum. As Dewey (1938) reminded us, kids are continually engaged in learning experiences although sometimes the lessons learned may be negative or miseducative ones.

Invitation 14.3

Individually or in groups, select a unit of study in an elementary school curriculum. Having assembled all the information, discuss how this information could be presented to other students in a written story form, either fiction or nonfiction, rather than a more traditional factual report. (There are many excellent examples of this genre in children's literature.) Students who choose to write fiction have the poetic license to create fantastic characters and stiuations, but like their nonfiction writing classmates, are required to faithfully adhere to what is historically or scientifically considered to be accurate wherever possible in the text or accompanying illustrations. A possible added feature to these history or science stories is to include an appendix detailing the factual information that the story is based upon. (During the process of writing the stories, much of the learning happens as author/illustrator teams consult, check their information, or engage in further research to give their stories added substance and accuracy.)

SOCIAL STUDIES AND OUR SENSE OF PLACE

Science slowly became more and more appealing to my fourth-grade students, thanks to the abundance of exciting literature available that they could now read on their own, and as a result of their fascination with playing around with scientific instruments such as microscopes and bioscopes. But, to my surprise, social studies quickly became the subject of choice for most of the students. We began by inviting different families to visit and explain the family history of each student through personal artifacts such as family keepsakes and photo albums.

To complement this family history project, we selected historical fiction stories and biographies that shared a setting, or at least were from the same time era, as the generation in our family that we had chosen to research. The biographies and historical fiction stories were read to capture the sense of their setting and social conditions. Our reader-response approach lent itself to this type of thinking very well. Many of the books were discussed with parents and grandparents and then became a springboard for generating written family stories and personal histories.

Linked to this family research was a geographical component. I wanted the students to trace the places where their family had lived and to try to ferret out what influences *place* had had on their family's history. It is my belief that having developed a sense of where and how important one's place is allows us to know better who we are and to understand more completely why others put so much value on their personal and community places.

To help build a case for the importance of obtaining an understanding and an attachment to our place, I turned to novelists such as Paton, environmental essayists such as Lopez and the wisdom of Momaday's poetry and prose. In *Cry, the Beloved Country*, Paton (1948) warned us of the need to protect our land: "Keep it, guard it, care for it, for it keeps men, guards men, cares for men. Destroy it and man is destroyed." (p. 3). Similarly, in *The Rediscovery of North America*, Lopez (1990) referred to a "crisis of culture" (p. 32) that he explains to be an attitude of looking on a place as a temporary home from which to extract as much material wealth as possible and then abandon it. What is missing is a collective or cultural sense of place. Momaday (1969) advised that this elusive sense of place will be obtained if an individual will "concentrate his mind upon the remembered earth, I believe. He ought to give himself up to particular landscape in his experience, to look at it from as many angles as he can, to wonder about it" (p. 83).

Through reflections about their experiences and discussions with their family members, I wanted my students to consider and further develop their sense of place. This past year, we read MacLachlan's *All the Places to Love* (1994) during read-aloud time and then we interviewed a parent or grandparent about their places to love. For many students, this project has led to their most successful writing piece of the year. Every student returned with notes, stories, and more questions. We spent one entire afternoon sitting with our chairs in a circle, telling each other what we had learned, oblivious of the passing time.

After having developed this notion of place as an influence on family and personal history, the students eagerly searched through encyclopedias and other geographical reference books to gain more knowledge and factual understanding of various places connected to their family's history. Our reading may have been efferent in that we were searching for information to take away from the texts, but it was colored by our heartfelt curiosity and our emotional attachment to the subject of our research. Moreover, this emotional aspect of the reading is of vital importance. Without this emotional layering, empathy would not have been possible. With it, the facts mattered. Without personal involvement our learning would have been another vacuous, academic nonevent in our lives as learners. With it, the reading of information texts transcends mere reading about and becomes an experience of the subject of our study.

One of our favorite read-aloud novels that year, and since, has been *Prairie Songs* by Conrad (1986). This was a novel that very strongly pulled most of the class under its narrative spell and transported us into the times and lives of its characters. At the same time, our factual knowledge about and genuine understanding of frontier conditions grew enormously through listening to, reflecting on, and discussing the story and our reactions to it. Later, I found an interview with Pam Conrad (Tunnell & Ammon, 1993), in which she divulged that she wrote this work of historical fiction without doing any initial research. She explained that she had no need for such research because, "I had been reading pioneer stories and old journals all my life . . . so when I sat down to write *Prairie Songs*, I knew the place as if I had been born and raised there myself" (p. 34). After finishing the novel, she did some follow-up research, "to check my information, and my information, I am pleased to tell you, was accurate" (p. 34). Clearly, her experiences reading pioneer stories and journals had strong aesthetic, or living through, and efferent, or carrying away, components blended together.

This spring, as a sixth-grade teacher, I observed many of the students choose to illustrate a picture book, based on our sea-life research, rather than write a formal research article. Most of the sixth graders chose to write fictional stories and yet they were very careful to make their texts and illustrations as scientifically accurate as possible. The stories were to be donated to the class library of our first-grade partner class. The sixth graders were very cognizant of the opportunity to teach their buddies a great deal of marine science through their stories. The project was a self-selected, self-directed assignment. Complaints were few and the accuracy and quality of the research and illustrations was exceptionally high. I am also certain that because the sixth graders had a real audience and because visual arts, language arts and science were combined, the amount and depth of real, lasting learning was greater than if each student had authored a lengthy scholarly paper.

Invitation 14.4

As a history and geography introductory activity, construct a family migratory map. Individually research your family history: Record the dates, places, and causes for the moves, and any significant consequences or results of these relocations. Conduct this research by interviewing parents, grandparents, or other knowledgeable family members. Then construct both individual maps and a group or whole-class map with each student's family being represented by a different color strand of yarn on a wall-sized world map. One of the more successful related assignments is to choose a particular place or region that was a part of our family's geographic history and perform factual research that relates to the time period or activities of our family when they were residing at that place.

READING WITH BOTH OUR EYES
AND OUR HEARTS

T. S. Eliot (1956) wrote that he did "not think of enjoyment and understanding as distinct activities, one emotional and the other intellectual" (Elliot, 1956, p. 16). Like Eliot, my students and I have discovered together that factual research and emotional involvement in our learning can be complimentary processes, perhaps even different sides of the same process. Eliot goes on to state that, "It is certain that we do not fully enjoy a poem unless we understand it; and, on the other hand, it is equally true that we do not fully understand a poem unless we enjoy it" (pp. 16–17). If taken seriously, Eliot's words have enormous implications for us as teachers.

Not only is it possible to simultaneously enjoy and understand, to merge aesthetic experience and critical, efferent thinking, but Eliot seems to be going a step further by claiming that both are necessary for a complete experience with literature. A lack of one diminishes the other.

One year ago a student in our class, Elvis Diaz, ended fifth grade by describing how, after two years with the same classmates, his biggest change as a reader was that, "before, I had learned to read with my eyes and now I know how to read with my eyes and my heart." I see Elvis's words as a tribute to Rosenblatt's positive influence on the teaching of literature and the increased richness that students are having in classrooms where her ideas are a reality.

As more teachers find ways to incorporate the insights that Rosenblatt provides for us, we may hope for a reversal of this trend. Seemingly, reader-response theory has taken a lasting hold on our literature instructional practices. It is my hope that as elementary teachers continue to discover the increased richness that a reader-response approach provides for students engaged in reading stories and poems, we will also find ways to extend these same insights into nonfiction reading experiences. My students have proven to me that Goethe's description of the ideal reading experience as being one where the reader both enjoys and judges is possible regardless of the topic or the genre, so long as the reader is personally experiencing the text aesthetically and efferently.

Invitation 14.5

Think back or skim back over this chapter and take note of those passages that brought up memories of past experiences or that triggered feelings of either agreement or disagreement. It is through these points of personal connection to your experiences and your degree of emotional involvement that will ultimately make the difference in deciding whether this chapter leads to useful insights and lasting ideas or whether it goes the way of your last fast food meal—consumed and quickly forgotten. Discuss your collection of passages with your peers to reflect on your personal associations and strongly felt beliefs about the nature and value of literature in your life.

REFERENCES

Dewey, J. (1938). *Experience and education*. New York: Macmillan.

Eisner, E. (1994). *Cognition and curriculum reconsidered*. New York: Longman.

Eliot, T. S. (1956). *The frontiers of criticism*. Minneapolis: University of Minnesota Press.

Heathcote, D. (1984). *Collected writings on education and drama*. London: Hutchinson.

Loban, W. (1087). *The California reader.* Berkley, University of California Press

Lopez, B. (1990). *The rediscovery of North America*. New York: Random House.

Momaday, M. S. (1969). *The way to Rainy Mountain*. Albuquerque: University of New Mexico Press.

Paton, A. (1948). *Cry the beloved country*. New York: Scribner's.

Rosenblatt, L. M. (1976). *Literature as exploration*. New York: Modern Language Association.

Rosenblatt, L. M. (1978). *The reader, the text, the poem*. Carbondale: Southern Illinios University Press

Slezak, E. (1993). *The book group book*. Chicago: Chicago Review Press.

Steinbeck, J. (1961). *The winter of our discontent*. New York: Penguin.

Tchudi, S. (1993). *The astonishing curriculum: Integrating science and humanities through language*. Urbana, IL: National Council of Teachers of English.

Tunnell, M. O., & Ammon, R. (1993). *The story of ourselves, Teaching history through children's literature*. Portsmouth, NH: Heinemann.

CHILDREN'S TEXTS

Carson, R. (1956). *The sense of wonder*. New York: Harper & Row.

Conrad, P. (1986). *Prairie songs*. New York: Harper & Row.

MacLachlan, P. (1994). *All the places to love*. New York: HarperCollins.

Zim, H. S., & Shaffer, R. R. (1957). *Rocks and minerals: A Guide to Familiar Gems, Ores and Rocks* (R. Perelman, Il.). New York: Golden Press.

PART IV

Professional Development

15

Reconsidering Teachers' Roles and Procedures: Developing Dialoguing Skills

Lee Karnowski
University of Wisconsin–River Falls

EDITOR'S OVERVIEW

In the final analysis, the making of a reader-response teacher depends on the recognition and acceptance of altered goals and roles for teachers. This change is represented in the procedures and processes adopted—as well as those rejected. Lee Karnowski, who consciously adheres to a process orientation in her classes, examines the ramifications of these roles and procedures. She provides signposts to aid you on your journey to become such a teacher.

Readers naturally want to share their responses to books with others. Sharing responses in a classroom provides situations ripe for learning. Such a sharing is illustrated and explored to establish the teacher-and-student goals and to evaluate the procedure and questions. A comparative evaluation of textbook questions and activities leads to a consideration of the presumed merits of these, in contrast to the values and learning engendered by the response approaches.

Karnowski's closing advice is to trust the literature, trust the students, trust yourself. This is easily said, but acting on it requires creative self-education and careful planning on the teacher's part. It further requires the preparation of the students, so they may fully experience.

Consider the following:

1. *Do you consider yourself a reader or a nonreader? If you're in between, analyze when and why you read—or not. When you read, where are you on the aesthetic–efferent continuum?*
2. *What seem to be the objectives of textbook questions and activities? What, then, are their presumed merits?*
3. *Compare these to the learning values projected for reader-response approaches.*

If you are an avid reader, congratulations. It will be easier for you to share the joys of reading with students.

If you are not a reader, you will need to become one. There is no shortcut. You, like your students, will become readers by reading. Teachers who have felt the effects literature can have on their lives are able to share these feelings with students. If you have never felt the relevance of literature to your personal life, you will not be able to model this. After all, this book has been about helping students respond to literature in a personal way. So, begin to explore books and find those that speak to your personal life. This chapter contains some activities to help you begin this journey.

There is a t-shirt that reads, "So many books . . . so little time." How do you choose the books you will bring into your classroom out of the thousands that are published each year? You must have some criteria in mind for making your choices. Karl (1987) described *true literature* as having "ideas that go beyond the plot of a novel or picture book story or the basic theme of a nonfiction book, but they are represented subtly and gently; good books do not preach; their ideas are wound into the substance of the book and are clearly a part of the book itself" (p. 507). On the other hand, Karl described mediocre books as ones that "over-emphasize their message or oversimplify or distort life" (p. 507). She cautions us to remember that "just as fast foods do not nourish completely, so fast books—obvious and superficial—do not nourish completely either" (p. 508).

Invitation 15.1

Take two books, one an award winner, and one a fast-food book, and compare them for these elements: picture quality, word choice, honesty of purpose, and potential for response. In addition, you might want to ask yourself the following questions after you have read each:

Is this a book I want to reread?

Could I strongly identify with the main character and did I care about what happened to him or her?

Did this book arouse a personal reaction like fear, sadness, happiness?

What was it that I liked about the writing of this author or the pictures of this illustrator?

Do I want to find another book by this author or illustrator?

Any book can stimulate book responses, including picture books, informational books, novels, and poetry. Therefore, start reading a variety of books. You might want to ask a children's librarian to suggest possible titles. You might want to read books that have won awards and honorable mentions, particularly the recipients of the Caldecott Medal for best illustrations, the Newbery Award for best text, the Coretta Scott King Award for Black authors and illustrators, and the Children's Choice Awards and the Teacher Choice Awards from the International Reading Association for best new titles chosen by children and teachers respectively. There are magazines that list new books such as *The School Library Journal, The Horn Book,* and *Book Links.* Of course, you might want to ask students what they are currently reading.

After you have begun reading and copying down titles, start collecting these books. You will need to have a large collection of books for your classroom so students will have a choice of reading materials. It should come as no surprise that students who have a library in their classroom read more than students in classrooms without a library. Once you are acquainted with the best in children's literature, you will be able to find these at inexpensive prices at garage sales or through school book clubs.

SHARING RESPONSES

If you are a reader, you know that when you have finished a great book, you want to talk with others who have also read the book. You'll first share with them your pure enjoyment of the book. You'll say things like, "I just loved the part when . . ." or "Wasn't that the funniest situation when . . ." or, "I cried when. . . ." You will understand that students need to have an opportunity to share their personal responses with others.

If you are not a reader, you may feel that the way to have students respond to literature is through a comprehension worksheet of fill-in-the-blank questions. Therefore, it is important to get with a group of people who like to read and discuss children's literature. If there is not a response group in your area, begin one. It is through discussions with others that you will begin to understand the pleasures books can bring, the book craft (plot, characterization, setting, theme, mood, and style), and the structure of various genres (mysteries, science fiction, historical fiction, and biographies).

Here is an example of a response group in session. *The Giver* (1993) Lowry's Newbery Award-winning novel for 1994, was my book choice for an undergraduate response group. This book was chosen not so much on its merits as a medal winner but because it is a gripping science fiction novel appropriate for middle schoolers, and interesting for adults as well. It is about a perfect world where everything is under control because no one is allowed any choices in life, including the choice of their life's work. At 12, Jonas is chosen to be the next Giver, the one who holds all the good and bad memories of life when choice was allowed. My undergraduate students began talking to one another before the date of the response group's meeting arrived. "This is one book I couldn't put down," said one of the students. "I was angry when someone interrupted my reading," said another. When our response group convened, everyone was ready to discuss the book, honestly wanting to know how others reacted to certain parts of the story.

My goal for leading this response group was to model the teacher's role and have the undergraduates practice the student's role in literary discussions. The following teacher or facilitator goals were the ones I hoped to model:

1. When to focus a discussion around a question and when to move on to a new question;
2. when to share thoughts and when to allow students to continue sharing their thoughts;
3. what kinds of questions produce more divergent student thinking.

For the students' role, the goals I hoped they would experience were:

1. Feeling they were actively involved in the discussion;
2. making meaning from the text based on their own experiences, feelings, and prior knowledge;
3. serving as catalysts for the discussion questions; taking over the traditional role of the teacher as questioner.

Here is a portion of our response discussion:

Student: I'll begin the discussion. I was disturbed by Jonas' world. I didn't like the fact that you were always being observed and chastised for breaking even insignificant rules.

Student: And what about the "Matching of the Spouses" and the "Placement of Newchild"—all the important choices of life were controlled by the Committee of Elders. There were no individual choices.

Teacher: I was, at first, taken in by the peacefulness of Jonas' world. I liked the fact that every evening children ate with their parents and discussed their feelings. I also liked the fact that the children did volunteer hours. They seemed to take good care of the old and the young. What was good that you might want to keep from Jonas' world?

Student: I like the part about having someone else cook my meals, deliver them, and then take the dirty dishes away!

Student: Money didn't matter to the community. Everyone had enough to eat, a bike, and a job to perform. There were no wars, poverty, or crime.

Student: There was no crime because someone was always watching you. I wouldn't mind if they watched everyone else, but not me.

Student: And if you did something really bad, you were probably released. Did you feel it was right to release someone because they just didn't fit in?

Student: I was shocked to discover what released meant. I was really upset by the release of the twin with the lower birthweight.

Student: Especially because it was done by Jonas' patient, caring father.

Teacher: Do we have anything like *release* in our world?

Student: I guess we do because we can pull the plug on people who are on life support.

Student: And some states have the death penalty.

Student: And some cultures control the number of children a family can have like in the book.

Student: Now we have people who release themselves when the pain of disease is too much.

Teacher: Which character surprised you most?

Student: Since we're talking about releasing, it was Jonas' father that surprised me the most. He was so nice around the family and so cruel, with no real remorse, when he released the twin.

Student: Jonas surprised me the most. First, I was surprised when he seemed willing to take on the painful as well as the pleasurable memories. And then, I was surprised when he decided to release the memories back to the people.

Student: I wonder if the plan for his escape would have worked.

Student: I think so because the Giver would have given him all the memories for courage and strength.

Student: Which bring us to the most important question for me. Did Jonas die at the end?

Student: Of course he died. The author used the writer's device of hallucinating—Jonas was freezing to death.

Student: Yes, the book ended with Jonas thinking that the music was perhaps only an echo.

Student: I don't think he died. I think he went sledding into a new community, a more caring community.

Student: Remember, both the Giver and Jonas thought there really was a place called Elsewhere.

Teacher: What significance do you think the name of the young child had on the ending? . . . I was thinking about Gabriel, the angel, in the Bible.

Student: Oh yeah. The angel who announced Christ's coming.

Teacher: A new beginning.

Student: I still think they both died.

Invitation 15.2

Take a few minutes and revisit the dialogue that occurred during this response group. Identify what the teacher is doing to create this dialogue? Where can you see the teacher focusing the dialogue around one question and encouraging various student responses? Where do you see the teacher moving on to a new question? Why do you think the teacher decided to do this? What kinds of questions produced more divergent student thinking? How are the students creating this dialogue? Do you see them as serving as catalysts for the discussion questions?

COMPARING DIFFERENT TYPES OF QUESTIONS

In this type of response group, a teacher's questions and responses about literature are crucial. Posing divergent critical thinking questions will develop divergent, critical thinking in students. But divergent, critical thinking questions demand careful thought and planning. They do not just pop into one's mind if you're reading the selection for the first time with your students.

I went into this response group with questions in mind, but I also wanted to listen to the students and build on their interests and on their responses. Let's consider an array of questions that could have been posed. Here are some useful efferent, in-text, questions we could have discussed:

Describe the relationship between Jonas and his family before his selection as the next Giver, and then after his selection.

Jonas has many rules and traditions to follow. What are some of these and how are they similar to rules and traditions we have to follow?

What thoughts did Jonas have when his selection as Receiver of Memories was being announced by the Chief Elder?

Here are some of the aesthetic, inside the reader, questions we could have discussed:

You have freely chosen to be a teacher. If it was left to the Committee of Elders, what assignment would be chosen for you?

What memories would you hope to keep forever? Are they all pleasant ones?

Jonas' community has chosen sameness. Are there times when sameness or conformity appeals to you? When?

Unfortunately, if you were not taught this way of responding to literature either in your early school years or in college, you may think that the way to conduct a reading session is with a basal approach. You probably learned to read using a reader and a matching workbook or two. Your teacher had a teacher's edition that was at least double the size of your reader, and it contained all of the questions and the answers related to the stories you would be reading. You probably began the reading session with flash cards to help you learn new vocabulary. You were then instructed to read in a round-robin fashion, sometimes only getting through part of a selection. You may have been admonished not to read ahead, but there really wasn't time to do that. There was a vocabulary worksheet page and a comprehension page or two to finish. The next day would begin by the correcting and the discussion of the workbook pages before beginning the whole cycle over again.

Publishers now have created better readers than before, with a variety of genres and excerpts from good literature. But the teacher's edition and workbooks still suggest a fragmented word study approach and a fill-in-the-blank right answer comprehension check. Writing activities have been added but these do not give the student a choice of responding to the text in an individual manner and are skill based.

Let's look at the new basal texts for vocabulary lessons, comprehension questions, and follow-up activities.

A unit still begins with a list of vocabulary words that need to be pretaught before reading of the selection begins. Here are three typical vocabulary worksheet activities:

> Read each group of words and fill in the word from the box that fits with each group.
> Read the following paragraph. Some words have been left out. Use the words in the box to complete it.
> Complete each sentence with the correct story word. Use each word once.

Next the reading and questioning begins. Text-centered questions are designed to tell teachers whether or not students have read the selection. The setting-the-purpose-for-reading question sets the stage for a purely efferent stance. Here are two examples:

> Read to find out what special skill the main character has and how he used that skill.
> Read to discover what problems the two friends had and how it is solved.

Questions on a worksheet or asked during reading by the teacher are mainly efferent questions that are based on someone else's reading of the selection and someone else's answer to those questions. Here are three examples of questions designed to help students identify with the main character:

What details on this page tell you how tired the main character was?
Who is the main character of the story? What new information did you learn about this character that you didn't know before reading this page?
How would you describe the main character?
Here is a worksheet question designed to check sequencing skills:
Read the sentences. Decide which event happened first and write it on the line.

After reading the selection, there are a variety of activities for the class to do, related to the selection. These often have a cross-curricular theme. Teachers often skip these activities in order to make it through all of the selections in the basal texts required for their grade level. Here are three examples of these activities:

Have students write word problems that relate to the story.
Have the students research an animal from the story.
Have students give a debate about courage.

When using the basal, the reward for reading is finishing. It is getting through the reading aloud without losing your place or missing a word. It is getting done with the workbook pages with few errors so that you don't need to go into a remedial skills group for further instruction and more workbook pages.

BASALIZING AND TRIVIALIZING
CHILDREN'S LITERATURE

Teachers are now turning to a new way to teach reading—through a literature-based approach. They are using books that were written not to teach reading skills but because the author had something to say. But some teachers are basalizing or trivializing children's literature by using the same basal format for reading sessions. They buy teacher's guides for literature books that contain the same kind of vocabulary workbook pages, the same kind of comprehension checks, and the same kind of teacher-directed activities as are found in basals.

This has led authors and teacher educators alike to criticize what is happening to children's literature. Babbitt (1990), author of many books including *Tuck Everlasting* (1975), wrote:

I know that there is a movement underway to stop using texts for the teaching of reading and to start using works of fiction. In the beginning that seemed to me to be a good idea. But now I'm not so sure. The texts had related workbooks with sentences to complete, quizzes, questions to think about, and all kinds of suggested projects. The feeling has been, as I understand it, that these texts and workbooks were making a dry and tedious thing out of learning to read at the very time when concern about literacy levels was growing more and more serious. So it seemed sensible to try using real stories in the classroom—stories that could grab the children's fancies and show them what the joy of reading is all about. But what I see happening now is that these real stories are being used in the same way that the old texts were used. . . . I worry that this will make a dry and tedious thing out of fiction. (pp. 696–697)

Huck (1992) discussed this trivialization of children's literature when she wrote:

Teachers do not have confidence in their own abilities to determine the strengths in these stories, nor do they have confidence in the stories to generate a wonderful response from children. It tells me what I already know—that many teachers do not know children's literature and yet are expected to use it with little or no inservice work. So use it they do—in ways years of teaching from basal readers have taught them, they basalize it and destroy it in the process. (p. 524)

Here are some examples of how the new literature units are still using the same format as did the basals. Let us start with vocabulary activities. The units begin with a list of predetermined words that are new to the students. Compare these activities to the ones cited under basal vocabulary worksheet activities:

Look up the underlined words in the dictionary and write the definition in the space next to the word.

The following words are from the story. Find the definition of the word and write the word under the correct category (vegetables, animals, etc.)

Here are additional activities for the teacher to lead:

Write these words on the chalkboard and choral read them. Point to a word and ask a student to tell you what it means and use it in a sentence.

Make vocabulary flashcards in the shape of some object from the story and use to review vocabulary.

Next there are the setting-the-purpose-for-reading questions that again, just as in the basal, set the stage for a purely efferent reading stance. Here are two examples:

Look at the picture on the cover of this book. Read to find out why the man and child are out in the snow.

Talk about what makes a friend. Tell students they should read the story and make notes of every sign of friendship that occurs in the story.

During and following the reading of the book, the teacher asks questions or there are questions on workbook pages that are mainly comprehension checks and are efferent in nature. These do not differ significantly from standard basal questions. Here are two questions checking character development:

Does the main character feel brave? Why or why not?

Characterize the main character in one well-written sentence.

Here is a worksheet question checking sequencing ability:

The following are events that happened in the story so far. Put a *1* next to the event that happened first, a *2* by the event that happened second, and so forth until all events are numbered according to how they happened in the story.

Finally, there are the activities to be done during and after the reading of the story. These are often cross-curricular. They are, as in the basal, teacher-led with little student choice. Here are two activities:

Paterson's book *Bridge to Terabithia* (1977), is a beautiful story about the relationship between Jess Aarons, a sensitive artistic child, and Leslie Burke, an active, imaginative child. Their friendship leads them to discover a world where they are king and queen. Jess must face life alone when Leslie drowns one day as she tries to cross to their special place. One literature unit suggests that Miss Bessie, a cow, played an integral part in Jessie's life and so the teacher should set up a cow that uses a milk-filled plastic glove so everyone can practice their milking skills.

No one who read the book in my classes suggested that the cow was important enough to the story to do this activity.

Natalie Babbitt's book, *Tuck Everlasting,* is a story about a family that drinks from the spring that gives them immortality. A 10-year-old, Winnie Foster, discovers the spring and must decide whether to drink from it or live a life that revolves around the natural cycle of life. One literature unit suggests that students will enjoy creating an interesting bulletin board by writing on a predesigned frog, with 11 lines printed across the body, whether they would drink the spring water.

I would imagine when this assignment is over and all the identical frogs are lined up on the bulletin board, no one will think it's interesting enough to give it a second glance.

TRUSTING THE LITERATURE, THE STUDENTS, AND YOURSELF

We must, as teachers, trust the literature and stop thinking we must teach and test every detail in a book. We must come to the realization that discussing books in genuine peer–teacher conversations allows students to think more deeply about what is being read than when students work alone to complete worksheets. Encouraging students to initiate these conversations with questions of their own and personal insights based on prior knowledge or experiences allows students to view themselves as active sources of meaning, rather than passive receivers of someone else's meaning. Langer (1994) suggested that the "thought-provoking literature class is an environment where students are encouraged to negotiate their own meanings by exploring possibilities, considering understandings from multiple perspectives, sharpening their own interpretations, and learning about features of literary style and analysis through the insights of their own responses" (p. 204).

The question, of course, is how do some teachers make quality discussions happen. Learning how to conduct effective discussions is something that takes work. Practicing being a group facilitator is important. Visit classrooms in which teachers have learned this art and ask to lead a small group.

You have begun your professional reading in this area by reading this book. Other books that give practical help in handling discussions and also developing divergent, critical thinking questions include: *Grand Conversations: Literature Groups in Action* by Peterson and Eeds (1990), *Book Talk and Beyond: Children and Teachers Responding to Literature* edited by Roser and Martinez (1995), and *Teaching With Children's Books: Paths to Literature-Based Instruction* edited by Sorenson and Lehman (1995).

We have discussed the need for the teacher to enjoy reading, to be a reader of children's literature, and the need for the teacher to be an effective facilitator/participant in reading discussions, but a teacher must also prepare the classroom for group, as well as individual, responses to literature. As Hickman (1995) wrote, "Much of that work goes on behind the scenes in careful planning for space, time, materials, and activities" (p. 3).

There must be a space for books and a quiet area for reading in your classroom. Morrow's (1989) research on library corners suggests the following:

- bookshelves that house books spines out as well as covers out, with books shelved by categories;
- chairs, tables, and throw pillows for reading alone or listening to taped stories, as well as writing one's own texts;
- posters and children's work advertising books;
- planning, clean-up, and rules for use, organized and posted by students so they have ownership of their library space.

Finding a space for response groups to meet, talk, and work collaboratively must also be planned. Perhaps you will have groups meet around individual tables, or move their chairs into a circle, or, perhaps, be seated on the floor on mats or rugs. Responding to literature may take the form of writing and/or art. The teacher has to plan where materials will be stored and where children will have the space to create and display their work.

Finally, the teacher must plan time for the reading, responding, and sharing of literature to occur. Many schools are moving toward a language arts block of time that will allow all of the language arts subject areas time to be integrated.

We are in a very exciting time in the teaching of reading. Use of authentic literature and the modeling of both efferent and aesthetic responses may bring us closer to the goal of each child being not only able to read, but wanting to read. Just as you will not expect perfection in your students' abilities to respond to the many layers of a story immediately, so you should not expect perfection in your own skills as a reader and facilitator. Good teaching takes time to develop. It also takes a reflective stance where one looks at the teaching that has occurred and determines what went right so that it can be repeated, and what could go better the next time so that improvement takes place. Good teaching also requires taking a good look at the beliefs that shape our teaching. Teaching is shaped by our personal philosophies about how students learn and how we should teach. As Peterson and Eeds (1990) wrote, "A teacher's view of literature and learning is the greatest determinant of what will happen in the classroom where children read real books" (p. 5).

REFERENCES

Babbitt, N. (1990). Protecting children's literature. *The Horn Book, 66,* 696–703.
Hickman, J. (1995). Not by chance: Creating classrooms that invite responses to literature. In N. I. Roser & M. G. Martinez (Eds.), *Book talk and beyond: Children and teachers respond to literature* (pp. 3–9). Newark, DE: The International Reading Association.

Huck, C. (1992). Literacy and literature. *Language Arts, 69,* November, 520–526.

Karl, J. E. (1987). What sells—What's good? *The Horn Book,* 63, July–August, 505–508.

Langer, J. (1994). A response-based approach to reading literature. *Language Arts, 71,* 203–211.

Morrow, L. M. (1989). *Literacy development in the early years.* Englewood Cliffs, NJ: Prentice-Hall.

Peterson, R., & Eeds, M. (1990). *Grand conversations: Literature groups in action.* New York: Scholastic.

Roser, N. L., & Martinez, M. G. (Eds.). (1995). *Book talk and beyond: Children and teachers respond to literature.* Newark, DE: The International Reading Association.

Sorensen, M., & Lehman, B. (Eds.). (1995). *Teaching with children's books: Paths to literature-based instruction.* Urbana, IL: National Council of Teachers of English.

CHILDREN'S TEXTS

Babbitt, N. (1975). *Tuck everlasting.* New York: Farrar, Straus, & Giroux.

Lowry, L. (1993). *The giver.* New York: Bantam Doubleday Dell Books for Young Readers.

Paterson, K. (1977). *Bridge to Terabithia.* New York: Crowell.

16

The Making
of a Bicultural Teacher:
A Classroom Case Study

Kathleen G. Velsor
Jossie O'Neill
State University of New York, College at Old Westbury

EDITOR'S OVERVIEW

Multicultural education has become a given in curriculum planning. Multicultural learning varies, of course, according to curricular setting, teacher preparedness and imagination, and other classroom dynamics. Kathleen G. Velsor and Jossie O'Neill are convinced that teachers must be prepared for such teaching by becoming themselves culturally alive, recognizing their own cultural heritage, and becoming cognizant of their own and others' cultural responses.

Journal writing is the immediate strategy used in their classroom, first to investigate personal cultural perspectives and then to respond to a novel, The Abduction *by Newth (1993). The journal writes are used to develop understanding of the text. More significant in this class's context, they are also used to cause students to reflect on the responses themselves. What do they reveal about the respondents to themselves and to each other? What then is the cultural community of the class? A follow-up retelling exercise helps the students to explore their responses to the novel.*

Another kind of follow-up is expressed: The classroom students become student teachers. A group of them, working as a team, designed a multicultural unit for a fourth-grade class. Their unit also models an integrated curriculum; it incorporates art, language and literature, mathematics, and social studies. Their planning procedures illustrate collaborative learning, a strategy they include in their unit for their students.

Consider the following:

1. *As you read this chapter, reflect on your own cultural background and cultural responsiveness to the other. How are you affected by your own sense (or lack) of cultural identity?*
2. *What is the import of journal writing in response to literature in the development of understanding of the readers of themselves and their cultural attitudes?*

3. *What is the nature and potential scope of an integrated curriculum? In what ways can a literature-based, response-oriented reading program function in an integrated curriculum?*

This is a sign of great literature. I cannot say that these thoughts were foreign to me before reading this novel, but now I feel as if I've walked a mile in a person's moccasins who was truly ostracized.

—Lauren Jacobs (Journal entry, 1994)

As professors of Reading in the Teacher Education Program at SUNY-College at Old Westbury, we are confronted with the challenge of preparing teachers to work with students in culturally rich learning environments. "The most culturally alive people," said Henderson (1984), are "those who are changing and recombining new attitudes all their lives." Our particular teaching goal is to encourage culturally alive people to enter the field of education so they can begin to interface in a more authentic relationship with students in their classrooms. We seek to engage future teachers in developing multicultural skills, beliefs, and knowledge about people in ways that enable them to see themselves as well as others.

We believe that literature engages students in an experience of making human connections beyond the classroom. The universal themes found in good literature give our student teachers a medium for validating their own individual culture. Furthermore, literature provides an opportunity for our student teachers to enter a new culture. When our students identify themselves with the characters of a particular novel, they begin to "challenge and redefine the substance and effects of cultural borders . . ." making it possible for them to cross the imaginary parameters of culture (Mitchell & Weiler, 1991). Igoa (1995) clearly stated in her book, *The Inner World of Immigrant Children,* that literature gives students "a sense of solidarity with all people making them transcend cultural attitudes."

THE EXPERIENCE

As we began teaching, it amazed us how "culturally disoriented" (Smalley, 1963) our student teachers were as people. Like recent immigrant children, our students felt alienated from their own cultural roots. This cultural disorientation caused our student teachers to view multicultural education as "only for those Others rather than for Us" (Barrett, 1993). If we want teachers to develop "an appreciative, non-exploitive relationship with another culture" (Gochenour, as cited in Barrett, 1993, p. 16), "conscious knowledge of oneself, as a center, as a cultural being" is a key. Schools, in particular teacher education schools, must help students discover "how we each have become cultured and gendered people, and how we can actively participate socially and remake ourselves" (Kalantzis & Cope, 1985).

Our student teachers desperately needed cultural validation if they were to embrace multicultural education. We began by approaching the reading course as an experience in becoming consciously responsive teachers. We viewed each of our student teachers as people of culture. Knowing the need for social closeness for constructing meaning, we built this context in our classroom.

On our first day of class, the students were asked to introduce themselves and identify their cultural background. Twenty-five college juniors formed a circle to accomplish this task. The process began with hesitation as they struggled to define themselves as people of culture. Even though they represented men and women ages 22 to 50 from African American, Latino, Northern European, and people from the Mediterranean cultures, they did not see themselves as cultured and gendered people. Many of our students are parents of school-age children that represent the many faces of cultures in the Long Island classroom. Although recent immigrants easily identified their cultural makeup, second and third generation students were lost in the cultural dialogue. How can a woman with a name like Romaine Snowden respond, "I have no culture!"

Romaine, initially, had no historical understanding of herself and neither did many other students in Room C118. How can these future teachers understand a student as a cultural being when they have no perception of their own cultural contexts? These levels of awareness of cultural identity opened our student teachers to different cultural perspectives and began to affect their views on teaching:

> I thought it was great when the whole class talked about their own culture. I always used to think that being raised in a different culture made me an outcast. Ever since I started College, I began to understand how important my culture is to me. Everything we do in life has a culture, so why should we avoid that culture while teaching.
>
> —*María Marques, (Journal entry, 1994)*

María Marques had rediscovered the truth that, "we create and are created by culture" (Barrett, 1993). Barrett explained that "knowing how culture affects us gives us more choices as well as a deeper understanding of why members of our society and world have different values, customs, and communication styles" (p. 20).

With this initial experience in mind, we searched for a book that was culturally rich and that provided a perspective of the commonality of human experiences as a cultural context in which to ground our student teachers. *The Abduction* by Newth (1993) was the literary medium we used to create a critical reflective process for our students to discover themselves and to respond to "the other." *The Abduction* tells the story of a clash of cultures (Newth, 1993). It is a historical novel for advanced middle school and older readers—set in the 1600s in Norway. Newth portrays a 13-year-old Inuit girl named Osuqo, living in Greenland with her family. One day, when the crew of a Norwegian ship lure Osuqo, her father, and her fiancé on board under the pretense of trading, they are all abducted. The crew treats them as animals, brutally murdering her father and repeatedly raping her. Osuqo and Poq are taken to Norway, where they are chained and thrown into a filthy dungeon, and accused of insanity and witchcraft. The language barrier and the narrow views of the people in the tiny village offer them little chance for survival until they meet Christine, a young servant girl who has been charged with guarding them.

We assigned two literacy activities that allowed our readers to respond to the literature. Each student was asked to individually keep a journal as they read the novel. The guiding principle for the journal was to keep our student teachers engaged in an ongoing critical reflection process of their individual beliefs, values, and prejudices as they learned about their own and other cultural realities. The journal provided a forum for views to emerge that were perceived as safe. In their journals, the students thought about the issues of the book, connected literature to their own lives, developed their own interpretations, and prepared the groundwork for their retellings, the second literacy activity.

Our students were told that they would be expected to retell the story in a creative way using a medium other than a book report. They had an opportunity to explore the numerous expressive languages within cultures using the Inuit and Norwegian people as an initial context. Our intention was to allow students to express their thoughts using a medium that they were familiar with and could best communicate their feelings while still utilizing the cultural aspects of the Inuit and Norwegian people. These retellings took the form of plays, poems, song tapes, story scopes, felt boards, mobiles, pop-up books, photographic essays, and many others.

THE JOURNALS

As we began our literary journey, we did not know what kinds of journal entries we would receive. What we did know and what we reaffirmed as teachers was the need to trust the process that great literature provides. It was critical for us to engage in a dialogue with students throughout the duration of the course (15 weeks). Dialogue journals provided an opportunity to sustain this type of interaction. Our students were asked to write weekly and to exchange their dialogue journals with us four times during the duration of the course. We made it clear to the students that they were free to react either positively or negatively in their journals to any issue in the book and course. They could complain, questions, request, share, instruct . . . in essence, students were encouraged to think, reflect, and, most important, to communicate that which they took time to ponder and evaluate. Our job, in turn, was to respond to their entries in such a way as to help our students, reason, imagine, focus, question—in short, help our students connect with their cultural realities, thus promoting their learning (Vygotsky, 1962). We would then return their journals for their next entries. In a way, we, students and teachers of ED 4220, became each other's audiences.

Our dialogue was based on sharing ideas and thoughts as we both experienced learning, rather than the traditional journal writing activities where the teacher controls content and development by assigning topics and then making corrections and comments based on the form of writing. Instead, in each journal entry, we responded by addressing the student teacher (writer) by name, making a comment on one or more issues in the entry, and then requesting more information or giving an alternative for the student teacher to consider. These procedures not only kept the conversation going but also invoked the purpose of the course, which was to have participants see culture from more than one perspective. Shete Saha's journal entry (see appendix) reveals a process of cultural understanding that mirrors Hanvey's (1979) model of cultural awareness. Sheta describes at length her difficulty in approaching the retelling assignment as she begins to intellectualize the cultural similarities between India and Norway and the cultural differences between the Indian and American educational systems. She seeks explanations for behavior and differentiates between behavior that she can assimilate versus that which she finds too different from the original culture, her own. She does not rebel, but instead accepts that differences must and do exist between cultures. Sheta retells her learning experience by creating her own personal diary as it related to *The Abduction*. Thus, she becomes at home with this retelling assignment and new culture, the American educational system.

As our students read, they became alive and their journals began to interact to the various themes and issues that the book discussed such as rape, gender oppression, and most significantly the foreigner—the stranger—the other.

> In *The Abduction*, Osuqo is physically raped but more importantly, she is raped of her culture. After hearing of her struggles, I felt empathetic. There is often a time when a feeling of alienation comes over all of us. . . . while I was reading the book, I did not constantly stop as the theme smacked me in the face, but instead became one with Osuqo.
>
> —*Lauren Jacobs (Journal entry, 1994)*

For Osuqo, her culture was her identity. What Lauren understood was the connection of culture and one's self as her "I am ness" (Bradshaw, 1990). Lauren saw herself in Osuqo. Lauren began to perceive "the other" as equal.

One student wrote a poem narrating Osuqo's rape in her journal. As a woman, she took Osuqo's voice and wrote:

I sensed the fear, the image haunts me.
The blackbird swooped down and enveloped me.
He brings an evil I never knew possible.
Darkness weighs heavy on my heart.
How do I feel?
He forced his way inside me.
My body is a lifeless empty shell.
My soul is trapped.
My innocence is lost forever.
How do I feel?
Happiness is distant memories.
The present is unbearable, the past is a memory, and the future is
    unknown.
Only a flicker of light remains, I must hold on.
How do I feel?

—Sheila Rafkind (Journal entry, 1994)

Certainly, Sheila has responded to the reading about Osuqo's world differently, given her gender. Nevertheless, great literature makes you construct social relationships that cross the borders of gender and culture:

The rape of Osuqo is devastating on many levels. First the physical violation of Osuqo takes place. This in itself is a horrible act. Second, it is the rape of her people. They seemed a peaceful people, now they will have to live in fear of all strangers. Thirdly, it is raping away of Christine's innocence. I say this because it is the actions of the men on the boat that ultimately cause the death of Christine's father. Christine waits at home (Norway) for her father who is supposed to bring with him proof of purity in the form of a unicorn. Instead, she receives only the news of her father's death and she is charged with the care of his "killers."

—Paul Bloom (Journal entry, 1994)

We could also see through our student teachers' journal entries how they began to perceive "the other" as a people of culture. They began to grow biculturally and affirm diversity and to show evidence of becoming culturally responsive individuals:

As I re-read through the book, the reference to "the natives" as wild beasts, make me want to be there saying,

"No, you don't understand! They love. They are people like us. They sing like us, enjoy things like us and try to survive like us.."

Just because their language is different, people assume they are wrong and less than human . . . It is so true. When people don't understand you, they think you are strange or less than them.

—Kerry Rollo (Journal entry, 1994)

In this reading course, it amazed us to see the natural progression which our students logically took in voicing their understanding of the human nature and experience:

As I am reading this book, I can't help but think about all the clashes of race discrimination and cultural conflict. These are not new but continual manifestations of the earliest of times when people of diverse backgrounds came into contact.

—Joanne Walker (Journal entry, 1994)

In concert with Joanne's reflections, Paul's entry voices a philosophical perspective on the human experience and its age of innocence. He even questioned its existence:

I am not sure, however, I doubt that an age of innocence ever existed; or if as individuals we are ever in a state of pure innocence. However, we each reach a point at which the world does not seem so pure anymore

—Paul Bloom (Journal entry, 1994)

If the world is not so pure, as Paul wants us to believe, our student teachers need to construct a new understanding of the human nature that talks about the commonality of "the other." Many of our students described this understanding in their journals:

The whole book projects a lesson on the unknown which we must try and learn from it. Just because someone is different from the majority of people around you does not give you reason to be cruel and mean.

—Michelle Bauman (Journal entry, 1994)

Our students are fearful of themselves as well as of others. They are culturally without a voice. Many have been silent for years. Literature requires people to "write, speak, and listen in the language of difference, a language in which meaning becomes multi-accentual, dispersed, and resists permanent closure" (Mitchell & Weiler, 1991). Our student teachers need rich cultural identities in which to ground their teaching and human development.

Reading is a cultural act. Our students responded to this culturally rich literature through writing. The process encouraged our students to interact with the other, understand the other as an equal and to begin to cross cultural borders. It was only at this point that we felt that our student teachers took their first steps to being bicultural. The journal became their individual voice for their inner worlds. Reflecting on their own words allowed for a personal reconstruction of their world view to adopt a more culturally responsive teaching behavior. Barbara responded to the students' voices in the class discussions:

It's interesting to hear (through each students' retellings) how different everyone's interpretation is about what we're reading (or similar)? That seems to me the key to this biliteracy approach to reading to learn. Everyone is different, and should be able to express what they've learned in their own creative way. Everyone should also have the chance to learn.

—Barbara Haines (Journal entry, 1994)

Like Barbara Haines, Barbara Cirello recaptured a teaching perspective when she wrote:

In the end
we will conserve
only what we love.
We will love
only what we
understand.
We will understand
only what we've
been taught. [author unknown]

—Barbara Cirello (Journal entry, 1994)

Invitation 16.1

Form a group of your peers to analyze and discuss these students' journal writes. How do they express the bicultural growth and affirmation of diversity alluded to by the authors? How does literature become such a catalyst?

THE RETELLINGS

When we discussed the second literacy activity with our students, they were, to say the least, very apprehensive. As we encouraged them to explore the numerous expressive languages within cultures, we were all led to surprising levels of cultural understandings and creativity. Each student validated their personal interpretation through a confirming process that allowed their human experiences to take form.

By doing this collage, it made me think about every point in the book because I had to decide which pictures to use . . . . After reading the book and completing the collage, I was very satisfied with myself. I completed a creative collage (which I never though I could do) and gained so much

knowledge of different cultures. I never knew you could learn and do so
many activities with just one book.

—Charlene Heeger (Journal entry, 1994)

It took a while to figure out what point (theme) I wanted to concentrate
on. There were a few that popped out to me, for example, the inhumane
treatment of Osuqo and her family; the violation of another human in an
incredibly cruel and barbaric fashion (the rape); the ignorance of people
who fear what they do not know; the religious aspect of how beliefs can be
drilled into people's minds once again separating and discriminating from
one another.

—Erika Shulman (Journal entry, 1994)

In retelling, Charlene and Erika had to explain to themselves and to
others what they were thinking and reflecting as they read *The Abduction*. The process of retelling helps readers to refocus their attention on
the work as an act of expression. Thus the range of expressive modes
(photography, mobiles, song texts, collages, paintings, life-size puppets
. . .) emerged.
Patrick's rendering of Osuqo's dream is lovely and creative.

The following is a dream shared by Osuqo to Christine, as she paddles out
to sea with Poq:

My sister, I feel as though our souls have been united through a dark and
treacherous journey, which allows me to call you that. I think of you often
as I dream, searching for the answers to this puzzling set of circumstances
which has brought us together.

Do not mourn for me, as I travel to a place which is far better than the one
from which I escaped.

I wanted to speak to you about your father. Without a spoken word
between us, you forgave me for what happened to him. He was a good man.
A man who stood firm in his belief of right and wrong in the face of his
peers and superiors. He is the light in your world of darkness, the unicorn
in your dreams. Be proud of him, as I'm sure he is of you, for you shall see
him once again in another place.

Be proud of your mother also, who treated an animal with love and respect
and found a human being instead. Her faith is her strength, and she is to
be admired for that. I will not forget her kindness. She returned to me the
part of me which had been stolen, my dignity.

As you receive this dream, the end of my journey is near. It reminds me
of the final journey I made with my grandparents. As a young girl I often
dreamt about the day Poq would come for me in the longhouse and the life
we would live together. I regret not being able to pass on the tales and
songs taught to me by my grandmother. Not being able to see Little

Brother grow into a great hunter and leader. Not being able to make him the pair of boots I promised to him. But the end of my journey ends exactly as I have seen it in my dreams. My soul shall wander with the souls of the animals and we shall sing beautifully about the mysteries of life and death. I will speak well of you and your mother to the Sea Woman, so that you will always have enough to eat.

The sun hung night-red on the horizon as Poq paddles on what he told Osuqo was their bridal procession. She smiled to herself, as before them lay the glittering expanse of sea. "This is where the journey ends," thought Osuqo. And her last thought was of Christine. "Don't ever forsake me in the unknown, my sister, as I will never forsake you."

At that moment, somewhere over the Inuit village, a beautiful young swan spread its wings and flew for the first time into that same sunset that Osuqo had gazed upon.

—Patrick Morris (Journal entry, 1994)

Invitation 16.2

Consider the traditional book report in contrast to this retelling exercise. What are the sources, implicit responsibilities, and potential outcomes of each?

The students began to reflect upon this literacy experience and to develop as culturally alive people. Their knowledge about people and themselves as equals brought these student teachers to make connections beyond the classroom and across imaginary cultural borders. Toni wrote in her journal that she felt the story spoke of perceptions that exist today.

The realities of this story will stay with me for quite a while. I hope these will provide a deeper respect for all human life, a better understanding of cultural differences, family pride as well as tolerance and acceptance.

—Toni Keatty (Journal entry, 1994)

THE APPLICATION

As wonderful as these retellings were, we knew our course was not over until our student teachers could demonstrate the application of this experience in their future classrooms. Once more, we asked them to go through the process of learning how to apply this new knowledge. Thus, our they embarked on designing curriculum units using children's literature as a vehicle for entering other cultures. Their task at hand was to work cooperatively to construct literacy activities in the elementary classroom that enable students: to see themselves as cultured and gendered people and to perceive the other as equal to themselves.

Our student teachers researched literature for children that was culture rich and that provided a perspective of the commonality of human experiences as a cultural context on which to ground their elementary grade level students. The literature research provided a selection of culturally dynamic children's books in which they planned and presented curriculum units from perspectives such as an immigrant experience (*Aekyung's Dream* by Pack, 1988): the culture of the blind (*Knots on a Counting Rope* by Martin, Jr. & Arckambault; 1987); an activist agenda (*The Woman Who Outshone The Sun / La Mujer Que Brillaba Aún Más Que El Sol* by Martinez, 1991); a human quality (*The Masquerader / El Vejigante* by Delacre, 1993), and an ecological outlook (*The Little Painter of Sabana Grande* by Markus, 1993)

A CROSS-CULTURAL, INTERDISCIPLINARY LANGUAGE ACTIVITY FOR FOURTH-GRADE TEACHERS' RESPONSE TO LITERATURE

Modeling the value of cooperative learning via team-teaching throughout the course engaged our students in cooperative planning activities from an interdisciplinary teaching perspective. Through their coursework, these student teachers have been trained in planning instructional activities that emphasize the interdisciplinary nature or problems. Characteristically, an interdisciplinary curriculum design deliberately brings together the full range of disciplines in the school's curriculum: language arts, math, social studies, science, art, music, and physical education. The main point is to bring together the discipline perspectives and focus them on the investigation of a target theme, issue, or problem (Jacobs, 1989). Jacobs (1989) has identified a step-by-step approach for developing integrated units of study that include the following process:

1. Select the topic
2. Brainstorm associations
3. Establish a guiding question to serve as a scope and sequence
4. Write activities for implementation

In designing an interdisciplinary unit for students to learn about themselves and others as equal to themselves, it was logical for our student teachers to investigate with their learners the multifaceted nature of cultural perceptions found in children's literature. It was on this premise that Michelle, Beverly, Diane, Maureen and Jeanne chose to work with *El Vejigante / The Masquerader.*

As they began to share their understanding of *El Vejigante*, many questions arose: "What is the central theme of this story?" "Who is the audience?" "How can we validate our students' work with this story?" "Where are we going to take our students?" The possibilities seemed limitless. The students identified a theme to discuss with elementary school children that focused on the commonality of human experiences, regardless of their cultural background. This book is ideal for understanding that all people persevere to achieve things that are important to them. Our student teachers designed literary experiences that helped to facilitate this theme in many activities in the integrated curriculum. Interestingly enough, as they brainstormed, a guiding question emerged: Why is perseverance an important part of planning and creating a *carnaval*? They began to act as researchers and the question became the central focus to their curriculum unit.

Our student teachers were motivated by the life of an African-American hero, Dr. Martin Luther King, who is honored during the month of January for his perseverance. They organized their *Vejigante* curriculum unit to follow Dr. King's holiday in February, carnival month in Puerto Rico and many Latin-American countries.

Ramón, the main character of this story, is portrayed as a boy who perseveres in becoming a *vejigante* for the *carnaval* festivities in Ponce, Puerto Rico. The unit takes a class of fourth-grade students through activities that provide an experience of what it means to persevere. The children are to engage in making their own masks, like Ramón, by studying the history, religion, literature, art, and music of the *carnaval* in Ponce. The fourth graders are to retell the story from their own perspectives either by drawing, an essay, a poster, collage, or poem. They are asked to research, collectively, the history of the Spanish influence in the *carnaval* in Ponce and its religious implications.

The initial research provided the foundation on which to ground their interdisciplinary unit. Beverly designed a science activity in which the fourth-graders discovered the most effective paste for making their *vejigante* masks. Jeanne explored the materials for making the mask as folk art with the fourth graders. Michelle created a *carnaval* based on the initial social studies research with the children. Maureen designed a culinary activity for food to be sold at the *carnaval*. Diane planned a math activity using the metric system to route the *carnaval*.

Invitation 16.3

Select one of the books from the young adult literature section for your classroom. Follow the literacy activities detailed in this chapter. Together with a group of peers, develop cross-cultural, interdisciplinary language activities that respond to the issues presented in the book that develop or enhance the readers' aesthetic responses. Implement the plan in your classroom. Keep a running log on your students' teaching-learning interactions. Reflect upon the literacy-teaching experience:

1. *What you learned using this approach . . .*
2. *What was difficult or confusing for you . . .*
3. *How you are going to learn what was different . . .*
4. *The most interesting thing about teaching literature this way . . .*

Finally, to evaluate the effectiveness of the learning experience in the unit, Michelle designed a reflective activity. The students would be asked to create books that retell their individual experiences in planning a *carnaval*; they would also be asked to reflect on the perseverance theme.

CONCLUSION

As professors in the teacher education program, it has become obvious to us that we must reflect upon and recreate learning environments that are alive and sensitive to culture. Through reading the novel *The Abduction*, our student teachers learned to reflect and to cross the fine line that divides the printed page from their own life experience. Through the use of their journals, they were able to record their cultural perceptions as they progressed. The presentation of the individual retellings helped our students to test the waters and to validate their culture with their peers. The greatest leaps of thought were made when our students began to be alive and sensitive to culture.

By being culturally honest, our students began to view themselves as bicultural teachers:

> I wanted to somehow bring a "positive" light into the situation. The idea I came up with was to focus on "us" as future educators, having the power to empower children with the knowledge of all types of people, cultures, religions, etc. so that events like *The Abduction* will no longer take place
>
> . . . I hope to create an attitude and stimulate the minds of our children so that they will use their minds to make decisions . . .
>
> —Erika Shulman (Journal entry, 1994)

Cultural ideas can become the foundation for learning when literature sets the stage to move beyond the day-to-day struggles. Our students crossed the border of culture when they reflected on the characters in this novel. Responding to literature facilitated the content for their meaningful learning. Journal notes and creative retellings provided the method to respond to literature. Our student teachers in turn recreated literature experiences for their students that allowed for culturally honest classrooms to emerge.

Reader-response is the spontaneous act of reflecting on literature. Engaging future teachers in an experience of responding to culturally rich literature prepares them to facilitate literacy activities in the elementary classroom that validate children's individual culture as well as their human connections.

APPENDIX: JOURNAL ENTRY AND RETELLING

Sheta Saha's Entry July 13, 1994

Today, I had to make my presentation to the class. I avoided the moment of reckoning for as long as I could. Each of my classmates had their own version of the story, some were really creative. I had no idea about what I should do and it depressed me that I didn't have something as creative but just a rehash of the facts. I tried discussing with my sister but somehow I didn't feel very happy with what I had done with the story.

When I read the book, I read it as a story. I did not consciously seek images or comparisons. The book being what it was, soon made me aware of them. To me, Christine was a person I could sympathize with. In India the dowry issue being what it is, I could understand the father's compulsions, I could empathize with Christine's feelings. In India, where marriages are still arranged and looks count, a physical deformity for a girl is the worst thing that could possibly happen. In fact, we have a saying which goes like this, "first check to see if the girl is worth a second glance, only then you should enter into a discussion about the girls' qualities." The other thing that affected me deeply was the treatment that Osuqo and Poq received in Vagen. I was revolted by what they had to endure. Usually people are suspicious of strangers and if they are weaker, they try to dominate them, but this went beyond that. I sympathized with Poq when he said, "they have taken our dignity from us." To me that is something which affects me deeply. I am from a country which has lived through three hundred years of British domination. They turned our society and our culture upside down. It is ironic that the average Indian speaks better English than his mother tongue. On an average two Indians communicate with each other in English. Most Indians can tell you more about the history of Europe or the world rather than their own. We know more about the Bible than our own scriptures. When I finished the book, I had to find a creative way to retell it.

My educational background has not encouraged independent thinking or innovative presentations. It is a totally content oriented system. if you can quote chapter and verse you are a good student. Most of our education doesn't either teach or encourage us to apply our learning to real life situations. It emphasizes factual correctness, adherence to a certain accepted point of view. As a child and student, I do recall trying to fight that system, but in several cases it got me nowhere. Over the years I have retained a fair amount of that rigidity. It isn't easy to come up with something truly innovative. After a while, I thought that I would write it up either as a sequel to the story or to literally retell it, for that is how I interpreted the instruction to retell the story. What I was not too clear about was whether I ought to retell it as an adult or as a child. Eventually I chose to retell it through Henrik's experiences. I dismissed the sequel idea. Try as hard as I might, I could not see a future for Osuqo and Poq. The way the story ends, I am convinced that they were going out to sea to die. The way the song begins, the sense of finality in Osuqo when she says, "Let's go home" adds to that conviction.

My sense is that they wanted to die because they had nothing to go back to, Osuqo had been raped and she felt that she was no longer worthy of him, as for Poq, he had been abused too but in a different way. He couldn't count on being accepted back. Also in the Inuit culture is the essential belief that you can take your life, if you feel you are a burden to your people you can follow the time honored custom and put an end to your life. A frail kayak, no provisions and none of their implements only adds to that sense. So I chose to look at it through Henrik's eyes.

To me he is more than an ill dressed, stammering son of master Mowinckel. he is compassionate, kind, generous and above all, he has a conscience. He is the one who tries to protect the Inuit from the moment he realized that the furry bundles were not animals but humans. So I wrote out a letter to the author telling her about a journal which Christine Mowinckel had found amongst her family papers. I began to retell my story through a series of journal entries. In the early entries I tried to highlight some of the issues I reacted to, or empathized with, in the novel. To me the waiting for the ship to return has a certain meaning. Christine's feelings and thoughts were important too, so I put that down as well. Once the ship returned, I put the focus on the unfair treatment that the Inuit received at the hands of the people of Vagen. Henrik, in a sense, became the guardian of Osuqo and Poq. He became the keeper of the stories. Since I wrote it up as a diary, and because of Henrik's particular role, I thought it necessary to draw some pictures. Once again, I was hampered by my upbringing. To me, stick figures, incorrectly drawn pictures, were difficult to do. I was miserable because at home in Indonesia I have an article on the Inuit which would have been so appropriate. Given my limitations in terms of inability to go to a library book or look for materials I may need, I found myself getting very frustrated. To add to it, my own sketches were not good enough as far as I was concerned and the quality of the presentations I had seen in class were way beyond anything that I was doing.

At that point I tried to talk to my sister. She pointed out to me that in this system, the process is more important than the product. It is essentially a system which encourages creative thinking. We talked quite a bit about what I had to do in class, what I was doing in Indonesia. She talked about her experiences as a teacher. Finally, at about 1:00 AM when I sat down to write up my last entry, it occurred to me that for Henrik, he is the interpreter of Poq's words, he has not seen what Poq describes so the pictures could be rough sketches and technically incorrect. A Narwhal could be dolphin with a large snout, or the long house could be a large log cabin. All that remained for me was to shade in what I had drawn. What I would have loved to draw was what I had seen in Dr. Velsor's book. It was an Eskimo word story, if I had the time, I would have added that onto the journal. Once that was done, I was prepared with my assignment. I must admit that once I got up to the present, I thoroughly enjoyed it. What I had done with my work had some validity. In its own way, it was a retelling, a different kind of retelling!

—*Sheta Saha (Journal entry, July 13, 1994)*

Kirsten Mowinckel's July 12, 1994 Entry

King Olaf II Road
Oslo 01 78465 Norway

Dr. M. Newth
Department of Anthropology
S.U.N.Y. at Old Westbury
New York, NY 11749 USA

12 July 1994

Dear Dr. Newth,

This letter follows the conversation I had with you on the telephone about a week ago. You may recall that Dr. Bjorg had given me your telephone number and asked me to speak to you. Enclosed with this letter is the diary of my great grandfather, Henrik Mowinckel.

Some weeks ago, I chanced upon a boxful of papers at the back of the armoire in my grandfather's room. Amongst his sketches and notes was this bundles of papers. I almost threw it out but when I glanced through it, I discovered that it was part of his father's diary written when he was about 18 years old. Once I began reading it, I realized that he was writing about what possibly might have been the first attempt in Norway to study and understand the Inuit as a people, rather than as one of Nature's freaks. For a while I thought that I might keep it, for it helps me know a little more about my father's family. Dr. Bjorg, however, mentioned that you are currently working on a project which documents the oral traditions of the Inuit so I thought that you might have a use for it.

I do hope that some of what is in the diary will be of use to you. I have sent you copies of the entries which relate to this encounter with the two Inuit: Osuqo and Poq. I look forward to hearing from you soon. Thank you.

Yours sincerely.

Kirsten Mowinckel

REFERENCES

Barrett, M. B. (1993). Preparation for cultural diversity: Experiential strategies for educators. *Equity and Excellence in Education, 26*(1), 19–26.

Bradshaw, J. (1990). *Homecoming: Reclaiming and championing your inner child.* New York: Bantam.

Hanvey, R. (1979). *Cross-cultural awareness. Toward internationalism: Readings in cross-cultural communication.* Rowley, MA: Newbury House.

Henderson, J. L. (1984). *Cultural attitudes in psychological perspective.* Toronto: Inner City Books.

Igoa, C. (1995). *The inner world of immigrant children.* New York: St. Martin's Press.

Jacobs, H. H. (Ed.). (1989). *Interdisciplinary curriculum: Design and implementation.* Alexandria, VA: Association for Supervision and Curriculum Development.

Kalantzis, M., & Cope, B. (1985). Pluralism and equitability: Multicultural curriculum strategies for schools. *Social Literacy Monograph, 16.*

Mitchell, C., & Weiler, K. (Eds). (1991). *Rewriting literacy: Culture and the discourse of the other.* New York: Bergin & Garvey.

Newth, M. (1993). *The abduction.* New York: Farrar, Straus & Giroux.

Smalley, W. A. (1963). Culture shock, language shock and the shock of self-discovery. *Practical Anthropology, 7,* 177–182.

Vygotsky, L. S. (1962). *Thought and language.* Cambridge, MA: MIT Press.

CHILDREN'S TEXTS

Children's Literature

Castañeda, O. (1993). *Abuela's weave.* New York: Lee & Low Books.

Czernecki, S., & Rhodes, T. (1992). *Pancho's Piñata.* New York: Hyperion Books for Children.

Delacre, L. (1993). *Vejigante / Masquerader.* New York: Scholastic.

Jacobs Altman, L. (1993). *Amelia's road.* New York: Lee & Low Books, Inc.

Maloney Markun, P. (1993). *The little painter of sabana grande.* New York: Bradbury Press.

Mandelbaum, P. (1990). *You be me I'll be you.* California: Kane/Miller.

Martin, B., Jr., & Archambault, J. (1987). *Knots on a counting rope.* New York: Holt & Co.

McKissack, P. C. (1988). *Mirandy and brother wind.* New York: Knopf.

Paek, M. (1988). *Aekyung's dream.* California: Children's Book Press.

Wynn, M. (1993). *The eagles who thought they were chickens.* Georgia: Rising Sun Pulishers.

Zubizarreta, R. (1991). *The woman who outshone the sun.* California: Scholastic/Children's Book Press.

Young Adult Literature

Baillie, A. (1994). *Little brother.* New York: Puffin Book.

Burnford, S. (1977). *Bel ria.* Boston, MA: Little, Brown.

Collier, J. L., & Collier, C. (1974). *My brother Sam is dead.* New York: Scholastic.

Fisher-Staples, S. (1989). *Shabanu, daughter of the wind.* New York: Random House.

Fox, P. (1991). *Monkey island.* Illinois: Dell Yearling Book.

Greene, B. (1973). *Summer of my German soldier.* New York: The Dial Press.

Hotze, S. (1988). *A circle unbroken*. New York: Clarion Books.
Kincaid, J. (1986). *Annie John*. New York: Plume Fiction.
Laird, E. (1991). *Kiss the dust*. New York: Puffin Book.
Lee, M. G. (1992). *Finding my voice*. Boston, MA: Houghton Mifflin.
Mori, K. (1993). *Shizuko's daughter*. New York: Henry Holt & Co.
Naidoo, B. (1988). *Journey to Jo'burg*. New York: Harper Trophy.
Newth, M. (1993). *Abduction*. New York: Farrar, Straus & Giroux.
Richter, C. (1975). *The light in the forest*. New York: Bantam.

17

Reader Response:
One District's Initiatives

Connie Russell
Eau Claire Area School District

EDITOR'S OVERVIEW

One teacher making the decision to adopt a reader-response process in conjunction with a literature-based reading curriculum requires significant attitude and assumption shifting. It necessitates training to engage students' responses. When the personnel of a school district make this decision, the action implications may seem formidable.

For the Eau Claire Area School District, the change has been carefully planned and staged by a committee of teachers and reading/language arts specialists. They concentrated first on curriculum developing and book selection. The reorientation of instructional practices came next—and continues. Connie Russell, the district's reading/language arts coordinator, explains the procedures used to ready and train the teachers; she identifies some of the problems and pitfalls, the misconceptions and obstacles about theory and practice. She also explores the ways in which these factors were (and are) attended to and how appropriate practices are being developed.

There are evident successes as well. Examples of these—the veteran first-grade teacher combining the teaching of reading with literature discussion; a fourth-grade teacher modeling response techniques through the use of picture story books; a fifth-grade teacher integrating language arts and social studies and having her students respond with journal writes and small group discussions—reveal that effort and dedication pay off.

Consider the following:

1. *Imagine that you have accepted a position in this or a comparable school district. Where would you place yourself on a reader-response teaching continuum? What would you want to learn to successfully adapt to and practice these principles?*

2. *What teaching strategies for developing readers' responses do you feel comfortable using? How would you proceed? How would you get your students ready?*

Five years ago, the Eau Claire Area School District had a basal-driven curriculum with every teacher using reading workbooks. Our goal was to move toward an integrated language arts curriculum based on current research in the areas of reading and language arts. To do this, we needed to provide teachers with a written integrated curriculum guide and staff development in the areas of strategic reading strategies for both narrative and expository texts, integration of the language arts, and reader-response theory. We were already moving toward the elimination of tracking. We had offered staff development on heterogeneous flexible grouping, showing teachers how to move from ability grouping to a combination of whole group and small group instruction. However, we knew the new curriculum and additional resources would further facilitate grouping according to student needs and interests.

The changes would take time. The Eau Claire Area School District is a district of approximately 11,500 students. About 6,000 preschool through fifth-grade students are housed in a total of 16 buildings ranging from one section to four sections of each grade. Approximately 300 teachers, including the special education teachers, serve the pre-kindergarten through grade 5 students. Four elementary reading/language arts specialists serve the preschool and elementary teachers. Depending on the number of sections in a building, these specialists are in the elementary buildings from a half day to one and a half days a week to work with teachers and students. Hmong students comprise 8% of the total student population. The Hmong students coming into the district often arrive with little or no English. The balance of the population is nearly all Caucasian. Elementary schools range from schools with an upper middle class population to a low socioeconomic status.

Eau Claire is a midsized city with surrounding rural areas totaling about 100,000 people. Retail, service, and medical fields provide the majority of jobs for people in the community. In fact, the Eau Claire Area School District is the third largest employer in the city. The University of Wisconsin–Eau Claire provides many of the teachers for the school district.

Today, although the district still uses a basal, teachers use that basal selectively as a resource along with hundreds of trade books. About 5% of the teachers use workbooks; they will be phased out after the 1996–1997 school year. This chapter focuses on reader response; it outlines the changes that have taken place in our district as well as the problems we faced, and projects the changes yet to come with regard to reader-response theory and practices.

CURRICULUM PLANNING

A committee of teachers and reading/language arts specialists began by rewriting the language arts curriculum guide. In order to write a state-of-the-art guide, we had to work as a team, citing the research and deciding how that research could be incorporated into our written guide in a practical manner. We relied heavily on the *Wisconsin Guide to Curriculum Planning in Reading* (Wisconsin Department of Public Instruction, 1987) and *The Wisconsin Guide to Curriculum Planning in English Language Arts* (Wisconsin Department of Public Instruction, 1987). A skills-based curriculum no longer served our goals in reading/language arts. We needed a balanced program of comprehension strategies, reader response, and interpretation development in an integrated language arts program. We discussed, we brainstormed, we argued, and we learned! Our students needed to learn how to read and then use reading to learn but, as important, they needed the support to become lifelong readers for enjoyment as well as learning. To do this, we had to get them into good literature and honor their choices as well as their thoughts about books. One change, then, mandated the use of a minimum of three novels yearly. This mandate applied to only a small percentage of teachers, as most already used many trade books during a school year.

Once the curriculum was written, we looked at materials. We first added to our collection of trade books. We purchased sets of trade books for all reading levels that would accommodate small and large groups. Teachers needed multiple copies of books in order to flexibly group students and offer reader-response opportunities. Several steps helped teachers with the selection of trade books for use in their classrooms. Teachers have been and continue to be invited to submit titles of books they would like ordered. The elementary language arts specialists and I keep updated as much as possible on books and routinely order fiction with appeal and literary quality as well as nonfiction that complements the science, social studies, math, and health curricula. Through inservices, suggestions from elementary language arts specialists who knew the collection, and a reading newsletter published quarterly, teachers became familiar with novels, picture books, and big books that were available. Our district adopted Media Minder, a program whereby teachers, using their code number, dial the Central Administration Office from their schools or from their homes at night to request the trade books they want. Books are delivered to the schools twice a week. This program greatly eased the task of ordering books, and the collection kept in a central book room meant that we could have a bigger selection. With 16 elementary schools, we would not find it effective to house duplicate sets of all titles in schools.

In addition, the teachers have formed grade level committees for the past three years and select trade books in sets of six each year in place of workbooks. These books function as resources for math, science, social studies, and health and provide a balance of fiction and nonfiction. These books stay in the schools.

REVISING INSTRUCTIONAL PRACTICES

These were only initial steps, however. Once the materials and written curriculum were in place, we had to begin looking at instructional practices. Long before teachers can use reader response, they must understand the meaning of aesthetic reading (Rosenblatt, 1978) and examine their methodology. If, in aesthetic reading, "the reader's attention is centered directly on what he is living through during his relationship with that particular text," (pp. 22–30) then chapter questions on the story elements or plot structure cannot be considered reader response—even when they're used with a children's novel rather than with a basal reader. Probst (1988) tells us that, while "it [literature] may be studied in scholarly and professional ways, that is not its primary function. We must keep in mind that the literary experience is fundamentally an unmediated, private exchange between a text and a reader, and that literary history and scholarship are supplemental" (p. 7). There would be a continual struggle between the need to build comprehension strategies and the need to provide lifelong readers who enjoyed literature. As district reading/language arts coordinator, I knew that most teachers who were using trade books used no more reader-response theory than those teachers using the basal exclusively. Teachers merely wrote their own questions or purchased a ready-made set for the trade books they were using. The teacher-made questions duplicated those contained in basal manuals and workbooks; they examined literal comprehension. For example, in the book *Stone Fox* (Gardiner, 1987), questioning why Willy wanted to race his dog is a literal comprehension question. Certainly, students must understand the basic story, but we can assess their comprehension through inferential questioning as well as through their responses to the moral issues in this book. In his speech on "Research on Reader Response and the National Literature Initiative" at the National Council of Teachers of English Convention in Baltimore, Squire (1990) said that,

> too many practitioners today seem to be using response to literature as an umbrella term to refer to any aspect of literature and its teaching: the study of literature, the study of the teaching of literature (which may or may not be designed to elicit response), or studies about and around literature—the author, the genre, the history, the cultural period from which the work emerged, and so forth. (p. 2)

Without a clear understanding of the difference between information-oriented efferent and aesthetic responses (Rosenblatt, 1978), teachers were calling any work revolving around a trade book reader response. We would not quickly undo years of working with a basal where the majority of the manual questions asked only for information from the text.

Our elementary language arts department, made up of four elementary language arts specialists and me, knew we would need an ongoing staff development plan. Seeds were planted with theoretical background on reader response during inservices held during the elementary inservice day and during 1-hour sessions after school. The Early Literacy Inservice Course (ELIC), offered for teachers of grades K through 3 and taught by two of our elementary reading specialists, helped many teachers examine their teaching philosophy. However, most of the staff development occurred, and still occurs, one-on-one when the elementary language arts specialists visit the buildings weekly. The specialists, who have #317 Wisconsin Department of Public Instruction reading licenses and expertise in process writing, continue to help the teachers apply what they heard during inservices and classes. These language arts specialists have continually modeled through the use of literature circles (see chapters 8, 9, 19, and 13 in this book). They have also shown teachers how to use dialogue or other response journals. In some instances, study groups were formed with the language specialists leading the teachers as they studied *Transitions* or *Invitations* (Routman, 1991). Staff development in the area of critical thinking and interpretive questioning within the district also helped teachers examine the ways they had students respond to literature. Although literal questioning still occurs, we believe we continue to improve.

We could also draw on the success of teachers reading orally to their students, a practice that occurs across the district. I remembered my own classroom experiences: Patti, my romantic, dreaming over the Oscar Wilde fairy tales after I had read *The Happy Prince* (Wilde, 1980); Brian, taking *Incident at Hawk's Hill* (Eckert, 1987) home because he couldn't wait for the next day's oral reading time. Patti would respond in her writing over the next few weeks, trying to imitate Wilde with her own fairy tale that she illustrated in the manner of the art of this beautiful picture book. Brian wanted more books by Eckert, and I spent weeks trying to find another of his books that was out of print. Sean, a struggling reader, was a master in creative dramatics as we all became shipmates of Christopher Columbus.

Invitation 17.1

Select a favorite book (picture story or chapter) appropriate to be read aloud to children. (You choose the age). Read this to your peers to practice your delivery and to develop a response discussion or read it to children, again, to engage their responses.

Over the years I have seen students from preschool age through high school respond aesthetically to books the teachers read orally. We needed to take the magic from this practice and apply it to our instruction in the classroom. As teachers read to their students, especially in the upper grades, they should expect more than attention. We needed to promote the idea of oral responses to literature read to students at all grades. This is especially critical for those students for whom reading and writing is a struggle, and it would be a good place to start. Just as we enjoy discussing books with other adults, students enjoy dialoguing about the books read to them.

CONNECTING THEORY AND PRACTICE

We also needed to know more about connecting theory and practice. As language specialists, our department continued to study the area of reader response. I gained a deeper understanding as I watched very young children.

Perhaps the most natural responses to books come from preschoolers in our Head Start, Preschool English as a Second Language, and Early Education Needs programs. The children applaud, move their bodies in response to rhyme and rhythm, and draw and pretend write during and after they are read stories. We needed to examine the ways young children respond to literature and take our cue from them for the early grades. Pugh (1988) told us that "for children, encounters with literature should retain characteristics of play, children's most natural activity" (p. 1). This means a combination of creative dramatics, structured play, and art work are natural ways for young children to respond to literature. Their responses reveal the strength of play in helping them figure out their world and the world of books. They often choose the words that elicit noise or images to repeat, and their drawings may or may not have something to do with the story. Sometimes the story triggers memories of their own lives, and they depict these in their drawings. Rosenblatt told us that "the notion that first the child must 'understand' the text cognitively, efferently, before it can be responded to aesthetically is a realization that must be rejected" (Holland, 1993, p. 14).

I found this to be true of preschool children in a English as a Second Language program who, with limited English, still participated gleefully as we acted out a book about ducklings. I began with an oral reading while the bilingual aide repeated each sentence in Hmong. These children needed to build on vocabulary and experiences in their first language while they learned a second language. Their favorite words were the action verbs as they mimicked my actions while I circled around the room and they followed me, being ducks. They loved the word *quack* for its noisiness. However, even as they responded aesthetically, they were beginning to see the link between oral and written language. When we finished our little drama, I showed them the story I had read to them on a large chart. Nearly all of the children could use the pointer to find the word *duckling*. When I asked them how they knew the word, some told me it started with *d*. Others used the title word as a pattern for matching. I also knew the children for whom print still had little or no meaning. Paula, their classroom teacher, would monitor these children carefully. I found that these children, as well as the other children in our early education programs, love to write, and that many of them are well on their way to understanding that print carries meaning and to paying attention to letter formation before they enter kindergarten. This learning takes place very naturally as children respond to stories and assures me that the skills needed for reading can occur through immersing these children in literature and allowing them to respond aesthetically.

Mary Catherine, at 4, moved from drawings (see Fig. 17.1) with an adult providing the text to experimentation with letters and marks that resemble letters (see Fig. 17.2) as she responded to the story of Cinderella. At 5, she continued to draw but ended her minibook with a pattern she noticed in books read to her (see Fig. 17.3).

Slowly, teachers began to examine their use of trade books in the classroom. Mary, a veteran first-grade teacher, begins the year combining the teaching of reading with literature discussion. Students begin by drawing pictures about the books read to them or read by themselves. After a time, Mary teaches her first graders to respond in writing by typing questions on paper in primary type and cutting them into strips. The students choose a question that appeals to them and respond to it

Cinderella hid in the bushes and Jack counted to ten.

FIG. 17.1. Mary Catherine's drawing when an adult provided text.

FIG. 17.2. Mary Catherine's experimentation with letters and marks that resemble letters in response to the story of Cinderella.

FIG. 17.3. Mary Catherine's pattern ending to her minibook.

in their journals (See chapters 8, 9, and 13 on journaling). They paste the question at the top of their response. The children begin with retellings and feelings but, by the end of the year, these first graders respond to the story characters and the plot of the stories. More important, they relate the stories to their own lives (see Figs. 17.4, 17.5, and 17.6).

Organization is important in classrooms using reader response, especially when groups of students are using different books. Phyllis and Judy, in second-grade classrooms, organize their literature circles by teaching students how to work in cooperative groups. Directions to the students and charts, on which the groups decide on responsibilities and keep track of how well the literature circle went, help students manage time well and stay on task as they discuss trade books in small groups (see Figs. 17.7 and 17.8).

Denise begins the use of reader response in her fourth grade classroom by orally reading strong picture books to her students. She and the building reading specialist team up initially to model the technique for the students. After reading a book, both write responses and then talk about their responses with the students. Once students know the difference between a response and a retelling or summary of the story, they are ready to respond to picture books that Denise reads orally. In Laura's

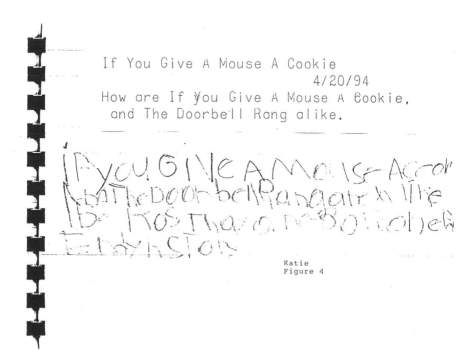

FIG. 17.4.　Katie's response to *If You Give a Mouse a Cookie.*

response to *The Wall* (Bunting, 1990), she demonstrates an understanding of personal response to a story:

> When I was listening to it [*The Wall*], I felt sad. Seeing people around me that seemed like my grandfather would make me cry. If I was the grandfather and I was listening to the little boy, I would either cry or wish I could put my hand on his shoulder and say, "It's all right, it's all right." If

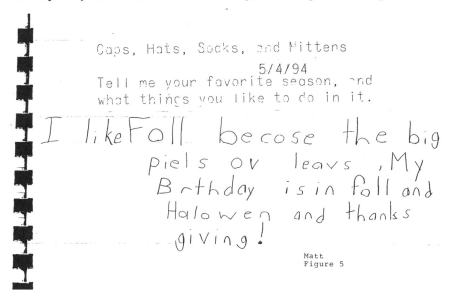

Caps, Hats, Socks, and Mittens
5/4/94
Tell me your favorite season, and
what things you like to do in it.

I like Fall becose the big
piels ov leavs, My
Brthday is in foll and
Halowen and thanks
giving!

Matt
Figure 5

FIG. 17.5.   Matt's response to *Caps, Hats, Socks, and Mittens.*

The Three Billy-Goats Gruff   3/24/94
Illustrate your favorite character,
tell who it is and why you like him.

The big pily goat
Becose he is snort

Matt

FIG. 17.6.   Matt's response to *The Three Billy Goats Gruff.*

When your group is ready to start
everyone will...

1. Share their reading journals
   one at a time.

2. Tell about his or her favorite
   character in the story. What
   made him or her your favorite?

3. Talk about the story together.
   Who liked the story? Why?
   Who didn't like the story? Why?

When your group is done, talk
about how well you worked
together.

S - Secretary - writes the
      date and + or - on the chart.

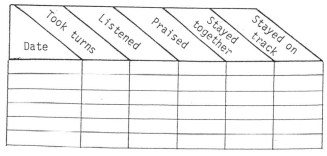

Figure 7

FIG. 17.7. Chart to help guide discussion groups.

I was the dad, I would never want to go there. It would be so sad but then
again it might be a happy moment because I would know that he did a
good thing and served the country. I think I would die right away in a war,
but the grandfather probably died at the very end of the war. I think the
grandfather was very brave and strong.

Invitation 17.2

*Select a quality picture book that evokes emotion. Read it orally to
upper elementary students. Model a response for them and then
have them do their own. Do this a few times to help students
understand how a response is different than a book report or review.*

There are many eloquent books to use: The Wall, The Faithful
Elephants, Pink and Say, *and* Rose Blanche *are good examples of
books that work well for modeling.*

Older children need modeling and instruction if their responses to
literature are not to look like book reports. Used to paraphrasing the
plot of library books, students must learn how to respond to books. As
Deb, one of the elementary language arts specialists puts it, "We might
better use the term 'react' than 'respond' since we want to know how
children feel and think about books." Whichever term we use, we find
that beginning with discussion of books and students' understandings
and interpretations about those books is a way to begin. When question-

Group Jobs

```
R  -  Reader  -  reads comments and questions
M  -  Mechanic  -  operates the tape recorder
C  -  Coordinator  -  makes sure everyone has
          a chance to talk and keeps the group
          on track
S  -  Secretary  -  writes group members'
          names and jobs
```

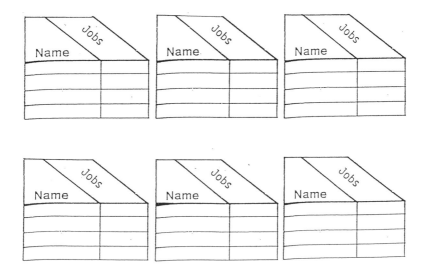

FIG. 17.8. Group jobs.

ing evolves from literal questions about the text to different aspects of involvement with literature, teachers and children begin to see what reader response is all about. Moss (1984), in *Focus Units in Literature: A Handbook for Elementary School Teachers,* helped us guide teachers to formulate better discussion with students about literature. Her eight levels of questioning range from basic discussion of the story to "building bridges between the child's world and the story world" (p. 27). Questions move from asking students literal questions about the story elements of character, setting, and plot sequence to questions like, "What do these stories say about the nature of courage" (p. 25)? or "Has this ever happened to you" (p. 27)?

We also have many Junior Great Books groups, and the leader guides that come with the literary selections have been a model for interpretive questioning. We find the training associated with this program spills over into other classroom activities. Further, we discourage the basalizing of literature, continually expounding on the fact that children learn to read and learn to enjoy reading by reading. By using these examples, we try to show how students can use more depth in their reading, going beyond the surface elements of a book.

MANAGING PROBLEMS AND MISCONCEPTIONS

But, as we saw successes in our district, we also encountered problems. However, we needed to look at these problems as transitional. Several of the novel sets in our bookroom had sets of questions with them, either teacher-made or commercial. We removed these questions that focused on literal comprehension. Teachers began to use story maps or other graphic organizers with novels or stories. These activities would still be regarded as efferent responses because the students were responding with information from the text. However, this practice has merit in teaching comprehension strategies and literary analysis. As adult learners, we use these organizers, and we want our students to move toward using them independently. However, we did not want this to be the entire program. Just recently, in an inservice for second-grade teachers, we offered a formula to help them manage their instructional time. We suggested that they think of dividing their reading time over a week into thirds. One third would involve work with reading comprehension strategies, one third would involve work with reader response, and one third would be independent reading by the student. Although this formula may change, the language arts specialists and I are comfortable for the time being with this division for an elementary program.

We have seen many misconceptions about reader-response theory. One of the most challenging has been the equation of reader-response theory with Readers/Writers Workshop. Many of our teachers have read Atwell's (1987) *In the Middle* at our suggestion. It has given the teachers practical advice. However, we find they carry one misconception back to the classroom. They believe they must use reader response in the same way, with each student in a different book. Although students should freely choose books for part of their reading, we needed to show teachers that response to reading can be carried out with the whole class reading the same novel or with small groups reading the same book. If we are to balance the social aspects of reading with individual aspects, there must be time for students to share ideas about the same book. This interaction gives students opportunities to learn from each other, to exchange responses and expand personal interpretations. They, thus, come to understand that learning to read includes learning how to understand broadly and interpret deeply. In small and large group settings, and with a teacher's coaching, students move from answers that look like book reports to answers that connect their own lives with the literature. Although one student is adept at connecting two books, another may connect all the works by one author. Hearing one another and being asked to rationalize responses by the teacher leads each student to accept more challenges in reading.

Some teachers also believed they were committing a sin if they used their basal, a newer edition of the D. C. Heath text. We had to assure them that they could use reader response with basal stories that have depth and that evoke emotion. These are often the only short stories available for intermediate grades, and they might be compared to the anthologies used in middle and secondary schools. While the stories help teachers assist students' development of comprehension strategies and literary analysis skills, they also ease the transition into reader response theory with materials the teachers know. At the same time, the teachers are making decisions instead of allowing the basal manual to totally guide their instruction.

A third misconception was the idea that this approach to teaching literature allows any response on the part of the student. This misconception can rightfully bring questions from parents who wonder what students are learning if anything goes.

If we consider the transactive model of reading whereby the reader, text, and context in which the reader reads come together to bring about meaning, we quickly realize that the text imposes constraints. Karolides (1992) claimed

> [the] adequacy of interpretations can be measured against the constraints of the text: to what degree does the individual response include the various features of the text and the nuances of language; to what degree does it include aspects that do not reflect the text; to what degree has the reading evoked a coherent work? (pp. 24, 25)

By teaching and modeling for students the concept of support from the text for their interpretations, this problem can be avoided. On the other hand, we need to recognize that there will be a range of interpretations for stories (see chapter 1, this volume).

Another problem that has been constant is the task of trying to integrate response theory with the skills and strategies that elementary-age children must be taught in order that they learn to read both efferently and aesthetically. If we are to give our young students what they need, we know that we cannot overemphasize one method. Squire (1990) pointed out that "in a very real sense the aims of reading instruction and the aims of a literary education are in conflict." He asked "if we must apply them (skill and strategies) in literature-centered reading programs, do we not run the risk of teaching children to read but destroying the desire to read?" (p. 27).

We believe our district is meeting this challenge in several ways. In addition to the teaching strategies identified and illustrated earlier, one way has been to move toward language arts blocks whenever possible rather than separate reading, writing, and spelling blocks. In order to gain larger blocks of time, some grades have had to move this block away from the morning where reading was traditionally taught. Principals have had to monitor the scheduling of music, art, and physical education to give as many large blocks of time as possible to the language arts. With larger blocks of time, students can spend part of the time in literature circles or in responding to reading through writing, and part of the time being coached in skills and strategies. As mentioned earlier in this chapter, giving teachers a formula to manage their time during a week has helped eliminate worries about giving students the reading instruction they need while encouraging aesthetic responses to books. And, in most instances, working through an integrated language approach has allowed students to learn the skills they need without isolated drill.

INTEGRATING THE CURRICULUM

We also encourage integration of subjects and language arts across the curriculum so that instruction in reading takes place in social studies, math, and science, as well as during the language arts block. In fact, there is emphasis on reading across the curriculum in grades 3 through 5 in response to the knowledge that students need to learn different strategies for reading expository text than they learn for narrative text. This leaves more time for aesthetic response to literature during the language arts block.

LaVonne, in her fifth-grade classroom, used the basal and workbooks for many years. Although she has always read to her students and has used novel sets since they have been available, she has recently examined how she teaches language arts as well as social studies. She now integrates language arts and social studies, selectively using some stories in the basal along with nonfiction and fiction trade books. This year, in a unit on historical fiction, she began in a unique way. The students carved faces from apples and dried them. The faces were then put aside to dry over time. As she blended the teaching of historical fiction with historical facts and events, the students read many books on their own or in small groups. She had opted for trade books in place of workbooks, and the trade books complemented the fifth grade social studies curriculum to a large extent. Students responded in journals and discussed the books in small groups. Many of their responses were what we would consider efferent responses as the books were largely biographical or factual. As Anjali read *Why Don't You Get a Horse, Sam Adams?* (Fritz, 1982), she connected her reading to what she knew about the Boston Tea Party:

> Samuel Adams is a man who hates the King of England, dresses the way no one else does, and never rides a horse! He has a dog named Queue. He (Adams) was elected as a representative in the Massachusetts Legislature.
>
> I was very surprised when I read about when people dressed up as Indians and dumped tea out of the ships, because I knew that was the Boston Tea Party.

We recognize that Anjali is making a connection between what she has learned from her social studies text and what she now reads in *Why Don't You Get a Horse, Sam Adams?* Obviously, she is surprised to find that historical fiction is based on historical fact.

Joanna's entries were much the same although she adds some personal opinions as she read *The Bloody Country* (Collier & Collier, 1976):

> So far Ben and Joe went out to pick berries, and they got caught by an Indian. The Indian was going to kill them, but the Indian would have been killed himself so he didn't. The book is kind of tense, but also at times it's boring. I hope it becomes exciting.

In her second entry she wrote, "Well, Ben, Joe, and Annie had to hide in the cellar so the British wouldn't scalp them. Isaac and Ben's mom are dead, because they got scalped. It was gross. This book is exciting."

By the time the students had read about several historical figures, either in their social studies text or in the various trade books, they took their apple heads and, deciding which characters the faces best resembled in their opinion, added bodies and dressed and decorated the dolls to represent the figure. We might look at their art as an aesthetic experience.

At the same time that the students were reading biographies and nonfiction by themselves or in small groups, they were reading *Sarah Bishop* (O'Dell, 1980) as a class. They were not asked to complete any written assignments with this book; they responded orally, interpreting the story under LaVonne's considering leadership. They connected the story of Sarah to the information they had read in their social studies text and in the biographies and tradebooks they used as part of their unit on the Revolutionary War. Finally, they wrote their own historical fiction. Brian began his story, "Jimmy Cal was a very strong man. He was an eighteen year old man who loved the land he lived on. It was on a bay in Virginia. He had a wonderful life. That was before the war...."

Invitation 17.3

Considering the several issues and pitfalls discussed in this chapter, reflect on this teacher's efforts to join the efferent and aesthetic responses. How might she proceed to enhance the aestheitc, given the dominance of the efferent? What will the students gain?

As LaVonne continues to explore her use of trade books in the area of social studies, she will make the transition to having students respond aesthetically in their journals. Students need to see their teacher modeling responses to books. However, we also need to realize that LaVonne has maintained the integrity of the social studies curriculum as students gained knowledge through efferent responses while moving toward aesthetic responses.

PROBLEMS OF ASSESSMENT AND BALANCE

LaVonne and other teachers like her struggle with another area that has impacted their teaching and the use of reader response. This is the area of assessment. Teachers know that they need to continually assess comprehension/strategies, and the easiest way to assess is through questions about the selections students read. District and school administrators must let teachers know they can assess in less traditional ways. Our work in alternative assessment in the Eau Claire Area School district is leading teachers to assess through classroom observation, through listening to students read, through group projects, and through examining responses to literature. However, teachers in grades 4 and 5 must still transfer this knowledge to letter grades on a report card. They find it difficult to grade personal responses to literature; this fact alone keeps some teachers from using this theory to its fullest degree. We need to develop standards for assessment of responses. We know that responses vary in their sophistication. While some students are merely discussing their likes and dislikes, others are relating the story to their own lives, and some are comparing the theme of one book to another. This is an area where we need to grow. One way will be to develop rubrics for reader response. We must decide whether there is a hierarchical sense about responses.

We also continue to work for balance in the language arts program. Jett-Simpson (1994) used a schematic to demonstrate the key events in a balanced literary program for young readers (see Fig. 17.9). The competition for time is always present. As students move into the intermediate grades, reading in the content areas becomes critical, adding one more dimension to an already overcrowded curriculum. We wrote a syllabus for and initiated a new class, Content Area Strategies for Learning (CASL), which addresses reading and writing in content areas. This class works with efferent reading skills and strategies. Our goal is to have teachers develop reading strategies during the teaching of all subjects. If efferent reading skills can be better integrated with content areas, we believe teachers will be comfortable using more reading response during the language arts block.

At the same time, the reading specialists and gifted and talented resource teachers (see chapter 8) continue to model and work with students in the area of reader response. We realize that change will occur slowly, but we remain confident that teachers will continue to examine their teaching practices and balance their language arts program to include aesthetic response to literature.

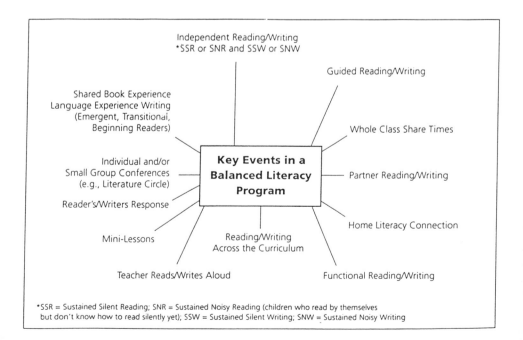

FIG. 17.9. Key events in a balanced literacy program.

APPENDIX

Content Area Strategies for Learning (CASL). This course originated in the Eau Claire Area School District based on the need for ongoing staff development in content area reading/writing. The course is taught as an Outreach course in conjunction with the University of Wisconsin–Eau Claire.

Early Literacy Inservice Course (ELIC). This course originated in Australia for teachers of grades K through 3 and is now sponsored by Rigby Education. Following 12 2-hour training sessions, districts can send graduates of this course for further training as facilitators of ELIC. Materials and licensing are purchased from Rigby.

Jett-Simpson, Mary, and Lauren, Leslie. Ecological Assessment Under Construction. This book begins with the Wisconsin State Reading Association Position Statement on Assessment in Reading and goes on to provide foundations, rationale, and advice for providing authentic assessment in the area of reading and writing. Useful forms for teachers are included in this practical but research-based guide.

Routman, Regie. Invitations: Changing as Teachers and Learners K–12. Routman's follow up to *Transitions* refines the process begun in her earlier book. Chapters on responding to literature and authentic contexts for writing are included in this book on becoming a whole language teacher. Annotated listings of professional and children's literature as well as other materials are included in a useful appendix.

Routman, Regie. Transitions. In this earlier book, Routman, an experienced teacher, recounts her own experiences as she moved away from basal texts and worksheets toward literature-based reading and process writing.

REFERENCES

Atwell, N. (1982). *In the middle*. Portsmouth, NH: Heinemann Educational Books.

Holland, K., Hungerford, R. A., & Ernst, S. B. (Eds.). (1993). *Journeying: Children responding to literature*. Portsmouth, NH: Heinemann Educational Books.

Jett-Simpson, M., & Leslie, L. (1994). *Ecological assessment under construction*. Schofield, WI: Wisconsin State Reading Association.

Karolides, N. J. (Ed.). (1992). *Reader response in the classroom*. New York: Longman Publishing Group.

Moss, J. F. (1984). *Focus units in literature: A handbook for elementary teachers*. Urbana, IL: National Council of Teachers of English.

Probst, R. (1988). *Response and analysis: Teaching literature in junior and senior high school*. Portsmouth, NH: Boynton Cook Publishing.

Pugh, S. L. (1988). Teaching children to appreciate literature. *ERIC Digest, 2*.

Rosenblatt, L. M. (1978). *The reader, the text, the poem*. Carbondale: Southern Illinois University Press.

Routman, R. (1991). Invitations. Portsmouth, NH: Heinemann Educational Books.

Routman, R. (1988). *Transitions: From literature to literacy*. Portsmouth, NH: Heinemann.

Simpson, M. J., & Leslie, L. (1994). *Ecological assessment under construction*. Schofield, WI: Wisconsin State Reading Association.

Squire, J. (1990, November). *Research on reader response and the national literature initiative*. Paper presented at the National Council of Teachers of English Convention, Baltimore, MD.

Wisconsin Department of Public Instruction. (1987). *Guide to curriculum planning in english language arts*. (1987). Madison, WI: Author.

Wisconsin Department of Public Instruction. (1987). *Guide to curriculum planning in reading*. (1987). Madison, WI: Author.

CHILDREN'S TEXTS

Bunting, E. (1990). *The wall*. New York: Clarion Books.

Collier, J. L., & Collier, C. (1976). *The bloody country*. New York: Four Winds Press.

Cooper, S. (1987). *The grey king*. NY: Harpercollins Children's Books.

Eckert, A. (1987). *Incident at Hawk's Hill*. New York: Bantam Books.

Fritz, J. (1982). *Why don't you get a horse, Sam Adams?* New York: Putnam Publishing Group.

Gardiner, J. R. (1987). *Stone fox*. New York: HarperCollins Children's Books.

Innocenti, R. (1987). *Rose Blanche*. Orlando, FL: Harcourt Brace.

O'Dell, S. (1980). *Sarah Bishop*. New York: Scholastic.

Polacco, P. (1987). *Pink & say*. New York: Putnam.

Tsuchiya, Y. (1987). *The faithful elephants*. Boston, MA: Houghton Mifflin.

Wilde, O. (1980). *The happy prince and other tales*. Boulder, CO: Shambhala Publications.

About the Contributors

Shelly Allen Shelly Allen, a former elementary school teacher, is currently a Postdoctoral Research Associate at Peabody College of Vanderbilt University. She coordinates a reading research project in the Department of Special Education. Her areas of interest include literature-based teaching at the elementary school level, children's literature, and classroom discourse.

Anne Barry Anne Barry, an experienced first grade teacher in the Chicago Public Schools, is interested in doing teacher research and especially enjoys being connected to the University of Illinois at Chicago. She feels that there is much need for research in urban education, particularly in neighborhood schools with much cultural diversity. She believes that by opening her classroom to student questions, comments, thought, ideas, beliefs, opinions, and feelings, she is better able to understand how her students are connecting to the real world.

Paul Boyd-Batstone Paul Boyd-Batstone, an experienced bilingual teacher from Long Beach, CA, has worked as a teacher educator at California State University, Long Beach and is Doctoral Fellow at the Claremont Graduate School. Currently he is conducting teacher action research in a bilingual classroom in Long Beach Unified School District. A composer at heart, he has collaborated with his students to compose literally dozens of children's songs. His latest creation is a recording of an original musical based on *The Great Kapok Tree* by Lynne Cherry.

Carole Cox Carole Cox is a professor in the College of Education at California State University, Long Beach. A former elementary teacher and faculty member at Louisiana State University, she has authored two textbooks—*Teaching Language Arts: A Student- and Response-Centered Classroom* and *Teaching Reading with Children's Literature* with James Zarrillo—as well as journal articles and book chapters on language and literacy education. She is in the seventh year of a longitudinal study of the development of childrens' response to literature, K–6.

Elizabeth Jackowski Davis Liz Davis teaches fifth grade Language Arts at Lakeway Elementary School, in Austin, TX. As a whole, she is no ordinary teacher. Ms. Davis loves to experiment with creative ways of teaching by using Reader's Theatre in both her Language Arts and Social Studies classes. Her emphasis is "Bringing Literature to Life," and it very well fits her character. Ms. Davis tries to establish a special bond with her students, which helps her teach easier throughout the year. She makes learning fun, while still being a teacher at the same time. Through her students' eyes, Ms. Davis is truly a teacher to remember.

–Written by Matt Dominy
5th grade student, 1995–1996

Alan Dean   Alan Dean teaches first grade in Giles County in Southwest Virginia. He has served on programs of the Conference on English Education and the Virginia Association of Teachers of English.

Brian Edmiston   Brian Edmiston, an assistant professor at the University of Wisconsin–Madison, teaches courses in the use of drama across the curriculum. Born in Ireland, he was a secondary teacher of English and Head of Drama in England as well as an elementary teacher in the United States. He has received several honors: the 1992 American Alliance for Theatre and Education Research Award and the 1995–1996 Lilly Endowment Teaching Fellowship. In addition to writing about drama and response to literature he is writing a book about his monster–hero play with his 6-year-old son, Michael.

Patricia Enciso   Patricia Enciso is an assistant professor at the University of Wisconsin–Madison where she teaches courses in reading and children's literature and graduate courses in culture, reading and response to literature. She is currently studying preservice teachers' interpretations of award-winning Latina literature and their plans for mediating this literature in the classroom.

Nyanne J. Hicks   Nyanne Hicks has taught sixth-grade language arts and social studies for 9 years at Blacksburg Middle School in Montgomery County, VA. A 20-year classroom veteran, she previously taught preschool through sixth grades in Indiana, Illinois, and West Virginia. Nyanne has presented papers at local, state, and national conferences and coauthored a journal article. She takes groups of students to Europe over summer breaks.

Karen Hirsch   Karen Hirsch, in her 30-year teaching career, has taught elementary, middle, and high school students. Additionally, Hirsch spent 6 summers teaching conversational English and American culture to young people in Poland, Hungary, Italy, and Russia. Hirsch published two children's picture books, *My Sister* and *Becky*. The latter was anthologized in the third-grade reader of the Houghton Mifflin Reading Series. Her 1994 juvenile novel, *Ellen Anders On Her Own*, won the Arthur Tofte Juvenile Fiction first place award from the Council for Wisconsin Writers.

Lee Karnowski Lee Karnowski began her elementary teaching career in California; subsequently, she traveled to Europe and taught in American schools in France and Belgium and in the British primary schools in England before returning to the United States to continue her elementary teaching in Colorado and Ohio. Now a professor at the University of Wisconsin–River Falls, she teaches Language Arts method courses and Emergent Literacy courses. In 1995, she was awarded the university's Distinguished Professor award.

Nicholas J. Karolides Nicholas J. Karolides, professor of English, University of Wisconsin–River Falls, frequently consults. about curriculum development and reader-response classroom applications. His experiences include middle-school teaching. His major publications include *The Pioneer in the American Novel, Focus on Physical Impairments* and *Focus on Fitness* (coauthored with daughter Melissa), *Reader Response in the Classroom* (editor), and *Censored books: Critical Viewpoints* (coeditor), which in 1995 was named Outstanding Book by the Gustavus Myers Center for the Study of Human Rights in North America. He was honored in 1994 with the University of Wisconsin Regents Excellence in Teaching Award.

Rick Meyer Rick Meyer taught young children for more than 16 years. An assistant professor at the University of Nebraska–Lincoln, he is involved in teaching literacy courses. His research interests include emergent literacy and teacher change. At present, he is working with a group of primary teachers dedicated to studying change in their classrooms and their lives as they discover their voices

Arlene Harris Mitchell Arlene Harris Mitchell, an Associate Professor of Literacy and English Education at the University of Cincinnati, is Associate Dean of Academic Affairs. Prior to joining the university, she was a classroom teacher for 16 years. Her areas of research and writing focus on issues related to cross-cultural and ethnic literature, children's and young adult prose and poetry, and home–school connections in learning. She is coeditor of an anthology of poetry across Black cultures.

Irma Josefina O'Neill Irma Josefina O'Neill (Jossie) is a former elementary school teacher who has had extensive experience with bilingual students and students with learning disabilities and severe reading problems in Puerto Rico, Connecticut, and New York. She now teaches courses in reading, special education, and bilingual education at SUNY–College at Old Westbury. Dr. O'Neill has served as a reading consultant and curriculum developer. Her most recent research and copublications focus on multicultural literacy, facilitating the teaching–learning process, social development curriculum, and teaching Spanish through authentic literature and traditional art.

Christine Pappas Christine Pappas is a professor at the University of Illinois at Chicago, where she teaches classroom discourse and various language and literacy course. For the past 6 years she has been involved in collaborative work with Chicago teacher-researchers who have been studying their efforts to move away from transmission-oriented teaching-learning in literacy to develop more collaborative interaction with their urban students.

Elizabeth Poe Elizabeth Poe is an associate professor of English education at Radford University in Virginia where she teaches young adult and children's literature. She previously taught high school English for 13 years in Colorado and English education courses for 4 years at the University of Wisconsin–Eau Claire. A past president of NCTE's Assembly on Literature for Adolescents and the current editor of IRA's *Signal Journal*, Elizabeth wrote two books for ABC-CLIO's Teenage Perspective series, *Focus on Sexuality* and *Focus on Relationships*.

Connie Russell Connie Russell is the K–12 Reading/Language Arts Coordinator for the Eau Claire Area School District, a district of about 11,500 students, in Wisconsin. Connie has served as an elementary reading resource teacher and an elementary grade teacher. She has published in Learning, Wisconsin English Journal, and Language Arts. Most recently, she wrote a chapter for Whole Learning in the Middle School. Past president of the Wisconsin Council of Teachers of English, she received the Pooley Research Award in the 1980s for her classroom research on peer conferencing and WCTE's 1994 Chisholm Award for Meritorious Service.

Robert Small Robert Small has chaired the NCTE Conference on English Education and the Assembly on Literature for Adolescents. He is the current chair of the NCTE Standing Committee on Teacher Preparation and Certification.

Elizabeth Smith Elizabeth Smith is currently an assistant professor of children's literature and multicultural education at Otterbein College in Westerville, OH. She has conducted research in several classrooms in the Columbus vicinity focusing on African American students' responses to African American literature. Additionally, she has facilitated and participated in presentations and workshops across the country that focus on topics such as diversity, children's literature and students' responses to multicultural literature.

Kevin Spink Kevin Spink has taught grades kindergarten through sixth grade in Anchorage, AK since 1986, as well as teacher education courses for the University of Alaska since 1991. His school, Mountain View Elementary, has a wealth of ethnic diversity among both staff and students and through his students, their families, and his colleagues, he is gaining an increasing awareness of the enormous influence which culture has in our learning experiences.

Kathleen G. Velsor Kathleen G. Velsor is a professor at State University of New York at Old Westbury. She teaches courses in child development, children's literature, and reading. Professor Velsor's career in education includes Head Teacher for the Arts for the School of Performing Arts in Ohio and visual arts teacher in New York. She also taught in special education programs for emotionally disturbed students. She is currently an educational consultant and works with school districts in curriculum evaluation research. Her most recent research and copublications focus on assertiveness training for women, mentoring, and multicultural literacy.

Author Index

Subject Index

A

Aesthetic stance, 13–14, 31, 89, 196. *See also* Efferent–aesthetic continuum
  defined, 31–32
African American church tradition
  call and response, 130–131
Assessment. *See* Evaluation
Attention, selective. *See* Selective attention

B

Basal texts, working with, 29, 192–193, 307–311, 336, 348
Behaviorist tradition of learning, 34–35
Berlin, Robert, 4–5
BEV. *See* Black English
Black English
  paralinguistic traits of, 127–128
  teaching appropriate use of, 132–133
Blending. *See* Identification by reader
Body language. *See* Responses
Book Presentation. *See* Reading-aloud curriculum genre
Bottom–up approach to learning. *See* Behaviorist tradition of learning
Brainstorming, 104–105
British integrated day model, 55

C

Child authors, 169–183
  metatextual awareness of, 179–180
Classifying information for students, 92
Classroom
  activities, 244–247, 255–257

atmosphere, 15, 42, 128–129, 133
process, 24–27, 119–120, 140–152, 156–161, 211, 218–233, 267–275, 336–338. *See also* Recording; Transcription
Connotative aspects of language, 13
Consensus, reaching, 65
Constructivist theories of learning. *See* Social constructivist perspective
Convergence among readers, 24–27
"Correct" meaning of text, 30
Culturally aware education, 26, 126–135, 261, 316
  disorientation of teachers, 134, 316–318, 321–322
  ethnic-based texts, 10–11
  variation, importance of, 10
Curriculum
  genres, 216, 232. *See also* Reading-aloud curriculum genre
  integrating, 347–359
  requirements, satisfying, 96, 101
  units, designing, 324–327, 334–335, 351

D

DEAR/W. *See* Drop Everything and Read/Write (DEAR/W)
Decision making, cooperative, 119–120, 122
Democratic ideal, promoted by humanistic studies, 25–27
Denotative aspects of language, 14
Dialogue writing. *See* Scripting
Discussion, 19–23, 53–67, 115–120, 144–151, 161–163, 218–231, 246–251, 304–305
  level of, 64